ASSISTED DYING AND
LEGAL CHANGE

Assisted Dying and Legal Change

PENNEY LEWIS

OXFORD

UNIVERSITY PRESS

OXFORD
UNIVERSITY PRESS

Great Clarendon Street, Oxford OX2 6DP

Oxford University Press is a department of the University of Oxford.
It furthers the University's objective of excellence in research, scholarship,
and education by publishing worldwide in

Oxford New York

Auckland Cape Town Dar es Salaam Hong Kong Karachi
Kuala Lumpur Madrid Melbourne Mexico City Nairobi
New Delhi Shanghai Taipei Toronto

With offices in

Argentina Austria Brazil Chile Czech Republic France Greece
Guatemala Hungary Italy Japan Poland Portugal Singapore
South Korea Switzerland Thailand Turkey Ukraine Vietnam

Oxford is a registered trade mark of Oxford University Press
in the UK and in certain other countries

Published in the United States
by Oxford University Press Inc., New York

© P. Lewis, 2007

The moral rights of the author have been asserted

Crown copyright material is reproduced under Class Licence
Number C01P0000148 with the permission of OPSI
and the Queen's Printer for Scotland

Database right Oxford University Press (maker)

First published 2007

British Library Cataloguing in Publication Data

Data available

Library of Congress Cataloging in Publication Data

Data available

Typeset by Newgen Imaging Systems (P) Ltd., Chennai, India
Printed in Great Britain
on acid-free paper by
Biddles Ltd., King's Lynn

ISBN 978–0–19–921287–3

1 3 5 7 9 10 8 6 4 2

For Alan and Frumie and Rael

Preface

In 1993, I was working as a law clerk to Mr. Justice Frank Iacobucci when the Sue Rodriguez case reached the Supreme Court of Canada. My exposure then to the first attempt to strike down a criminal prohibition on assisted suicide using constitutional rights was the start of my interest in legal change on assisted suicide and euthanasia. I am indebted to Mr. Justice Iacobucci for that opportunity.

I am grateful to those colleagues who kindly read and commented on drafts of earlier articles: Alex Bood, Stacey Pastel Dougan, Linda Fentiman, Andrew Grubb, Maleiha Malik, and Rosamund Scott. Alex Nolet provided valuable research assistance in France and Bastiaan Hoogendoorn helped with problems of translation from Dutch to English. Sabine Michalowski offered sound advice and helpful information on German law. Most importantly, I would not have been able to write about the Netherlands and Belgium without relying on colleagues in those countries who generously read and commented on drafts of chapters: John Griffiths, Ubaldus de Vries, Heleen Weyers, and Guy Widdershoven in the Netherlands; and Robert Cliquet and Herman Nys in Belgium. The responsibility for all errors of fact or interpretation of course remains my own.

My friends and family have provided unfailing support and encouragement during the research and writing of this book; in particular, Melissa Ruth, whose perceptive grasp of the bigger picture is invaluable in moments of doubt. I am truly fortunate in the love of my family, to whom this book is dedicated.

The article on which Chapters Two and Three are based was originally written as an LL.M. thesis at Columbia University, during which time I was generously supported by a Fellowship from the Social Sciences and Humanities Research Council of Canada and by a MacKenzie King Open Scholarship. Later research in France was assisted by a Small Research Grant from the British Academy and valuable writing time was provided by a Visiting Research Fellowship at the Institute of Advanced Legal Studies in London. The Research Leave Scheme of the Arts and Humanities Research Council gave me the time to write the bulk of the manuscript.

I would also like to thank Rael Lewis, who found the image used on the cover, and Kuakoon Kessuwan, who cross-referenced the cases and statutory provisions with great care. I am grateful to the staff of Oxford University Press for their efficiency and helpfulness, particularly to Gwen Booth and Fiona Stables.

Finally, I acknowledge the kind permission of the American Society of Law, Medicine and Ethics to reproduce in adapted form in Chapters Two and Three, Penney Lewis, 'Rights Discourse and Assisted Suicide' (2001) 27(1) *American Journal of Law and Medicine* 45–99. Blackwell Publishing obligingly allowed me to use portions of Penney Lewis, 'The Dutch Experience of Euthanasia' (1998) 25(4) *Journal of Law and Society* 636–649 and Oxford University Press kindly granted permission to use portions of Penney Lewis, 'The evolution of assisted dying in France: A third way?' (2005) 13(4) *Medical Law Review* 44–72.

Penney Lewis

King's College London
July 2006

Summary Table of Contents

Detailed Table of Contents

Table of Cases

GERMANY

IRELAND

NETHERLANDS

NEW ZEALAND

U.S.A.

Table of Statutory Material

INTERNATIONAL

AUSTRALIA

Federal

State

AUSTRIA

BELGIUM

[1] English translations can be found at (2003) 10 *Eur. J. Health L* 329; (2002) 9(2–3) *Ethical Perspectives* 182; Appendix I in Paul Schotsmans & Tom Meulenbergs, eds., *Euthanasia and Palliative Care in the Low Countries* (Leuven: Peeters, 2005) 245 and www.kuleuven.ac.be/cbmer/viewpic.php?LAN=E&TABLE=DOCS&ID=23, accessed 24 July 2006.

CANADA

Constitutional

Federal

Provincial

EUROPE

FRANCE

GERMANY

IRELAND

ITALY

NETHERLANDS

NEW ZEALAND

PORTUGAL

SPAIN

[2] English translations can be found at (2001) 8 *Eur. J. Health L.* 183 and as an appendix to Jurriaan de Haan, 'The New Dutch Law on Euthanasia' (2002) 10 *Med. L. Rev.* 57, 68–75.

SWITZERLAND

U.S.A.

Constitutional

Federal

State

URUGUAY

List of Abbreviations

A.C.	Appeal Cases (decisions of the House of Lords)
Alb. L. Rev.	Albany Law Review
All E.R.	All England Law Reports
A.L.R.	American Law Reports
Alta. L. Rev.	Alberta Law Review
Am. College of Surgeons Bull.	American College of Surgeons Bulletin
Annals Internal Med.	Annals of Internal Medicine
Arch. Pediat. Adol. Med.	Archives of Pediatric and Adoloscent Medicine
Ariz. L. Rev.	Arizona Law Review
B.M.L.R.	Butterworths Medico-Legal Reports
Boston Coll. Int' l & Comp. L. Rev.	Boston College International and Comparative Law Review
Br. Med. J.	British Medical Journal
Buff. L. Rev.	Buffalo Law Review
Bull. Crim.	Bulletin Criminel
Cal. App.	Californian Appeals
Cal. L. Rev.	California Law Review
Cal. Rptr.	California Reporter
Camb. L.J.	Cambridge Law Journal
Camb. Q. Healthcare Ethics	Cambridge Quarterly of Healthcare Ethics
Campbell L. Rev.	Campbell Law Review
Can. Crim. L. Rev.	Canadian Criminal Law Review
Can. J. L. & Juris	Canadian Journal of Law and Jurisprudence
Cardozo L. Rev.	Cardozo Law Review
Colum. L. Rev.	Columbia Law Review
Common L. World Rev.	Common Law World Review
Const. Comment	Constitutional Commentary
Cornell J. L. & Pub Pol'y	Cornell Journal of Law and Public Policy
Cornell L. Rev.	Cornell Law Review
Cr. App. R.	Criminal Appeal Reports (decisions of the Court of Appeal of England and Wales, Criminal Division)

Crim L.R.	Criminal Law Review
Crim. Rep	Criminal Reports
D.L.R.	Dominion Law Reports
D.P.P.	Director of Public Prosecutions
Duq. L. Rev.	Duquesne Law Review
E.H.R.R.	European Human Rights Reports
Emory Int'l L. Rev.	Emory International Law Review
Eur. Comm. H.R.	European Commission of Human Rights
Eur. Ct. H.R.	European Court of Human Rights
Eur. J. Health L.	European Journal of Health Law
E.W.H.C. Admin.	England and Wales High Court (decisions of the Queen's Bench Division (Divisional Court))
F.3d (etc.)	Federal Reporter (Third Series)
F. Supp.	Federal Supplement
Fordham Urb. L.J.	Fordham Urban Law Journal
Gaz. Pal.	Gazette du Palais
Gen. Hosp. Psychiatry	General Hospital Psychiatry
Geo. L.J.	Georgetown Law Journal
Gonz. J. Int'l L.	Gonzaga Journal of International Law
Harv. Civ. Rts. – Civ. Lib. L. Rev.	Harvard Civil Rights – Civil Liberties Law Review
Harv. L. Rev.	Harvard Law Review
Harv. Women's L.J.	Harvard Women's Law Journal
Hastings Center Rep.	Hastings Center Report
Health L.J.	Health Law Journal
Indus. Rel. L.J.	Industrial Relations Law Journal
J. Am. Geriatrics Soc.	Journal of the American Geriatrics Society
J. Am. Med. Ass'n.	Journal of the American Medical Association
J. Contemp. Health L. & Pol'y	Journal of Contemporary Health Law and Policy
J.C.P.	Juriclasseur Périodique
J. L. Med. & Ethics	Journal of Law, Medicine & Ethics
J. Law & Med.	Journal of Law and Medicine
J. Marshall L. Rev.	John Marshall Law Review
J. Med. Phil.	Journal of Medicine and Philosophy
J. Value Inquiry	Journal of Value Inquiry

King's Coll. L.J.	King's College Law Journal
Ky. L.J.	Kentucky Law Journal
Law & Hum. Behav.	Law & Human Behavior
L.C.E.W.	Law Commission of England and Wales
Loy. L.A. Int'l & Comp. L. Rev.	Loyola of Los Angeles International and Comparative Law Review
L.R.C.C.	Law Reform Commission of Canada
Md. L. Rev.	Maryland Law Review
Méd. & Droit	Médecin et Droit
Med. & L.	Medicine and Law
Med. L. Int'l	Medical Law International
Med. L. Rev.	Medical Law Review
Mich. L. Rev.	Michigan Law Review
Midwest Stud. Phil.	Midwest Studies in Philosophy
Milbank Q.	Milbank Quarterly
Minn. L. Rev.	Minnesota Law Review
Mod. L. Rev.	Modern Law Review
Monash U. L. Rev.	Monash University Law Review
Nebraska L. Rev.	Nebraksa Law Review
New Eng. J. Med.	New England Journal of Medicine
N.J.	Nederlandse Jurisprudentie
New L.J.	New Law Journal
Notre Dame L. Rev.	Notre Dame Law Review
N.S.R.	Nova Scotia Reports
N.Y.U. L. Rev.	New York University Law Review
Ohio N.U. L. Rev.	Ohio Northern University Law Review
Ox. J. Legal Stud.	Oxford Journal of Legal Studies
Phil. & Pub. Aff.	Philosophy and Public Affairs
Phil. Forum	Philosophy Forum
Phil. Rev.	The Philosophical Review
Q.B.D.	Queen's Bench Division (England and Wales)
Rev. Dr. Sanit. Soc.	Revue de droit sanitaire et social
Rutgers L.J.	Rutgers Law Journal

Sask. L. Rev.	Saskatchewan Law Review
S.C.R.	Supreme Court Reports (decisions of the Supreme Court of Canada)
So. 2d(etc.)	Southern Reporter (2nd series)
So. Cal. L. Rev.	Southern California Law Review
Soc. Theory & Prac.	Social Theory & Practice
Stan. L. Rev.	Stanford Law Review
St. John's L. Rev.	St John's Law Review
Stud. Hist. Phil. Biol. & Biomed. Sci.	Studies in History and Philosophy of Biological and Biomedical Sciences
Sw. L.J.	Southwestern Law Journal
Tenn. L. Rev.	Tennessee Law Review
Tex. L. Rev.	Texas Law Review
U. Chi. L. Rev.	University of Chicago Law Review
U.S.	United States Reports (decisions of the United States Supreme Court)
Vill. L. Rev.	Villanova Law Review
Wis. L. Rev.	Wisconsin Law Review
W.L.R.	Weekly Law Reports
Wm. & Mary L. Rev.	William and Mary Law Review
Yale L.J.	Yale Law Journal

1

Introduction

The question whether assisted dying should be legalized is often treated, by judges and commentators alike, as a question which transcends national boundaries and diverse legal systems. One obvious example is the use made of the 'Dutch experience' in other jurisdictions. By treating the issue as a transcendent, global ethical question, the important context in which individual jurisdictions make decisions about assisted dying and the significance of the legal methods chosen to carry out those decisions is often lost. Work in this field is dominated by partisan exhortation by proponents or opponents of legalization. Although comparative work exists, it tends to focus on the experience of assisted dying in practice, rather than on the process of legalization and its effects. This book concentrates not on the issue of whether assisted dying should be legalized, but rather on the impact of the choice of a particular legal route towards legalization.

Legal change on assisted dying may be achieved in a variety of ways: challenges to criminal prohibitions using constitutionally entrenched rights; the use of defences available to defendants who are prosecuted for assisting a death; legislative change; or referenda or ballot measures proposed by individual citizens or interest groups. The examination in this book of the impact of these different alternatives suggests that greater caution is needed before relying on the experience of one jurisdiction when discussing proposals for regulation of assisted dying in others, and the possible consequences of such regulation. The book seeks to demonstrate the need to explore the legal environment in which assisted dying is performed or proposed in order to evaluate the relevance of a particular legal experience to other jurisdictions.

This introductory chapter provides some context for the assisted dying debate; defines the important terms; and canvasses the current legal position in most major Western jurisdictions. Chapters 2 and 3 concentrate on rights as a mechanism for legal change on assisted dying. There have been unsuccessful attempts to use constitutionally entrenched rights claims to challenge criminal prohibitions on assisted suicide in Canada, the United States, and the United Kingdom. These challenges, brought by patients, reached the highest courts in Canada, the United States, and Europe. Their failure makes unlikely – in any major common law or European jurisdiction – the legalization of assisted suicide or euthanasia using challenges based on constitutionally entrenched rights.

What can we learn about the use of rights as a mechanism for legal change on assisted dying from the debate which surrounded these cases? Chapter 2 canvasses the use of rights in litigation and debate over the legalization of assisted suicide, including the rights to liberty, autonomy, privacy, dignity, equality, freedom of conscience and religion, life and property. The presentation of a multitude of conflicting and seemingly irresolvable rights-based claims suggests the need to examine more closely the phenomenon of rights-based arguments in the context of assisted suicide. In Chapter 3, the problems associated with such arguments are illuminated by looking at some of the critiques of rights which have gained popularity in recent years, and by discussing their applicability to the rights-based arguments used in the assisted suicide debate, which was ignited by the unsuccessful constitutional challenges in Canada, the United States, and the United Kingdom.

The focus in the next two chapters turns to other possible mechanisms of legal change. Chapter 4 examines the use of the defence of necessity as a mechanism of legal change. It was by this route that euthanasia was effectively legalized in the Netherlands. The chapter begins with an examination of the evolution of the Dutch use of necessity, focusing on the key conflict between the duty to preserve life and the duty to relieve suffering. The chapter also considers the purpose and impact of the eventual decision to codify the parameters of the defence in the Termination of Life on Request and Assisted Suicide (Review Procedures) Act 2001. The Dutch approach is then contrasted with the common law refusal to allow the defence of necessity to be used in murder cases, which has been re-affirmed recently in both England and Wales and Canada. The chapter then examines the differing choices made by these jurisdictions regarding the use of rights and necessity as mechanisms of legal change on assisted dying. Two central questions are asked. First, why is the common law defence of necessity apparently unavailable to defendants who have assisted another to die? Secondly, why did the Dutch not use constitutionally entrenched rights as the mechanism of legal change?

Chapter 5 examines compassion as a driver for legal change on assisted dying. Compassion was put forward explicitly as an agent for legal change in a recent proposal by the French National Bioethics Advisory Committee to enact a 'euthanasia exception' which would entail diversion from the criminal process following a 'plea of defence of euthanasia' which would then be subject to investigation by an interdisciplinary commission. After scrutinizing this proposal, Chapter 5 concludes by considering the reasons why neither rights nor the defence of necessity are likely candidates to drive forward legal change on assisted dying in France.

Chapter 6 examines the contours of the legal regulation of assisted dying resulting from the use of the three mechanisms of legal change that have been canvassed in Chapters 2 and 3, 4 and 5: constitutionally entrenched rights; the defence of necessity based on the conflicting duties to preserve life and relieve suffering; and compassion. After separate examination, the second half of Chapter 6 brings the three mechanisms of legal change together, contrasting the contours of their resulting regimes in relation to their key features. Legislative approaches in Oregon, Belgium, and the Northern Territory of Australia are also introduced to see if they mirror, in any significant respect, the regimes produced by the three mechanisms of legal change.

In the assisted dying context, the legal significance of the dispute over the slippery slope argument is enormous. Evidence of a Dutch 'slippery slope' was invoked by judges of both the Canadian and U.S. Supreme Courts in their decisions rejecting a constitutional right to assisted suicide. Chapter 7 evaluates comparatively how slippery slope arguments work in the context of the different mechanisms of legal change discussed in Chapter 6. Both the logical and empirical versions of the slippery slope argument are examined in some detail, with particular attention paid to the comparative evidence.

I. The Background to the Legalization Debate

The upsurge in interest in assisted dying has occurred against a backdrop of growing concern over 'modern medical death',[1] often preceded by an 'extended deteriorative decline'[2] which seems to 'strip [individuals] of choice and dignity'.[3] The use of advance directives or living wills[4] and the judicial or statutory acceptance of the right to refuse (even life-saving or life-sustaining) treatment[5]

---

[1] Daniel Callahan, *The Troubled Dream of Life: Living With Mortality* (New York: Simon & Schuster, 1993) 23. See also, Sherwin B. Nuland, *How We Die: Reflections on Life's Final Chapter* (New York: A.A. Knopf, 1994) xv ('Modern dying takes place in the modern hospital, where it can be hidden, cleansed of its organic blight, and finally packaged for modern burial.'); Philippe Ariès, *Western Attitudes Toward Death: From the Middle Ages to the Present* (Patricia M. Ranum, trans.) (Baltimore, Md.: The Johns Hopkins University Press, 1974).

[2] Margaret Pabst Battin, *Ethical Issues in Suicide* (Englewood Cliffs, N.J.: Prentice-Hall, 1995) 201, 225–6.   [3] Callahan, above n. 1, 23.

[4] For a comparative study, see Cristiano Vezzoni, 'Engineering Rights: The Legal Status and Social Practice of Advance Directives' in Albert Klijn et al., eds., *Regulating Physician-Negotiated Death* (Amsterdam: Elsevier, 2001) 67. The relevant provisions in England and Wales, the United States, and Canada are discussed in Chapter 6, Section V.A.

[5] The strongest vindications of this right are found in the major common law jurisdictions and some continental European countries. Vezzoni, ibid. 69–70. In the United States, see *Cruzan v. Director, Mo. Dep't of Health* (1990) 497 U.S. 261, 278 ('a competent person has a constitutionally protected liberty interest in refusing unwanted medical treatment'). In England and Wales, see *Sidaway v. Board of Governors of Bethlem Royal Hospital* [1985] A.C. 871, 882, 888; *Airedale NHS Trust v. Bland* [1993] A.C. 789, 864; *Re M.B. (Medical Treatment)* [1997] 2 F.L.R. 426, 432 (C.A.) ('A mentally competent patient has an absolute right to refuse to consent to medical treatment for any reason, rational or irrational, or for no reason at all, even where that decision may lead to his or her own death). In Canada, see *Ciarlariello v. Schacter* [1993] 2 S.C.R. 119; *Nancy B. v. Hôtel-Dieu de Québec* (1992) 86 D.L.R. (4th) 385 (Qué. S.C.); *Malette v. Shulman* (1990) 72 O.R. (2d) 417 (Ont. C.A.); *Rodriguez v. British Columbia (Attorney-General)* [1993] 3 S.C.R. 519, [41] (recognizing a common law right of patients to refuse consent to medical treatment). In Australia, see *Rogers v. Whitaker* (1992) 175 C.L.R. 479, 486–7 (H.C. Aust.). In Ireland, see *Ryan v. Attorney General* [1965] I.R. 294 (Irish S.C.); *Re A Ward of Court (withholding medical treatment) (No. 2)* [1996] 2 I.R. 79, 156 (Irish S.C., Denham J.); *North Western Health Board v. W.(H.)* [2001] I.E.S.C. 90 (Irish S.C.). In the

have failed to diminish public anxieties surrounding this modern reality of dying.[6]

Physicians' attitudes characterized by 'a worry about malpractice, a zest for technology, a deep-seated moral belief in the need to prolong life, and the pressure of families and others, still often lead to overtreatment and an excessive reliance on technology.'[7] The result may be that dying has become, in some cases, longer and more difficult. 'An inadvertent and unintended side effect of medicine's growing effectiveness is that the dying process has been elongated . . . . [F]or those who are suffering greatly . . . it has become harder and harder to die.'[8] As the European Court of Human Rights observed in *Pretty v. United Kingdom,* 'in an era of growing medical sophistication combined with longer life expectancies, many people are concerned that they should not be forced to linger on in old age or in states of advanced physical or mental decrepitude which conflict with strongly held ideas of self and personal identity.'[9] Desire to take control of this modern dying process has manifested itself in renewed calls for the legalization of assisted suicide and voluntary active euthanasia.[10]

II. Definitions

A. Euthanasia

There are many definitions of euthanasia.[11] The *Oxford English Dictionary* states:

Euthanasia: . . . The action of inducing a gentle and easy death. Used [especially] with reference to a proposal that the law should sanction the putting painlessly to death of those suffering from incurable and extremely painful diseases.[12]

The House of Lords Select Committee on Medical Ethics adopted a different definition, emphasizing the actor's intention: 'a deliberate intervention under-taken with the express intention of ending a life to relieve intractable suffering'.[13]

Netherlands, see Law on Contracts for Medical Care, Art. 450(1), discussed by L.F. Markenstein, 'The Codification in the Netherlands of the Principal Rights of Patients: A Critical Review' (1995) 2(1) *Eur. J. Health L.* 33. In Belgium, see Law concerning the rights of the patient of 22 Aug. 2002, Art. 8, discussed by Herman Nys, 'Recent Developments in Health Law in Belgium' (2006) 13(2) *Eur. J. Health L.* 95. In Denmark, see Patients' Rights Act of 1 July 1998 No. 482, §§ 6, 7, translated in Jørn Vestergaard, 'Medical Aid in Dying under Danish Law: Mainly Regarding Living Wills and Other Forms of Renouncing Life Prolonging Treatment' (2000) 7(4) *Eur. J. Health L.* 405, 409.

[6] Callahan, above n. 1, 39–40.   [7] Ibid. 39.

[8] Timothy E. Quill, *Death and Dignity: Making Choices and Taking Charge* (New York: W.W. Norton, 1993) 50.   [9] *Pretty v. U.K.* (2002) 35 E.H.R.R. 1, [65] (Eur. Ct. H.R.).

[10] Callahan, above n. 1, 39–40.

[11] See the helpful discussion in Margaret Otlowski, *Voluntary Euthanasia and the Common Law* (Oxford: Oxford Univ. Press, 1997) 4–7.

[12] *Oxford English Dictionary* (2nd edn.) (Oxford: Oxford Univ. Press, 1989).

[13] House of Lords Select Committee on Medical Ethics, *Report,* HL Paper 21-I (Session 1993–1994) [20].

Preferring to emphasize motive rather than intention, Peter Singer defines euthanasia as 'the killing of those who are incurably ill and in great pain or distress, for the sake of those killed, and in order to spare them further suffering or distress.'[14] The classic example is the administration of a fatal dose of potassium chloride to a dying patient. The drug has no palliative or curative effect and produces death extremely rapidly.[15]

Euthanasia is voluntary when it is 'carried out at the request of the person killed.'[16] Euthanasia is 'involuntary when the person killed is capable of consenting to her own death, but does not do so, either because she is not asked, or because she is asked and chooses to go on living.'[17] Non-voluntary euthanasia occurs when the individual is incompetent to consent to or refuse euthanasia and has made no prior decision.[18]

The distinction between active and passive euthanasia, although problematic, is widely used.[19] This book deals predominantly with active euthanasia, that is, a 'deliberate act to end . . . life'.[20] The term passive euthanasia is often used to refer to the withdrawal or withholding of life-saving or life-sustaining treatment. Its use can be misleading, and will be avoided in this work.

It is important to note that in the Dutch and Belgian context,[21] the term 'euthanasia' is used to refer to the termination of life upon request or voluntary active euthanasia.[22] Assisted suicide is often included in this term.[23]

B. Assisted suicide

Assisted suicide can be any act which intentionally helps another to commit suicide, for example by 'providing him with the means to do so'.[24] Examples of such conduct could include: providing a prescription for lethal medication;[25] supplying such medication;[26] or setting up the elaborate machine created by Dr. Jack Kevorkian.[27]

---

[14] Peter Singer, *Practical Ethics* (2nd edn.) (Cambridge: Cambridge Univ. Press, 1993) 175. In Chapter 6 we will see that although euthanasia usually is performed in cases where there is severe, unrelievable suffering, this is not always a specific requirement in regulatory regimes. See Chapter 6, Sections V.C and VI.A.2 (discussing the absence of a suffering requirement in Oregon).

[15] See, e.g., *Cox* (1992) 12 B.M.L.R. 38 (Winchester (Eng.) Crown Ct.).

[16] Singer, above n. 14, 176.   [17] Ibid. 179.   [18] Ibid.

[19] Otlowski, above n. 11, 5–7.   [20] Ibid. 5.

[21] See Chapter 4, Section I.A. and Chapter 6, Section VI.B.

[22] The Dutch definition is discussed in Chapter 4, text accompanying n. 6. See also, John Griffiths, Alex Bood & Heleen Weyers, *Euthanasia and Law in the Netherlands* (Amsterdam: Amsterdam Univ. Press, 1998) 17. In Belgium, see Act on Euthanasia of 28 May 2002, s. 2.

[23] Griffiths, Bood & Weyers, above n. 22, 17. The situation is less clear in Belgium. See Chapter 6, text accompanying n. 216.

[24] Termination of Life on Request and Assisted Suicide (Review Procedures) Act 2001 (Neth.), s. 1(b). See the criminal provisions cited in Section III.B, below.

[25] See, e.g., Death with Dignity Act, Ore. Rev. Stat. § 127.800–§ 127.995 (1996).

[26] See, e.g., the situation in Switzerland, discussed in Andreas Frei et al., 'Assisted suicide as conducted by a "Right-to-Die"-society in Switzerland: A descriptive analysis of 43 consecutive cases' (2001) 131 *Swiss Med. Wkly* 375, 376.   [27] See Chapter 2, Section I.A.

C. Assisted dying

For ease of use, I use the term 'assisted dying' as a compendium that refers to both voluntary active euthanasia and assisted suicide.[28]

D. Other medical behaviour that (potentially) shortens life

The withdrawal or withholding of life-saving or life-sustaining treatment (sometimes referred to as passive euthanasia) and the provision of adequate pain relief may all bring about or hasten the patient's death. Although there are very strong reasons in favour of regulating *all* medical behaviour that potentially shortens life, rather than solely assisted dying,[29] this debate is outside the scope of this work. Most of the jurisdictions under consideration here criminalize only assisted dying – it is the issue of legalizing this practice which is the focus of this work.

III. Criminal Prohibitions[30]

A. Euthanasia

1. *Murder*

Most common law[31] and some civil law[32] jurisdictions treat termination of life on request or voluntary active euthanasia as murder. That is, the presence of a request does not affect the charge brought: termination of life on request is treated

---

[28] See, e.g., Assisted Dying for the Terminally Ill Bill, House of Lords, HL Bill 36, 9 Nov. 2005, www.publications.parliament.uk/pa/ld200506/ldbills/036/2006036.pdf, accessed 27 July 2006. The Bill is further discussed below, n. 43.

[29] Griffiths, Bood & Weyers, above n. 22, 252–7, 296–8; Helga Kuhse, 'From Intention to Consent: Learning from Experience with Euthanasia' in Margaret P. Battin et al., eds., *Physician Assisted Suicide: Expanding the Debate* (New York: Routledge, 1998) 252, 264.

[30] Interesting comparative analyses include Dana Elizabeth Hirsch, 'Euthanasia: Is it Murder or Mercy Killing? A Comparison of the Criminal Laws in the United States, the Netherlands and Switzerland' (1990) 12 *Loy. L.A. Int'l & Comp. L.J.* 821; Mustafa D. Sayid, 'Euthanasia: A Comparison of the Criminal Laws of Germany, Switzerland and the United States' (1983) 6 *Boston Coll. Int'l & Comp. L. Rev.* 533; Lesley Vickers, 'Assisted dying and the laws of three European countries' (1997) 147(6789) *New L.J.* 610 (discussing the Netherlands, Switzerland, and Germany); Herman Nys, 'Physician Involvement in a Patient's Death: A Continental European Perspective' (1999) 7 *Med. L. Rev.* 208; Timothy Stoltzfus Jost & Danuta Mendelson, 'A Comparative Study of the Law of Palliative Care and End-of-Life Treatment' (2003) 31 *J. L. Med. & Ethics* 130.

[31] In England and Wales, see, e.g., *R. (on the application of Pretty) v. D.P.P.* [2002] 1 A.C. 800, [5]; *Airedale NHS Trust v. Bland* [1993] A.C. 789, 865–6 (Lord Goff), 882, 885 (Lord Browne-Wilkinson), 892–3 (Lord Mustill); *Cox* (1992) 12 B.M.L.R. 38 (Winchester Crown Ct.) (instructing the jury that if the primary purpose of the administration of potassium chloride was to hasten death then it was murder). In Canada, see Criminal Code R.S. 1985, c. C-46, s. 14. The position is similar in the United States. See the cases cited in Laura Dietz et al., 'Consent; humanitarian purpose' (2006) 40A *Am. Jur. 2d Homicide* § 105. In Australia, see Criminal Code (N.Terr.), s. 26(3); Criminal Code (Tas.), s. 53(a); Criminal Code (W.A.), s. 261; Otlowski, above n. 11, 21. In New Zealand, see Crimes Act 1961, s. 63.

[32] See, e.g., Penal Code (Belg.), Art. 394; Penal Code (Fr.), Art. 221-1. In Belgium, see Bert Broeckaert, 'Belgium: Towards a Legal Recognition of Euthanasia' (2001) 8 *Eur. J. Health L.* 95.

similarly to termination of life without request,[33] although sentencing may reflect the presence of a request.[34] Separate offences of pre-meditated murder[35] and poisoning[36] or administering a noxious substance[37] are also available in some jurisdictions. These offences could be used in cases with or without a request.

2. Consensual homicide

Some civil law jurisdictions have a separate, lesser offence of consensual homicide or termination of life on request. In Switzerland, for example, Article 114 of the Penal Code provides that: 'Every person who shall for honourable reasons, especially mercy, kill a person on his or her serious and pressing request, shall be liable to imprisonment.'[38] Omitting any reference to the defendant's motive, Article 293(1) of the Dutch Criminal Code states: 'Any person who terminates another person's life at that person's express and earnest request shall be liable to a term of imprisonment not exceeding twelve years or a fifth-category fine.'[39] This offence is now qualified by an explicit defence of necessity available to a physician who fulfils the statutory due care criteria and reports the death appropriately.[40] In Spain, the offence of consensual homicide is specifically limited to cases involving terminal illness or severe, unbearable, and permanent suffering.[41] In Uruguay, the Penal Code provides that the defendant who commits consensual homicide motivated by compassion may be completely exonerated.[42]

A few recent investigations are described by Freddy Mortier & Luc Deliens, 'The Prospects of Effective Legal Control on Euthanasia in Belgium: Implications of recent end-of-life studies' in Klijn, above n. 4, 179, 181. See also, Heleen Weyers, 'Legal recognition of the right to die' in Austen Garwood-Gowers et al., eds., *Contemporary Issues in Healthcare Law and Ethics* (Edinburgh: Elsevier Butterworth-Heinemann, 2005) 253, 256, n. xi ('In Belgium... there were a few prosecutions of family members of the patient for killing on request or out of compassion'). Consent is no defence to murder under French criminal law. *Roubignac*, Cour de Cassation, Criminal Chamber, 2 July 1835, (1935) 1 *Sirey* 861; *Copillet*, Cour de Cassation, Criminal Chamber, 23 June 1838, (1838) 1 *Sirey* 625, concl. Dupin, note L.-M. Dev.; *Dénain*, Cour de Cassation, Criminal Chamber, 21 Aug. 1851, (1851) 5 *D.P.* 237; *P.*, C.A., Toulouse, 9 Aug. 1973, (1974) *Dalloz* 452. A few prosecutions have been reported. See Penney Lewis, 'The evolution of assisted dying in France: A third way?' (2005) 13(4) *Med. L. Rev.* 44, 46.

[33] See, e.g., *Arthur* (1993) 12 B.M.L.R. 1 (Leicester (Eng.) Crown Ct.); *Latimer* [2001] 1 S.C.R. 3, [28] discussed in Chapter 4, Section II.B; *Morrison* (1998) 174 N.S.R. (2d) 201 (N.S.S.C.).

[34] See, e.g., *Cox* (1992) 12 B.M.L.R. 38 (Winchester (Eng.) Crown Ct.) (doctor convicted of attempted murder given a one year suspended sentence).

[35] See, e.g., Penal Code (Fr.), Art. 221-3 (assassinat).

[36] See, e.g., Penal Code (Fr.), Art. 221-5; Penal Code (Belg.), Art. 397.

[37] See, e.g., Criminal Code R.S. 1985 (Cda.), c. C-46, s. 245.

[38] Penal Code (Switz.), Art. 114. See also, Penal Code (Ger.), Art. 216; Penal Code (Croatia), Art. 94; Penal Code (Den.), Art. 239; Penal Code (Italy), Art. 579; Criminal Code (Portugal), Art. 134.

[39] Criminal Code (Neth.), Art. 293(1), as amended by the Termination of Life on Request and Assisted Suicide (Review Procedures) Act 2001 (Neth.), s. 20A. A fifth-category fine is now € 45000, Criminal Code (Neth.), Art. 23.

[40] Criminal Code (Neth.), Art. 293(2) as inserted by the Termination of Life on Request and Assisted Suicide (Review Procedures) Act 2001 (Neth.), s. 20A. The Dutch law is discussed in depth in Chapter 4. See particularly, Chapter 4, Section I.C.

[41] Penal Code 1995 (Spain), Art. 143(4).   [42] Penal Code (Uruguay), Art. 37.

Although proposals have been made in England and Wales[43] and New Zealand[44] to adopt similar provisions, they have not been successful. In 1995, the Northern Territory of Australia passed legislation legalizing physician-performed voluntary active euthanasia (as well as physician-assisted suicide). The Act was overturned by the Australian Federal Parliament in 1997.[45]

3. Compassionate homicide

Some civil law jurisdictions have separate offences of compassionate homicide. In Germany, compassionate killing in the absence of a request is prosecuted as the lesser offence of manslaughter.[46] Similarly, in Colombia, a separate lesser offence of compassionate homicide is available to a defendant who killed another in order to end intense suffering stemming from injury or serious and incurable illness.[47]

B. Assisted suicide

1. Complete prohibitions

Most jurisdictions have criminal prohibitions on assisted suicide.[48] A majority of U.S. states impose criminal penalties on one who assists another in committing

---

[43] See Criminal Law Revision Committee, *Working Paper on Offences Against the Person* (1976) [82]. The lesser offence of 'mercy' killing would have applied in cases where the victim was '(1) permanently subject to great bodily pain or suffering, or (2) permanently helpless from bodily or mental incapacity, or (3) subject to rapid and incurable bodily or mental degeneration'. No request requirement was proposed in order to allow the offence to encompass cases where the victim was incompetent. The proposal was dropped owing to lack of support from consultees. See Criminal Law Revision Committee, *Offences Against the Person*, Report No. 14 (1980) [115]. Numerous private members' bills have failed to gain Parliamentary support. See Hazel Biggs, *Euthanasia, Death with Dignity and the Law* (Oxford: Hart Publishing, 2001) 13. The most recent of these was the Assisted Dying for the Terminally Ill Bill, which was recently defeated in the House of Lords. Assisted Dying for the Terminally Ill Bill, House of Lords, HL Bill 36, 9 Nov. 2005, www.publications.parliament.uk/pa/ld200506/ldbills/036/2006036.pdf, accessed 27 July 2006; *Hansard*, House of Lords, 12 May 2006, cols. 1184–1295. See also, House of Lords Select Committee on the Assisted Dying for the Terminally Ill Bill, *Report*, HL Paper 86-I (2005) www.publications.parliament.uk/pa/ld200405/ldselect/ldasdy/86/86i.pdf, accessed 27 July 2006; Hazel M. Biggs, 'The Assisted Dying for the Terminally Ill Bill 2004: Will English law soon allow patients the choice to die?' (2005) 12(1) *Eur. J. Health L.* 43.

[44] A 1995 private member's Bill which would have allowed voluntary active euthanasia for the terminally ill was unsuccessful. Roger S. Magnusson, *Angels of Death – Exploring the Euthanasia Underground* (New Haven, Conn.: Yale Univ. Press, 2002) 66.

[45] Rights of the Terminally Ill Act 1995 (N.Terr.); Euthanasia Laws Act 1997 (Cth.). See Chapter 6, Section VI.C.

[46] Penal Code (Ger.), Arts. 211–213. See also, Penal Code (Switz.), Arts. 63–64, 111.

[47] Penal Code 2000 (Colombia), Art. 106. A decision of the Colombian Constitutional Court in 1997 carved out a defence to the predecessor of this provision for a doctor who terminates the life of a terminally ill, intensely suffering patient with the informed consent of the patient. *In re Artículo 326 del Código Penal (Re Article 326 of the Penal Code)*, Decision C-239 of 1997, discussed in Justice Manuel José Cepeda-Espinosa, 'Judicial Activism in a Violent Context: The Origin, Role, and Impact of the Colombian Constitutional Court' (2004) 3 *Wash. U. Global Stud. L. Rev.* 529, 580–1.

[48] *Rodriguez v. British Columbia (Attorney-General)* [1993] 3 S.C.R. 519, [48] (observing that no western democracy expressly permits assisted suicide and that most countries impose criminal penalties for such acts of assistance).

suicide.[49] The United States now also prohibits the use of federal funds in support of physician-assisted suicide.[50] Across the rest of the common law world, the criminalization of assisted suicide is widespread, including England,[51] Ireland,[52] Canada,[53] all Australian states,[54] and New Zealand.[55] Many civil law jurisdictions have similar provisions, including Austria,[56] Italy,[57] Spain,[58] and Portugal.[59]

2. Limited prohibitions

A minority of jurisdictions restrict the scope of criminalization of assistance in suicide, including Switzerland, which criminalizes assistance only where the assister's motive was selfish rather than compassionate,[60] and Denmark, which punishes any person who assists another in committing suicide with a fine or simple detention, but subjects assistance with suicide committed for 'reasons of personal interest' to imprisonment.[61] In the Netherlands, the crime of assisted suicide is now qualified by an explicit defence of necessity available to a physician who fulfils the statutory due care criteria and reports the death appropriately.[62] In Oregon, the Death with Dignity Act allows terminally ill persons with less than six months to live to request a prescription of a lethal dose of drugs.[63]

3. Absence of prohibition

In theory, in the absence of any prohibition against assisting suicide, the act of assisting will not constitute a criminal offence if there is no criminal prohibition

---

[49] *Cruzan v. Director, Mo. Dep't of Health* (1990) 497 U.S. 261, 280 (noting that a majority of states have laws imposing criminal penalties on assisted suicide); *Compassion in Dying v. Washington* (1994) 850 F. Supp. 1454, 1464, n. 9 (W.D. Wash.); *Kevorkian* (1994) 527 N.W.2d 714, 731, n. 51 (Mich. S.C.) (listing state statutes criminalizing assisted suicide). See generally, Neil M. Gorsuch, 'The Legalization of Assisted Suicide and the Law of Unintended Consequences: A Review of the Dutch and Oregon Experiments and Leading Utilitarian Arguments For Legal Change' [2004] *Wis. L. Rev.* 1347, App. A. See also, Model Penal Code § 210.5(2) cmt.5 (1980).

[50] Assisted Suicide Funding Restriction Act of 1997, 42 U.S.C. §§ 14401–14408 (2000).

[51] Suicide Act 1961 (Eng.), s. 2(1). See *Attorney General v. Able* [1984] 1 All E.R. 277 (Eng. Q.B.); *Chard*, The Times, 23 Sept. 1993 (Central Crim. Ct.); *Re Z (Local Authority: Duty)* [2005] 1 W.L.R. 959 (Eng. H.C.).   [52] Criminal Law (Suicide) Act 1993 (Ire.), s. 2(2).

[53] Criminal Code R.S. 1985 (Cda.), c. C-46, s. 241.

[54] Crimes Act 1900 (A.C.T.), s. 17; Crimes Act 1900 (N.S.W.), s. 31C; Criminal Code (Qld.), s. 311; Criminal Law Consolidation Act 1935 (S.A.), s. 13A(5); Criminal Code (Tas.), s. 163; Crimes Act 1958 (Vic.), s. 6B(2); Criminal Code (W.A.), s. 288; Criminal Code (N.Terr.), s. 168.

[55] Crimes Act 1961 (N.Z.), s. 179.   [56] Penal Act (Austria), s. 139b.

[57] Penal Code (Italy), Art. 580.   [58] Penal Code 1995 (Spain), Art. 143(2).

[59] Criminal Code (Portugal), Art. 135. See also, Penal Code (Croatia), Art. 96; Penal Code 2000 (Colombia), Art. 107.

[60] Penal Code (Switz.), Art. 115. See Olivier Guillod & Aline Schmidt, 'Assisted suicide under Swiss law' (2005) 12 *Eur. J. Health L.* 25; Samia A. Hurst & Alex Mauron, 'Assisted suicide and euthanasia in Switzerland: allowing a role for non-physicians' (2003) 326 *Br. Med. J.* 271.

[61] Penal Code (Den.), Art. 240.

[62] Criminal Code (Neth.), Art. 294, as amended by Termination of Life on Request and Assisted Suicide (Review Procedures) Act 2001 (Neth.), s. 20B. See Chapter 4, Section I.C.

[63] Death with Dignity Act, Ore. Rev. Stat. § 127.800–§ 127.995 (1996). See Chapter 6, Section VI.A.

on attempting suicide. Other offences may, however, come into play. For example, in France, although neither suicide itself nor assisting suicide are criminal offences,[64] anyone who intentionally provides assistance could be prosecuted for failing to assist a person in danger[65] or even involuntary homicide.[66] Following the publication of a suicide manual in 1982[67] and the prosecution of one of its authors for failing to assist a person in danger,[68] new provisions were inserted into the Penal Code. Article 223-13 prohibits 'provocation to suicide' when followed by a successful or attempted suicide. Article 223-14 prohibits 'propaganda or advertising . . . in favour of products, articles or methods recommended as a means to procure one's death.'[69] The doctrine has strongly criticized the new provisions for failing to include a specific prohibition against assisting a suicide.[70]

In Germany, there is no specific provision in the Penal Code prohibiting assistance in suicide. The assister will not be liable for homicide provided that the individual who committed suicide with assistance determined her own fate and retained control over the final act.[71] The assistee must have acted of her own free will upon a sincere wish to die. Physician-assisted suicide is more problematic. If the patient falls unconscious in the presence of her doctor following the final act,

---

[64] *Assoc. Défense contre l'incitation au suicide c. Moreau*, Tribunal de Grande Instance, Paris, 16th Chamber, 11 Apr. 1995, (1996) *J.C.P. G.* II [22729], note Lucas-Gallay. See also, J. Borricand, 'La répression de la provocation au suicide: de la jurisprudence à la loi' ('The repression of provocation of suicide: from the jurisprudence to the law') (1988) *J.C.P.* I [3359], § 12; G. Levasseur, 'Le suicide en droit pénal' ('Suicide in criminal law') in F. Terré, ed., *Le suicide* (Paris: Presses Universitaires de France, 1994) 121, 125–6.

[65] Penal Code (Fr.), Art. 223-6. See Chapter 5, Section III.B.

[66] *P.*, CA Toulouse, 9 Aug. 1973, (1974) *Dalloz* 452.

[67] C. Guillon & Y. Le Bonniec, *Suicide, mode d'emploi (Histoire, technique, actualité) (Suicide, how to do it (history, techniques, news))* (Paris: Editions Alain Moreau, 1982).

[68] *X.*, Tribunal de Grande Instance, Paris, 16th Correctional Chamber, 20 Nov. 1985, (1986) *Dalloz* 369, note Calais; (1987) *Rev. Sci. Crim. (J. of Criminal Sciences)* 202, note Levasseur; *Le Bonniec*, Cour de Cassation, Criminal Chamber, 26 Apr. 1988, *Bull. crim.* no. 178, (1990) *Dalloz* Juris. 479, note Fenaux. An initial attempt to prosecute both authors had failed. See *Époux M.*, Tribunal de Grande Instance, Paris, 23 Jan. 1985, (1985) *Dalloz* Juris. 418, note Calais and see also, *L. et ADMD*, Tribunal de Grande Instance, Paris, 25 Jan. 1984, (1984) *Dalloz* Juris. 486, note Mayer. The subsequent prosecution was only possible because one of the authors of the manual had entered into a correspondence with the victim which had alerted him to the risk that he would take his own life. See Levasseur, above 203. More than 70 people killed themselves using this manual before it was withdrawn from publication. Levasseur, above n. 64, 128.

[69] See *Assoc. Défense contre l'incitation au suicide c. Moreau*, Tribunal de Grande Instance, Paris, 16th Chamber, 11 Apr. 1995, (1996) *J.C.P. G.* II [22729], note Lucas-Gallay (publisher of new edition of *Suicide, mode d'emploi* found guilty); *C., T.*, Court of Appeal, Paris, 11th Chamber, 18 Jan. 2001, no. 2001-137734, (2001) 84 *Droit pénal* 12; *C., T.*, Cour de Cassation, Criminal Chamber, 13 Nov. 2001, no. 01-81.418, (2002) *J.C.P.* IV 105 (newspaper publisher found guilty over advertisement for Derek Humphry, *Final Exit: The Practicalities of Self-Deliverance and Assisted Suicide for the Dying* (Secaucus, N.J.: Hemlock Society, 1991)).

[70] See the sources cited in Levasseur, above n. 64, 129. Nevertheless, the dearth of assisted suicide cases suggests that assisted suicide is less prevalent than active euthanasia in France. See above n. 32.

[71] Kathrin Becker-Schwarze, 'Legal Restrictions of Physician-Assisted Suicide' (2005) 12 *Eur. J. Health L.* 11, 16–17; Marc Stauch, 'Euthanasia and assisted suicide in German law' (2005) 7(3) *Contemp. Issues in Law* 301, 312–13.

the doctor may have a duty to rescue her.[72] However, the doctor's duty to rescue may not apply 'in a specific case when the patient himself only experiences his life as a burden and wants to be freed from it'.[73]

It is noteworthy that Oregon is the only common law jurisdiction that provides a limited exception to the otherwise widespread total prohibition on both assisting suicide and active euthanasia.[74] In the common law world, the most serious attempts at legal change on assisted dying have been made by challenging criminal prohibitions on assisted suicide on the grounds that such prohibitions violate patients' constitutional rights. The next chapter considers the range of such challenges.

---

[72] *Wittig*, Federal Supreme Court (Bundesgerichtshof), 4 July 1984, BGHSt 32, 367, discussed in Becker-Schwarze, above n. 71, 18–19; Stauch, above n. 71, 313–15. See Penal Code (Ger.), Art. 323.

[73] Nys, above n. 30, 233. See also, Margaret P. Battin, 'Assisted Suicide: Can We Learn from Germany?' (1992) 22(2) *Hastings Center Rep.* 45, 45–6; Jost & Mendelson, above n. 30, 135–6.

[74] See above, text accompanying n. 63.

2

Rights to Assisted Dying

I. Introduction

The first part of this Chapter provides some context for the rights debate over assisted suicide in Canada, the United States, and the United Kingdom. It was in these jurisdictions that unsuccessful challenges to criminal prohibitions on assisted suicide were brought using constitutionally entrenched human rights.

A. Individual cases

The debate surrounding the legalization of assisted suicide was galvanized by reports of specific cases of assisted suicide in the United States, primarily involving physicians such as Kevorkian and Quill. National and international media attention on criminal trials of individuals accused of assisting in a suicide has heightened public awareness of the issue.[1] In particular, the legal proceedings surrounding retired pathologist Dr. Jack Kevorkian, who assisted in over one hundred suicides in Michigan between 1990 and 1999, captured the public imagination in the United States and around the world and did much to bring the issue of assisted suicide to public attention.[2] Kevorkian was initially unsuccessfully charged with murder, and Michigan enacted a criminal prohibition on assistance in suicide in response to his actions.[3] Kevorkian was charged under the new law and both he and the Michigan chapter of the American Civil Liberties Union unsuccessfully challenged its constitutionality.[4] Both lower courts held that the right to commit suicide is guaranteed by the U.S. Constitution, but the Michigan Court of Appeals reversed on the federal constitutional issue, finding no constitutional right to commit suicide.[5] The Michigan Supreme Court affirmed on this

[1] See, e.g., the case discussed by the Second Circuit Court of Appeals in *Quill v. Vacco* (1996) 80 F.3d 716, 723, n. 1. See also, Gerald Jacobs, 'Assisted Suicide Cases Difficult to Prosecute; Defendants Have Little Chance of Facing Prison' *Hartford Courant*, 29 Sept. 1994, A3 (describing five separate cases of assisted suicide in New England).

[2] See generally, Neal Nicol & Harry Wylie, *Between the Dying and the Dead: Dr Jack Kevorkian, the Assisted Suicide Machine and the Battle to Legalise Euthanasia* (London: Vision, 2006); Lori A. Roscoe et al., 'Dr. Jack Kevorkian and Cases of Euthanasia in Oakland County, Michigan, 1990–1998' (2000) 343(23) *New Eng. J. Med.* 1735.   [3] Mich. Comp. Laws § 752.1027 (1993).

[4] *Kevorkian* (1993) No. 93–11482, 1993 WL 603212, *1 (Mich. Cir. Ct.); *Hobbins v. Attorney Gen.* (1993) No. 93-306-178 CZ, 1993 WL 276833, *7 (Mich. Cir. Ct.).

[5] *Hobbins v. Attorney General* (1994) 518 N.W.2d 487 (Mich. C.A.).

issue, holding that the U.S. Constitution does not prohibit a state from imposing criminal penalties for assistance in suicide.[6] In addition, in 1991 an 'Order of Permanent Injunction' enjoining Kevorkian from assisting in a suicide was entered, and later affirmed by the Michigan Court of Appeals,[7] relying on the Michigan Supreme Court's 1994 decision which had affirmed that assisted suicide was a common law crime.[8]

At the same time, Kevorkian brought an action for injunctive and declaratory relief against the Oakland County Prosecutor preventing him from prosecuting Kevorkian for 'his assisted suicide activities'.[9] The court rejected the plaintiffs' claims based on the constitutional rights to due process and equal protection, but held that the Michigan Supreme Court's interpretation of the common law as prohibiting assisted suicide prior to the statutory prohibition enacted in December 1992 was unconstitutionally vague.[10] Kevorkian was later jailed for second-degree murder following the broadcast on the television programme *60 Minutes* of a videotape depicting Kevorkian giving a lethal injection to Thomas Youk.[11] Extensive media coverage focused on Kevorkian. His trials were carried on the cable network Court TV and he was the subject of numerous newspaper and television reports, including a *Frontline* documentary.[12]

A less controversial case involved the doctor Timothy Quill, who described, in an article in the *New England Journal of Medicine*, his relationship with a patient called 'Diane', who had been diagnosed with terminal leukaemia. Quill wrote of his decision to accede to her request to provide her with sufficient pills to enable her to take her own life when she felt the time was right.[13] Quill was subject to a 'very public criminal investigation' following the publication of this article.[14]

---

[6] *Kevorkian* (1994) 527 N.W.2d 714, 732–3 (Mich. S.C.), *certiorari* denied, *Hobbins v. Kelley* (1995) 514 U.S. 1083.

[7] *Kevorkian* (1995) 534 N.W.2d 172 (Mich. C.A.), leave to appeal denied, (1996) 549 N.W. 2d 566 (Mich. S.C.), *certiorari* denied, *Kevorkian v. Michigan* (1996) 519 U.S. 928.

[8] *Kevorkian* (1994) 527 N.W.2d 714, 732–3 (Mich. S.C.), *certiorari* denied, *Hobbins v. Kelley* (1995) 514 U.S. 1083.

[9] *Kevorkian v. Thompson* (1997) 947 F. Supp. 1152, 1154 (E.D. Mich.). The district court concluded, relying on the abstention rule from *Younger v. Harris* (1971) 401 U.S. 37 that it should abstain from adjudicating the plaintiff Kevorkian's claims, but would adjudicate those of the plaintiff Good, who was not facing a pending state action. Ibid. 1164–6.

[10] *Kevorkian v. Thompson* (1997) 947 F. Supp. 1152, 1167–74, 1179 (E.D. Mich.).

[11] Dirk Johnson, 'Kevorkian Sentenced to 10 to 25 Years in Prison' *N.Y. Times*, 14 Apr. 1999, A1.

[12] *The Kevorkian File*, P.B.S. television broadcast, (first) 5 Apr. 1994. See, e.g., David Margolick, 'Kevorkian's Trial Has Come to End But Debate on Assisted Suicide Hasn't' *N.Y. Times*, 4 May 1994, A16; David Margolick, 'Jury Acquits Dr. Kevorkian of Illegally Aiding a Suicide' *N.Y. Times*, 3 May 1994, A1; Edward Walsh, 'Kevorkian Acquitted in Suicide: Former Pathologist Vows Continued Fight for Assisted Deaths' *Wash. Post*, 3 May 1994, A1; James A. McClear & Mark Truby, 'Judge "Stops" Kevorkian with Jail' *Detroit News*, 14 Apr. 1999, A1.

[13] Timothy E. Quill, 'Death and Dignity: A Case of Individualized Decision Making' (1991) 324(10) *New Eng. J. Med.* 691, 693–4. See also, Timothy E. Quill, 'Doctor, I Want to Die. Will You Help Me?' (1993) 270(7) *J. Am. Med. Ass'n* 870; Peter A. Ubel, 'Assisted suicide and the case of Dr Quill and Diane' (1993) 8(4) *Issues in Law & Med.* 487.

[14] Quill, 'Death and Dignity', above n. 13. See also, *Quill v. Koppell* (1994) 870 F. Supp. 78, 80 (S.D.N.Y.).

Quill and other witnesses testified before the grand jury, but no indictment was handed down.[15]

Unlike in the United States, in the United Kingdom and Canada there have been no highly publicized trials of medical practitioners for assisting their patients' suicides. Although important assisted dying prosecutions have occurred in these jurisdictions, they have tended to involve active euthanasia, and thus the medical practitioners involved have been tried for murder or attempted murder, rather than for assisted suicide.[16]

B. Constitutional challenges to criminal prohibitions on assisted suicide

The legalization debate was also stimulated by impassioned pleas for legalization and assistance in suicide from individuals suffering in the throes of terminal or agonizing diseases, such as Sue Rodriguez and Dianne Pretty, who were both suffering from terminal amyotrophic lateral sclerosis or motor neurone disease. Rodriguez petitioned the Canadian courts for a declaration that the criminal prohibition on assisted suicide violated her constitutional rights to life, liberty and security of the person, to freedom from cruel and unusual treatment, and to equality.[17] She was unsuccessful at all levels including the Supreme Court of Canada. In 1993, a decision dismissing her appeal was rendered by a 5–4 majority, which concluded that the criminal prohibition on assisted suicide does not violate a terminally ill patient's constitutional rights.[18] Rodriguez later committed physician-assisted suicide in the presence of a Member of Parliament with the assistance of an as-yet unnamed physician in early 1994.[19] No charges were brought in connection with the death, although a special prosecutor was appointed to look into the matter.[20]

In a similar case in England, Dianne Pretty requested an assurance in advance from the Director of Public Prosecutions (D.P.P.) that her husband would not be prosecuted if he assisted her suicide. Mrs. Pretty relied on her rights to life, freedom from torture and inhuman or degrading treatment, respect for her private and family life, freedom of thought, conscience and religion, and freedom from discrimination under the European Convention on Human Rights.[21] She appealed

---

[15] See *Quill v. Koppell* (1994) 870 F. Supp. 78, 80 (S.D.N.Y.).

[16] On the distinction between euthanasia and assisted suicide and the relevant legal provisions, see Chapter 1, Sections II and III. For individual cases in the United Kingdom, see, e.g., *Adams (Bodkin)* [1957] Crim. L.R. 365 (Central Crim. Ct.); *Cox* (1992) 12 B.M.L.R. 38 (Winchester Crown Ct.); Anthony Arlidge, 'The Trial of Dr David Moor' [2000] *Crim. L.R.* 31. In Canada, see, e.g., *Latimer* [2001] 1 S.C.R. 3, [28] discussed in Chapter 4, Section II.B; *Morrison* (1998) 174 N.S.R. (2d) 201 (N.S.S.C.). See also, Chapter 4, Section III.A.1.

[17] Canadian Charter of Rights and Freedoms, ss. 7, 12, 15.

[18] *Rodriguez v. British Columbia (Attorney-General)* [1993] 3 S.C.R. 519, 521–2.

[19] Miro Cernetig, 'Police Suspect Rodriguez Suicide' *Globe and Mail*, 14 Feb. 1994, A1.

[20] 'Lawyer to Probe Rodriguez Suicide' *Globe and Mail*, 11 Jan. 1995, A1; 'Passages' *MacLean's*, 10 July 1995, 9 (stating that a politician was cleared of criminal charges after observing an assisted suicide).

[21] European Convention on Human Rights, Arts. 2, 3, 8, 9, 14.

against the D.P.P.'s refusal to provide such assurance through the English courts to the European Court of Human Rights but was unsuccessful at every level.[22]

In 1997, challenges in the United States brought by doctors and patients' groups were also unsuccessful at the United States Supreme Court in the companion cases of *Washington v. Glucksberg* and *Vacco v. Quill*.[23] In contrast to the Canadian and English cases, though, the applicants in *Washington v. Glucksberg* and *Vacco v. Quill* had succeeded at the interim appellate level (in the Ninth and Second Circuits) on the basis of the liberty interest protected by the Due Process clause[24] and the right to equal protection respectively.[25]

C. The rights debate over assisted suicide

Individuals and organizations on both sides of the debate over the legalization of assisted suicide were quick to frame their arguments in terms of rights. Attracted by the trumping[26] and attention-getting[27] effects of rights discourse and the powerful political impact of rights-based arguments, proponents and opponents of assisted suicide claimed a battery of different rights to support their various positions, many of which were used in the constitutional challenges described in the previous section.

In general terms, those in favour of the legalization of assisted suicide stressed a 'revitalized argument for self-determination, pushing the idea of autonomy and patient rights as far as they can go.'[28] Those against such legalization relied upon arguments concerning the right to life and, to a lesser extent, the right to equality or equal protection.[29]

---

[22] *R. (on the application of Pretty) v. D.P.P.* [2001] E.W.H.C. Admin. 788; *R. (on the application of Pretty) v. D.P.P.* [2002] 1 A.C. 800; *Pretty v. U.K.* (2002) 35 E.H.R.R. 1 (Eur. Ct. H.R.). The constitutionality of the English prohibition on assisting a suicide had been previously considered by the European Commission on Human Rights in *R. v. U.K.* (1983) 6 E.H.R.R. 140 (affirming a conviction of conspiring to aid and abet suicide where the defendant had facilitated contact between individuals desiring assistance in suicide and an individual willing to provide such assistance). The European Commission upheld the prohibition as necessary in a democratic society to prevent abuses and protect health. Ibid. 144.

[23] *Vacco v. Quill* (1997) 521 U.S. 793, 799; *Washington v. Glucksberg* (1997) 521 U.S. 702, 735. A later challenge in Alaska was similarly unsuccessful. *Sampson v. Alaska* (2001) 31 P3d 88 (Alaska S.C.). See also, *Donaldson v. Van de Kamp* (1992) 4 Cal. Rptr. 2d 59, 64 (Cal. C.A.) (holding that the cancer-afflicted plaintiff, seeking pre-mortem cryogenic preservation, had no constitutional right to state-assisted death); *Krischer v. McIver* (1997) 697 So. 2d 97, 100 (Fla. S.C.) (following the U.S.S.C. holding that there is no fundamental right to assisted suicide and holding the state statute criminalizing assisted suicide constitutional); *Kevorkian* (1994) 527 N.W.2d 714 (Mich. S.C.) (holding that the state statute banning assisted suicide conformed with both the state and federal constitutions).

[24] *Compassion in Dying v. Washington* (1996) 79 F.3d 790, 839 (9th Cir. en banc). This decision is discussed in detail in Chapter 6, Section II.D.

[25] *Quill v. Vacco* (1996) 80 F.3d 716, 729 (2nd Cir.). This decision is discussed in detail in Chapter 6, Section II.C.

[26] Ronald Dworkin, *Taking Rights Seriously* (Cambridge, Mass.: Harvard Univ. Press, 1977) xi.

[27] Martha Minow, 'Interpreting Rights: An Essay for Robert Cover' (1987) 96 *Yale L.J.* 1860, 1899.

[28] Daniel Callahan, 'Can We Return Death to Disease?' (1989) 19(1) *Hastings Center Rep.* S4.

[29] Ibid.

The next section of this chapter enumerates different formulations of a right to suicide or assisted suicide. The discussion then moves from the *kind* of right claimed, to the *basis* of such a right, requiring a canvass of rights-based arguments both in favour of and against the legalization of assisted suicide. Included, where appropriate, is a brief mention of any conceptual difficulties or limitations associated with the right at issue in the context of assisted suicide. The presentation of a multitude of conflicting and seemingly irresolvable rights-based claims suggests the need to examine more closely the phenomenon of rights-based arguments in the context of assisted suicide. In Chapter 3, the problems associated with such arguments are illuminated by looking at some of the critiques of rights which have gained popularity in recent years, and by discussing their applicability to the rights-based arguments used in the assisted suicide debate. These critiques suggest particular difficulties with claims using rights in this context.

II. Rights in the Assisted Suicide Debate

A. Right to suicide or right to assisted suicide?

As a preliminary matter, it must be noted that claims to legalize assisted suicide using rights can be couched in terms of either a right to suicide[30] or a right to assisted suicide.[31] Interestingly, the lead opinion in the Michigan Supreme Court case rejecting the federal constitutional arguments in favour of legalization began with the assertion that what is at issue is the existence of a fundamental right to commit suicide, from which a right to assistance *may* be derived:

An attempt to find a liberty interest in assisted suicide independent of a liberty interest in suicide itself cannot succeed. If the Due Process Clause does not encompass a fundamental right to end one's life, it cannot encompass a right to assistance in ending one's life.[32]

Levin J., dissenting, argued that

[b]y framing the question in this manner, the lead opinion foreordains the answer. . . . The real issue is not whether the state can generally prohibit suicide. The real issue is whether the state may deny a competent, terminally ill person, facing imminent, agonizing death, medical assistance to commit suicide.[33]

Proponents of assisted suicide who rely on a right to suicide assert that such a right necessarily entails the impermissibility of prohibitions on assisted

---

[30] See, e.g., Samuel E. Wallace & Albin Eser, 'The Rights of Personhood' in Samuel E. Wallace & Albin Eser, eds., *Suicide and Euthanasia: The Rights of Personhood* (Knoxville, Tenn.: Univ. Tenn. Press, 1981) 99, 101.

[31] See, e.g., Note, 'Physician-Assisted Suicide and the Right to Die with Assistance' (1992) 105 *Harv. L. Rev.* 2021, 2023–31.

[32] *Kevorkian* (1994) 527 N.W.2d 714, 726, n. 35 (Mich. S.C., Cavanagh C.J. & Brickley & Griffin JJ.).

[33] *Kevorkian* (1994) 527 N.W.2d 714, 748 (Mich. S.C., Cavanagh C.J. & Brickley & Griffin JJ.).

suicide.[34] Similarly, arguments against the legalization of assisted suicide may reject either or both the right to suicide[35] or the right to assisted suicide.[36] In this book, I will maintain consistency with individual commentators' formulations. When speaking generally, I will refer to the 'right to suicide or assisted suicide'.

B. Different types of rights to suicide or assisted suicide

Margaret Pabst Battin distinguishes three different ways in which a right to suicide can be formulated.[37] First, as a liberty right: the individual is free to commit suicide – she has no obligation not to do so. Secondly, as a right to non-interference: others have a duty not to interfere with the individual's suicide. Thirdly, as a positive or welfare right: others have a duty to assist the individual with her suicide. This typology can also be applied to a right to assisted suicide. The liberty right would be a freedom to commit assisted suicide. The right to non-interference would mean that others have a duty not to interfere with the assisted suicide, that is, with either the individual or the assister. The positive right would involve a duty on the part of others to *be* the assister.[38]

Most analyses of a right to suicide or assisted suicide either assume or assert that such a right must be either a liberty right[39] or a right to non-interference. For example, one commentator writes:

the right to die with assistance would provide only a right against state interference, not a right to force an unwilling physician to assist in a patient's suicide. . . . Similarly, patients

---

[34] 'It is argued that, because suicide is a constitutional right, laws that forbid assisting the commission of suicide can no more be constitutional than could the imposition of criminal penalties for assisting another to reach a voting booth or a place of worship.' Thomas J. Marzen et al., 'Suicide: A Constitutional Right?' (1985) 24 *Duq. L. Rev.* 1, 8.

[35] See, e.g., Michael Ariens, 'Suicidal Rights' (1988) 20 *Rutgers L.J.* 79. See also, *Washington v. Glucksberg* (1997) 521 U.S. 702, 723 (Rehnquist C.J.) ('the question before us is whether the "liberty" specially protected by the Due Process Clause includes a right to commit suicide which itself includes a right to assistance in doing so'); *Kevorkian* (1994) 527 N.W.2d 714, 730, n. 47 (Mich. S.C.); John Keown, 'European Court of Human Rights: Death in Strasbourg – assisted suicide, the *Pretty* case, and the European Convention on Human Rights' (2003) 1(4) *Int'l J. Const'l L.* 722, 728.

[36] See, e.g., James Bopp, Jr., 'Is Assisted Suicide Constitutionally Protected?' (1987) 3 *Issues in Law & Med.* 113, 129; *Quill v. Vacco* (1996) 80 F.3d 716, 724 (2nd Cir.) ('The right to assisted suicide finds no cognizable basis in the Constitution's language or design.').

[37] Margaret Pabst Battin, *Ethical Issues in Suicide* (Englewood Cliffs, N.J.: Prentice-Hall, 1995) 184–5. Other typologies are of course possible. See Isaiah Berlin, 'Two Concepts of Liberty' in *Four Essays on Liberty* (Oxford: Oxford Univ. Press, 1969) 118, 121–2 (distinguishing between positive and negative liberty); H.L.A. Hart, 'Are There Any Natural Rights?' (1955) 64 *Phil. Rev.* 175, reprinted in David Lyons, ed., *Rights* (Belmont, Calif.: Wadsworth, 1979) 14, 20 (distinguishing between general and special rights); Wesley Newcomb Hohfeld, *Fundamental Legal Conceptions As Applied in Judicial Reasoning* (New Haven, Conn.: Yale Univ. Press, 1919) 36 (distinguishing between claim-rights, liberties, powers, and immunities). For the purposes of this work, the distinctions between liberty rights, rights to non-interference, and positive rights prove most helpful.

[38] See Battin, above n. 37, 185.

[39] See, e.g., Antje Pedain, 'The Human Rights Dimension of the Diane Pretty Case' (2003) 62(1) *Camb. L.J.* 181, 185, 187.

have no right to force unwilling physicians to withdraw life-sustaining treatment....
Instead, a physician may make arrangements for the patient's transfer to another physician
or hospital that will withdraw treatment.[40]

This formulation of the right to suicide or assisted suicide can be contrasted
with a positive or welfare right, which would necessarily and controversially entail
a corresponding duty to assist.[41] Such a positive right could be formulated as
a right to assistance in suicide. In the context of euthanasia, a positive right
formulation would be that if a person has a right to be killed, then another has a
duty to kill him.[42] Similarly, if a person has a right to assistance in suicide, then
another has a duty to provide that assistance. This kind of rights claim faces stiff
opposition. For example, Robert Weir argues that patients should *not* request
physician-assisted suicide on the grounds of the distinction between positive and
negative rights:

A decision made by a patient to forgo mechanical ventilation, feeding tubes, or some other
life-sustaining treatment involves the negative right (or liberty right) of treatment refusal.
A correlate of this negative right is the obligation of the patient's physician not to interfere
with or thwart that negative right unless the physician has some overriding obligation of
another sort. By contrast, a request by a patient for a physician's assistance in committing
suicide can be interpreted as involving a positive right (or welfare right), or at least a claim
to that effect. The difference is important: the patient does not merely request to be left
alone by the physician, but tries to impose a moral obligation on the physician to help the
patient accomplish the desired end of self-destruction. That claim, whether based on merit
or need, is weak, and certainly need not be regarded as imposing an obligation on the
physician who receives it.[43]

One commentator who does propose a positive right to suicide is Steven
Neeley, who observes that '[g]ravely ill, competent patients who wanted to die,

---

[40] Note, above n. 31, 2024, n. 29 (citations omitted). See also, H. Tristram Engelhardt, Jr. &
Michele Malloy, 'Suicide and Assisting Suicide: A Critique of Legal Sanctions' (1982) 36 *Sw. L.J.*
1003, 1013; Maurice A.M. de Wachter, 'Euthanasia in the Netherlands' (1992) 22(2) *Hastings
Center Rep.* 23, 26 (reporting remarks of Professor William J. Winslade); Leon R. Kass, 'Is There a
Right to Die?' (1993) 23(1) *Hastings Center Rep.* 34, 39–42 (examining various perspectives on the
liberty interest in the right to die); Ronald Dworkin et al., 'Assisted Suicide: The Philosophers' Brief'
(1997) 44(5) *N.Y. Rev. of Books* 41, 45, reprinting with an introduction the *amici curiae* brief filed in
the Supreme Court by a group of moral philosophers prior to the hearing of *Vacco v. Quill* (1997) 521
U.S. 793 and *Washington v. Glucksberg* (1997) 521 U.S. 702. The brief itself is also found at 1996 WL
708956. On rights to non-interference generally, see John L. Mackie, 'Can There Be a Right-Based
Moral Theory?' (1978) 3 *Midwest Stud. Phil.* 350, reprinted in Jeremy Waldron, ed., *Theories of
Rights* (Oxford: Oxford Univ. Press, 1984) 168; Hart, above n. 37, 185.

[41] Battin, above n. 37, 181.

[42] See Peter Williams, 'Rights and the Alleged Right of Innocents to Be Killed' in Elsie L.
Bandman & Bertram Bandman, eds., *Bioethics and Human Rights* (Boston: Little, Brown, 1978) 141;
Marian H.N. Driesse et al., 'Euthanasia and the Law in the Netherlands' (1987–88) 3 *Issues in Law &
Med.* 385, 396 (translation by Walter Lagerwey of Marian H.N. Driesse et al., *Op leven en dood* (*A
Matter of Life and Death*) (Dieren: Blok & Zonen, 1986) ch. 6).

[43] Robert F. Weir, 'The Morality of Physician-Assisted Suicide' (1992) 20 *Law, Med. & Health
Care* 116, 121.

even if not ensnared by invasive life-support apparatus, could compel the administration of lethal agency, and arguably, present certain positive claims against others.'[44] The possibility of recognizing a positive right to assisted suicide in the United States is even less likely since the passing of a federal law prohibiting the use of federal funds for assisted suicide.[45]

Other commentators are less clear about the type of right they are proposing. Ronald Dworkin, who at least implicitly bases an argument in favour of euthanasia on the right to dignity, uses both a negative (liberty or non-interference) formulation, and a positive (welfare) formulation of that right. Dworkin first discusses the limited idea 'that people have a right not to suffer *indignity*, not to be treated in ways that in their culture or community are understood as showing disrespect. Every civilized society has standards and conventions defining these indignities, and these differ from place to place and time to time.'[46] Later, a more expansive (positive) formulation is provided: 'The right to dignity . . . requires the community to deploy whatever resources are necessary to secure it.'[47]

Constitutional rights are most often formulated in terms of negative liberty rights or rights to non-interference, rather than as positive entitlements or welfare rights.[48] Thus the right to freedom of expression or speech is traditionally interpreted to prohibit some or all interference with an individual's protected expression, but not to require that the state provide funds to facilitate the dissemination of protected expression.[49] Positive rights to shelter or necessities are found

---

[44] G. Steven Neeley, *The Constitutional Right to Suicide: A Legal and Philosophical Examination* (New York: Peter Lang, 1994) 83.

[45] Assisted Suicide Funding Restriction Act of 1997, 42 U.S.C. §§ 14401–14408 (2000).

[46] Ronald Dworkin, *Life's Dominion: An Argument About Abortion, Euthanasia, and Individual Freedom* (New York: A.A. Knopf, 1993) 233.   [47] Ibid. 233–4.

[48] See, e.g., *DeShaney v. Winnebago County Dep't of Social Servs.* (1989) 489 U.S. 189, 195–6 (holding that the Due Process Clause of the Fourteenth Amendment does not constitute 'a guarantee of certain minimal levels of safety and security . . . [and] confer[s] no affirmative right to governmental aid, even where such aid may be necessary to secure life, liberty, or property interests of which the government itself may not deprive the individual').

[49] In the United States, see Daniel A. Farber, *The First Amendment (Concepts and Insights)* (2nd edn.) (New York: Foundation Press, 2003) 205–10; J.M. Balkin, 'Frontiers of Legal Thought II The New First Amendment: Some Realism about Pluralism: Legal Realist Approaches to the First Amendment' [1990] *Duke L.J.* 375, 402. The generally 'negative' conception of free speech contained in the First Amendment can be contrasted with the positive right to free expression found in some state constitutions. See Evan G.S. Siegel, 'Closing the Campus Gates to Free Expression: The Regulation of Offensive Speech at Colleges and Universities' (1990) 39 *Emory L.J.* 1351, 1394–5 (describing positive free speech provisions in 38 state constitutions). Under the European Convention on Human Rights, see Clare Ovey & Robin C.A. White, *Jacobs & White on the European Convention on Human Rights* (2nd edn.) (Oxford: Oxford Univ. Press, 2002) 278. In Canada, see *Haig v. Canada* [1993] 2 S.C.R. 995, 1035, 1039 ('The traditional view, in colloquial terms, is that the freedom of expression contained in s. 2(b) [of the Canadian Charter of Rights and Freedoms] prohibits gags, but does not compel the distribution of megaphones.'); *Native Women's Association of Canada v. Canada* [1994] 3 S.C.R. 627, [52], [73]; *Delisle v. Canada (Deputy Attorney-General)* [1999] 2 S.C.R. 989, [26]–[27].

in some constitutional[50] and quasi-constitutional documents such as the United Nations Universal Declaration on Human Rights.[51]

Claims of a constitutional right to suicide or assisted suicide have generally been formulated in terms of a liberty right or right to non-interference.[52] Physicians involved in constitutional cases have asserted their own corresponding right to assist in a constitutionally protected activity without fear of prosecution.[53]

C. Rights-based arguments in favour of assisted suicide

Rights-based arguments in favour of assisted suicide are generally derived from some combination of the interrelated rights of self-determination, autonomy, privacy, and liberty. Other such arguments include: the right to suicide or assisted suicide as one element of a fundamental right to dignity; the right to assisted suicide as a part of a commitment to equality rights; the right to suicide or assisted suicide as implicit in the right to freedom of conscience and religion; and the right to suicide as a necessary concomitant of the individual's property rights in her body or her life.[54]

1. *Right to liberty*

Liberty-based derivations of a right to suicide or assisted suicide can be in the form of either an intrinsic or instrumental justification. The intrinsic argument is that freedom is a basic good, and thus in the absence of harm to others which could

---

[50] For example, some U.S. state constitutions require government to provide certain services to citizens. See James K. Langdon & Mark A. Kass, 'Homelessness in America: Looking for the Right to Shelter' (1985) 19 *Colum. J. L. & Soc. Probs.* 305, 332–5 ('In most states, the poor have no explicit constitutional right to receive aid . . . only six state constitutions contain language which unambiguously obligates the government to provide for the needs of the poor.').

[51] G.A. Res. 217, U.N. Doc. A/811 (1948), Arts. 22–25 (recognizing rights to work, free education, reasonable limitation of working hours, social security, and adequate standard of living including food, clothing, housing, and medical care).

[52] See, e.g., *Compassion in Dying v. Washington* (1994) 850 F. Supp. 1454, 1459 (W.D. Wash.); *Quill v. Koppell* (1994) 870 F. Supp. 78 (S.D.N.Y.).

[53] See, e.g., *Compassion in Dying v. Washington* (1994) 850 F. Supp. 1454, 1459 (W.D. Wash.); *Quill v. Koppell* (1994) 870 F. Supp. 78, 82 (S.D.N.Y.) (concluding that 'if such a constitutional right resides in the patient, then there would be a corresponding constitutional right of the physician not to be prosecuted for assisting in the exercise of the patient's constitutional right').

[54] Although not generally used in the U.S. context and of limited interest to commentators, the right to be free from inhuman and degrading or cruel and unusual treatment has also been proposed as a basis for a right to assisted suicide in both the Canadian and U.K. constitutional challenges to criminal prohibitions on assisted suicide. The appellant in the U.K. case of *Pretty* relied upon the right to be free from inhuman and degrading treatment under Article 3 of the European Convention on Human Rights. Similarly, Sue Rodriguez claimed that the criminal prohibition on assisted suicide violated her right to be free from cruel or unusual treatment under section 12 of the Canadian Charter. Both attempts failed as the judges rejected the idea that the presence of the criminal prohibition on assisted suicide or the refusal to waive its application in advance could amount to 'treatment' within the meaning of the constitutional guarantees. See *Rodriguez v. British Columbia (Attorney-General)* [1993] 3 S.C.R. 519, [62]-[68]; *R. (on the application of Pretty) v. D.P.P.* [2002] 1 A.C. 800, [14]; *Pretty v. U.K.* (2002) 35 E.H.R.R. 1, [54]–[55] (Eur. Ct. H.R.).

outweigh the commitment to freedom in the particular instance,[55] individuals must be let alone to do as they wish.[56] An alternative formulation of this argument is that individuals have a (natural) equal right to be free.[57] In the right to die context, Robert Risley has argued that 'Americans must fight to win the right to a humane and dignified death . . . the right to be free to decide our own fate; a fundamental concept of Western civilization.'[58] Prohibitions on assisted suicide are restrictions on the individual liberty of both the person desiring assistance, and any potential assister as 'everyone necessarily has th[e] right [to commit suicide] as part of his or her freedom.'[59] Thus, 'there is a standing *prima facie* case for legaliz[ation] . . . , and it is up to [its] opponents to show why [it] should be forbidden.'[60]

The instrumental argument is that a commitment to freedom or liberty (again in the absence of direct and significant harm to others) protects another fundamental value such as moral pluralism or dignity.[61] The recognition that a pluralism of moral convictions exists in a secular society prompts the argument that individual freedom must be the pre-eminent value: 'although one may not be able to agree about what constitutes good life, or good death, one can agree to let each make his own choices, as long as those choices do not involve direct and significant violence against others.'[62]

Alternatively, a commitment to dignity mandates a parallel commitment to freedom. Dignity, intimately connected with self-respect, requires that the individual lead her own life and make her own decisions. Ronald Dworkin explains:

a true appreciation of dignity argues . . . for individual freedom, not coercion, for a regime of law and attitude that encourages each of us to make mortal decisions for himself. Freedom is the cardinal, absolute requirement of self-respect: no one treats his life as having any intrinsic, objective importance unless he insists on leading that life himself, not being ushered along it by others, no matter how much he loves or respects or fears them.[63]

Dignity is cited as one possible basis for the right to liberty, from which a right to suicide or assisted suicide could be derived. Such a right may also be derived directly from the right to dignity.[64]

---

[55] See John Stuart Mill, *On Liberty* (Currin V. Shields, ed.) (Indianapolis: Bobbs-Merrill, Library of the Liberal Arts, 1956) (1st edn. 1859) 13 ('the only purpose for which power can be rightfully exercised over any member of a civilized community, against his will, is to prevent harm to others'). See *Brophy v. New England Sinai Hosp., Inc.* (1986) 497 N.E.2d 626, 633 (Mass. S.J.C.); *In re Caulk* (1984) 480 A.2d 93, 100 (N.H.S.C., Douglas J., dissenting) (both citing this passage from Mill in support of a 'right to die'). On the question of 'harm,' see Chapter 3, Section II.A.2.c.

[56] See *French Declaration of the Rights of Man and of Citizens IV*, found in Thomas Paine, *Rights of Man* (Mattituck, N.Y.: Amereon, 1976) (1st edn. 1792) 133.   [57] See Hart, above n. 37, 175.

[58] Robert L. Risley, 'Legal and Ethical Issues in the Individual's Right to Die' (1994) 20 *Ohio N. U. L. Rev.* 597, 609–10.   [59] Wallace & Eser, above n. 30, 101.

[60] Alister Browne, 'Assisted Suicide and Active Voluntary Euthanasia' (1989) 2 *Can. J. L. & Juris.* 35, 38. See also, Glanville Williams, *The Sanctity of Life and the Criminal Law* (New York: A.A. Knopf, 1957) 341, 346.   [61] Engelhardt & Malloy, above n. 40, 1010–11.

[62] Ibid. 1010.   [63] Dworkin, above n. 46, 239.   [64] See below, Section II.C.4.

Whatever the foundation of the liberty-based right to suicide or assisted suicide, it is subject to the criticism that it is logically incoherent owing to a fundamental paradox. This argument relies on the familiar slavery example from John Stuart Mill's *On Liberty*. Mill writes:

by selling himself for a slave, [a person] abdicates his liberty, he foregoes any future use of it beyond that single act. He therefore defeats, in his own case, the very purpose which is the justification of allowing him to dispose of himself.... The principle of freedom cannot require that he should be free not to be free. It is not freedom, to be allowed to alienate his freedom.[65]

In the context of suicide, critics argue that suicide necessarily involves the complete renunciation of one's freedom and that it cannot be an exercise of one's right to liberty to alienate one's liberty.[66] For example, Richard Doerflinger writes:

suicide is not the ultimate exercise of freedom but its ultimate self-contradiction: A free act that by destroying life, destroys all the individual's future earthly freedom. If life is more basic than freedom, society best serves freedom by discouraging rather than assisting self-destruction. Sometimes one must limit particular choices to safeguard freedom itself, as when American society chose over a century ago to prevent people from selling themselves into slavery even of their own volition.[67]

2. Right to autonomy or self-determination

A commitment to autonomy or self-determination is generally considered inherent in any rights-based morality:

Rights-based views emphasize a view of persons as capable of forming purposes, of making plans, of weighing alternatives according to how well they fulfill those plans and purposes, and of acting on the basis of this deliberation. Rights protect our exercise of these capacities, capacities whose exercise is often associated with the notion of autonomy, independent of how doing so promotes goals specified as valuable.[68]

---

[65] Mill, *On Liberty*, above n. 55, 173. For a critique of this conception of negative liberty, see Margaret Jane Radin, 'Market-Inalienability' (1987) 100 *Harv. L. Rev.* 1849, 1902–3.

[66] See New York State Task Force on Life and the Law, *When Death Is Sought: Assisted Suicide and Euthanasia in the Medical Context* (1994) 88; Callahan, above n. 28, 5; T. Douglas Kinsella et al., 'Legalized Active Euthanasia: An Aesculapian Tragedy' (1989) 74(12) *Am. College of Surgeons Bull.* 6, 7.

[67] Richard Doerflinger, 'Assisted Suicide: Pro-Choice or Anti-Life?' (1989) 19(1) *Hastings Center Rep.* 16, 17.

[68] Dan Brock, *Life and Death* (Cambridge: Cambridge Univ. Press, 1993) 98. See also, David A.J. Richards, 'Constitutional Privacy, The Right to Die and The Meaning of Life: A Moral Analysis' (1981) 22 *Wm. & Mary L. Rev.* 327, 339–43. Richards summarizes the neo-Kantian position on human rights, derived from a commitment to autonomy and treating people as equals: 'to express equal respect for personal autonomy is to guarantee the minimum conditions requisite for autonomy; ethical principles of obligation and duty rest upon and insure that this is so and correlatively define human rights. Without such rights, human beings would lack, inter alia, the basic opportunity to develop a secure sense of an independent self.' Ibid. 343.

In a rights-based morality, individuals have the freedom to define their own conception of the good within limits necessary for peaceful co-operation.[69] The derivation of a right to suicide from a general right to autonomy is self-evident: 'The decision to exit life by one's own decree is more fundamental to the concepts of autonomy, freedom, and liberty than any other, for pivotal to the control of one's own life is the choice of electing to forego continued life.'[70] The concurring opinion of Compton J. in the well-known *Bouvia* case contains a similarly confident assertion: 'The right to die is an integral part of our right to control our own destinies so long as the rights of others are not affected. That right should... include the ability to enlist assistance from others, including the medical profession, in making death as painless and quick as possible.'[71] In an article entitled 'The Last Fearsome Taboo: Medical Aspects of Planned Death', Jack Kevorkian advanced an absolutist autonomy rationale for the legalization of planned death: '[p]erhaps the greatest advantage would be the further unshackling of the primal human right of what should be absolute personal autonomy within the bounds of reasonable law.'[72]

Both Sue Rodriguez and Dianne Pretty successfully persuaded the Supreme Court of Canada and the European Court of Human Rights, respectively that their rights to autonomy were engaged by the criminal prohibition on assisting suicide. In *Rodriguez*, Mr. Justice Sopinka held that:

> There is no question, then, that personal autonomy, at least with respect to the right to make choices concerning one's own body, control over one's physical and psychological integrity, and basic human dignity are encompassed within security of the person, at least to the extent of freedom from criminal prohibitions which interfere with these.[73]

The provision in question was section 7 of the Canadian Charter of Rights and Freedoms, which guarantees the 'right to life, liberty and security of the person and the right not to be deprived thereof except in accordance with the principles of fundamental justice'. The *Rodriguez* majority found that the deprivation of the right *was* in accordance with the principles of fundamental justice.[74] In *Pretty v. U.K.*, the court held that 'the notion of personal autonomy is an important principle underlying the interpretation' of the right to respect for private and family life found in Article 8(1) of the European Convention on Human Rights.[75]

---

[69] Brock, above n. 68, 126–7; Dworkin, above n. 46, 224. See generally, Gerald Dworkin, *The Theory and Practice of Autonomy* (Cambridge: Cambridge Univ. Press, 1988).

[70] Neeley, above n. 44, 80.

[71] *Bouvia v. Superior Court (Glenchur)* (1986) 179 Cal. App. 3d 1127, 1147 (Cal. C.A.). See also, George C. Garbesi, 'The Law of Assisted Suicide' (1987) 3 *Issues in Law & Med.* 93, 108 (arguing that international human rights law protecting individual autonomy encompasses the right to assisted suicide for the terminally ill).

[72] Jack Kevorkian, 'The Last Fearsome Taboo: Medical Aspects of Planned Death' (1988) 7 *Med. & L.* 1, 9. See also, *Hobbins v. Attorney General* (1994) 518 N.W.2d 487, 490 (Mich. C.A.) (finding that the Fourteenth Amendment right of self-determination includes the right to choose to cease living).   [73] *Rodriguez v. British Columbia (Attorney-General)* [1993] 3 S.C.R. 519, [21].

[74] Ibid., [23]–[60].   [75] *Pretty v. U.K.* (2002) 35 E.H.R.R. 1, [61] (Eur. Ct. H.R.).

However, the court went on to find that any interference with Mrs. Pretty's right was compatible with the saving provision in Article 8(2) as it was necessary 'in pursuit of the legitimate aim of safeguarding life and thereby protecting the rights of others'.[76]

Failure to respect the right to autonomy in the extreme cases of decisions involving life and death may impoverish the individual's other, perhaps less momentous, choices. 'If one must . . . live or die as the state dictates, how much are the remaining choices worth?'[77] In the context of assisted suicide, the argument from a right to autonomy is closely linked to the concept of individual control of the dying process.[78]

Most proponents of an autonomy-based right to suicide are careful to articulate that not all suicides can be considered autonomous. For example, David Richards argues that there can be autonomous, rational suicide only when 'the person's plans, assessed and subject to revision in terms of standards and arguments to which he or she gives free and rational assent, are better satisfied by death than by continued life.'[79] These kinds of limitations on self-determination are subject to vigorous debate from both ends of the legalization spectrum. For example, Yale Kamisar, a consequentialist opponent of the legalization of assisted suicide on the grounds of the danger of abuses and slippery slopes, observes that 'unless we carry the principle of self-determination or personal autonomy to its logical extreme – assisted suicide by any competent person who clearly and repeatedly requests it for *any* reason *she* deems appropriate – we have to find a "stopping point" somewhere along the way.'[80]

The issue of whether a suicide can be autonomous has generated significant debate in legal, bioethical, and medical circles. Some opponents of the legalization of assisted suicide argue that autonomous, rational suicide does not exist, and that a desire for death is a sign of mental illness, and not of rational choice.[81] Timothy Quill, one of the central players in the debate over the legalization of assisted suicide, disagrees: 'it is not idiosyncratic, selfish, or indicative of a psychiatric disorder for people with an incurable illness to want some control over how they die. The idea of a noble, dignified death, with a meaning that is deeply personal and unique, is exalted in great literature, poetry, art, and music.'[82]

---

[76] *Pretty v. U.K.* (2002) 35 E.H.R.R. 1, [69]–[78] (Eur. Ct. H.R.).

[77] Wallace & Eser, above n. 30, 101.

[78] See, e.g., Margaret A. Somerville, 'The Song of Death: The Lyrics of Euthanasia' (1993) 9 *J. Contemp. Health L. & Pol'y* 1, 18; Weir, above n. 43, 124; Note, above n. 31, 2026; Daniel Callahan, *The Troubled Dream of Life: Living With Mortality* (New York: Simon & Schuster, 1993) 16–17; *Pretty v. U.K.* (2002) 35 E.H.R.R. 1, [64] (Eur. Ct. H.R.).

[79] Richards, above n. 68, 359–60.

[80] Yale Kamisar, 'Are Laws Against Assisted Suicide Unconstitutional?' (1993) 23(3) *Hastings Center Rep.* 32, 39 (emphasis in original).

[81] See, e.g., Victor D. Rosenblum & Clarke G. Forsythe, 'The Right to Assisted Suicide: Protection of Autonomy or an Open Door to Social Killing?' (1990) 6 *Issues in Law & Med.* 3, 23.

[82] Timothy E. Quill et al., 'Care of the Hopelessly Ill: Proposed Clinical Criteria for Physician-Assisted Suicide' (1992) 327(19) *New Eng. J. Med.* 1380, 1380.

The autonomy-based derivation of a right to suicide or assisted suicide is also subject to an argument that such a rights claim is paradoxical. Many critics of assisted suicide argue that it is self-contradictory to exercise one's autonomy in such a way as to destroy the capacity for autonomy and its future exercise: 'if autonomy and dignity lie in the free exercise of will and choice, it is at least paradoxical to say that our autonomy licenses an act that puts our autonomy permanently out of business.'[83]

A further problematic aspect of the right to autonomy as the basis for a right to suicide or assisted suicide is the phenomenon that the possession of rights may encourage their exercise. If, as Joel Feinberg argues, it is the act of *claiming* one's rights which gives them their special moral significance,[84] then this phenomenon is not a surprising one. Feinberg suggests that human dignity is intimately connected with the recognizable capacity to assert such claims, and that the activity of claiming builds self-respect and respect for others and gives a sense to the notion of personal dignity.[85] Without denying the necessary connection with the act of exercising or claiming one's rights and one's dignity and self-respect, a more circumspect attitude towards the exercise of one's rights might be appropriate in the context of personal rights,[86] and particularly with regard to a right to suicide or assisted suicide. While knowledge that the individual possesses the right to suicide or assisted suicide may in fact help her to continue living[87] (as the Oregon evidence appears to show)[88] autonomy proponents must be slightly wary of this tendency towards exercising one's rights when that exercise results in the individual's

---

[83] Kass, above n. 40, 39–40. See also, John A. Alesandro, 'Physician-Assisted Suicide and New York Law' (1994) 57 *Alb. L. Rev.* 819, 923, n. 559; Bopp, above n. 36, 128; Doerflinger, above n. 67, 17 ('[A]n unqualified "pro-choice" defense of assisted suicide lacks coherence because corpses have no choices. A particular choice, that of death, is given priority over all the other choices it makes impossible, so the value of choice as such is not central to the argument.'); *Pretty v. U.K.* (2002) 35 E.H.R.R. 1 (Eur. Ct. H.R.), Intervention of the Catholic Bishops' Conference of England and Wales pursuant to Art. 36 § 2 of the European Convention on Human Rights, [33], www.catholic-ew.org.uk/resource/pretty/DPEurope.htm, accessed 29 July 2006.

[84] Joel Feinberg, 'The Nature and Value of Rights' (1970) 4 *J. Value Inquiry* 243, 252, reprinted in Joel Feinberg, *Rights, Justice, and The Bounds of Liberty* (Princeton, N.J.: Princeton Univ. Press, 1980) 143, 151 ('Having rights . . . makes claiming possible; but it is claiming that gives rights their special moral significance.').

[85] Ibid. See also, A.L. Melden, *Rights and Persons* (Berkeley, Calif.: Univ. Cal. Press, 1977) 25 ('to demand our rights, to assert ourselves as the moral agents we are, is to be able to demand that we be dealt with as members of the community of human beings. This is what moral dignity involves . . .').

[86] See Carl Schneider, 'Rights Discourse and Neonatal Euthanasia' (1988) 76 *Cal. L. Rev.* 151, 164.

[87] See F.G. Miller & J.C. Fletcher, 'The Case for Legalized Euthanasia' (1993) 36 *Perspectives in Biology & Med.* 163, 163–4; Quill, above n. 82, 1382; David T. Watts & Timothy Howell, 'Assisted Suicide Is Not Euthanasia' (1992) 40 *J. Am. Geriatrics Soc.* 1043, 1044–5. James K. Rogers, 'Punishing Assisted Suicide: Where Legislators Should Fear to Tread' (1994) 20 *Ohio N.U. L. Rev.* 647, 656 ('The discussion [of assisted suicide] could . . . give the patient a sense of control; an important factor in emotional and physical well-being.').

[88] For example, in 2005, 50% of 64 prescriptions for lethal doses of medication written in 2005 were not used by the patients who had requested them; 27% of these non-users were still alive at the end of 2005. Oregon Department of Human Services, *Eighth Annual Report on Oregon's Death with Dignity Act*, 9 Mar. 2006, http://oregon.gov/DHS/ph/pas/docs/year8.pdf, accessed 24 July 2006.

death, and ensure that dignity and self-respect are fostered by continued life, for as long as that is possible. To take a specific example, suicide might be legalized for the physically disabled on the basis of their autonomy rights – that is, on the grounds of increasing the range of options available to them.[89] But claims to fostering autonomous choice, or to state neutrality as between those options – while its format *as a right* encourages the choice of that particular option – might ring distinctly false.

3. Right to privacy

Arguments in favour of a right to suicide or assisted suicide derived from the right to privacy are closely related to those derived from the rights to autonomy and liberty.[90] Indeed, the interpretation by the European Court of Human Rights of the right to respect for private life in Article 8(1) of the European Convention as including a right to 'personal autonomy in the sense of the right to make choices about one's own body'[91] suggests that the right to autonomy subsumes considerations of the right to privacy in the context of assisted suicide.[92]

In the American constitutional context, however, the right to privacy may have greater independent content. Suicide has been described as 'the ultimate exercise of one's right to privacy.'[93] Alan Sullivan uses the absence of a clearly articulated principled basis for the constitutional right to privacy to argue that one can infer from U.S. Supreme Court decisions connecting privacy with constitutionally protected liberty interests that 'the right protects personal choices in areas historically screened from the state's interference.'[94] Sullivan asserts that the decision whether to continue living is the quintessential example of a decision which demands protection under the right to privacy.[95]

In the United States, privacy-based arguments now rely on the Supreme Court's decision in *Cruzan.*[96] Proponents of the legalization of assisted suicide have argued:

If the right to privacy protects the right to die naturally, it should also protect the competent, terminal patient's right to choose a quick and painless death. The difference between a terminal patient's choosing to refuse treatment and choosing a faster means of dying does

---

[89] Note that this argument would also apply if the right to assisted suicide for the physically disabled were derived from the right to equality. See below Sections II.C.5 and II.D.2 and Chapter 3, Section II.A.1.c.

[90] See, e.g., John D. Arras, 'The Right to Die on the Slippery Slope' (1982) 8(3) *Soc. Theory & Prac.* 285, 298–9.

[91] *Pretty v. U.K.* (2002) 35 E.H.R.R. 1, [61]–[66] (Eur. Ct. H.R.). See above n. 78.

[92] See also, *Rodriguez v. British Columbia (Attorney-General)* [1993] 3 S.C.R. 519, [91] (McLachlin J., dissenting) '(Security of the person has an element of personal autonomy, protecting the dignity and privacy of individuals with respect to decisions concerning their own bodies.').

[93] *Bouvia v. Superior Court (Glenchur)* (1986) 179 Cal. App. 3d 1127, 1144 (Cal. C.A.).

[94] Alan Sullivan, 'A Constitutional Right to Suicide' in Margaret Pabst Battin & David J. Mayo, eds., *Suicide: The Philosophical Issues* (New York: St. Martin's Press, 1980) 229, 231.

[95] Ibid. 240–1.

[96] See *Cruzan v. Director, Mo. Dep't of Health* (1990) 497 U.S. 261, 278, 279 (holding that state restrictions on the withdrawal of hydration and nutrition from patients in a persistent vegetative state

not offer a basis for legal distinction. When a competent terminal patient chooses to die, the state interests balanced against that patient's right to privacy are virtually the same regardless of the means chosen.[97]

The privacy-based argument derived from *Cruzan* was accepted by the District Court and by Justice Wright, dissenting in the first Ninth Circuit decision in *Compassion in Dying v. Washington*. Justice Wright held that terminally ill, mentally competent adults have a fundamental privacy right to choose physician-assisted death.[98]

4. Right to dignity

While more commonly cited in moral philosophy circles[99] than in legal circles, the right to dignity may also provide an argument in favour of the legalization of assisted suicide. Justice Stevens has referred to the individual's interest in dignity as part of the basic concept of freedom.[100] One legal scholar who does emphasize the right to dignity is Ronald Dworkin.

Dworkin discusses whether indignity is contrary to our experiential interests (in the quality of our future experiences) or our critical interests (in the 'character and value of our lives as whole').[101] This distinction will affect how the right to dignity is framed: on the experiential theory it is supposed that 'indignity causes its victims distinctive and especially severe mental pain, that people resent and therefore suffer more from indignity than from other forms of deprivation. People denied dignity may lose the self-respect that dignity protects, moreover, and then suffer an even more serious form of distress: self-contempt or self-loathing.'[102] Dworkin contends that 'this experiential theory of indignity is unpersuasive... because it does not explain central features of our convictions about dignity.'[103]

(requiring clear and convincing evidence of the incompetent patient's wishes) are not unconstitutional and assuming for the purposes of the case that the Constitution 'would grant a competent person a constitutionally protected right to refuse life-saving hydration and nutrition'). Although Chief Justice Rehnquist was careful to state that the decision centred not on the right to privacy but on a Fourteenth Amendment liberty interest, ibid. 279, n. 7, the decision has been widely interpreted as involving the right to privacy.

[97] Steven J. Wolhandler, 'Voluntary Active Euthanasia for the Terminally Ill and the Constitutional Right to Privacy' (1984) 69 *Cornell L. Rev.* 363, 375. Wolhandler argues further that the constitutional right to privacy includes the right to *assistance* in suicide within the 'constitutional penumbra of protection.' See also, Richards, above n. 68.

[98] *Compassion in Dying v. Washington* (1995) 49 F.3d 586, 595–6 (9th Cir.). See also, *Compassion in Dying v. Washington* (1994) 850 F. Supp. 1454, 1461–2 (W.D. Wash.). The argument that there is no legal distinction between the right to refuse treatment and the right to suicide or assisted suicide is discussed in greater detail in Chapter 3, Section II.A.1.d. See also, Chapter 6, Section V.A.

[99] See, e.g., Battin, above n. 37, 176–91; William T. Blackstone, 'Human Rights and Human Dignity' (1971) 9 *Phil. Forum* 3; Herbert Spiegelberg, 'Human Dignity: A Challenge to Contemporary Philosophy' (1971) 9 *Phil. Forum* 39; Arnold S. Kaufman, 'A Sketch of a Liberal Theory of Fundamental Human Rights' (1968) 52 *The Monist* 595; Michael S. Pritchard, 'Human Dignity and Justice' (1972) 82 *Ethics* 299.

[100] *Washington v. Glucksberg* (1997) 521 U.S. 702, 743; *Cruzan v. Director, Mo. Dep't of Health* (1990) 497 U.S. 261, 278, 344, 356 (Stevens J., dissenting). [101] Dworkin, above n. 46, 235.
[102] Ibid. 234. [103] Ibid. 235.

As an example, Dworkin cites the fact that we do not think indignity does not exist when its subject is not aware of the indignity; for Dworkin, therefore, the right to dignity is connected to an individual's critical interests: 'A person's right to be treated with dignity ... is the right that others acknowledge his genuine critical interests: that they acknowledge that he is the kind of creature, and has the moral standing, such that it is intrinsically, objectively important how his life goes. Dignity is a central aspect of the ... intrinsic importance of human life.'[104]

A right to suicide can be based on a right to dignity,[105] or a right to be free from indignity.[106] Margaret Pabst Battin argues that dignity is the foundational basis of fundamental rights:

Individuals have fundamental rights to do certain sorts of things just because doing those things tends to be constitutive of human dignity.... [B]ecause fundamental rights are rooted in human dignity, they are not equally distributed.... [W]e have a right to suicide (if and when we do) because it can be constitutive of human dignity, and ... this ... is the same [basis] on which we have all other fundamental human rights. Even though it may be very markedly unequally distributed, the right to suicide is not an 'exception' or a 'special' right, or a right that is to be accounted for in some different way; it is of a piece with the other fundamental human rights we enjoy.[107]

Perhaps the most powerful endorsement of rights as connected to human dignity is found in Feinberg, who writes:

Having rights ... makes claiming possible; but it is claiming that gives rights their special moral significance.... To think of oneself as the holder of rights is not to be unduly but properly proud, to have that minimal self-respect that is necessary to be worthy of the love and esteem of others. Indeed, respect for persons ... may simply be respect for their rights, so that there cannot be the one without the other; and what is called 'human dignity' may simply be the recognizable capacity to assert claims. To respect a person then, or to think of him as possessed of human dignity, simply is to think of him as a potential maker of claims.[108]

A right to suicide derived from a right to dignity is a more limited creature than the expansive rights derived from autonomy, liberty,[109] or privacy discussed above. Such a right to suicide would be overridden in cases where the suicide does

---

[104] Dworkin, above n. 46, 236.

[105] See, e.g., Margaret Pabst Battin, *The Least Worst Death: Essays in Bioethics on the End of Life* (New York: Oxford Univ. Press, 1994) 280–1; Battin, above n. 37, 187.

[106] See, e.g., Dworkin, above n. 46, 233 ('people have a right not to suffer indignity, not to be treated in ways that in their culture or community, are understood as showing disrespect').

[107] Battin, *The Least Worst Death*, above n. 105, 280–1. See also, Dworkin, above n. 26, 198 (basing his account of rights on 'the vague but powerful idea of human dignity' and the 'more familiar idea of political equality').   [108] Feinberg, above n. 84, 151.

[109] Dignity was also discussed as one possible basis for a general right to liberty, from which a right to suicide or assisted suicide could be derived. See above, text accompanying n. 63. It is interesting to note that a liberty-based right to suicide or assisted suicide would arguably be potentially unlimited (in the absence of harm to others) as all suicides could be seen as an exercise of liberty. However, not all suicides can be seen as an exercise of the right to dignity. See below, text accompanying nn. 110–112. This apparent inconsistency is discussed in Chapter 3 in the context of critiques concerned with the lack of articulation of the basis of personal rights. See Chapter 3, Section II.B.1.

not promote dignity, on the grounds of the individual's lack of competence to exercise the right in a way designed to attain its end.[110]

A central problem with a 'right to dignity' approach to suicide or assisted suicide would undoubtedly be the difficulty of distinguishing dignity-constitutive suicides (or proposed suicides) from those which do not promote the individual's dignity.[111] This distinction may be easier to make retrospectively (looking back on the individual's life and death after her death) than prospectively.[112]

It should be noted that the problem of the paradoxical nature of rights claims based on liberty or autonomy and involving death may be circumvented by the use of the right to dignity, if one accepts that an individual's dignity does not necessarily end at death,[113] and that living does not necessarily involve more dignity than dying or death. These arguments do not hold true for an individual's autonomy or liberty. Autonomy and liberty necessarily end at the time of the individual's death, and therefore death could not possibly increase autonomy or liberty.

5. Right to equality

a. Using the legality of suicide

Equality rights arguments in favour of the legalization of assisted suicide generally focus on those individuals or groups who are physically unable to commit suicide without assistance, such as the severely physically disabled, or some terminally ill persons. Given that suicide is now a legal act in most jurisdictions, the basic premise of such arguments is that individuals who would require assistance in order to carry out a decision to end their lives are denied the *choice* which is available to all other mentally competent adult persons. Such persons may argue that the criminal prohibition on assisted suicide has a disparate impact on them by virtue of their physical disability and thus violates their right to equality or equal protection.[114] For most people who wish to commit suicide, the effect of the criminal prohibition on assisted suicide is to deny them the *option* of choosing a method that would require the assistance of another person. However, for persons who because of illness or disability are physically unable to kill themselves

---

[110] Battin, above n. 37, 188. For some commentators, such a limited right would not be worthy of the appellation 'right': 'A constitutional right that cannot be freely exercised by all persons without state interference lacks the most essential indicia of a "right" in our legal order.... A "right" so limited is no right at all.' Marzen, above n. 34, 104.

[111] Margaret Pabst Battin attempts to do this in *The Least Worst Death*, above n. 105, 282–5 (discussing different types of suicide and their motivations).

[112] Ronald Dworkin suggests that 'the emphasis we put on dying with "dignity" . . . shows how important it is that life ends *appropriately*, that death keeps faith with the way we want to have lived.' *Life's Dominion*, above n. 46, 199 (emphasis in original). My point here is that determinations about whether a life will end 'appropriately' may be more difficult to make in advance than after the fact.

[113] Feinberg argues that certain interests of persons continue after their death. Joel Feinberg, 'The Rights of Animals and Unborn Generations' in *Rights, Justice and the Bounds of Liberty*, above n. 84, 159; Joel Feinberg, *Harm to Others* (New York: Oxford Univ. Press, 1984) vol. I, ch. II.

[114] *Rodriguez v. British Columbia (Attorney-General)* [1993] 3 S.C.R. 519, 544–57 (Lamer C.J.C. dissenting). See Chapter 6, Section II.B.

unassisted, the effect of such a prohibition is quite different. For this group, the option of lawful suicide has been completely removed.[115] This forms the basis of the argument that such a prohibition has a disparate impact on persons with severe physical disabilities who are unable to commit suicide without assistance, which violates their right to equality. An example of this argument is found in the dissenting judgment of Chief Justice Lamer in *Rodriguez*, holding that a blanket prohibition on assisted suicide results in disparate treatment of those who cannot physically commit suicide without assistance.[116] It is important to note that this argument would support *only* a right to assisted suicide for those unable to commit suicide without assistance, and would not entail acceptance of a more general right to suicide.

Even disabled-rights advocates who oppose assisted suicide in the current environment of discrimination against the disabled recognize that '[i]t is important to acknowledge the necessity of assistance in the suicides of persons with disabilities.'[117] Paul Steven Miller writes:

for many people with disabilities, the 'right to commit suicide' can be realized only with assistance due to the individual's own physical . . . limitations. Unlike able-bodied persons who can quietly end their lives alone, persons with disabilities often require, due to the physical limitations of their bodies, the assistance and intervention of assisters.[118]

b. Using the right to refuse life-saving or life-sustaining treatment

Equal protection arguments are also made in reliance on the right to refuse life-saving or life-sustaining medical treatment. The District Court in *Quill v. Koppell* described this argument made by proponents of assisted suicide, who

argue that such refusal of treatment is essentially the same thing as committing suicide with the advice of a physician [and] that for the State to sanction one course of conduct and criminalize the other involves discrimination which violates the Equal Protection Clause of the Fourteenth Amendment.[119]

The District Court rejected this argument, but it met with success upon appeal to the Second Circuit:

it seems clear that New York does not treat similarly circumstanced persons alike: those in the final stages of terminal illness who are on life-support systems are allowed to hasten

---

[115] The European Court of Human Rights recognized this distinction in *Pretty v. U.K.* (2002) 35 E.H.R.R. 1, [87]–[88], although the court concluded that the difference in treatment was not discriminatory under Article 14 of the European Convention as there was 'objective and reasonable justification' for it. Ibid. [89]. For criticism of this position, see Pedain, above n. 39, 201–3. See also, Meredith Blake, 'Physician-Assisted Suicide: A Criminal Offence or a Patient's Right?' (1997) 5(3) *Med. L. Rev.* 294, 313–16.

[116] *Rodriguez v. British Columbia (Attorney-General)* [1993] 3 S.C.R. 519, 544 (Lamer C.J.C., dissenting).

[117] Paul Steven Miller, 'The Impact of Assisted Suicide on Persons with Disabilities – Is It A Right Without A Freedom?' (1993) 9 *Issues in Law & Med.* 47, 50.   [118] Ibid.

[119] *Quill v. Koppell* (1994) 870 F. Supp. 78, 84 (S.D.N.Y.).

their deaths by directing the removal of such systems; but those who are similarly situated, except for the previous attachment of life-sustaining equipment, are not allowed to hasten death by self-administering prescribed drugs.[120]

This argument was also accepted by the District Court in *Compassion in Dying v. Washington*:

Washington law, by creating an exception for those patients on life support, yet not permitting competent, terminally ill adult patients such as plaintiffs the equivalent option of exercising their rights to hasten their deaths with medical assistance, creates a situation in which the fundamental rights of one group are burdened while those of a similarly situated group are not. Therefore, this court finds that [the Washington ban on assistance in suicide] violates the equal protection guarantee of the Fourteenth Amendment.[121]

Dissenting in the Ninth Circuit, Justice Wright agreed on this point with the District Court.[122]

6. *Right to freedom of conscience and religion*

Although not often asserted as the basis of a right to suicide or assisted suicide,[123] the right to freedom of conscience has been relied upon in the abortion context in the United States by both commentators and judges. For example, Ronald Dworkin argues that 'any government that prohibits abortion commits itself to a controversial interpretation of the sanctity of life and therefore limits liberty by commanding one essentially religious position over others, which the First Amendment forbids.'[124] Judicial adoptions of this approach have been rare. Justice Stevens did suggest that only theological dogma could support the view that life begins at conception,[125] and that religious dogma underlies opposition to the 'right to die'.[126] In *Casey*, the plurality opinion stated:

At the heart of liberty is the right to define one's own concept of existence, of meaning, of the universe, and of the mystery of human life. Beliefs about these matters could not define the attributes of personhood were they formed under the compulsion of the State.[127]

---

[120] *Quill v. Vacco* (1996) 80 F.3d 716, 729 (2nd Cir.).
[121] *Compassion in Dying v. Washington* (1994) 850 F. Supp. 1454, 1467 (W.D. Wash.).
[122] *Compassion in Dying v. Washington* (1995) 49 F.3d 586, 597 (9th Cir., Wright J., dissenting).
[123] One example is found in Matthew P. Previn, 'Assisted Suicide and Religion: Conflicting Conceptions of the Sanctity of Human Life' (1996) 84 *Geo. L.J.* 589, 590.
[124] Dworkin, above n. 46, 165 and generally 160–8. For an argument opposing Dworkin's position that the First Amendment protects abortion decisions, see Gerard V. Bradley, '*Life's Dominion*: A Review Essay' (1993) 69 *Notre Dame L. Rev.* 329, 369–74 (relying on *Harris v. McRae* (1980) 448 U.S. 297, 319–21 and *Oregon v. Smith* (1990) 492 U.S. 872).
[125] *Webster v. Reproductive Health Services* (1989) 492 U.S. 490, 566–72 (Stevens J., concurring in part and dissenting in part). In the Canadian context, see *Morgentaler* [1988] 1 S.C.R. 30, 175–80 (Wilson J., concurring).
[126] *Cruzan v. Director, Mo. Dep't of Health* (1990) 497 U.S. 261, 355–6 (Stevens J., dissenting).
[127] *Planned Parenthood of Southeastern Pennsylvania v. Casey* (1992) 505 U.S. 833, 851 (O'Connor, Kennedy & Souter JJ.).

Linda McClain has argued that this opinion

echoes judicial and scholarly interpretations of constitutional rights that appeal to the idea that a certain realm of freedom with respect to fundamental decisions, which typically implicates ethical or religious convictions, is critical to respect for decisional autonomy or liberty of conscience and to the development of personality and a sense of moral responsibility.[128]

This idea also appears at the end of the Ninth Circuit en banc decision in *Compassion in Dying v. Washington*: 'Under our constitutional system, neither the state nor the majority of the people in a state can impose its will upon the individual in a matter so highly "central to personal dignity and autonomy" '.[129] Not surprisingly, Justice Stevens wrote in *Casey* that 'a woman's decision to terminate her pregnancy is nothing less than a matter of conscience.'[130]

In general terms, the argument in the assisted suicide context would be that for the state to interfere in the *moral* decision of an individual to take her life violates her right to freedom of conscience. One might argue that, as is the case with abortion, the decision whether or not to commit suicide is essentially a matter of conscience. Evidence for this assertion could be drawn from the many arguments against the legalization of assisted suicide centred on the sanctity of life.[131] Although such arguments can be formulated in ostensibly secular terms,[132] their religious origins are still present in many modern uses, arguably reflecting an underlying belief that suicide is a sin.[133] For freedom of conscience proponents,

---

[128] Linda C. McClain, 'Rights and Irresponsibility' (1994) 43 *Duke L.J.* 989, 1076.

[129] *Compassion in Dying v. Washington* (1996) 79 F.3d 790, 839 (9th Cir. en banc).

[130] *Planned Parenthood of Southeastern Pennsylvania v. Casey* (1992) 505 U.S. 833, 916 (Stevens J., concurring in part and dissenting in part). For state court use of state constitutional freedom of conscience guarantees in the abortion context, see, e.g., *Preterm Cleveland v. Voinovich*, No. 92CVHO1-528, 1992 Ohio Misc. LEXIS 1, *14, *15 (Franklin Cty. C.P.) (holding that the freedom of conscience guarantee protects against state interference in decisions involving 'deeply-held moral' and philosophical convictions including the decision to terminate a pregnancy), rev'd (1993) 627 N.E. 2d 570 (Ohio C.A.). The decisions centred on section 7 of the Ohio Constitution, which reads: 'All men have a natural and indefeasible right to worship Almighty God according to the dictates of their own conscience. No person shall be compelled to attend, erect, or support any place of worship, or maintain any form of worship, against his consent; and no preference shall be given, by law to any religious society; nor shall any interference with the rights of conscience be permitted...' Ohio Const. Art. I, § 7.

[131] Dworkin, above n. 46, 214; Williams, above n. 60. For examples of such arguments, see Rosenblum & Forsythe, above n. 81, 21; Byron L. Sherwin, 'Jewish Views of Euthanasia' in Marvin Kohl, ed., *Beneficent Euthanasia* (Buffalo, N.Y.: Prometheus, 1975) 3, 7. See Chapter 3, Section II.A.2.c.   [132] See, e.g., Dworkin, above n. 46, 81–4, 237–9.

[133] See, e.g., Joseph V. Sullivan, 'The Immorality of Euthanasia' in *Beneficent Euthanasia*, above n. 131, 12, 19 (describing how Christianity from the beginning opposed self-destruction and homicide); J. Gay-Williams, 'The Wrongfulness of Euthanasia' in Ronald Munson, ed., *Intervention and Reflection: Basic Issues in Medical Ethics* (Belmont, Calif.: Wadsworth, 1983) 156, 157 (writing that religion interprets suicide as an act against God). Alexander Capron, a leading bioethicist, describes the sanctity of life argument as one which 'smacks of religious dogma'. Alexander Morgan Capron, 'The Burden of Decision' (1990) 20(3) *Hastings Center Rep.* 36, 37. Ronald Dworkin contends that 'a belief in the objective and intrinsic importance of human life has a distinctly religious content.' Dworkin, above n. 46, 163.

such an argument must be recognized as representative of one conscientiously-held view, based on deeply felt religious values.[134] To accede to it would be 'to endorse [and] also to enforce, on pain of a further loss of liberty through actual imprisonment, one conscientiously-held view at the expense of another.'[135] The possibility exists that an individual seeking assistance in suicide in a jurisdiction in which such assistance constitutes a criminal act could be found guilty of the crime of conspiracy or as a party to an offence being committed by those assisting her. In the *Rodriguez* case, the British Columbia Court of Appeals found that the appellant Sue Rodriguez could be guilty of an offence if she participated in the planning or attempted execution of her own assisted suicide.[136]

In other words, to accept this argument would be to impose a certain set of religious values on individuals, in circumstances where there is no impingement on the rights of others to hold different beliefs.[137] The decision whether to take one's life is a deeply personal, moral decision. As Justice Stevens remarked in *Cruzan*, '[n]ot much may be said with confidence about death unless it is said from faith, and that alone is reason enough to protect the freedom to conform choices about death to individual conscience.'[138] For the state to endorse and enforce one particular moral standpoint in any manner, where there is no countervailing interest (such as protecting the freedom of conscience, or indeed any other guaranteed freedom of other individuals) could therefore be argued to violate the individual's right to freedom of conscience and religion.[139] This argument would be subject to the limit also exposed in *Casey* in which Justices O'Connor, Kennedy and Souter stated that 'though the abortion decision may originate within the

---

[134] See Jean-Louis Baudouin, 'Le droit de refuser d'être traité' ('The right to refuse treatment') in Rosalie S. Abella & Melvin L. Rothman, eds., *Justice Beyond Orwell* (Montréal: Éditions Y. Blais, 1985) 207, 209. Baudouin describes an evolution of thought and law in this area. He acknowledges that during a particular historical period human beings were denied the power to decide their lives and deaths, as life was considered to be loaned by God and not given to the individual, who was required to return the loan, and was not free to dispose of his life as he desired. Baudouin situates the sanctity of life argument as a historical one and argues that modern legal systems have moved away from it towards a recognition of personal autonomy on many levels including constitutional rights protection. See also, Previn, above n. 123, 604–5.

[135] *Morgentaler* [1988] 1 S.C.R. 30, 179 (Wilson J., concurring).

[136] *Rodriguez v. British Columbia (Attorney-General)* (1993) 76 B.C.L.R. (2d) 145, [43], [120] (B.C.C.A.).

[137] *Compassion in Dying v. Washington* (1996) 79 F.3d 790, 839 (9th Cir. en banc) ('Those who believe strongly that death must come without physician assistance are free to follow that creed, be they doctors or patients. They are not free, however, to force their views, their religious convictions, or their philosophies on all the other members of a democratic society, and to compel those whose values differ with theirs to die painful, protracted, and agonizing deaths.'). See also, Geoffrey Lee Martin, 'Australians In Dispute Over Euthanasia' *Daily Telegraph*, 3 Feb. 1995, 16 (discussing remarks of Marshall Perron, Chief Minister of Australia's Northern Territory).

[138] *Cruzan v. Director, Mo. Dep't of Health* (1990) 497 U.S. 261, 343 (Stevens J., dissenting).

[139] For a discussion of freedom of conscience as including the autonomy to make such decisions, see James E. Fleming, 'Constructing the Substantive Constitution' (1993) 72 *Tex. L. Rev.* 211, 253–6, 294–7. For the argument that freedom of conscience protects only religious obligation and not the autonomy to make 'moral' decisions, see Michael W. McConnell, 'Religious Freedom at a Crossroads' (1992) 59 *U. Chi. L. Rev.* 115, 172–5.

zone of conscience and belief, it is more than a philosophic exercise.'[140] Indeed, such arguments were summarily rejected by both the U.S. Supreme Court and the European Court of Human Rights in the assisted suicide context.[141]

An alternative (and more limited) argument based on the right to freedom of conscience and religion is put forth by Matthew Previn. He argues that the humanist conception of the sanctity of life is a religious belief.[142] This belief would be consistent with assisted suicide in certain circumstances, when those capacities central to the humanist conception of the sanctity of life – freedom, rationality, and conscience – are in serious danger.[143] Thus individuals holding this belief would be eligible for exemption from any law which would burden the exercise of that belief, such as criminal prohibitions on assisted suicide.[144]

7. Right to property

The right to suicide has also been framed in terms of the individual's property right in her own life or body. Such a formulation is uncommon,[145] and is most often used in rebuttal against the assertion of a property right in the individual's life or body held by either God or the state.[146] In its simplest form, the argument is based on the assertion 'it's *my* body' or 'it's *my* life' to dispose of as I choose.[147] Leon Kass discusses the philosophical antecedents of this argument, focusing his attention on the writings of John Locke, who contended that '[t]hough the earth and all inferior creatures be common to all men, yet every man has a property in his own person; this nobody has a right to but himself. The labor of his body and the work of his hands we may say are properly his.'[148] Kass argues that this property right 'is less a metaphysical statement of self-ownership, more a political

---

[140] *Planned Parenthood of Southeastern Pennsylvania v. Casey* (1992) 505 U.S. 833, 852 (O'Connor, Kennedy & Souter JJ.).

[141] *Washington v. Glucksberg* (1997) 521 U.S. 702, 727–8 (Rehnquist C.J.); *Pretty v. U.K.* (2002) 35 E.H.R.R. 1, [82]–[83] (Eur. Ct. H.R.) ('not all opinions or convictions constitute beliefs in the sense protected by Article 9 § 1 of the Convention' which guarantees the 'right to freedom of thought, conscience and religion').

[142] 'According to [the humanist] conception of life's sanctity, reverence for life derives not from God, but from the ability to exercise the distinctly human qualities of freedom, rationality, and conscience.' Previn, above n. 123, 598. The humanist view of the sanctity of human life is discussed in depth in Part III of Previn's article.   [143] Ibid. 599.

[144] Ibid. 611.

[145] See, e.g., Roger F. Friedman, 'It's My Body and I'll Die If I Want To: A Property Based-Argument in Support of Assisted Suicide' (1995) 12 *J. Contemp. Health L. & Pol'y* 183 (arguing that a property-based argument provides suffering people the legal and moral ammunition to exercise their rights to commit suicide and to have others assist them in doing so).

[146] See, e.g., Battin, above n. 37, 178–80; Engelhardt & Malloy, above n. 40, 1033, n. 150.

[147] See *Thornburgh v. American Coll. of Obst. & Gyn.* (1986) 476 U.S. 747, 777, n. 5 (Stevens J., concurring) (referring to the 'moral fact that a person belongs to himself and not others nor to society as a whole,' quoting Charles Fried, Correspondence (1977) 6 *Phil. & Pub. Aff.* 288, 288–9). See also, Mary Ann Glendon, *Rights Talk: The Impoverishment of Political Discourse* (New York: Free Press, 1993) 45 (discussing claims of property rights and individual freedom in the context of the human body and mandatory seat-belt laws).

[148] John Locke, *Second Treatise on Civil Government* (Thomas P. Peardon, ed.) (New York: Macmillan, 1952) (1st edn. 1690) [27].

statement denying ownership by another.'[149] According to Kass, the right is limited to prevention of use of the property by others, and does not include the right of the 'owner' to 'dispose' of the property.[150] In support of this assertion, Kass relies on a later passage in Locke concerning legislative power: 'nobody has an absolute arbitrary power over himself or over any other, to destroy his own life or take away the life or property of another.'[151]

This right-based argument suffers from certain conceptual difficulties, particularly the problem of whether life can be the object of a property right.[152] This is especially problematic in the case of suicide, which involves the destruction of the object of the purported property right – life. In this case, the destruction of the object presupposes or includes the owner's destruction, which is not usually the case when property is destroyed.[153] That is, 'the owner *is* the destroyed property.'[154]

The right to property argument in favour of suicide or assisted suicide may also be subject to certain limitations. Individuals do not have unlimited rights regarding the use of their property. For instance, one may not use one's property to harm another person or to destroy another's property.[155] Similarly, 'some [acts of] suicide[or assisted suicide] may violate the rights of *other* persons, though equally certainly some suicides do not.'[156] Thus a parent of a young child may owe a duty of care to that child, or the child may have a *right* to be cared for which could override the parent's property right of disposition in this context.[157]

D. Rights-based arguments against assisted suicide

Rights-based arguments against assisted suicide cluster around the right to life and the problem of its inalienability. Other rights-based arguments include: the right to equality or equal protection; property rights in the individual's life or body held by either God or the state; and the right to autonomy.

1. Right to life

Opponents of the legalization of assisted suicide derive support from human rights documents such as the U.S. Declaration of Independence, which describe

---

[149] Kass, above n. 40, 38.   [150] Ibid. 39.   [151] Locke, above n. 148, [135].
[152] Battin, above n. 37, 180.
[153] '[I]n ordinary property-destruction cases the owner of the property continues to exist (and be benefited or harmed) after destroying his or her property.' Ibid. 184.   [154] Ibid.
[155] See Joel Feinberg, 'Voluntary Euthanasia and the Inalienable Right to Life' (1978) 7 *Phil. & Pub. Aff.* 93, 119.   [156] Ibid.
[157] Whether such a duty in fact exists depends on a case's particular facts, and may depend on factors such as the presence or absence of alternative care-giving arrangements for the child and the child's age. See, e.g., *Norwood Hosp. v. Munoz* (1991) 564 N.E.2d 1017, 1025 (Mass. S.J.C.) (holding that a mother who was one of Jehovah's Witnesses was entitled to refuse a life-saving blood transfusion where her child would not be abandoned upon her death); *Public Health Trust v. Wons* (1989) 541 So. 2d 96, 97 (Fla. S.C.) (holding that a refusal of a life-saving blood transfusion does not constitute abandonment of teenage children who could be cared for by their father). See generally, Rosamund Scott, 'Autonomy and Connectedness: A Re-Evaluation of Georgetown and its Progeny' (2000) 28 *J. L. Med. & Ethics* 55.

the right to life as inalienable.[158] Proponents of this view often conclude that the right to life is of a special character, and does not possess the characteristic of waivability,[159] which is customarily assumed to be an aspect of any right in a rights-based morality.[160] The non-waivability of the right to life renders any decision to take one's own life an attempt 'to alienate the inalienable, to give away what cannot properly be given away.'[161]

This position reflects a particular view of the meaning of inalienability. As Margaret Jane Radin has observed, 'there is no one sharp meaning for the term "inalienable." '[162] For proponents of the inalienable right to life in the context of assisted suicide, an inalienable right is a *mandatory* right. That is, the right-holder has no discretion regarding the exercise of the right – 'only one way of exercising it is permitted.'[163] A mandatory right to life imposes a duty on the right-holder to remain alive as long as possible, 'or, at least, a duty not to take one's own life or not to cooperate with others in its taking.'[164]

In contrast, assisted suicide proponents argue that the inalienability of a right does not make that right a mandatory one. According to this view, the right to life would be a *discretionary* right which can be voluntarily waived.[165] The inalienability of the right to life would refer to the right's non-relinquishable nature – that is, the individual would not be able to relinquish the *right* to life, although one form of exercise of the right would include the relinquishment of the *object* of the right – one's life.[166] '[T]he individual who chooses to die does not lose his or her *right* to

---

[158] '[All humans are] endowed by their Creator with certain unalienable Rights, that among these are Life, Liberty and the Pursuit of Happiness.' *The Declaration of Independence* (1776), [2]; *Martin* (1946) 37 S.E.2d 43, 47 (Va. S.C.A.) (discussing in a homicide case that the right to life is sacred and inalienable). See Leon R. Kass, 'Neither for Love nor Money: Why Doctors Must Not Kill' (1989) 94 *Public Interest* 25, 27; Maria T. CeloCruz, 'Aid-in-Dying: Should We Decriminalize Physician-Assisted Suicide and Physician-Committed Euthanasia?' (1992) 18 *Am. J. L. & Med.* 369, 387–8.

[159] See, e.g., Rosenblum & Forsythe, above n. 81, 21; CeloCruz, above n. 158, 387; Daniel Callahan, 'When Self-Determination Runs Amok' (1992) 22(2) *Hastings Center Rep.* 52. This argument is described under the heading 'paternalist' in Feinberg, above n. 155, 120–1.

[160] For example, the right to privacy or security of the person is frequently waived in the medical context to allow for examinations, treatment, and even surgical interventions. See generally, Feinberg, above n. 84; Hart, above n. 37; Brock, above n. 68, 105 (arguing that waivability is a central characteristic of rights); Browne, above n. 60 (asserting that rights are by definition waivable).

[161] Feinberg, above n. 155, 93.   [162] Radin, above n. 65, 1849.

[163] Feinberg, above n. 155, 105. See, e.g., Jonathan T. Smies, 'The Legalization of Euthanasia in the Netherlands' (2003–04) 7 *Gonz. J. Int'l L.* 1, 56–63.

[164] Feinberg, above n. 155, 110. Many commentators are critical of the imposition of a duty to live. See, e.g., Eike-Henner W. Kluge, *Biomedical Ethics in a Canadian Context* (Scarborough, Ont.: Prentice-Hall Canada, 1992) 264–5; Battin, above n. 105, 287, n. 15; H.J.J. Leenen, 'Assistance to Suicide and the European Court of Human Rights: the Pretty Case' (2002) 9 *Eur. J. Health L.* 257, 259; Pedain, above n. 39, 204.

[165] See Jozef H.H.M. Dorscheidt, 'Assessment Procedures Regarding End-of-Life Decisions in Neonatology in the Netherlands' (2005) 24 *Med. & L.* 803, 812–18 (describing the position of the Dutch Government during the debates preceding the enactment of the Termination of Life on Request and Assisted Suicide (Review Procedures) Act 2001).

[166] 'In exercising my own choice in these matters, I am not renouncing, abjuring, forswearing, resigning, or relinquishing my right to life; quite the contrary, I am acting on that right by exercising it one way or the other.' Feinberg, above n. 155, 121.

life. To commit suicide is not to abridge one's right to life; it is to abridge one's life.... Thus refusal to exercise one's right to life by committing suicide does not entail that one loses that right.'[167]

To encapsulate the distinction between these two versions of inalienability, on the mandatory view both the right and its object are not relinquishable, while on the discretionary view, the right is not relinquishable, but its object may be relinquished.[168] In response to those who argue in favour of the *discretionary* inalienable right to life, mandatory right to life proponents often cite the special, primary character of the right to life, arguing that as a necessary precursor to the possession of all other rights, its special mandatory character of non-waivability is both explicable and warranted.[169]

2. Right to equality or equal protection

a. The impact of legalization on marginalized groups

Opponents of the legalization of assisted suicide rely on two separate but related arguments based on the right to equality or equal protection. The first focuses on the impact such legalization may have on already-marginalized and discriminated-against groups, particularly the physically disabled. Policy-makers and commentators also suggest that legalization could have a disparate impact on the indigent (especially indigent women), people of colour, minors, and the mentally disabled.[170] Marginalized groups such as these may already be at greater risk of suicide prompted by some form of mental illness: 'the ranks of those who attempt suicide are disproportionately filled with marginal members of our society – the aged, the poor, the ill or disabled – and with those who are isolated and lacking in personal and social support – the single or recently bereaved, the alienated and unhelped young.'[171]

Members of marginalized groups may be more likely to receive inadequate pain treatment, and thus more likely to view assisted death as their only option:

A recent study found that patients treated at centers that serve predominantly minority patients were three times more likely than those treated elsewhere to receive inadequate

---

[167] Battin, above n. 37, 190. [168] See Feinberg, above n. 155, 114–15.

[169] See, e.g., Doerflinger, above n. 67, 16. On the priority of the right to life, see Chapter 3, Section II.A.1.a.

[170] See House of Lords Select Committee on Medical Ethics, *Report*, HL Paper 21-I (Session 1993–1994) [239]; Diane Coleman, 'Withdrawing Life-Sustaining Treatment from People with Severe Disabilities Who Request It: Equal Protection Considerations' (1992) 8 *Issues in Law & Med.* 55, 78 (arguing that assisted suicide legislation for people with disabilities would probably not survive a strict scrutiny equal protection analysis); Rosenblum & Forsythe, above n. 81, 29–31. See also, *Compassion in Dying v. Washington* (1995) 49 F.3d 586, 592 (9th Cir.) (voicing concern regarding the protection of the poor and minorities from exploitation). For an interesting debate on this issue, see Ronald A. Lindsay, 'Should We Impose Quotas? Evaluating The "Disparate Impact" Argument Against Legalization of Assisted Suicide' (2002) 30 *J. L. Med. & Ethics* 6; Carl H. Coleman, 'The "Disparate Impact" Argument Reconsidered: Making Room For Justice In The Assisted Suicide Debate' (2002) 30 *J. L. Med. & Ethics* 17. [171] Marzen, above n. 34, 4.

pain treatment. Elderly individuals and women were also more likely than others to receive poor pain treatment.[172]

In its 1994 report entitled *When Death Is Sought: Assisted Suicide and Euthanasia in the Medical Context*, the New York State Task Force on Life and the Law argued:

No matter how carefully any guidelines are framed, assisted suicide and euthanasia will be practiced through the prism of social inequality and bias that characterizes the delivery of services in all segments of our society, including health care. The practices will pose the greatest risks to those who are poor, elderly, members of a minority group, or without access to good medical care.[173]

The New York State Task Force was relied on in this regard by the three judge panel of the Ninth Circuit in *Compassion in Dying v. Washington*.[174] The panel's use of this argument was rejected as 'disingenuous', 'fallacious', and 'meretricious' by the majority of the Ninth Circuit sitting en banc:

The argument that disadvantaged persons will receive more medical services than the remainder of the population in one, and only one, area – assisted suicide – is ludicrous on its face. So, too, is the argument that the poor and the minorities will rush to volunteer for physician-assisted suicide because of their inability to secure adequate medical treatment.[175]

Indeed, the evidence from Oregon is that those who are better educated (and therefore expected to have higher incomes) are most likely to request a prescription under the Death with Dignity Act.[176]

The public statement made by legalization might inappropriately encourage individuals to exercise their new option to commit assisted suicide.[177] The pressure on many physically disabled persons to forgo expensive and time-consuming care is already an unfortunate societal reality: 'The legalization of assisted suicide will only increase this pressure. If legalized, it will become available, and if available, it will become standard for anyone, and anyone who declines to take advantage of what is reasonably available to all will be seen as unreasonable.'[178]

---

[172] New York State Task Force, above n. 66, 90, n. 46, quoting Charles S. Cleeland et al., 'Pain and its treatment in outpatients with metastatic cancer' (1994) 330(9) *New Eng. J. Med.* 592.

[173] New York State Task Force, ibid. xiii. See also, Herbert Hendin, 'Seduced by Death: Doctors, Patients, and the Dutch Cure' (1994) 10 *Issues in Law & Med.* 123, 165 ('without comprehensive [health] care for sickly, poor, and older persons, euthanasia will tend to become their only option').

[174] *Compassion in Dying v. Washington* (1995) 49 F.3d 586, 592 (9th Cir.).

[175] *Compassion in Dying v. Washington* (1996) 79 F.3d 790, 825 (9th Cir. en banc).

[176] Oregon Department of Human Services, *Eighth Annual Report on Oregon's Death with Dignity Act*, 9 Mar. 2006, Table 2, http://oregon.gov/DHS/ph/pas/docs/year8.pdf, accessed 24 July 2006.

[177] See Kamisar, above n. 80, 37; Marzen, above n. 34, 108 (describing the 'social legitimacy' that would attach to suicide following the constitutional recognition of suicide as a right).

[178] Rosenblum & Forsythe, above n. 81, 27. See also, *Compassion in Dying v. Washington* (1995) 49 F.3d 586, 592 (9th Cir.) (articulating concern regarding coercion and psychological pressure on the elderly and infirm); Mary Johnson, 'Voluntary Active Euthanasia: The Next Frontier?' (1992) 8 *Issues in Law & Med.* 343, 344 (emphasis in original): 'It seems all too likely that the high moral ground of "right to die" has been appropriated as a cover for what appears to be occurring with an increasing number of mentally alert, but physically disabled, people. It is not the protection of a freely chosen right but the encouragement, perhaps by coercion, to exercise that "right" as the *only* option.'

Without denying the autonomy-based arguments in favour of a right to suicide or assisted suicide, the equality-based response suggests that such a right may be meaningless if the choice between available options is more apparent than real.[179] For those with physical disabilities who are not terminally ill, if the choice to continue living is illusory owing to lack of care, financial constraints, or gross societal indifference,[180] then an autonomy-based right to assisted suicide may itself be transformed, in effect, into a duty, in violation of the individual's equality rights (and indeed, her right to life).[181]

b. The form of legalization

A different formulation of the right to equality in opposing legal assisted suicide concerns the form which legalization might take. If assisted suicide were legally restricted to certain groups of individuals, such as the terminally ill and those with severe physical disabilities, as is often proposed,[182] some have argued that such distinctions would be impermissible on equal protection grounds.[183] That is, to allow assisted suicide solely for the physically disabled, for example, could constitute 'prejudicial treatment'[184] of the disabled – whose right to life might be seen as less worthy of protection than the right to life of the physically able – thus violating constitutional guarantees of equal protection. Chief Judge Hogan accepted this equal protection argument in *Lee v. Oregon*, holding that the Oregon Death with

---

[179] See, e.g., Miller, above n. 117.

[180] See Gina Kolata, 'Saying Life Is Not Enough, the Disabled Demand Rights and Choices' *N.Y. Times*, 31 Jan. 1991, B7 (describing the choice of some severely disabled persons to die rather than to live a 'numbing life in a nursing home'). See also, *Compassion in Dying v. Washington* (1995) 49 F.3d 586, 592 (9th Cir.); Marzen, above n. 34, 132 (describing some suicides and suicide attempts by individuals who are physically ill and/or socially disabled as attempts to escape 'from the rejection they suffer from others'); Carol J. Gill, 'Suicide Intervention for Persons with Disabilities: A Lesson in Inequality' (1992) 8 *Issues in Law & Med.* 37, 38–9.

[181] See Johnson, above n. 178, 358. See also, Stanley S. Herr et al., 'No Place to Go: Refusal of Life-Sustaining Treatment by Competent Persons with Disabilities' (1992) 8 *Issues in Law & Med.* 3, 7 ('Will the effects of these "right to die" cases undermine the struggle of many persons with severe disabilities to enjoy a right to life with dignity?').

[182] See Susan M. Wolf, 'Holding the Line on Euthanasia' (1989) 19(1) *Hastings Center Rep.* S13, S14. For examples of such proposals, see Kluge, above n. 164, 264 (restriction of assisted suicide to the terminally ill and those whose life is 'qualitatively atrocious, even torturous, by ordinary standards, and . . . quite unacceptable'); Browne, above n. 60, 55 (advocating only a restriction to the competent).

[183] See Bopp, above n. 36, 116; Coleman, above n. 170, 79 (stating that judicial and legislative actions may be challenged on an equal protection basis); Marcia Pearce Burgdorf & Robert Burgdorf, Jr., 'A History of Unequal Treatment: The Qualifications of Handicapped Persons as a "Suspect Class" Under the Equal Protection Clause' (1975) 15 *Santa Clara Lawyer* 855, 908 (arguing that individuals with handicaps are a 'suspect' class); Robert A. Destro, 'Quality-of-Life Ethics and Constitutional Jurisprudence: The Demise of Natural Rights and Equal Protection for the Disabled and Incompetent' (1986) 2 *J. Contemp. Health L. & Pol'y* 71, 130 (arguing that equal protection doctrine should prevent the law from making quality of life judgments); Walter M. Weber, 'What Right to Die?' (1988) 18 *Suicide & Life-Threatening Behavior* 181, 183–6 (citing equal protection considerations which would result in such a right being available to any competent adult, mature minors, and possibly even incompetent individuals).

[184] *McKay v. Bergstedt* (1990) 801 P.2d 617, 635 (Nev. S.C., Springer J., dissenting).

Dignity Act violates the Equal Protection Clause because the terminally ill are deprived of a benefit afforded to those who are not terminally ill, namely the protection of the statutory ban on assisted suicide.[185]

3. Right to property

Two separate property right claims can be advanced against the legalization of assisted suicide. The first, neatly encapsulated in the oft-cited declaration that 'we are but stewards of what God has entrusted to us',[186] argues that God has property rights in our bodies and our lives.[187] Thus the individual's sovereignty over her body and her life is strictly limited, by definition excluding the right to commit suicide, which would destroy God's property. Although many may see this kind of argument as simply a metaphor, its formulation in terms of property rights, rather than as a 'sanctity of life' or 'duty to live' argument is significant.[188] Such a property right would necessarily be stronger than the conventional notion of property rights which does not absolutely prohibit the destruction of another's property. In certain cases, for example, such destruction may be necessary to avoid greater harm to another.[189]

Obvious problems with an argument intimately connected to religious beliefs stem from the pluralistic nature of our society, exemplified by the right to freedom of conscience and religion.[190] Many commentators argue that religious arguments have no special force in a pluralist, constitutional democracy.[191] '[T]he concern not to offend God . . . is an inappropriate consideration for a pluralistic society in which divergent and irreconcilable opinions concerning the desires or the existence of a deity exist.'[192]

---

[185] *Lee v. Oregon* (1995) 891 F. Supp. 1429, 1438 (D. Or.), overturned by *Lee v. Oregon* (1997) 107 F.3d 1382, 1392 (9th Cir.), *certiorari* denied by *Lee v. Harcleroad* (1997) 522 U.S. 927. See also, Chapter 3, Sections II.A.5.b and II.B.2; Chapter 6, Section VI.A.

[186] See New York State Task Force, above n. 66, 90 (discussing the notion of 'stewardship'); Helga Kuhse, *The Sanctity-of-Life Doctrine in Medicine: A Critique* (Oxford: Oxford Univ. Press, 1987) 18–19.

[187] See Dworkin, above n. 46, 214 (describing this argument); Richards, above n. 68, 373–6 (summarizing and rebutting this argument); Baudouin, above n. 134, 209 (describing this argument as one found in historical materials, rather than as a present-day contention). However, present-day formulations of this argument still abound. See, e.g., Sullivan, above n. 133, 12–33; Gay-Williams, above n. 133, 157 ('Man as trustee of his body acts against God, its rightful possessor, when he takes his own life.'). The argument can be traced back to Thomas Aquinas, *Summa Theologiae* (Fathers of the English Dominican Province, trans.) (London: Burns, Oates & Washbourne, 1918) II-II, 64.

[188] See Locke, above n. 148, [6] on the state of nature: 'But though this be a state of liberty, yet it is not a state of license; though man in that state have an uncontrollable liberty to dispose of his person or possessions, yet he has not liberty to destroy himself... [F]or men being all the workmanship of one omnipotent and infinitely wise Maker... they are his property whose workmanship they are... Every one... is bound to preserve himself and not to quit his station wilfully.'

[189] See Browne, above n. 60, 41–2. Browne provides the example of the destruction of property in order to prevent the spread of fire. See also, Feinberg, above n. 155, 102.

[190] See above, text accompanying nn. 124–137.   [191] See Richards, above n. 68, 373–6.

[192] Engelhardt & Malloy, above n. 40, 1021.

The second property right claim used in opposition to legalization of assisted suicide substitutes the state for God as the holder of a property right in individuals' lives. The argument that the state has a property right in individuals' lives has little currency.[193] It is most often presented only to be brusquely rejected in favour of an individual property right in life, or a general right of self-determination.[194] Given the prevalence of state interest analysis in the constitutional context, opponents of the legalization of assisted suicide often prefer to speak in terms of the 'state interest in the preservation of life,' rather than the state's property right in individuals' lives.[195]

4. *Right to autonomy*

To counteract the derivation of a right to suicide from the general right to autonomy, opponents of the legalization of assisted suicide sometimes argue that such legalization poses a *threat* to the individual's right to autonomy rather than enhancing or being consonant with it.[196] The concern is with the quality of autonomous choice in the context of decisions to commit suicide, along a spectrum ranging from the spectre of outright coercion,[197] to the problem of the social construction of choice in an environment in which legal assisted suicide is known to be an option.[198] 'Each personal choice [regarding assistance in suicide] will be formed by societal and interpersonal forces that must be acknowledged, even though they cannot be perfectly counterbalanced. The societal context includes financial barriers to the choice of palliative and community-based care and a culture that is saturated with media images of trivialized and superficially justified killings.'[199]

The problem is seen as particularly acute if assisted suicide is enshrined as a right.[200] The fear is that the legalization of assisted suicide, especially in a rights-based formulation, would send a message to already marginalized members of

---

[193] See Richards, above n. 68, 376–8. The argument stems from the Aristotelian conception of duties to the state. See Aristotle, *Nichomachean Ethics* 1138a4-1138b14, cited in Richards, ibid. 376. At common law, suicide constituted a crime against the Crown as it deprived the monarch of a subject. See *Hales v. Petit* (1562) 75 Eng. Rep. 387, 399–400 (C.B.) and the excellent discussion in Marzen, above n. 34, 56–63.

[194] See, e.g., Battin, above n. 37, 183–4; Richards, above n. 68, 376–8.

[195] One exception is found in Bopp, above n. 36, 132 (referring to the state's interest in the preservation of life as a 'right'). [196] See Dworkin, above n. 46, 190.

[197] See Johnson, above n. 178, 344; Browne, above n. 60, 46 (discussing the problem of coercion and possible regulatory safeguards to avoid it); Bopp, above n. 36, 138–40.

[198] Edmund D. Pellegrino, 'Compassion Needs Reason Too' (1993) 270(7) *J. Am. Med. Ass'n* 874, 875.

[199] Steven H. Miles, 'Physicians and Their Patients' Suicides' (1994) 271(22) *J. Am. Med. Ass'n* 1786, 1787. See also, Marzen, above n. 34, 146 ('a climate of societally sanctioned suicide could well lead to pressure on the otherwise nonsuicidal elderly and disabled, who are marginal in our society, to end their lives').

[200] See J. David Velleman, 'Against the Right to Die' (1992) 17 *J. Med. & Phil.* 665. See also, Bopp, above n. 36, 126, presenting the rather overblown factual scenario of a request for suicide assistance at a hospital emergency room, followed by immediate compliance.

society that suicide is an acceptable, responsible or even expected option.[201] Such a message might potentially override the hitherto unconsciously accepted autonomous choice to continue living. 'The social legitimacy and easy availability of effective assistance to commit suicide that would necessarily follow recognition of suicide as a "right" would . . . contribute to a climate in which both subtle and obvious forms of duress would cause many who would not otherwise do so to choose suicide, whether or not they are mentally or emotionally disturbed.'[202]

[201] See Kamisar, above n. 80, 37.

[202] Marzen, above n. 34, 108. Evidence that suicides have the potential to be 'contagious' may exacerbate this problem. See ibid. 139–46 (describing phenomena of 'cluster' suicides amongst teenagers and suicide epidemics within communities).

3

The Effects of Rights

I. Introduction

Having enumerated the various kinds and different formulations of rights-based arguments in the debate surrounding the legalization of assisted suicide, the difficulties presented are self-evident: how can such competing and seemingly irreconcilable claims be resolved with any kind of societal agreement? Paralysis is an understandable response in the face of vociferous, strident, and conflicting claims of individual rights. If we are not to simply throw up our hands and abandon the rights-based debate, or at least its present incarnation, then some way to move forward through the thicket of competing claims must be found.

We may be understandably reluctant to renounce the use of rights altogether, seeing much that is of actual and potential value in rights claims. '[O]n an individual level, a claim of right can be an assertion of one's self-worth and an affirmation of one's moral value and entitlement.'[1] Mary Ann Glendon rejects the radical attack on rights (which advocates their abandonment) in favour of a re-evaluation of

certain thoughtless, habitual ways of thinking and speaking about rights. Let us freely grant that legally enforceable rights can assist citizens in a large heterogeneous country to live together in a reasonably peaceful way. They have given minorities a way to articulate claims that majorities often respect, and have assisted the weakest members of society in making their voices heard.[2]

Even the major schools of the critique of rights see some value in rights discourse. For example, the Critical Legal Studies scholar Duncan Kennedy argues:

the critique of rights as liberal philosophy does not imply that the left should abandon rights rhetoric as a tool of political organizing or legal argument. Embedded in the rights notion is a liberating accomplishment of our culture: the affirmation of free human subjectivity against the constraints of group life, along with the paradoxical countervision of a group life that creates and nurtures individuals capable of freedom. We need to work at the slow transformation of rights rhetoric, dereifying it, rather than simply junking it.[3]

---

[1] Elizabeth M. Schneider, 'The Dialectic of Rights and Politics: Perspectives from the Women's Movement' (1986) 61 *N.Y.U. L. Rev.* 589, 625.

[2] Mary Ann Glendon, *Rights Talk: The Impoverishment of Political Discourse* (New York: Free Press, 1993) 15.

[3] Duncan Kennedy, 'Critical Labor Law Theory: A Comment' (1981) 4 *Indus. Rel. L.J.* 503, 506. For an alternative view, see Mark Tushnet, 'An Essay on Rights' (1984) 62 *Tex. L. Rev.* 1363, 1383.

Similarly, some feminist scholars, while critiquing current rights discourse, do not advocate its wholesale abandonment.[4]

At least in the present political environment, most would agree, even if only on a superficial level, that there is some value in claims of rights.[5] The wholesale abandonment of rights discourse would have its most devastating impact on historically oppressed and marginalized groups in society. The Critical Race Theorist Patricia Williams responds to Critical Legal Studies proposals to abandon rights discourse, observing that:

> The vocabulary of rights speaks to an establishment that values the guise of stability, and from whom social change for the better must come (whether it is given, taken, or smuggled).... The subtlety of rights' real instability thus does not render unusable their persona of stability....
>
> In discarding rights altogether, one discards a symbol too deeply enmeshed in the psyche of the oppressed to lose without trauma and much resistance.[6]

Williams suggests that '[w]hat is needed . . . is not the abandonment of rights language for all purposes, but an attempt to become multilingual in the semantics of evaluating rights.'[7] Before any progress can be made towards a way forward through the assisted suicide debate, and decisions reached on the appropriate mechanisms for legal change, a more detailed analysis of the problems of rights discourse in this context must be undertaken.

In the following sections I attempt to identify common arguments or points of agreement among the various schools of rights critiques. I focus on specific critiques to the extent that they apply in the context of the debate on assisted suicide, rather than recount the positions of the various schools of rights critique[8] – such as the Critical Legal Studies (CLS),[9] Feminist,[10] and Critical Race Theory

---

[4] See, e.g., Lucinda M. Finley, 'Transcending Equality Theory: A Way Out of the Maternity and the Workplace Debate' (1986) 86 *Colum. L. Rev.* 1118, 1172, n. 208. Finley rejects the more extreme criticisms of rights. She sees rights as important even as they have been traditionally defined, although she acknowledges that we may need to re-conceive or redefine them to fit experience or needs as appropriate. See also, Frances Olsen, 'Statutory Rape: A Feminist Critique of Rights Analysis' (1984) 63 *Tex. L. Rev.* 387, 391.

[5] That is, in contrast to some future, utopian ideal, which for some would not include the concept of rights. See Deborah L. Rhode, 'Feminist Critical Theories' (1990) 42 *Stan. L. Rev.* 617, 631–2. Rhode discusses the problem associated with a move towards a legal system based on care and empathy, rather than adversarial and hierarchical dispute-resolution. 'Norms appropriate to our vision of justice in an ideal state may not be the best way to get us there.' Ibid. 632.

[6] Patricia J. Williams, *The Alchemy of Race and Rights* (Cambridge, Mass.: Harvard Univ. Press, 1991) 149, 165.   [7] Ibid. 149.

[8] See Rhode, above n. 5, 617 (commenting that attempting to summarize either feminism or CLS 'risks homogenizing an extraordinarily broad range of views').

[9] See generally, Peter Gabel, 'The Phenomenology of Rights-Consciousness and the Pact of the Withdrawn Selves' (1984) 62 *Tex. L. Rev.* 1563, 1563 (characterizing the CLS movement as developing a consciousness of how legal institutions and ideas have an effect on society); Peter Gabel & Paul Harris, 'Building Power and Breaking Images: Critical Legal Theory and the Practice of Law' (1982–83) 11 *N.Y.U. Rev. L. & Soc. Change* 369, 374–5 (outlining how attorneys can apply CLS in practice to achieve social change); Tushnet, above n. 3.

[10] See generally, Schneider, above n. 1; Elizabeth Kingdom, *What's Wrong with Rights? Problems for Feminist Politics of Law* (Edinburgh: Edinburgh Univ. Press, 1991) (discussing the relevance of rights

(CRT)[11] critiques. I divide the critiques into two broad categories. The first contains arguments regarding the inadequacies associated with rights discourse when attempting to solve complex social problems, and particularly in the context of personal rights. This category includes the problems of indeterminacy, absolutism, and the prevalence of slippery slopes, to name only the more familiar critiques. The second category questions the underlying assumptions of current rights discourse, querying the focus on individualism and autonomy, and raises concerns about the 'missing language'[12] of community.

II. Failure to Provide Solutions to Complex Social Problems

The critiques in this category focus on flaws in rights discourse which impede progress toward solutions to complex social problems. When considering such defects of rights discourse in the context of the debate over assisted suicide, it is helpful to divide the critiques into those which point out problems with rights discourse generally – such as indeterminacy, absolutism, and lack of room for compromise – and those which focus on specific problems with rights discourse in the context of personal (as opposed to civil) rights.

A. Problems with rights discourse generally

From the various critiques of rights one can identify certain general themes which resonate in the context of the assisted suicide debate, requiring further examination. These themes include critiques that rights discourse is indeterminate; rights discourse suppresses and transforms certain forms of argument and thereby distorts the debate; rights discourse is uncompromising and tends to impede the accommodation of (inevitably) competing interests; rights discourse is conclusory and over-simplifying; and rights discourse is absolutist.

1. The indeterminacy critique

The critique that rights discourse is profoundly indeterminate is most often associated with the CLS movement. These critics argue that rights discourse does

discourse to feminist legal theory); Carol Smart, *Feminism and the Power of Law* (London: Routledge, 1989); Judy Fudge, 'The Effect of Entrenching a Bill of Rights Upon Political Discourse: Feminist Demands and Sexual Violence in Canada' (1989) 17 *Int'l. J. Soc. L.* 445, 445; Olsen, above n. 4, 389, n. 7; Catharine MacKinnon, 'Feminism, Marxism, Method, and the State: Toward a Theory of Law and Patriarchy' (1983) 8 *Signs: J. of Women in Culture & Soc'y* 635; Janet Rifkin, 'Toward a Theory of Law and Patriarchy' (1980) 3 *Harv. Women's L.J.* 83, 84 (developing a theory on how law contributes to the permanence of the patriarchal social order); Clare Dalton, 'Book Review' (1983) 6 *Harv. Women's L.J.* 229, 229 (reviewing Davis Kairys, ed., *The Politics of Law* (New York: Pantheon Books, 1982) as a 'manifesto' of CLS).

[11] See, e.g., Williams, above n. 6; Patricia J. Williams, 'Alchemical Notes: Reconstructing Ideals from Deconstructed Rights' (1987) 22 *Harv. Civ. Rts.–Civ. Lib. L. Rev.* 401 (discussing CLS and rights-based theory as applied to the civil rights struggle).　　[12] Glendon, above n. 2, 76.

not provide a mechanism for resolving inevitable conflicts between rights which stem from the perpetual friction between the principles of freedom and security:[13]

Only by ignoring at least half the rights that could be asserted can rights rhetoric even appear to solve concrete problems.... If we recognize the [ ] multiple rights claims [that can be asserted in any given situation] and try to 'balance' the conflicting rights or to choose between them, we wind up talking politically about how we want to live our lives, not abstractly about rights.[14]

a. Conflicts between competing rights

In the assisted suicide debate, such irresolvable conflicts between competing rights are manifold. The conflict between the right to life and the right to liberty provides one example of two rights pitted against each other in a battle which neither can win within a rights-based framework. Those who favour the right to life argue that the priority of life over liberty (and liberty over happiness) is instrumental. That is, the protection of life is needed in order to ensure liberty, just as the protection of liberty is needed to ensure happiness.[15] A variant on this argument contains echoes of sanctity of life arguments: 'Our societal regard for the value of an individual life... would never countenance an assertion of liberty over life' in the circumstances of a physically healthy person.[16] The contrary argument favouring the right to liberty over the right to life argues that the latter loses meaning without the individual's liberty to make fundamental decisions concerning her life (and death).[17] Without freedom, one cannot truly live, thus the individual's right to liberty must take precedence.[18] The 'absence of a[n] [accepted] hierarchy of rights'[19] renders such conflicts both irresolvable and interminable.

---

[13] See Olsen, above n. 4, 388–9, citing Joseph William Singer, 'The Legal Rights Debate in Analytical Jurisprudence from Bentham to Hohfeld' [1982] *Wis. L. Rev.* 975, 1059. See also, Dalton, above n. 10, 235; Mark G. Kelman, 'Trashing' (1984) 36 *Stan. L. Rev.* 293; Kennedy, above n. 3, 506; Karl Klare, 'Labor Law as Ideology: Toward a New Historiography of Collective Bargaining Law' (1981) 4 *Indus. Rel. L.J.* 450, 478; Schneider, above n. 1, 596; Tushnet, above n. 3, 1375.

[14] Olsen, above n. 4, 391. Martha Minow responds to this charge with the interpretevist assertion that 'legal rules are applied in specific contexts, and by reference to specific contextual features we can resolve, at least for that instant case, the tension between, say, freedom and security.' Martha Minow, 'Interpreting Rights: An Essay for Robert Cover' (1987) 96 *Yale L.J.* 1860, 1864, n. 14. A choice between these competing principles, though, is still required, rather than mandated by the rights claimed.

[15] Richard Doerflinger, 'Assisted Suicide: Pro-Choice or Anti-Life?' (1989) 19(1) *Hastings Center Rep.* 16. Similarly, James Bopp argues that in the event of a conflict between the rights to life and liberty, the right to life has priority, relying on Justice Brennan's description of the right to life as 'the right to have rights'. James Bopp, Jr., 'Is Assisted Suicide Constitutionally Protected?' (1987) 3 *Issues in Law & Med.* 113, 126, citing *Furman v. Georgia* (1971) 408 U.S. 238, 290 (Brennan J., concurring). See also, Pope John Paul II, 'The Prayer Vigil' (1993) 23 *Origins* 182, 184 (describing the right to life as God's first gift, and the right on which all other rights are based).

[16] *McKay v. Bergstedt* (1990) 801 P.2d 617, 625 (Nev. S.C.). On sanctity of life arguments, see Chapter 2, Section II.D.1.

[17] See Samuel E. Wallace, 'The Right to Live and the Right to Die' in Samuel E. Wallace & Albin Eser, eds., *Suicide and Euthanasia: The Rights of Personhood* (Knoxville, Tenn.: Univ. Tenn. Press, 1981) 86.　　　　　　　　　　　　　　　　　　　　　　　　　　　[18] See ibid.

[19] Carl Schneider, 'Rights Discourse and Neonatal Euthanasia' (1988) 76 *Cal. L. Rev.* 151, 175.

To avoid belabouring this point I will mention only one other such conflict in the assisted suicide debate with particular application to the physically disabled: the tension between the right to autonomy (to choose death, if desired) and the right to equality (which may be negatively affected by the presence of an autonomy-based right to suicide or assisted suicide).[20]

b. Conflicts between rights and their limiting features

Other insoluble conflicts occur not only between competing rights, but between rights and their inherent or articulated limiting features. This is particularly evident in the context of state interest balancing. Carl Schneider refers to the impossibility of balancing incommensurable interests within a state interest framework.[21] Thomas Mayo also makes this point bluntly, in terms of the right to die, rather than the right to suicide or assisted suicide:

the 'right to die' formulation of the patient treatment problem...merely pits one set of preferences against another: the patient's choice of a hastened death versus the state's traditional role of preserving and protecting life. The claimed right to die unavoidably bumps up against the state's duty to protect and preserve life. It...is a conflict that lacks rules and standards for decision. When this clash of naked preferences occurs in litigation, there is precious little legal content to guide decision-makers but, rather, a subjective choice by a judge whose own preferences are the likeliest guide to a result.[22]

As a result, commentators and judges often simply assert their preference for either the individual right at issue,[23] or the countervailing state interest.[24]

c. Levels of generality

Another related critique is that 'rights discourse is indeterminate...because one can always appeal to a broader or narrower level of generality in order to secure or refuse to protect any particular right.'[25] From the rights-based arguments in favour of and against the legalization of assisted suicide arrayed in Chapter 2, it

---

[20] See Chapter 2, Section II.D.2.a. See also, Lois Shepherd, 'Sophie's Choices: Medical and Legal Responses to Suffering' (1996) 72 *Notre Dame L. Rev.* 103, 145–6.

[21] See Schneider, above n. 19, 172.

[22] Thomas Mayo, 'Constitutionalizing the "Right to Die"' (1990) 49 *Md. L. Rev.* 103, 105.

[23] See, e.g., Steven J. Wolhandler, 'Voluntary Active Euthanasia for the Terminally Ill and the Constitutional Right to Privacy' (1984) 69 *Cornell L. Rev.* 363, 375 (asserting that the individual's right to privacy outweighs any state interest that could oppose assisted suicide); *Kevorkian* (1994) 527 N.W.2d 714, 748 (Mich. S.C., Levin J., concurring in part and dissenting in part).

[24] See, e.g., Margaret A. Somerville, 'The Song of Death: The Lyrics of Euthanasia' (1993) 9 *J. Contemp. Health L. & Pol'y* 1, 26–7 (stating, albeit in the euthanasia context, '[i]t is proposed that euthanasia is not acceptable at the societal level, even if one has no personal moral inhibitions against it at the individual level, and that its unacceptability at the societal level outweighs the acceptability of the best case argument for it at the individual level'). See generally, Laurence H. Tribe & Michael C. Dorf, 'Levels of Generality in the Definition of Rights' (1990) 57 *U. Chi. L. Rev.* 1057, 1096–7 (discussing Justice Scalia's attempt to engage in such reasoning more generally).

[25] Michael Ariens, 'Suicidal Rights' (1988) 20 *Rutgers L.J.* 79, 83. See also, Tribe & Dorf, above n. 24, 1096–7.

is clear that the same general right can be and is used on either side of the debate. This is particularly true of the rights to autonomy[26] and equality.[27] With regard to the latter, Frances Olsen's critique of the indeterminacy of equality rights is apposite: 'the strategy of promoting equality runs afoul of the conflict between formal equality of opportunity and substantive equality of outcome.'[28] We appear to be required to make a choice between formal equality (all individuals, including those who are physically unable to take their own lives, should have an equal opportunity to commit suicide) and substantive equality of opportunity (all individuals should have the opportunity to live an independent, dignified life). According to Olsen, this choice is not determined by examining the right concerned, but rather 'rest[s] upon sociological calculations and political and moral commitments.'[29]

Similarly, Carl Schneider argues that situations in which two opposing sides claim to speak for the 'rights' of the disabled are not uncommon, 'and the only way to decide what those rights [are is to] return to "substantive" questions about what methods of care and treatment best serve the [disabled].'[30] For example, in the *Rodriguez* case, the Intervenor British Columbia Coalition of People with Disabilities (BCCPD) argued that the criminal prohibition on assisted suicide violated the constitutional guarantee of equality in that it denied equality before the law and under the law to persons who have such severe physical disabilities that they are unable to carry out a decision to terminate their lives without assistance. BCCPD contended that the criminal prohibition:

has the effect of imprisoning the appellant and all other mentally competent adult persons with severe physical disabilities who no longer wish to continue living in what for them has become a life of unbearable and unrelenting physical or mental suffering. It converts their 'right to life' into a burden, or "duty to live," and thereby deprives them of equality before and under the law, which allows able-bodied persons the choice of ending their suffering.[31]

Similar arguments were made by the Intervenor Coalition of Provincial Organizations of the Handicapped.[32] However, the Intervenor People in Equal Participation Inc. (PEP), an organization for persons with severe disabilities

---

[26] See Chapter 2, Sections II.C.2 and II.D.4.

[27] See Chapter 2, Sections II.C.5 and II.D.2. The right to property also appears on both sides of the debate, although its inherent conceptual weaknesses in this context, coupled with the notion of different right-holders (the individual, the state, God) make the indeterminacy argument perhaps less significant for the right to property. See Chapter 2, Sections II.C.7 and II.D.3. In the case of Dianne Pretty, the right to life also appeared on both sides of the debate, but the use of the right to life in support of legalization was given short shrift by all of the judges involved. See *Pretty v. U.K.* (2002) 35 E.H.R.R. 1, [37]–[42] (Eur. Ct. H.R.); *R. (on the application of Pretty) v. D.P.P.* [2002] 1 A.C. 800, [3]–[9], [59], [86]–[88]; *R. (on the application of Pretty) v. D.P.P.* [2001] E.W.H.C. Admin. 788, [39]–[44].   [28] Olsen, above n. 4, 412.

[29] Ibid.   [30] Schneider, above n. 19, 170.

[31] *Rodriguez v. British Columbia (Attorney-General)* [1993] 3 S.C.R. 519, Factum of the Intervenor the B.C. Coalition of People with Disabilities, [21].

[32] *Rodriguez v. British Columbia (Attorney-General)* [1993] 3 S.C.R. 519, Factum of the Intervenor Coalition of Provincial Organizations of the Handicapped.

dedicated to enhancing quality of life for the disabled, strongly disagreed with these disability rights organizations. PEP relied on the equal protection argument against legalization canvassed in Chapter 2,[33] namely that legalization would have an adverse impact on vulnerable and already discriminated against groups, particularly the severely physically disabled.[34]

d. Definitional vagueness

Another pertinent argument focuses on the inherent definitional vagueness associated with rights discourse. Both the type of right claimed (whether liberty right, right to non-interference, or positive right) and the basis upon which the right is founded can have a determinative effect on the policy to be adopted once the particular formulation of the right is accepted. As an instance of the former case, one can observe that acceptance of a liberty right to assisted suicide would simply mandate the removal of criminal prohibitions on assistance in suicide; while recognition of a positive right could require that the state provide suicide assistance 'on demand'.

Definitional vagueness of the latter sort is exemplified by a comparison between the rights to dignity and equality as bases for the right to suicide. A dignity-based formulation would authorize only those suicides which promote the individual's dignity.[35] In contrast, the equality-based version of the right to suicide would permit not only assisted suicide but voluntary active euthanasia for those physically disabled persons not able to perform the actions necessary to take their own life, even with appropriate assistance.[36] If the right to suicide or assisted suicide is asserted without clarity as to the basis from which it is derived,[37] or if multiple bases are claimed,[38] confusion regarding the policy to be adopted will be inevitable.

Definitional vagueness and confusion are both inherent in rights discourse and deliberately fostered by its users. The intrinsic vagueness means that even if one frames a right in a specific fashion in order to avoid or achieve a certain policy outcome, there is no guarantee that other jurists, policy drafters or commentators

---

[33] See Chapter 2, Section II.D.2.a.

[34] *Rodriguez v. British Columbia (Attorney-General)* [1993] 3 S.C.R. 519, Factum of the Intervenor People in Equal Participation, Inc., 7–19.   [35] See Chapter 2, Section II.C.4.

[36] See, e.g., G. Steven Neeley, *The Constitutional Right to Suicide: A Legal and Philosophical Examination* (New York: Peter Lang, 1994) 153; Franklin Miller et al., 'Regulating Physician-Assisted Death' (1994) 331(2) *New Eng. J. Med.* 119, 120; *Rodriguez v. British Columbia (Attorney-General)* [1993] 3 S.C.R. 519, [234] (Lamer C.J.C., dissenting). See also, *R. (on the application of Pretty) v. D.P.P.* [2002] 1 A.C. 800, [5] (Lord Bingham). Examples of the use of the right to equality as a mechanism of legal change are canvassed in Chapter 6, Sections II.B and II.C. See also, Chapter 6, Section V.D.

[37] See, e.g., *Kevorkian* (1994) 527 N.W.2d 714, 752, n. 2 (Mich. S.C., Mallett J., dissenting) ('Whether physician-assisted suicide is characterized as a liberty right or a privacy right, the proper constitutional analysis is found in *Casey* and the right to die cases.').

[38] See, e.g., Neeley, above n. 36, 79–80 (relying on liberty, autonomy, and privacy); *Compassion in Dying v. Washington* (1994) 850 F. Supp. 1454, 1461 (W.D. Wash.) (describing the liberty interest at stake as 'the freedom to make choices according to one's individual conscience about those matters which are essential to personal autonomy and basic human dignity').

will continue that definitional plan. Thus one might intentionally frame a right to assisted suicide as a liberty right or a right to non-interference – in opposition to a positive or welfare right – in order to avoid the imposition of a corresponding duty to assist in suicide.[39] This position will nevertheless be prone to re-casting in order to suit a different agenda. Opponents of assisted suicide often formulate it in positive right terms in order to decrease its palatability to both doctors and lay-persons. For example, Michael Ariens argues that acceptance of the liberty-based Mill paradigm in the context of suicide *necessarily* entails a positive right formulation of the right to suicide which 'requires the community to facilitate requests to commit suicide.'[40] Richard Fenigsen uses a similar tactic, albeit in the context of active euthanasia rather than assisted suicide. He argues that a right to euthanasia could only be formulated as a positive or welfare right:

The right to voluntary euthanasia (were we to recognize such a right) would . . . include not only the right to exert control over one's own person, but over other persons as well, over their acts and their consciences. The person requesting his own death would also have the right to make killers of other people and accomplices to killing of those who expressed their consent.[41]

Deliberate use of the definitional vagueness which plagues rights discourse is prevalent in the assisted suicide debate. Participants in the debate may carefully define a particular right in such a way as to achieve a certain desired policy outcome, or to make their position appear more moderate, anticipating later, more radical, transformations of the right in question once a more moderate position has found societal acceptance.[42] Particular concern in this regard has focused on the promotion of the right to refuse life-sustaining or life-saving treatment – popularly known as the 'right to die' – which may later be transformed into a right to suicide or assisted suicide using various different means. Perhaps the most familiar of such techniques is the argument that recognition of the former

---

[39] See, e.g., Robert F. Weir, 'The Morality of Physician-Assisted Suicide' (1992) 20 *Law, Med. & Health Care* 116, 121. On corresponding duties to assist, see Chapter 2, Section II.B.

[40] Ariens, above n. 25, 84, n. 18.

[41] Richard Fenigsen, 'A Case Against Dutch Euthanasia' (1989) 19(1) *Hastings Center Rep.* S22, S29. See also, Lois Snyder & Daniel P. Sulmasy for the Ethics and Human Rights Committee, American College of Physicians – American Society of Internal Medicine, 'Physician-Assisted Suicide' (2001) 135 *Annals Internal Med.* 209, 211; Maurice A.M. de Wachter, 'Euthanasia in the Netherlands' (1992) 22(2) *Hastings Center Rep.* 23, 30 (reporting the remarks of Alexander Capron); Marian H.N. Driesse et al., 'Euthanasia and the Law in the Netherlands' (1987–88) 3 *Issues in Law & Med.* 385, 396 (translation by Walter Lagerwey of Marian H.N. Driesse et al., *Op leven en dood* (*A Matter of Life and Death*) (Dieren: Blok & Zonen, 1986) ch. 6) ('A right to kill almost leads as a matter of course to a duty to kill!').

[42] See, e.g., 'Derek Humphry Discusses Death with Dignity with Thomasine Kushner' (1993) 2 *Camb. Q. Healthcare Ethics* 57, 59 (noting that after assisted suicide for the terminally ill is legalized, assisted suicide for incompetent patients with advance directives and for the elderly must be examined more fully). See also, Leon R. Kass, 'Is There a Right to Die?' (1993) 23(1) *Hastings Center Rep.* 34, 36; Yale Kamisar, 'Are Laws Against Assisted Suicide Unconstitutional?' (1993) 23(3) *Hastings Center Rep.* 32, 36 (describing the tactical use of restrictions of a right to assisted suicide to the terminally ill as 'good advocacy' but otherwise unjustifiable).

right logically and rationally compels acceptance of the latter.[43] For example, Steven Wolhandler argues:

If the right to privacy protects the right to die naturally, it should also protect the competent, terminal patient's right to choose a quick and painless death. The difference between a terminal patient's choosing to refuse treatment and choosing a faster means of dying does not offer a basis for legal distinction. When a competent terminal patient chooses to die, the state interests balanced against that patient's right to privacy are virtually the same regardless of the means chosen.[44]

Another such technique focuses on the correlation between the asserted basis of the 'right to die' and the right to suicide or assisted suicide, particularly the right to autonomy.[45]

Definitional vagueness and confusion contribute to the problem of the indeterminacy of rights discourse. Constantly shifting and easily manipulated definitions of rights claims preclude satisfactory and conclusive resolution of conflicts and prevent closure in this socially and politically divisive debate.

2. *The critique of suppression and distortion*

The powerful force of rights-based arguments makes their use exceedingly attractive to all sides in any contested debate. Leon Kass, an ardent and articulate euthanasia and assisted suicide opponent, describes his political adversaries as deliberately using the powerful language of rights to accomplish a sinister objective:

Many people have seen the advantage of using the language of individual rights, implying voluntary action, to shift the national attitudes regarding life and death, to prepare the way for the practice of terminating 'useless' lives.... These advocates understand all too well that the present American climate requires one to talk of rights if one wishes to have one's way in such moral matters.[46]

The attractions of rights discourse are evident to both sides of the debate on assisted suicide, as is clear from the arguments enumerated in Chapter 2.[47]

---

[43] See Somerville, above n. 24, 9–11 (detailing ways in which the right to suicide may flow from the right to die).

[44] Wolhandler, above n. 23, 375. See also, *Compassion in Dying v. Washington* (1996) 79 F.3d 790, 816 (9th Cir. en banc) ('*Cruzan [v. Director, Mo. Dep't of Health* (1990) 497 U.S. 261], by recognizing a liberty interest that includes the refusal of artificial provision of life-sustaining food and water, necessarily recognizes a liberty interest in hastening one's own death.'); *Compassion in Dying v. Washington* (1994) 850 F. Supp. 1454, 1461 (W.D. Wash.) ('From a constitutional perspective, the court does not believe that a distinction can be drawn between refusing life-sustaining treatment and physician-assisted suicide by an uncoerced, mentally competent, terminally ill adult.'); *Kevorkian* (1994) 527 N.W.2d 714, 759 (Mich. S.C., Mallett J., dissenting) ('There is no adequate distinction between the right of a terminally ill person to refuse unwanted medical treatment and the right to physician-assisted suicide.').

[45] See below, text accompanying n. 73. See, e.g., Note, 'Physician-Assisted Suicide and the Right to Die with Assistance' (1992) 105 *Harv. L. Rev.* 2021, 2024–31 (arguing that current right to die jurisprudence based on the right to self-determination 'can be interpreted to protect patients' interests in receiving suicide assistance from their physicians'). Ibid. 2024.

[46] Kass, above n. 42, 37.   [47] See Chapter 2, Sections II.C and II.D.

My concern under this rubric is with the potentially all-encompassing nature of such discourse. The political and popular power of rights often partially or wholly eliminates other forms of moral discourse, particularly arguments about duties.

a. Focus on the self

Such arguments may be suppressed because of the overwhelming focus of rights discourse on the self and what may be claimed by it. Frances Olsen argues that 'rights theory conceptualizes a society composed of self-interested individuals whose conflicting interests are mediated by the state.'[48] Carl Schneider suggests that the use of rights encourages selfish behaviour since rights are self-concerning rather than other-concerning.[49] 'Thinking in terms of rights encourages us to ask what we may do to free ourselves, not to find ourselves. It encourages us to think about what constrains us from doing what we want, not what obligates us to do what we ought.'[50] Schneider notes that there are limits to this liberal conception of rights to non-interference, such as conflicts with other rights, and also moral considerations such as needs, or supererogatory duties such as compassion or generosity: 'But rights discourse encourages us to think of the claims of others on us in terms of their legal rights; the danger is that it may thereby encourage us to feel those rights fully describe the limits of what we owe them.'[51]

b. Equality rights

The dilemma of equality rights for the physically disabled in the assisted suicide debate is relevant here. In the context of the indeterminacy critique of rights discourse, I discussed the forced and indeterminate choice between formal equality (all individuals, including those who are physically unable to take their own lives, should have an equal opportunity to commit suicide) and substantive equality of opportunity (all individuals should have the opportunity to live an independent, dignified life).[52] If the effect of thinking about claims and obligations in terms of rights is to negate other possible obligations, then once assisted suicide has been legalized, we may discount other possible claims of the physically disabled, particularly those which are more costly and difficult to meet. 'There is no room for severely impaired children or adults in a society where it is permissible for others always to behave in a narrowly self-interested way, always to deny any moral imperative for self-sacrifice in the service of others, always to prefer self-serving actions at the expense of communal bonds.'[53] Thus we must be aware of the concern that '[t]he [current] debate over assisted suicide emphasizes "death with dignity," but it ignores the possibility . . . of recognizing the dignity of a disabled person's existence while living with that disability.'[54]

---

[48] Olsen, above n. 4, 389.   [49] Schneider, above n. 19, 162.   [50] Ibid. 162–3.

[51] Ibid. 163.   [52] See above, text accompanying nn. 28–30.

[53] Robert A. Burt, 'The Ideal of Community in the Work of the President's Commission' (1984) 6 *Cardozo L. Rev.* 267, 281.

[54] Paul Miller, 'Conference Transcript: Socially-Assisted Dying: Media, Money & Meaning' (1998) 7 *Cornell J. L. & Pub. Pol'y* 267, 298.

c. Transformation of duties

The problem of the distortion of rights discourse is related to the tendency of rights rhetoric to monopolize the relevant debate and thereby suppress other forms of argument. Arguments which are not in the form of rights, such as those premised on duties, do not truly disappear from the debate, but rather are transformed into rights discourse while their original form remains covert and unrecognized. The best example of this phenomenon involves religious-based argumentation. In the context of the debate on assisted suicide, the sanctity of life argument is the obvious concern here.[55]

There are two distinct reasons for the transformation of religious-based arguments into rights rhetoric. The first stems from the political power associated with rights discourse. Transforming an argument into the form of a right increases its palatability and persuasive force.[56] Rights constitute a 'powerful strategic tool,' inhibiting resistance to one's agenda by virtue of the consensus engendered by their use.[57] Expressing duty-based arguments in the form of the correlative right gives the argument more force and legitimacy in current political discourse.[58]

The second reason for the transformation inheres in any pluralist society in which certain enumerated human rights are constitutionally entrenched or simply conventionally protected. Such protections generally include some form of guarantee of freedom of religion and/or conscience,[59] which may pre-empt the use of explicitly religious argumentation in public debate.[60]

Many of the rights-based arguments already canvassed reveal that sanctity of life arguments are often cloaked in the language of rights. The controversy surrounding the inalienable right to life and the problem of waiver is one possible

[55] In the case of sanctity of life arguments, the transformation into rights rhetoric is partial, rather than total. That is, deontological arguments invoking the sanctity of life are present in the literature surrounding assisted suicide. See, e.g., Victor D. Rosenblum & Clarke G. Forsythe, 'The Right to Assisted Suicide: Protection of Autonomy or an Open Door to Social Killing?' (1990) 6 *Issues in Law & Med.* 3, 21 (arguing that the principle of the sanctity of life is paramount, and that respect for that principle – rather than the right to autonomy – promotes individual dignity).

[56] 'In America, when we want to protect something, we try to get it characterized as a right.' Glendon, above n. 2, 31. See also, Schneider, above n. 1, 625–6; Olsen, above n. 4, 391; Schneider, above n. 19, 154.

[57] Vasuki Nesiah, 'Toward a Feminist Internationality: A Critique of U.S. Feminist Legal Scholarship' (1993) 16 *Harv. Women's L.J.* 189, 194, n. 17.

[58] See Schneider, above n. 19, 153–4 (noting that 'in our intellectual and social life, rights thinking has achieved a currency unmatched in our history' and that rights solutions can 'greatly simplify the political battles . . . [as] rights are the "trumps" of legal analysis, and . . . can often be easily implemented nationally and not just state by state').

[59] See, e.g., U.S. Constitution, First Amendment; Canadian Charter of Rights and Freedoms, s. 2(a); European Convention on Human Rights, Art. 9.

[60] See, e.g., H. Tristram Engelhardt, Jr. & Michele Malloy, 'Suicide and Assisting Suicide: A Critique of Legal Sanctions' (1982) 36 *Sw. L.J.* 1003, 1021 ('the concern not to offend God . . . is an inappropriate consideration for a pluralistic society in which divergent and irreconcilable opinions concerning the desires or the existence of a deity exist'). Whether explicitly religious argumentation is inappropriate in the context of rights formulation in a pluralistic society is a contentious issue beyond the scope of this work. This section is concerned only with the effect on rights discourse of religious argumentation which is hidden for the reasons discussed in the text above.

example.[61] If waivability is considered an intrinsic property of rights, as is generally the case,[62] then it would seem that the right to life should necessarily have this property. One might infer that proponents of the inalienability/non-waivability of the right to life may be masking or transforming a duty-based sanctity of life argument. This connection can be seen explicitly in Samuel Adams' *The Rights of Colonists*. Adams wrote that it would be

the greatest absurdity to suppose it in the power of one or any number of men at the entering into society, to renounce their essential natural rights, or the means of preserving those rights when the great end of civil government . . . is for the support, protection, and defence of those very rights: the principal of which . . . are life, liberty, and property. If men through fear, fraud, or mistake, should in terms renounce and give up any essential natural right, the eternal law of reason . . . would absolutely vacate such renunciation; the right to freedom being the gift of God Almighty, it is not in the power of Man to alienate this gift, and voluntarily become a slave.[63]

The argument masquerades in the language of rights in order both to increase its power and persuasive force and to avoid the problems posed by the constitutional guarantee of freedom of religion.[64] The difficulty posed goes further than simply the covert nature of the argument: an additional concern must be the distortion of rights discourse, in this case by omitting the concept of waivability. If waivability begins to lose its status as an inherent property of rights, the conversion of other waivable rights into duties may be easier to achieve in future debates.

Other fully or partially concealed sanctity of life arguments are found in the rights discourse on assisted suicide. Perhaps the most obvious example is the property right formulation contending that God holds a property right in individuals' lives.[65] As Ronald Dworkin observes, this is a 'straightforward formulation' of the sanctity of life argument.[66]

Sanctity of life arguments are found not only in the form of specific rights (such as the inalienable right to life or the right to property), but also in the context of the limiting words contained in some rights formulations. For example, the rights to autonomy and liberty are generally articulated with an inherent 'harm principle'. That is, autonomy and liberty are guaranteed only to the extent that no (direct or

---

[61] See Chapter 2, Section II.D.1.

[62] See Dan Brock, *Life and Death* (Cambridge: Cambridge Univ. Press, 1993) 125–6 (arguing that the waivability aspect of rights provides a compelling argument in favour of a rights-based account of morality, in that it better promotes people's actual interest in life which may not always be a strong or present one); Philippa Foot, 'Euthanasia' (1977) 6 *Phil. & Pub. Aff.* 85, 105 (assuming that the right to life is waivable).

[63] Samuel Adams, 'The Rights of Colonists' quoted in B.A. Richards, 'Inalienable Rights: Recent Criticism and Old Doctrine' (1969) 29 *Phil. & Phenomenological Research* 398, 398, n. 33.

[64] See Chapter 2, Section II.C.6 for discussion of such problems.

[65] See Chapter 2, Section II.D.3.

[66] Ronald Dworkin, *Life's Dominion: An Argument About Abortion, Euthanasia, and Individual Freedom* (New York: A.A. Knopf, 1993) 214 ('In its most straightforward formulation . . . the appeal to the sanctity of life uses the image of property: a person's life belongs not to him but to God.').

significant) harm comes to another from the exercise of the right.[67] Opponents of assisted suicide argue that death constitutes a 'harm' to the deceased individual, and thus assisted suicide cannot be brought within the scope of the right to liberty or autonomy.[68] This type of argument entails an underlying assumption, based on a belief in the sanctity of life, that life is always and intrinsically a 'good,' thus death must always be a harm to the individual.[69]

In addition to the long-term consequences for future rights-based debates, the presence of hidden duty-based arguments and distorted rights claims may exacerbate the problems posed by the indeterminacy of rights discourse discussed in the previous section. Recognition of these tools and techniques may enable the unpacking of some apparently rights-based claims, thereby focusing the debate more clearly on points of disagreement.

3. The critique of rights discourse as simplistic and conclusory

Much of our current rights discourse is overly simplistic,[70] and conclusory.[71] Rights discourse often pre-empts social debate on a contentious issue by arriving at the apparently inevitable conclusion before the debate has even begun.[72] Generally accepted rights are quickly and stridently asserted to mandate the conclusion that the more specific right to engage in the contested activity at issue is entailed by the general right upon which reliance is placed. Debate is thereby discouraged, as it appears to necessarily involve the questioning of hitherto accepted basic rights. Thus proponents of assisted suicide declare the self-evidence of the necessary derivation of the right to suicide from the rights to liberty, autonomy, or privacy.[73] Their opponents proclaim the manifest priority of the inalienable right to life, which necessarily excludes the possibility of a right to

---

[67] See Chapter 2, Sections II.C.1 and II.C.2.

[68] See, e.g., Bopp, above n. 15, 126 ('If the Mill formulation is accepted, . . . it is readily apparent that a prohibition of assisted suicide is warranted because a homicidal act (by the assister) directed against another who consents to the homicidal act results in death which is clearly a "harm" to another.').

[69] The contrary argument assumes that whether life is a 'good' is individually determined, rather than presumptively the case. See, e.g., Dan Brock, 'Voluntary Active Euthanasia' (1992) 22(2) *Hastings Center Rep.* 10, 11 (arguing that at some point, for some people, life ceases to be a good (for the person) and instead becomes a burden); David A.J. Richards, 'Constitutional Privacy, The Right to Die and The Meaning of Life: A Moral Analysis' (1981) 22 *Wm. & Mary L. Rev.* 327, 359–60 (arguing that when the individual has a rational interest in dying, the termination of her life would not constitute a harm).   [70] See Glendon, above n. 2, x, 15.

[71] See Schneider, above n. 19, 174. The use of simplistic and conclusory rights talk has also contributed to 'deadlock' in the abortion debate. See Glendon, above n. 2, 66 ('Prolife and prochoice advocates have overwhelmingly opted for rights talk, a choice that has forced the debate into a seemingly nonnegotiable deadlock between the fetus' "right to life" and the pregnant woman's "right to choose." ').

[72] See Cass R. Sunstein, 'Right Talk' *New Republic*, 2 Sept. 1991, 34 (suggesting that discussions about rights 'can be conclusions masquerading as reasons').

[73] 'The decision to exit life by one's own decree is more fundamental to the concepts of autonomy, freedom, and liberty than any other, for pivotal to the control of one's own life is the choice of electing to forego continued life.' Neeley, above n. 36, 80.

suicide.[74] Debate appears to be both unnecessary[75] and futile, and resolution impossible.[76] The absence of debate has a distancing effect:[77] it is difficult for individuals to feel involved in or responsible for a decision when the decision is seen as inevitable and beyond argument.

The pre-emption of societal debate has a discernible effect in the context of life and death decision-making. Coupled with a natural and understandable reluctance to engage in discussions reminding individuals of their own mortality,[78] the pre-emptive and distancing effects of rights discourse allow us to avoid confronting the inevitability of death[79] and the reality of the current experience of dying.[80] 'In trying to batter our way through the human condition with the bludgeon of personal rights, we allow ourselves to be deceived about the most fundamental matters: about death and dying, about our unavoidable finitude, and about the sustaining interdependencies of our lives.'[81]

4. The absolutist critique

The critique that rights discourse is absolutist is a familiar one.[82] 'A penchant for absolute formulations... promotes unrealistic expectations and ignores both

---

[74] See Chapter 2, Section II.D.1. See also, Leon R. Kass, 'Neither for Love nor Money: Why Doctors Must Not Kill' (1989) 94 *Public Interest* 25, 27; Maria T. CeloCruz, 'Aid-in-Dying: Should We Decriminalize Physician-Assisted Suicide and Physician-Committed Euthanasia?' (1992) 18 *Am. J. L. & Med.* 369, 388.

[75] The use of the term 'right to die' 'allows and encourages us to believe that when society makes significant and painfully difficult decisions about life and death, we are making no decision at all, but merely deferring to individual autonomy. In short, it allows us to mask decisions as non-decisions.' Donald L. Beschle, 'Autonomous Decision-Making and Social Choice: Examining the "Right to Die"' (1988–89) 77 *Ky. L.J.* 319, 322.

[76] See Margaret Pabst Battin, *Ethical Issues in Suicide* (Englewood Cliffs, N.J.: Prentice-Hall, 1995) 184–7; Glendon, above n. 2, 15.

[77] See Glendon, ibid. 172–3 (asserting that rights discourse 'distances itself from moral judgment').

[78] See Daniel Callahan, *The Troubled Dream of Life: Living With Mortality* (New York: Simon & Schuster, 1993) 30, 34, 80. As a subject, death does appear to be losing some of its taboo status, particularly as a result of the success of recent books dealing with issues of death and dying. See, e.g., Sherwin B. Nuland, *How We Die: Reflections on Life's Final Chapter* (New York: A.A. Knopf, 1994) (describing the process of dying of various illnesses); Derek Humphry, *Final Exit: The Practicalities of Self-Deliverance and Assisted Suicide for the Dying* (Secaucus, N.J.: Hemlock Society, 1991) (setting out instructions for suicide for the terminally ill); Timothy E. Quill, *Death and Dignity: Making Choices and Taking Charge* (New York: W.W. Norton, 1993).

[79] See Beschle, above n. 75, 343 (describing the existentialist insight regarding 'the importance of the ways in which people construct elaborate defenses to enable them to avoid feeling the full force of the presence of mortality'). The regulation of death and dying through the mechanism of rights may be one such defence mechanism. 'Instead of discussing openly how to think about death and what we might appropriately choose in our dying – a painful and difficult subject – we too frequently and too easily transform the issue into more distanced, comfortable language of rights and choices: not how or what we ought to choose, but that we have a right to choose.' Callahan, above n. 78, 36.

[80] '"[R]ights" language misrepresents and distorts this new experience of dying.' Mayo, above n. 22, 155. On the 'modern medical death,' see Chapter 1, Section I.

[81] Kass, above n. 42, 43. See also, Callahan, above n. 78, 36.

[82] See, e.g., Glendon, above n. 2, xi, 44–5. Leon Kass describes rights as 'in principle always absolute and unconditional.' Kass, above n. 42, 35. The absolutist critique may be less applicable to

social costs and the rights of others.'[83] Absolutist formulations of the right to suicide or assisted suicide are common, and are used by both sides of the debate.

a. Absolutist claims on both sides of the debate
The most extreme proponents of a right to suicide make absolutist claims regarding the right to autonomy. Kevorkian writes: 'Perhaps the greatest advantage [of the legalization of planned death] would be the further unshackling of the primal human right of what should be *absolute* personal autonomy within the bounds of reasonable law.'[84] Their opponents attempt to characterize all arguments in favour of a right to suicide or assisted suicide in absolutist terms, in order to more easily disparage such arguments. For instance, Leon Kass refers to the 'intransigent and absolute demands of a legal or moral right to die.'[85] James Bopp, in a lengthy diatribe against a constitutional right to assisted suicide, argues that assisted suicide advocates' 'uncompromising...insistence on an absolutist standard of' autonomy fails to square with basic elements and policies of our society and its jurisprudence.'[86]

b. The difficulty of limiting rights
The absolutist nature of much rights rhetoric makes limiting rights a difficult task. The right to autonomy is particularly problematic in this regard.[87] 'How can

constitutional rights discourse, in which balancing of rights and interests is prevalent. See Linda C. McClain, 'Rights and Irresponsibility' (1994) 43 *Duke L.J.* 989, 1050.

[83] Glendon, above n. 2, xi.

[84] Jack Kevorkian, 'The Last Fearsome Taboo: Medical Aspects of Planned Death' (1988) 7 *Med. & L.* 1, 9 (emphasis added). See also, G. Steven Neeley, 'Self-Directed Death, Euthanasia and the Termination of Life-Support: Reasonable Decisions to Die' (1994) 16 *Campbell L. Rev.* 205 (arguing that 'the current state of the law often makes it difficult, if not impossible, for the individual to exercise unfettered control over the act of dying'); *Bouvia v. Superior Court (Glenchur)* (1986) 179 Cal. App. 3d 1127, 1147 (Cal. C.A., Compton J., concurring) ('Elizabeth apparently has made a conscious and informed choice that she prefers death to continued existence in her helpless and, to her, intolerable condition. I believe she has an absolute right to effectuate that decision.'); Robert L. Risley, 'Legal and Ethical Issues in the Individual's Right to Die' (1994) 20 *Ohio N.U. L. Rev.* 597, 610 ('As long as we do not infringe upon or endanger the rights of others, we should have the unfettered right to determine our own destiny, especially at life's end.').

[85] Kass, above n. 42, 34. See also, Thomas J. Marzen et al., 'Suicide: A Constitutional Right?' (1985) 24 *Duq. L. Rev.* 1, 5 (describing jurisprudential arguments in favour of a right to suicide as based on 'an almost absolute respect for individual autonomy').

[86] Bopp, above n. 15, 138. In an article advocating capital punishment for Kevorkian, Charles Krauthammer argues that '[i]f suicide is a right, an inalienable expression of personal autonomy, should not every hospital have a Department of Killing where those who have had enough of life can come to have it ended?' Charles Krauthammer, 'Test Euthanasia on Dr. Kevorkian' *The Plain Dealer*, 5 Dec. 1993, D4.

[87] See Kamisar, above n. 42, 39 ('unless we carry the principle of self-determination or personal autonomy to its logical extreme – assisted suicide by any competent person who clearly and repeatedly requests it for any reason she deems appropriate – we have to find a "stopping point" somewhere along the way'); Marzen, above n. 85, 102 ('Any attempt to limit th[e] "right to suicide" to certain persons or circumstances, for example to persons who are terminally ill or elderly, would conflict with the "freedom of choice" or privacy theory that is advanced to assert the existence of such a "right" in the first place.'); John Keown, 'No Right to Assisted Suicide' [2002] *Camb. L.J.* 8, 10.

self-determination have any limits? Why are not the person's desires or motives, whatever they be, sufficient?'[88] Once an absolute right to autonomy is asserted, limits on the right to suicide derived from that right appear nonsensical, arbitrary, or unprincipled.[89] In *Compassion in Dying v. Washington*, the majority of the three judge panel of the Ninth Circuit found that proposed limitations on the right to the terminally ill were implausible:

The category created is inherently unstable. The depressed twenty-one year old, the romantically-devastated twenty-eight year old, the alcoholic forty year old who choose suicide are also expressing their views of existence, meaning, the universe, and life; they are also asserting their personal liberty. If at the heart of the liberty protected by the Fourteenth Amendment is this uncurtailable ability to believe and act on one's deepest beliefs about life, the right to suicide and the right to assistance in suicide are the prerogative of at least every sane adult. The attempt to restrict such rights to the terminally ill is illusory.[90]

Proposed limits often include criteria of competence, the presence of a terminal illness and intolerable pain or suffering.[91] The judicial decisions in the United States jurisprudence on refusal of life-sustaining treatment demonstrate that such limitations may be difficult to sustain within a rights-based analysis.[92] Judicial acceptance of refusals of life-sustaining treatment was initially restricted to terminally ill patients, and over time was extended by judges and legislators who

[88] Callahan, above n. 78, 107–8.
[89] See Bopp, above n. 15, 117, 130–2 (discussing constitutional prohibitions which could prevent the imposition of limits on the right to suicide or assisted suicide); New York State Task Force on Life and the Law, *When Death Is Sought: Assisted Suicide and Euthanasia in the Medical Context* (1994) 100; Marzen, above n. 85, 101, 103, 104 (arguing that once a constitutional right to suicide were accepted, restricting the right 'to a narrow class of persons or set of circumstances would be perverse').
[90] *Compassion in Dying v. Washington* (1995) 49 F.3d 586, 595–6 (9th Cir.). See also, *Washington v. Glucksberg* (1997) 521 U.S. 702, 731–2, n. 23 (Rehnquist C.J.); *Krischer v. McIver* (1997) 697 So. 2d 97, 108 (Fla. S.C.); *R. (on the application of Pretty) v. D.P.P.* [2001] E.W.H.C. Admin. 788, [59]. For examples of apparently arbitrary limitations of rights to suicide or assisted suicide, see Wolhandler, above n. 23, 369–70 (simply asserting the limitation of a privacy-based right to euthanasia to those with less than six months to live without offering a justification for it); *Kevorkian* (1994) 527 N.W.2d 714, 746 (Mich. S.C., Levin J., concurring in part and dissenting in part) (restricting the right to assisted suicide to terminally ill, competent individuals), 756–7 (Mallett J., concurring in part and dissenting in part) (restricting the right to assisted suicide to terminally ill, competent individuals who are suffering from great pain). See Chapter 6, Section V for discussion of whether using rights as a mechanism of legal change on assisted dying mandates any of these (or other) restrictions.
[91] Susan M. Wolf, 'Holding the Line on Euthanasia' (1989) 19(1) *Hastings Center Rep.* S13, S14. See, e.g., Eike-Henner W. Kluge, *Biomedical Ethics in a Canadian Context* (Scarborough, Ont.: Prentice-Hall Canada, 1992) 264 (restricting assisted suicide to the terminally ill and those whose life is 'qualitatively atrocious, even torturous, by ordinary standards, and . . . quite unacceptable'); Alister Browne, 'Assisted Suicide and Active Voluntary Euthanasia' (1989) 2 *Can. J. L. & Juris.* 35, 55 (advocating only a restriction to the competent).
[92] Wolf, above n. 91, 14; Daniel Wikler, 'Not Dead, Not Dying? Ethical Categories and Persistent Vegetative State' (1988) 18(1) *Hastings Center Rep.* 41 (discussing *In re Quinlan* (1976) 429 U.S. 922 and *Conroy* (1985) 486 A.2d 1209 (N.J.S.C.)).

concluded that such criteria were inappropriate or unworkable.[93] Robert Risley describes the development of the jurisprudence:

Since the *Quinlan* decision, a patient's right to refuse life-sustaining medical treatment has been upheld by virtually every state appellate court which has been faced with the issue. Each state has followed an almost identical course of development in this area of the law, with the caselaw progressing in three stages. First, the cases established the patient's right to refuse treatment based on either the constitutional right to privacy or the doctrine of informed consent, or both. The second was judicial recognition of the patient's or guardian's right to refuse life-support systems, usually a respirator. Finally, the cases expanded the right to the removal of feeding tubes; a decision made by the patient who is competent or by a surrogate when the patient is incompetent.[94]

These cases may also be used in the assisted suicide context to exclude potential limits. Steven Neeley, an ardent advocate of the constitutional right to suicide, embraces these uses of the refusal of life-saving treatment cases in order to reject the limiting factors of both terminal illness[95] and competence.[96] Neeley's conclusion rests on his contention that such a result would protect individuals' autonomy rights in situations where the ability to exercise the right has been lost.[97] Opponents of the legalization of assisted suicide also foresee this use of the 'right to die' cases to exclude competence as a criterion for assisted suicide cases, but are far less sanguine about the consequences of such a possibility:

If individuals have a constitutional 'right to die' by withholding of life-support systems that is not diminished when they are incompetent and their wishes are unknown, a right

---

[93] See *Cruzan v. Director, Mo. Dep't of Health* (1990) 497 U.S. 261, 278, 280 (recognizing that 'a competent person has a constitutionally protected liberty interest in refusing unwanted medical treatment' and extending that principle to incompetent patients in certain circumstances); *In re Quinlan* (1976) 355 A.2d 647, 672 (N.J.S.C.) (holding that a comatose individual has a constitutional privacy right to be free from bodily invasion, that this right is not diminished by the individual's incompetence and could be exercised by a parent on her behalf); *Garger v. New Jersey* (1976) 429 U.S. 922; *Conroy* (1985) 486 A.2d 1209, 1250 (N.J.S.C.) (applying the substituted judgment and best interests tests to determine whether life-sustaining treatment should be withheld from an incompetent person who is not terminally ill); *Fosmire v. Nicoleau* (1990) 75 N.Y. 2d 218, 227 (N.Y.C.A.) (rejecting the contention that the right to refuse life-sustaining treatment should be limited to the terminally ill).

[94] Risley, above n. 84, 599–600. See generally, Alan Meisel & Kathy L. Cerminara, *The Right to Die: The Law of End-of-Life Decisionmaking* (3rd edn.) (Frederick, Md.: Aspen, 2004) (outlining the history and legal tenets of the right to die).

[95] 'The *Bartling*, *Bouvia*, and *Bergstedt* decisions...exemplify the proposition that there are no practical or logical lines of demarcation to be drawn between autonomy rights for the terminal and non-terminal patient.' Neeley, above n. 36, 107, citing *Bartling v. Superior Court* (1984) 163 Cal. App. 3d 186 (Cal. C.A.); *Bouvia v. Superior Court (Glenchur)* (1986) 179 Cal. App. 3d 1127 (Cal. C.A.); *McKay v. Bergstedt* (1990) 801 P.2d 617 (Nev. S.C.).

[96] 'If suicide were to become a constitutional right, then – under certain circumstances – the doctrine of substituted judgment could conceivably apply to allow a guardian ad litem to assert this right on behalf of comatose or otherwise incompetent patients.' Neeley, ibid. 155.

[97] Ibid., citing *Superintendent of Belchertown State Sch. v. Saikewicz* (1977) 370 N.E.2d 417 (Mass. S.J.C.).

that may be exercised by third parties by way of substituted judgment under such circumstances, then it would logically seem to follow that a recognized 'right to die' by suicide would also survive incompetence and that third parties would likewise be empowered to exercise this 'right' on their behalf. Put another way, if the 'right to die' recognized in present case law were deemed to encompass a 'right to suicide,' then suicide by substituted judgment – constitutionally sanctioned active, involuntary euthanasia – of incompetent persons would be a logical consequence.[98]

The enthusiastic rejection of limits by certain assisted suicide proponents – and the ease with which rights rhetoric enables such rejection – may simply serve to confirm their opponents' absolutized characterization of arguments in favour of assisted suicide,[99] thus 'fuel[ing] resentments, . . . breed[ing] hatreds'[100] and further polarizing the debate.

5. The critique of rights discourse as uncompromising

The indeterminate nature of rights discourse results in a further problem: as we have seen, rights discourse is marked by irresolvable conflicts within individual broad rights; between conflicting rights; and between rights and competing interests. The potential for conflict is increased by the absolutist, simplistic, and conclusory nature of rights discourse.[101] The presence of inevitable and frequent insoluble conflicts within rights discourse forms the basis of the critique that the discourse hinders compromise and impedes accommodation of competing interests.[102] Compromise is seen as unacceptable when rights are at stake because of the stark opposition in political discourse between guaranteed constitutional or moral rights, and consequentialist balancing. Rights 'form [ ] a kind of moral property of individuals to which they are as individuals entitled,'[103] and this moral property must not be trespassed upon for reasons of social costs and benefits.[104]

---

[98] Marzen, above n. 85, 102. See also, Michael McGonnigal, 'This is who will die when doctors are allowed to kill their patients' (1997) 31 *J. Marshall L. Rev.* 95, 99–100 ('Once the right to be killed is created, even by statute, courts may extend this blessing to the profoundly disabled on equal protection grounds'). See Chapter 6, Section V.A and especially the discussion in Chapter 6, Section V.A.1 of the Ninth Circuit's apparent acceptance of this possibility in *Compassion in Dying v. Washington* (1996) 79 F.3d 790, 832, n. 120 (9th Cir. en banc), quoted disapprovingly by the majority in *Washington v. Glucksberg* (1997) 521 U.S. 702, 733.

[99] See, e.g., Bopp, above n. 15, 117 ('Ostensibly, a broad constitutional right to assisted suicide would encompass the consensual killing of, at a minimum, any competent adult.'); Marzen, above n. 85, 7 ('Under the "autonomy" argument . . . the suicide of an autonomous individual for any reason, and under any circumstances, should never be prevented.').   [100] Kass, above n. 42, 37–8.

[101] See Glendon, above n. 2, 44.

[102] For examples of this critique, see Glendon, ibid. xi, 15; Schneider, above n. 19, 175.

[103] H.L.A. Hart, 'Are There Any Natural Rights?' (1955) 64 *Phil. Rev.* 175, reprinted in David Lyons, ed., *Rights* (Belmont, Calif.: Wadsworth, 1979) 14, 19. See also, John L. Mackie, 'Can There Be a Right-Based Moral Theory?' (1978) 3 *Midwest Stud. Phil.* 350, reprinted in Jeremy Waldron, ed., *Theories of Rights* (Oxford: Oxford Univ. Press, 1984) 168 (drawing a sharp contrast between right- and goal-based moral reasoning); Ronald Dworkin, *Taking Rights Seriously* (Cambridge, Mass.: Harvard Univ. Press, 1977) 269 (describing a strong sense of rights as 'anti-utilitarian').

[104] '[E]ach person possesses an inviolability founded on justice that even the welfare of society as a whole cannot override.' John Rawls, *A Theory Of Justice* (Cambridge, Mass.: Belknap Press, 1971) 3.

Compromise and accommodation are associated with utilitarian balancing, and are therefore seen as inappropriate when dealing with conflicts between fundamental rights.

a. The right to equality

For example, in the assisted suicide context, the right to equality or equal protection may inhibit compromise between proponents and opponents of assisted suicide. Any compromise limiting legalization to certain groups, such as the terminally ill, may encounter difficulties stemming from the right to equality or equal protection. This right may invalidate such limits as discriminatory on grounds of age, illness or mental capacity.[105]

b. Devaluation of opposing rights or interests

The problem of the uncompromising nature of rights discourse is exacerbated by a tendency to justify the choice of one right over another right or competing interest by devaluing or rejecting the opposing right or interest entirely.[106] This tendency is explicable in terms of the either/or choice which it seems necessary to make. If compromise is 'odious'[107] and a choice must be made, then any merits of the opposing view must be ignored.[108] In the assisted suicide context, examples of such argumentation are manifold. For example, proponents of an autonomy-based right to suicide often belittle any argument based on the right to life or the sanctity of life.[109] In response, advocates of the inalienability of the right to life often disparage current autonomy formulations as exaggerated, extreme and even dangerous.[110] For instance, Leon Kass writes:

An examination of the 'right to die'... reveals the dangers and the limits of the liberal – that is, rights-based – political philosophy and jurisprudence to which we Americans are

---

[105] See Chapter 2, Section II.D.2.b. This kind of equal protection argument has been used by proponents of the legalization of assisted suicide to expand the scope of the right to assisted suicide. See Frances Graves, 'Address at the Hemlock Society's Second National Voluntary Euthanasia Conference' 8 Feb. 1985, cited in Marzen, above n. 85, 8, n. 26 (arguing that restricting euthanasia to competent adults would be a form of 'age discrimination or discrimination against a type of illness').

[106] See Glendon, above n. 2, 154 (describing a tendency towards such justificatory reasoning in U.S. Supreme Court opinions). [107] Schneider, above n. 19, 175.

[108] The abortion debate provides a good example of this propensity. See generally, Howard Brody, 'Assisted Death – A Compassionate Response to a Medical Failure' (1992) 327(19) *New Eng. J. Med.* 1384 (citing Hilary Putnam). See also, Glendon, above n. 2, 154 (describing *Roe v. Wade* (1973) 410 U.S. 113 as 'troubling' with regard to the decision's unintentional 'appearance of leaving developing fetuses... outside the community for which we Americans have a common concern').

[109] See, e.g., Albin Eser, '"Sanctity" and "Quality" of Life in a Historical-Comparative View' in Wallace & Eser, above n. 17, 103, 114: 'Were we to give the sanctity principle absolute priority, a person longing for death would be degraded to an object doomed to live for the exclusive interest of the state. If we do not want to apotheosize the state as a life-giving divinity, we scarcely can deny the power of every person over his or her living and dying.'

[110] See, e.g., Thomas G. Dailey, 'Choosing Death: Exploring Assisted Suicide' *Our Family*, Sept. 1992, 12, 13; Catholic Health Association, 'Care of the Dying: A Catholic Perspective, Part I, Cultural Context' (1993) 74(2) *Health Progress* 34, 37 (criticizing the notion of complete autonomy in the context of religion, society, and sickness); Bopp, above n. 15, 138.

wedded. As the ultimate new right, grounded neither in nature nor in reason, it demonstrates the nihilistic implication of a new ('postliberal') doctrine of rights, rooted in the self-creating will.[111]

This problematic feature of rights discourse – the devaluation of opposing rights or interests – can also be exploited as a tactic within the discourse. Opponents of the legalization of assisted suicide argue that the concept of a right to suicide denies the sanctity of life[112] and ignores the spectre of abuse and the potential of harm to others.[113] Margaret Pabst Battin provides an example of a more balanced view in response to such arguments:

to say that the right to suicide overrides other objections to suicide does not show these objections to be erroneous or unfounded. For instance, to say that the right to suicide overrides the inherent value of human life is not to say that human life is not of value – it may be of great value, great enough so that one person may not destroy another's life; it may be only to say that the value of human life is not so great that one may not bring one's own life to an end. Similarly, to say that the right to suicide overrides objections that may be made on grounds of harms to others is not to say that such harms do not occur or should not be noticed. And to say that the right to suicide overrides the risk of abuse and manipulation is not to say that these risks are not real, but only that we ought not compromise the choices of some individuals in order to protect others.[114]

Clearly, decisions have to be reached in the face of conflicting rights and interests. What must also be clear is that the resolution reached by ignoring one side of a particular conflict is likely to be neither politically nor socially acceptable. 'We cannot resolve these moral tensions by making one side of the tension disappear. Instead, we must learn to live with these tensions within a pluralistic society.'[115] Rights discourse must adapt to allow for principled compromise between competing rights and interests.

B. Problems with rights discourse associated with personal rights

Until now, the various critiques of rights discourse under consideration have been widely applicable to rights discourse generally. The focus now shifts to critiques with particular application to discourse involving personal rights, as distinguished from civil or political rights.[116] Perhaps the central problem concerns the lack of

---

[111] Kass, above n. 42, 34.

[112] 'A constitutional right to kill oneself, once unleashed, would have far-reaching impacts. In essence, recognition of such a right would relegate life to a merely optional course legally equivalent to death.' Walter M. Weber, 'What Right to Die?' (1988) 18 *Suicide & Life-Threatening Behavior* 181, 183.   [113] See, e.g., Kamisar, above n. 42, 38–9.

[114] Battin, above n. 76, 180.

[115] Brody, above n. 108, 1384. Brody continues: 'This requires more reliance on negotiation, compromise, and practical reasoning, and less on abstract ethical theory.'

[116] An example of a personal right would be the right to privacy, while an example of a civil or political right would be the right to vote. See Mayo, above n. 22, 126–9; Schneider, above n. 19, 158–60.

articulation of the basis of personal rights, which has serious ramifications for their scope and limits. This section will also address briefly the problem of slippery slopes associated with rights discourse, particularly in the realm of personal rights.

1. Lack of articulation of basis of personal rights

H.L.A. Hart has argued that 'a sufficiently detailed or adequately articulate theory showing the foundation for [personal] rights and how they are related to other values which are pursued through government' is missing from our rights discourse.[117] In the United States, the absence of judicial consensus on the origin and purpose of those personal rights not specifically enumerated in the Constitution exacerbates this problem.[118] The use of differing justifications for personal rights, including appeals to broad values such as the protection of moral pluralism[119] or human dignity,[120] coupled with reliance on vague notions of 'societal consensus'[121] creates significant problems for rights discourse in the context of personal rights.[122] Some of these difficulties can be illuminated by examining the extent to which the right to suicide or assisted suicide suffers from the lack of an adequately articulated basis, and the effect of this conceptual weakness.[123]

---

[117] H.L.A. Hart, 'Utilitarianism and Natural Rights' in H.L.A. Hart, *Essays in Jurisprudence and Philosophy* (New York: Oxford Univ. Press, 1983) 181, 195.

[118] See Mayo, above n. 22, 128–9; Schneider, above n. 19, 171–2.

[119] See Schneider, ibid. 160–1; Engelhardt & Malloy, above n. 60, 1004–5, 1010.

[120] See Dworkin, above n. 66, 233–7; Dworkin, above n. 103, 198; Neeley, above n. 36, 197–8; Joel Feinberg, *Harm to Self* (New York: Oxford Univ. Press, 1986) 354. In the Canadian context, the most ardent adoption of dignity as a basis for personal rights is found in *Kindler v. Canada* [1991] 2 S.C.R. 779, 813–14 (Cory J., dissenting and Lamer C.J.C., concurring in the dissent) ('It is the dignity and importance of the individual which is the essence and the cornerstone of democratic government.'). See also, *Oakes* [1986] 1 S.C.R. 103, 136 (Dickson C.J.C.); *Re s. 94(2) of the Motor Vehicle Act of British Columbia* [1985] 2 S.C.R. 486, 512 (Lamer J.); *Andrews v. Law Society of British Columbia* [1989] 1 S.C.R. 143, 171 (McIntyre J.); *Law v. Canada (Minister of Employment and Immigration)* [1999] 1 S.C.R. 497, [51]–[54]; *Morgentaler* [1988] 1 S.C.R. 30, 166 (Wilson J., concurring) ('The idea of human dignity finds expression in almost every right and freedom guaranteed in the Charter.').

[121] Mayo, above n. 22, 128–30 (examining and accepting the judicial adoption of the standard of 'some evolving societal consensus' as a basis for justification of personal rights including the constitutional right to privacy).

[122] A full analysis of these difficulties associated with personal rights, and in particular with the right to privacy in U.S. constitutional law is beyond the scope of this work. See Henry T. Greely, 'A Footnote to "Penumbra" in *Griswold v. Connecticut*' (1989) 6 *Const. Comment.* 251, 264–5 (criticizing Justice Douglas' finding of the source of the right to privacy in the 'penumbras' of the Bill of Rights); Louis Henkin, 'Privacy and Autonomy' (1974) 74 *Colum. L. Rev.* 1410 (discussing constitutional treatment of the confrontation between private rights and public goods); Jed Rubenfeld, 'The Right of Privacy' (1989) 102 *Harv. L. Rev.* 737, 751, 795 (analysing how legal prohibitions contrary to the right of privacy dictate an individual's life); Gary L. Boswick, 'Comment, A Taxonomy of Privacy: Repose, Sanctuary, and Intimate Decision' (1976) 64 *Cal. L. Rev.* 1447 (arguing that the right of privacy is composed of three subdivisions: repose, sanctuary, and intimate decisions).

[123] A further problem may be the refusal to even examine potential bases for a right to suicide or assisted suicide: 'The question presented in this case . . . is not whether a person has a constitutional right of self-determination, or a right to define personal existence, or a right to make intimate and personal choices, or a right not to suffer. Rather, the question that we must decide is whether the

Many of the differing personal rights from which a right to suicide or assisted suicide can be derived suffer from an absence of an articulated or accepted theoretical justification. The central problem which arises from this deficiency concerns the *scope* of the right to suicide or assisted suicide, which may veer from essentially unlimited to strictly limited, depending on the particular difficulty associated with the justification of the right from which the right to suicide or assisted suicide is derived. Limiting personal rights may be difficult owing to the lack of an adequately articulated basis which both inhibits agreement on the scope of the right, and fails to provide a check on its 'uncommon expansive potential'.[124] Conversely, the right may be readily overridden by competing justifications or interests if its underlying theoretical justification is vague or ill-defined.

As an example let us take the right to liberty, which can be grounded on, *inter alia*, the protection of moral pluralism, or human dignity, or simply asserted as a *prima facie* good.[125] A right to suicide or assisted suicide derived from the right to liberty may be overly broad or unduly weak. If moral pluralism is asserted as the basis for the right to liberty, the lack of articulated limits to the value of moral pluralism,[126] and its tendency to overwhelm other values[127] (on the grounds that to impose other moral values on individuals would be contrary to respect for moral pluralism) will permit the derivation of a broad, virtually unlimited right to suicide or assisted suicide.[128] On the contrary, if the *prima facie* good formulation of the right to liberty is used to ground a right to suicide, then its associated limitation preventing its exercise in the face of harm to others[129] threatens to overwhelm the right to suicide almost entirely:

If suicide is a right simply as a function of one's freedom to do as one chooses, then it will be very difficult to show why, in any case in which others are at all adversely affected, the right to suicide is not always almost immediately overridden, and how it could ever impose claims for assistance upon others. Suicide might be a right, but only a right as substantial as the right to pick one's nose: something you may do just if nobody minds.[130]

Similar problems with scope and limits may arise with other rights used as bases for a right to suicide or assisted suicide. This suggests a need to step back from the immediate debate and to re-examine its foundations. At the very least, a recognition that the parameters of a right to suicide or assisted suicide are contingent upon the

---

Constitution encompasses a right to commit suicide, and, if so, whether it includes a right to assistance.' *Kevorkian* (1994) 527 N.W.2d 714, 730 (Mich. S.C., Cavanagh C.J. & Brickley & Griffin JJ.). This statement is reminiscent of Justice White's announcement in *Bowers v. Hardwick* (1986) 478 U.S. 186, 190 that the issue presented was 'whether the Federal Constitution confers a fundamental right upon homosexuals to engage in sodomy.'

[124] Schneider, above n. 19, 171.   [125] See Chapter 2, Section II.C.1.

[126] See Schneider, above n. 19, 161.

[127] See, e.g., Engelhardt & Malloy, above n. 60, 1004–5 (arguing that freedom must be the pre-eminent value in a pluralist, secular society, and thus advocating a libertarian approach which protects moral pluralism).   [128] See ibid. 1012–13.

[129] See Chapter 2, Sections II.C.1 and II.C.2 and above, text accompanying nn. 67–69.

[130] Battin, above n. 76, 183.

various formulations and bases of the personal rights used to justify such a right might result both in greater precision in debate and a more determined attempt to rationalize the parameters suggested.

2. The problem of the slippery slope

Slippery slope arguments are examined in depth in Chapter 7. For the purposes of this chapter, the concern is not the validity of slippery slope arguments, but rather their *effect* on rights discourse in the present context. Carl Schneider argues that we need to recognize:

> how genuine, numerous, and steep are the slippery slopes that complicate each rights-view. These slopes may work either to intensify a side's commitment to its rights view (by revealing ways in which such a commitment is necessary to protect other rights to which a side is committed), or to erode that commitment (by revealing ways in which that commitment conflicts with other rights the side espouses). But in either event a side's position is easily distorted by its efforts to cope with the surrounding slippery slopes.[131]

The former occurrence – intensification – can be observed among some right to life opponents of assisted suicide. Their commitment to the right to life acts to strengthen their commitment to equality rights for the disabled. That is, they reject the legalization of assisted suicide for those physically unable to commit unaided suicide on the grounds that the rights to life of the disabled and non-disabled are equally worthy of protection.[132]

The latter experience – erosion – may be encountered by autonomy-based proponents of a right to suicide who are also committed to the rights of the disabled. They may be forced to restrict their autonomy-based position because of slippery slope concerns about non-voluntary or involuntary euthanasia of the disabled. For example, restrictions to the terminally ill may appear necessary in order to avoid these concerns, although such proponents would prefer that competent physically disabled persons have available to them the option of assisted suicide. The discourse again becomes both distorted and uncompromising[133] because of the presence of slippery slopes.

III. Questioning the Underlying Assumptions

The critiques in this section question the underlying assumptions of current rights discourse. The primary focus will be the individualistic nature of rights discourse, its emphasis on individual autonomy, and its alleged opposition

---

[131] Schneider, above n. 19, 166–7.   [132] See Chapter 2, Section II.D.2.b.

[133] See Schneider, above n. 19, 175 ('defining interests as rights inhibits compromise because the pull of surrounding slippery slopes makes a whole system of rights, and not just [the particular question at issue,] seem to be at stake').

to community. It is important to note that these concerns focus not on the individualistic nature of rights discourse generally, but rather associate the problems of atomistic individualism with one side of the assisted suicide debate, and in particular with the right to autonomy formulation of the right to suicide.[134]

A. The individualist critique

In most rights-based systems, both theoretical and constitutionally entrenched, the unit of adjudication is the individual.[135] Rights discourse faces a barrage of criticism from all sides regarding its individualistic approach to solving conflicts and social change.[136] A full examination of the voluminous literature on this subject is beyond the scope of this work. Rather, I shall attempt to provide a flavour of the individualist critique and its varied permutations, while focusing on the applicability of the critique in the context of assisted suicide.

CLS adherents decry the atomistic, isolating effects of the individualistic rights-based approach, and reject the dichotomy between the individual and the community upon which liberal rights discourse is based.[137] 'Rights discourse tends to overemphasize the separation of the individual from the group, and thereby inhibits an individual's awareness of her connection to and mutual dependence upon others.'[138] Relatedly, some feminist theorists criticize rights discourse for erecting a separation between the individual and the community, the effect of which is to deny interdependence, connection, and both communal and

---

[134] This kind of critique is not commonly directed at the use of rights discourse against the legalization of assisted suicide, for example invoking the right to life or right to equal protection. See, e.g., Marzen, above n. 85, 135 (describing 'the "every man for himself" philosophy that typifies the right-to-suicide rhetoric').

[135] Occasionally exceptions are made for some type of group or communal rights. See, e.g., the limited protection of group rights in the Canadian Charter of Rights and Freedoms which contains sections protecting Canadians' multicultural heritage (s. 27), language and education rights (ss. 16–29), affirmative action programs (s. 15(2)), and gender equality (ss. 15, 28). See generally, Frank Iacobucci, 'Judicial Review by the Supreme Court of Canada Under the Canadian Charter of Rights and Freedoms: The First Ten Years' in David M. Beatty, ed., *Human Rights and Judicial Review: A Comparative Perspective* (Dordrecht: Kluwer, 1994) 93, 96–103. Group rights for 'the family' are found in the United Nations Universal Declaration on Human Rights, G.A. Res. 217, U.N. Doc. A/811 (1948), Art. 16.3, and in the European Social Charter, opened for signature 18 Oct. 1961, 529 U.N.T.S. 89 (entered into force 26 Feb. 1965), Arts. I-16, I-17. See David Harris & John Darcy, *The European Social Charter* (Ardsley, N.Y.: Transnational Publishers, 2001). On group rights generally, see Staughton Lynd, 'Communal Rights' (1984) 62 *Tex. L. Rev.* 1417.

[136] See Minow, above n. 14, 1862 (describing 'a charge from the right that rights promote conflict rather than community, and . . . a claim from the left that rights reinforce individualism at the expense of community').

[137] See, e.g., Ed Sparer, 'Fundamental Human Rights, Legal Entitlements, and the Social Struggle: A Friendly Critique of the Critical Legal Studies Movement' (1984) 36 *Stan. L. Rev.* 509, 516–17; Paul Brest, 'The Fundamental Rights Controversy: The Essential Contradictions of Normative Constitutional Scholarship' (1981) 90 *Yale L.J.* 1063, 1108; Duncan Kennedy, 'The Structure of Blackstone's Commentaries' (1979) 28 *Buff. L. Rev.* 209, 212–13.

[138] Schneider, above n. 1, 595.

individual responsibility, and to encourage self-interest. For example, Lucinda Finley writes:

Our legal system has tended to view the person who holds rights ... as an isolated, self-sufficient, autonomous actor. This conception of the self has little room in it for recognizing and embracing interconnectedness with and responsibility to others.... Autonomy, which is held out as the ideal for decontextualized human beings, is defined as the realization of self-fulfillment guided by the ultimate authority of self-judgment without interference from others. This underlying view of human nature has produced a negative, highly individualistic definition of rights.[139]

The communitarian critique of liberalism is also applicable to rights discourse.[140] Michael Sandel argues against the logical and temporal priority of individual over community implicit in liberal rights discourse, asserting that we cannot conceive of ourselves as 'unencumbered selves,' independent and wholly detached from our aims.[141] This 'unencumbered self' is the 'lone rights-bearer'[142] of liberal rights discourse. Mary Ann Glendon describes American rights discourse as paying 'extraordinary homage to independence and self-sufficiency, based on an image of the rights-bearer as a self-determining, unencumbered, individual, a being connected to others only by choice.'[143] Sandel argues that the self is not prior to its ends, and that certain of our roles and attachments are partly constitutive of the persons that we are.[144] The concept of a 'situated self' suggests that we are partly defined by the communities that we inhabit, and are implicated in both the purposes and ends of those communities.[145]

The rejection of an individualistic rights-based approach in favour of one that is more community oriented has not been whole-hearted or without criticism. Communitarianism has been criticized on the ground that it allows the trampling of individual rights in the name of community values.[146] The fear is that the community will usurp the will of the individual who will forfeit both autonomy and dignity as the community imposes the common good.[147] There may be

---

[139] Finley, above n. 4, 1159–60. See also, Olsen, above n. 4, 389, 429.

[140] For examples of this critique, see Robert N. Bellah et al., *The Good Society* (New York: Knopf, 1991); Robert N. Bellah et al., *Habits of the Heart* (Berkeley: Univ. of California Press, 1985); Amitai Etzioni, *The Spirit of Community: Rights, Responsibility, and the Communitarian Agenda* (New York: Crown Publishers, 1993); William Galston, *Liberal Purposes* (Cambridge: Cambridge Univ. Press, 1991); Glendon, above n. 2; Frank I. Michelman, 'The Supreme Court 1985 Term – Foreword: Traces of Self-Government' (1986) 100 *Harv. L. Rev.* 4, 66–73; Amy Gutmann, 'Communitarian Critics of Liberalism' (1985) 14 *Phil. & Pub. Aff.* 308, 314.

[141] Michael J. Sandel, *Liberalism and the Limits of Justice* (Cambridge: Cambridge Univ. Press, 1982) 48.   [142] Glendon, above n. 2, 47.

[143] Ibid. 48. See also, ibid. 191, n. 4 (making a connection between this critique and Sandel's concept of the 'encumbered self').   [144] Sandel, above n. 141, 133.

[145] That is, individuals rely on others to help determine the composition of their good. According to Sandel, the Rawlsian view of the self standing back from its constitutive attachments in order to decide its good alone is both impoverished and inaccurate. See ibid. 175–83. See also, Rawls, above n. 104.

[146] See generally, Finley, above n. 4, 1177; Daniel R. Ortiz, 'Categorical Community' (1998) 51 *Stan. L. Rev.* 769 (discussing the problems with communitarianism).   [147] See Ortiz, ibid.

individuals whose self-understandings are not shared by the community or its members, particularly individuals who differ in some way from the majority, whether on grounds of race, colour, or gender, for example, or in a more individualized manner. Thus some feminist theorists are extremely sceptical of claims that rights discourse destroys or weakens community. They are concerned about 'the impoverished forms of "community" forced on women.'[148] While the individualistic tendencies of rights discourse may be problematic, to embrace community as a solution may simply be to trade one impoverished discourse, and its effects, for another, differently flawed approach. '[W]hile isolation can be detrimental, too much community can be stifling or repressive, particularly if forced on individuals who might prefer to be alone or to be part of a community with different values.'[149]

Most critics who advocate some form of community rather than individually-based approach to solving moral or legal conflicts recognize that a wholesale adoption of the former approach will have to be tempered in order to avoid the excesses associated with majoritarianism. Thus Sandel recognizes that justice will be necessary in the presence of community, although it is unclear how the two will work together, that is, when justice will take over.[150] Leslie Bender stakes out similar ground, arguing not for the rejection of an ethic of justice and rights, but for its corrective effect only: 'Concepts of justice and rights should not be jettisoned when shifting to an alternative feminist analysis, but they should be used as correctives to an ethic of care when needed to make sure that power is not abused.'[151] How such a mechanism would work is again unclear.[152]

B. Applying the individualist critique to assisted suicide

Having sketched the broad contours of the various critiques of rights as overly individualistic, and the responses to them, the applicability of these critiques to the rights discourse surrounding assisted suicide must be examined.

1. Focus on community

Critics have bemoaned the exclusion of community from the assisted suicide debate in a variety of ways. Arguments in favour of a communitarian rather than individualistic approach to death and dying are often buttressed by the claim that dying, particularly assisted suicide, is a communal or social, rather than an individual or private act.[153] Medical personnel, family and friends, religious

---

[148] Olsen, above n. 4, 430.   [149] Finley, above n. 4, 1177.

[150] Sandel, above n. 141, 183.

[151] Leslie Bender, 'A Feminist Analysis of Physician-Assisted Dying and Voluntary Active Euthanasia' (1992) 59 *Tenn. L. Rev.* 519, 535.

[152] See McClain, above n. 82, 1053–4 (arguing that discussion of which costs to consider in a balancing test will result in substantial disagreement).

[153] See, e.g., Callahan, above n. 78, 103–4; Catholic Health Association, above n. 110, 37 (arguing that assisted suicide and euthanasia involve relinquishing power over oneself to the community).

representatives, health care proxies, and sometimes lawyers and judges may be involved.[154] Daniel Callahan argues that in any case of assisted dying, the involvement of the assister takes the action out of the realm of individual autonomy into what is 'essentially a form of concerted communal action, even though the community in question may only be two people.'[155]

Other arguments focus on the failure of individualized rights discourse to take account of the *impact* of the legalization of assisted suicide on 'the community'.[156] Margaret Somerville suggests that the individual rights approach in this context fails to adequately protect the community.[157] Michael Ariens strongly criticizes the liberal rights-based approach to suicide, particularly the concept of a right to suicide, rejecting this approach in favour of fostering 'an ideal of hope and reconciliation' for the community and its members.[158] Ariens sees rights-holders as atomistic and disconnected from their community.[159] He argues that the rights-based approach to suicide devalues and destroys the community, which is viewed not as a social entity which declares substantive goals and ideas, and acts to further those goals and ideals, but as a legal, ahistorical, and instrumental entity which may wield power only as a neutral (as between two rights-asserting individuals) rules-enforcer.[160] This view denies the community the chance to state a moral vision, and in the particular case of suicide, an opportunity to foster an ideal of hope and reconciliation for both the community and all of its members. This ideal is expressed both necessarily and limited through the unwieldy source of law. Indeed, it may require the community to facilitate individual choices otherwise disapproved of or condemned.[161]

The communitarian approach to suicide views a successful suicide as 'a blow to the larger community' which has lost one of its valuable members.[162] This view was echoed by Justice Stevens in his concurring opinion in the U.S. Supreme Court decision in *Washington v. Glucksberg*:

There is truth in John Donne's observation that 'No man is an island.' The State has an interest in preserving and fostering the benefits that every human being may provide to the community – a community that thrives on the exchange of ideas, expressions of affection, shared memories and humorous incidents as well as on the material contributions that its members create and support. The value to others of a person's life is far too precious to allow the individual to claim a constitutional entitlement to complete autonomy in

---

[154] See Fenigsen, above n. 41, 29.

[155] Daniel Callahan, 'Can We Return Death to Disease?' (1989) 19(1) *Hastings Center Rep.* S4, S5.

[156] See, e.g., Martin E. Marty & Ron P. Hamel, 'Some Questions and Answers' in Ron P. Hamel, ed., *Choosing Death: Active Euthanasia, Religion, and the Public Debate* (Philadelphia: Trinity Press International, 1991) 27, 46.

[157] See Somerville, above n. 24, 24. Somerville is concerned about 'the protection of human networks which . . . establish the web which constitutes society.' Ibid. 27.

[158] Ariens, above n. 25, 83.

[159] Ibid. 83, 112–13, 122. Ariens focuses mainly on non-terminal cases especially 'insane' suicides, and does not distinguish between suicide prompted by mental illness and suicide in the face of terrible physical and mental suffering caused by severe illness or disability.   [160] Ibid. 83.

[161] Ibid.   [162] Marzen, above n. 85, 135.

making a decision to end that life. Thus, I fully agree with the Court that the 'liberty' protected by the Due Process Clause does not include a categorical 'right to commit suicide which itself includes a right to assistance in doing so.'[163]

2. The problem of isolation

There is no shortage of individualistic and isolating rights-based approaches to the issue of assisted suicide, but three illustrative examples will suffice. In support of the individual's right to choose suicide, Steven Neeley describes a domain in which the individual is self-sovereign, into which neither the state nor other individuals may intrude.[164] When discussing the problem of defining 'competence' to exercise the right to choose death, Alan Sullivan argues that competence 'must be defined with a view to securing for the subject the right to choose to die despite the wishes of doctors, friends, psychologists, and judges.'[165] David Richards focuses on the autonomy-based right of rational agents to select their own life plans without regard to the desires and wants of other rational agents or the state, with the exception of serious harms to determinate third parties, such as young children.[166] These arguments in favour of a right to suicide or assisted suicide envision the individual as separate from and in opposition to those around her, able to reach a decision without assistance from and immune to the influence or wishes of her friends, family, and community.

In response to such isolating approaches, opponents of the legalization of assisted suicide echo communitarian writers and argue that individuals need and are partly defined by their communities.[167] Critiques abound of the picture of the decision-making process painted by proponents of the legalization of assisted dying.[168] Thomas Marzen et al. argue that 'the ideal of the atomistic individual freely and dispassionately making life and death choices free of societal influence is a myth.'[169]

---

[163] *Washington v. Glucksberg* (1997) 521 U.S. 702, 741.

[164] Neeley, above n. 84, 227. See also, Feinberg, above n. 120, 361 ('Why should a person be permitted to implement a "wrong" or "unreasonable" decision to die? The only answer possible is that it is his decision and his life, and that the choice falls within the domain of his morally inviolate personal sovereignty.').

[165] Alan Sullivan, 'A Constitutional Right to Suicide' in Margaret Pabst Battin & David J. Mayo, eds., *Suicide: The Philosophical Issues* (New York: St. Martin's Press, 1980) 229, 245.

[166] Richards, above n. 69, 387–91.

[167] Robert Destro warns that '[t]he danger in a rights-based approach lies in its myopic focus on the autonomy of the individual, without regard to the complex web of relationships that give each of our lives shape and meaning.' Robert A. Destro, 'The Scope of the Fourteenth Amendment Liberty Interest: Does the Constitution Encompass a Right to Define Oneself Out of Existence?' (1994) 10 *Issues in Law & Med.* 183, 211. See also, Somerville, above n. 24, 24; Richards, above n. 69, 387 ('Decisions to die do not occur in a vacuum: persons who express such wishes reasonably may be embedded in personal relationships which may relevantly alter our moral evaluation of the situation.').

[168] 'It is by no means obvious that the atomistic, individualist model of the patient on which a strong right to die would be based best reflects the position in which most people find themselves.' Jonathan Montgomery, 'Power Over Death: The Final Sting' in Robert Lee & Derek Morgan, eds., *Death Rites: Law and ethics at the end of life* (London: Routledge, 1994) 37, 50.

[169] Marzen, above n. 85, 147.

Other critiques focus on the unappealing nature of the deaths which often seem to be implicit in the writings of proponents of assisted suicide. Dying as a 'lone rights-bearer'[170] does not sound attractive. Leslie Bender provides an alternative analysis to the rights-based approach to death and dying. Drawing on the work of Carol Gilligan and her followers,[171] Bender argues that an approach focused on responsibility and care, rather than rights, is more aptly suited to the reality of death and dying:

A care-based ethic arises out of perceptions of human beings as relational, interdependent, and supportive as opposed to our current rights-based ethic in which people are separate, autonomous, and equally empowered actors. A care-based ethic acknowledges that emotions are as important as reason in our lives, decision-making, and dying, and that preserving relationships with and enabling others is as important as having rights to protect us from others.[172]

If the use of rights discourse in favour of assisted suicide has the effect of isolating the individual, that would seem to be cause for concern. Most of us prefer to think of dying while surrounded by our loved ones, rather than alone and isolated. In her relational feminist analysis of assisted dying, Bender paints an appealing picture of the communal process of dying:

Dying, particularly dying from illness or old age rather than from a sudden accident, is not a process involving only one person. Although the process focuses on the dying person's wants and needs, it is interactive, relational, and connected. It is social and communal. We show our love and care as a community when we act responsively and compassionately in accord with the dying person's needs. These are not abstract questions about isolated individuals. These are concrete processes in lives of interconnected people. Dying must be reconceived as the social, communal process it is. Decision-making about dying ought to grow out of ongoing conversations among interrelated people.[173]

This picture of dying, surrounded by loved ones, in a supportive, caring environment is an extremely attractive one. Nevertheless, we must be aware of the problems associated with a communal approach to dying, as well as its advantages. Communities may be accepting of only certain kinds of death and dying. The emotionally supportive, caring environment depicted by Bender may be withheld or unavailable when the type of death or mode of dying is unacceptable to the

---

[170] Glendon, above n. 2, 47.

[171] See Carol Gilligan, *In a Different Voice: Psychological Theory and Women's Development* (Cambridge, Mass.: Harvard Univ. Press, 1982) 3, 21 (discussing the Rights and Responsibilities Study the author conducted and reporting that many of the subjects focused on a responsibility to others and a duty to help others rather than their individual rights in living); Nel Noddings, *Caring, a feminine approach to ethics & moral education* (Berkeley, Calif.: Univ. California Press, 1984) 1–6 (analysing what it means to care and be cared for from the feminine view of practical ethics); Joan C. Tronto, 'Women and Caring: What Can Feminists Learn About Morality from Caring?' in Alison M. Jaggar & Susan R. Bordo, eds., *Gender/Body/Knowledge: Feminist Reconstructions of Being and Knowing* (New Brunswick, N.J.: Rutgers Univ. Press, 1989) 172, 173–6, 183–5 (discussing the types of caring, the approaches to caring by men and women, and the feminist approach to caring).

[172] Bender, above n. 151, 535.   [173] Ibid. 538.

community. Early attitudes towards those dying of AIDS in some jurisdictions come to mind.[174]

Current prohibitions on assisting suicide have resulted in the striking fact that almost all of the publicly reported cases of assisted suicide which have helped shape the legalization debate occurred either completely alone or in the absence of family and friends, in order to avoid the possible implication of loved ones in any potential criminal charges. Thus Timothy Quill's terminal leukaemia patient 'Diane' sent her husband and son out of the room when she took the barbiturates that Quill had prescribed for her.[175] At the end of his account of Diane's death, Quill decries the lonely nature of these kinds of suicides:

I wonder how many severely ill or dying patients secretly take their lives, dying alone in despair. I wonder whether the image of Diane's final aloneness will persist in the minds of her family, or if they will remember more the intense, meaningful months they had together before she died.... I wonder why Diane, who gave so much to so many of us, had to be alone for the last hour of her life.[176]

Similarly, Sue Rodriguez died in the presence of an unnamed doctor and a Member of Parliament. Her husband and son were not present.[177] Perhaps most disturbing were the assisted suicides presided over by Jack Kevorkian, which occurred in makeshift environments (including the back of a van) and in the absence of most family and friends, far from the communities to which the individuals concerned were connected.[178] Roger Magnusson's study in HIV+ communities in San Francisco and Australia suggests that this trend is not limited to cases which are publicly reported.[179]

Of course, the problem of the isolation of the dying is not limited to the use of rights discourse advocating a right to suicide or assisted suicide. Rather, the current legal position, in which assisted suicide seems to exist in a tenuous limbo, has resulted in the practice of assisted suicide being forced into isolating arenas in order to avoid criminal consequences.[180] 'Discussion of assisted death is an

---

[174] For example, a 1994 *New Yorker* article described the alienation and rejection experienced by HIV+ and AIDS patients in Japan, and the appalling lack of caring and compassion they suffered while dying. Stan Sesser, 'Hidden Death' *New Yorker*, 14 Nov. 1994, 62. However, this experience does not seem to have been generally replicated. For example, in the United States, see Nuland, above n. 78, 196 (quoting Dr. Alvin Novick, describing community-based approaches to care-giving for gay AIDS patients, which have been called the 'care-giving surround').

[175] Timothy E. Quill, 'Death and Dignity: A Case of Individualized Decision Making' (1991) 324(10) *New Eng. J. Med.* 691, 693.   [176] Ibid. 694.

[177] See Miro Cernetig, 'Police Suspect Rodriguez Suicide' *Globe and Mail*, 14 Feb. 1994, A1.

[178] In his book, Kevorkian proudly displays a photograph of his 1968 Volkswagen camper van in which a number of the deaths in which he assisted took place. Jack Kevorkian, *Prescription: Medicide The Goodness of Planned Death* (Buffalo, N.Y.: Prometheus Books, 1991) 224.

[179] Roger S. Magnusson, *Angels of Death – Exploring the Euthanasia Underground* (New Haven, Conn.: Yale Univ. Press, 2002) 137 ('A recurrent theme in interviews was that patients were concerned not to implicate those assisting them. The self-administration of stockpiled medications was one way of ensuring this. On some occasions, interviewees, friends or family were asked to leave, returning to find the patient dead.'). See also, ibid. 224, 254.

[180] See *Compassion in Dying v. Washington* (1996) 79 F.3d 790, 810–11 (9th Cir. en banc).

intimate, secret, hushed affair which contrasts sharply with the multidisciplinary approach to patient management in large hospitals.'[181]

Moreover, there is a danger that rights discourse may bear the brunt of criticism which would more appropriately be directed at the technological co-opting of the 'modern medical death',[182] with its associated isolating effects.

> [T]echnology... often distances us from the feelings and experiences of those who are dying. People seem less touchable, less human, and less real when connected to complicated medical equipment and tubing. They are often in intensive care or special hospital units, blocked off from visitors and all things familiar.[183]

The pursuit of 'futile', aggressive, highly invasive treatment 'often conspires to isolate the mortally ill.'[184] Thus it may be 'overkill' to blame rights discourse for the current isolating practice of death and dying.

3. Compromise between individual and community

The above discussion of isolation suggests that a re-conceptualization of how we die is clearly overdue, and rights discourse in its present state may not be well-suited to this task. Some rights critics have argued that current rights discourse often overlooks individuals' needs 'apart from disconnection and non-interference.'[185] Lucinda Finley writes:

> conflicts are inevitable between the need for a zone of individual freedom and the need for community. Not unique to the liberal conception of rights, this tension is endemic to the human condition.... The limitation of our traditional conception of rights and equality is that it slants the balance too far in the individualistic direction. A balanced conception of needs, acknowledging that human beings have both rights and responsibilities, can admit to the dynamic and contextual relationship between them. Thus, it will make us less uncomfortable with the idea that balancing solitude with community is an enterprise responsive to context and political values, rather than formal rules. Indeed, it may enable us to reconceive what making a decision between these needs means. Rather than every decision being an either-or choice, there may be options that satisfy both values, given their interdependent nature.[186]

Needs are of central importance in caring for the dying and the severely disabled. Such a reinvention of the process of dying *could* include assisted suicide without necessarily undermining community and condemning us to an individualistic,

---

[181] Magnusson, above n. 179, 80. See also, Chapter 7, Section III.B.4.

[182] Callahan, above n. 78, 23. See Chapter 1, Section I.

[183] Bender, above n. 151, 535.   [184] Nuland, above n. 78, 246.

[185] Finley, above n. 4, 1161. Michael Ignatieff has made this argument in greater depth: 'In the attempt to defend the principle that needs do make rights, it is possible to forget about the range of needs which cannot be specified as rights and to let them slip out of the language of politics. Rights language offers a rich vernacular for the claims an individual may make on or against the collectivity, but it is relatively impoverished as a means of expressing individuals' needs for the collectivity.' Michael Ignatieff, *The Needs of Strangers* (New York: Viking, 1985) 13. See also, Bender, above n. 151, 537–8.   [186] Finley, above n. 4, 1177.

atomistic, and isolating experience of dying and death. Dying, after all, is a process that affects the individual *most* profoundly, although others surrounding her, and the community more generally, are clearly also involved and affected. To conflate individual claims and needs with communal 'values' denies this reality. Prevailing formulations of rights discourse may not pay adequate attention to needs, but in the context of death and dying, there is evidence that current practice is not ideal in this regard either. Leslie Bender argues in favour of a need-centred approach to dying:

Caring for dying people requires careful attention to their particularized needs. The caregivers must discover what those needs are by listening to the patient; conversing with her and those who know her best and are responsible for her care; and learning about her options, beliefs, and her concerns for her well-being and the well-being of others about whom she cares.[187]

Once again, Bender's description sounds quite idyllic, but surely there will be conflicts about the content of a particular patient's needs. There is evidence that physicians often fail to believe patients' estimates and claims regarding the amount of pain they are suffering, and fail to treat pain seriously and effectively.[188] Without individual rights-based claims, it is difficult to envision the changes in such attitudes which would allow the patient to define and articulate her own needs.[189]

IV. Conclusion

I began the examination of the problems associated with rights discourse in the assisted suicide debate with the observation that paralysis would be an understandable response in the face of the multitude of conflicting rights-based claims

---

[187] Bender, above n. 151, 537–8.

[188] 'The failure to provide pain relief is a pervasive fault of current clinical practice.' New York State Task Force, above n. 89, 158. 'Pain is terribly real and immediately present for the person in pain, but can be less apparent to observers. This divergence can lead to a sense of isolation on the part of the patient, and to inadequate responses by others in alleviating pain.' Ibid. 18. The then President of the American Association of Bioethics stated that '[t]he best friend Dr. Kevorkian has is the undermedication of pain.' Ann Hardie, '"Morphine Drip" Has Little Opposition' *Atlanta Journal and Constitution*, 8 Mar. 1995, C3 (quoting Arthur Caplan). See also, James Rachels, *The End of Life: Euthanasia and Morality* (Oxford: Oxford Univ. Press, 1986) 152–4 (describing horrendous case of the undermedication of pain at the National Institutes of Health cancer clinic); Weir, above n. 39, 123–4; John Glasson, 'Report of the Council on Ethical and Judicial Affairs of the American Medical Association: Physician-Assisted Suicide' (1994) 10 *Issues in Law & Med.* 91; Kathleen Foley, 'Dismantling the Barriers: Providing Palliative and Pain Care' (2000) 283 *Med. Student J. of Am. Med. Ass'n*. 115; Linda Ganzini et al., 'Physicians' Experiences with the Oregon Death with Dignity Act' (2000) 342(8) *New Eng. J. Med.* 557, 559; Ronald Dworkin et al., 'Assisted Suicide: The Philosophers' Brief' (1997) 44(5) *N.Y. Rev. of Books* 41, 42, reprinting with an introduction the *amici curiae* brief filed in the Supreme Court by a group of moral philosophers prior to the hearing of *Vacco v. Quill* (1997) 521 U.S. 793 and *Washington v. Glucksberg* (1997) 521 U.S. 702. The brief itself is also found at 1996 WL 708956.

[189] Moreover, Bender unrealistically assumes that those around the patient will be in (or will be able to reach) some kind of agreement as to the content of the patient's needs. See Bender, above n. 151.

found in that debate. By focusing on and recognizing some of the problems associated with current rights discourse in the assisted suicide debate, we may be able to avoid continued reiteration of the same stalemated debate.

My strategy here has been to canvass some of the arguments made by participants in the present debate, and to consider the applicability of more generalized critiques of rights discourse to the debate, in order to better enable principled, systematic, and thoughtful evaluation of current and future rights claims for and against assisted suicide. These critiques may also offer the continuing debate suggestions for 'rules of engagement'[190] which may enable participants in the debate to avoid the 'thoughtless, habitual ways of thinking and speaking about rights' described by Mary Ann Glendon.[191]

My aim in this chapter has not been to suggest a 'solution' to the problems enumerated above, nor to advocate an alternative debate. In jurisdictions with constitutionally entrenched human rights, the debate over the legalization of both assisted suicide and voluntary active euthanasia is likely to continue in the form of rights discourse, having been sparked by the unsuccessful attempts to use constitutionally entrenched rights claims to challenge criminal prohibitions on assisted suicide in the United States, Canada, and the United Kingdom. The current failure of rights as a mechanism of legal change on assisted dying suggests that it is worth examining other modes of reasoning and potential mechanisms of legal change. The next two chapters examine the defence of necessity and compassion. The regimes produced by the various mechanisms, including rights, are then compared in Chapter 6.

---

[190] This phrase is borrowed from Andrew Ashworth, 'Crime, Community and Creeping Consequentialism' [1996] *Crim. L.R.* 220, 229.   [191] Glendon, above n. 2, 15.

4

Duties and Necessity

This chapter examines the defence of necessity as a mechanism of legal change on assisted dying. This is the basis on which euthanasia was effectively legalized in the Netherlands. The defence is available when the defendant faced a conflict between her duties to preserve life and relieve suffering. Section I describes the Dutch defence of necessity and how it has been recently codified. In contrast, although the defence of necessity exists at common law, it has not been used to permit euthanasia. Section II examines the common law refusal to allow the defence of necessity to be used in murder cases, which has been re-affirmed recently in both England and Canada. Section III then examines the differing choices made by these jurisdictions regarding the use of rights and necessity as mechanisms of legal change on assisted dying and proposes explanations for the different roads taken by Dutch judges and their common law counterparts. Two central questions are asked. First, why is the common law defence of necessity apparently unavailable to defendants who have assisted another to die? Secondly, why did the Dutch not use constitutionally entrenched rights as the mechanism of legal change?

I. The Dutch Defence of Necessity

The duty-based defence of necessity was the mechanism of legalization of euthanasia and assisted suicide in the Netherlands, developed through judicial interpretation of Criminal Code provisions governing the offences of taking life on request, assisting suicide, and the defence of necessity. Although the role of other influences should not be overlooked, in particular the medical profession (especially the position of the Royal Dutch Medical Association) and pro-euthanasia pressure groups,[1] the Dutch courts were the agent of formal legal change in the Netherlands.[2]

---

[1] See Heleen Weyers, 'Euthanasia: The process of legal change in the Netherlands' in Albert Klijn et al., eds., *Regulating Physician-Negotiated Death* (Amsterdam: Elsevier, 2001) 11, 13–21; John Griffiths, 'Self-regulation by the Dutch medical profession of medical behavior that potentially shortens life' in Hans Krabbendam & Hans-Martien ten Napel, eds., *Regulating Morality: A Comparison of The Role of the State in Mastering the Mores in the Netherlands and the United States* (Antwerp: Maklu, 2000) 173, 174–7.

[2] Jurriaan de Haan, 'The New Dutch Law on Euthanasia' (2002) 10 *Med. L. Rev.* 57, 59 ('The legal acceptance of euthanasia was based on jurisprudence'); Gerrit K. Kimsma & Evert van Leeuwen,

A. The Criminal Code provisions

Unlike many common law jurisdictions, the Dutch Criminal Code (Wetboek van Strafrecht) provides a specific lesser offence of consensual homicide.[3] Prior to the recent legislative reforms, Article 293 stated: 'A person who takes the life of another person at that other person's express and earnest request is liable to a term of imprisonment of not more than twelve years or a fine of the fifth category.'[4] The Criminal Code also contains a separate offence of assisting suicide.[5]

The term 'euthanasia', in the Dutch context, refers only to the termination of life *upon request*.[6] That is, 'euthanasia' cases *by definition* fall under Article 293. Prior to codification,[7] the legal basis on which Dutch doctors who performed euthanasia were either not prosecuted or acquitted (subject to certain 'requirements of careful practice')[8] was the defence of necessity. Article 40 of the Dutch Criminal Code provides that '[a] person who commits an offence as the result of a force he could not be expected to resist [*overmacht*] is not criminally liable.'[9] 'This defence has two variants in Dutch law: the excuse of duress and the justification of necessity.'[10]

'Euthanasia and Assisted Suicide in the Netherlands and the USA: Comparing Practices, Justifications and Key Concepts in Bioethics and Law' in David C. Thomasma et al., eds., *Asking to Die: Inside the Dutch Debate about Euthanasia* (Dordrecht: Kluwer, 1998) 35, 63 (the 'affirmative position of Dutch courts' was '[o]f primary and overruling importance').

[3] For other examples of such provisions, see Chapter 1, Section III.A.2.

[4] Louise Rayar & Stafford Wadsworth, trans., *The Dutch Penal Code* (Littleton, Colo.: Fred B. Rothman & Co., 1997) 200, reproduced in John Griffiths, Alex Bood & Heleen Weyers, *Euthanasia and Law in the Netherlands* (Amsterdam: Amsterdam Univ. Press, 1998) 308. A fine of the fifth category was ƒ100,000 and is now €45,000, Criminal Code, Art. 23.

[5] Criminal Code, Art. 294 ('A person who intentionally incites another to commit suicide, assists in the suicide of another, or procures for that other person the means to commit suicide, is liable to a term of imprisonment of not more than three years or a fine of the fourth category, where the suicide ensues.'). The translation is from Rayar & Wadsworth, above n. 4, 200. A fine of the fourth category was ƒ25,000 and is now €11,250, Criminal Code, Art. 23.

[6] As defined by the State Commission on Euthanasia in *Rapport van de Staatscommissie Euthanasie (Report of the State Commission on Euthanasia)* (The Hague: Staatsuitgeverij, 1985), discussed in Kimsma & Van Leeuwen, above n. 2, 43. For an English summary of the report, see J.K.M. Gevers, 'Final Report of the Netherlands State Commission on Euthanasia: An English Summary' (1987) 1(2) *Bioethics* 163. On the definition, see also, Griffiths, Bood & Weyers, above n. 4, 17; Jürgen Wöretshofer & Matthias Borgers, 'The Dutch Procedure for Mercy Killing and Assisted Suicide by Physicians in a National and International Perspective' (1995) 2(1) *Maastricht J. of Eur. & Comparative L.* 4, 5–7; Royal Netherlands Society for the Promotion of Medicine and Recovery, Interest Association of Nurses and Nursing Aids, 'Guidelines for Euthanasia' (1988) 3 *Issues in Law & Med.* 429, 430–1 (Walter Lagerwey, trans.). I use this definition throughout this chapter.

[7] Termination of Life on Request and Assisted Suicide (Review Procedures) Act 2001. English translations can be found at (2001) 8 *Eur. J. Health L.* 183 and as an appendix to de Haan, above n. 2, 68–75.

[8] In the new law, the term used is 'due care criteria'. Termination of Life on Request and Assisted Suicide (Review Procedures) Act 2001, Ch. II (translations listed ibid.).

[9] Rayar & Wadsworth, above n. 4, 73.

[10] Griffiths, Bood & Weyers, above n. 4, 62, 326. The excuse/justification distinction is discussed below at Section II.C.1.a. The unavailability of the defence of duress in euthanasia cases is discussed below at n. 27.

A doctor can rely on the defence of necessity when faced with conflicting duties, namely, the duty to preserve life, and her professional duty to relieve her patient's suffering.[11] 'If a person in such a situation chooses to prefer the value that from an objective standpoint is more important, even if this means doing something that in itself is forbidden, his conduct is justifiable.'[12]

B. The conflict of duties

What is the philosophical basis of this position? As we saw in Chapter 2, in jurisdictions such as the United States of America, Canada, and the United Kingdom, the right of autonomy is the primary tool of those who argue in favour of legalization of euthanasia and assisted suicide. Other rights are also cited in support of legalization, including the rights to privacy, dignity, and equality.[13] However, in the Netherlands, '[t]he duty of a doctor to alleviate "unbearable and hopeless suffering" has, via the justification of necessity recognized by the Supreme Court, become the principal legal basis for the legalization of euthanasia and assistance with suicide.'[14]

Prior to codification, the Dutch law developed through a series of court cases.[15] The first case to reach the Supreme Court (Hoge Raad) was the 1984 case of *Schoonheim*. Rejecting alternative defences,[16] the court accepted the defence of necessity based on a conflict of duties:

in accordance with norms of medical ethics, and with the expertise which as a professional he must be assumed to possess – [the defendant] balanced the duties and interests which,

---

[11] Maurice Adams & Herman Nys, 'Euthanasia in the Low Countries: Comparative Reflections on the Belgian and Dutch Euthanasia Act' in Paul Schotsmans & Tom Meulenbergs, eds., *Euthanasia and Palliative Care in the Low Countries* (Leuven: Peeters, 2005) 5.

[12] Griffiths, Bood & Weyers, above n. 4, 62; *Schoonheim*, Supreme Court, 27 Nov. 1984, N.J. 1985, no. 106.   [13] See Chapter 2, Section II.C.

[14] Griffiths, Bood & Weyers, above n. 4, 172.

[15] For detailed accounts of these cases, see Griffiths, Bood & Weyers, ibid. 51–67; Raphael Cohen-Almagor, *Euthanasia in the Netherlands: The Policy and Practice of Mercy Killing* (Dordrecht: Kluwer, 2004) 39–49; Barney Sneiderman & Marja Verhoef, 'Patient Autonomy and the Defence of Medical Necessity: Five Dutch Euthanasia Cases' (1996) 34 *Alta. L. Rev.* 374; Jonathan T. Smies, 'The Legalization of Euthanasia in the Netherlands' (2003–04) 7 *Gonz. J. Int'l L.* 1, 1–28; Julia Belian, 'Deference to Doctors in Dutch Euthanasia Law' (1996) 10 *Emory Int'l L. Rev.* 255, 261–72. It is not correct to say that euthanasia was simply 'tolerated' in the Netherlands prior to the enactment of the Termination of Life on Request and Assisted Suicide (Review Procedures) Act 2001. Heleen Weyers has argued convincingly that 'pragmatic tolerance' does not appropriately describe the Dutch legal position since the 1984 decision of the Supreme Court in *Schoonheim*. See Weyers, above n. 1, 21–3.

[16] The defendant argued that his patient's consent meant that he had not 'taken' her life. He also relied on 'absence of substantial violation of the law'. *Schoonheim*, Supreme Court, 27 Nov. 1984, N.J. 1985, no. 106, translated in Griffiths, Bood & Weyers, above n. 4, App. II-1, 324–6. The latter doctrine encapsulates 'the idea that behavior that violates the letter but not the purpose of the law does not constitute an offence.' Griffiths, Bood & Weyers, ibid. 61. The defendant argued that no offence had been committed because 'in ever wider circles the right of self-determination in the matter of terminating one's life is accepted; that it is a commonly known fact that in order to terminate one's

in the case at hand, were in conflict, and made a choice that – objectively considered, and taking into account the specific circumstances of this case – was justifiable.[17]

For the Supreme Court, the crucial finding of the appeals court that the patient was 'experiencing her suffering as unbearable' triggered the applicability of the defence of necessity.[18] The case was remanded to a different appeals court for further consideration of the facts. The appeals court was instructed to consider: the risk of 'increasing loss of personal dignity and/or worsening of [the patient's] already unbearable suffering'; the risk that had the defendant waited, his patient would 'no longer [have been] in a position to die in a dignified manner'; and 'whether, and if so to what extent, there were any remaining ways of relieving her suffering.'[19]

The substantive pillars of the defence of necessity in euthanasia cases are that the patient was experiencing unbearable and hopeless suffering and that no reasonable alternative to relieve her suffering existed. The patient's suffering need not be related to a terminal illness.[20] Indeed, the source of the patient's suffering may be either somatic (that is, stemming from a physiological disorder) or

---

own life in an acceptable, nonviolent manner, the assistance of third parties is often necessary; and that consequently the rendering of assistance in voluntary life termination, even though in a formal sense that assistance is in violation of Article 293 or 294 of the Penal Code, (nevertheless) material illegality can be absent, if and in so far as that action can not legally be deemed undesirable.' H.R.G. Feber, 'The Vicissitudes of article 293 of the Penal Code from 1981 to the Present' in Gerrit van der Wal, ed., *Euthanasie: Knelpunten in Een Discussie (Euthanasia: Bottlenecks in a Discussion)* (Baarn: Ambo, 1987) 54 (in Dutch), an English summary by Walter Lagerwey is found at (1988) 3 *Issues in Law & Med.* 455, 456. See also, Belian, above n. 15, 268–9. The 'medical exception', a further alternative defence, was rejected by the Hoge Raad in *Pols*, Supreme Court, 21 Oct. 1986, N.J. 1987, no. 607, 2124, English summary in Barry Bostrom & Walter Lagerwey, 'The High Court of the Hague Case No. 79065, October 21, 1986' (1987–1988) 3 *Issues in Law & Med.* 445, 445–6. The defendant argued that her actions were justified 'since she acted in accordance with the demands of appropriate professional practice'. Ibid. 445 (2122–3 of the original). The court held that no medical exception for euthanasia existed, as it was 'evident that even in medical circles in the Netherlands there is no general agreement regarding the permissibility of euthanasia and the manner in which, and the conditions under which, it might be carried out.' Ibid. 446 (2123 of the original). The medical exception is discussed in H.J.J. Leenen, 'The Development of Euthanasia in the Netherlands' (2001) 8 *Eur. J. Health L.* 125, 126; Jos V.M. Welie, 'The Medical Exception: Physicians, Euthanasia and the Dutch Criminal Law' (1992) 17(4) *J. of Med. & Philosophy* 419, 429–32; Griffiths, Bood & Weyers, above n. 4, 91–7; Weyers, above n. 1, 19; Adams & Nys, above n. 11, 14, n. 21.

[17] *Schoonheim*, Supreme Court, 27 Nov. 1984, N.J. 1985, no. 106, translated in Griffiths, Bood & Weyers, above n. 4, App. II-1, 326–7.   [18] Ibid. 328.

[19] Ibid. The Court of Appeals, The Hague allowed the defendant's plea of necessity and he was acquitted. 10 June & 11 Sept. 1986, N.J. 1987, no. 608.

[20] *Admiraal*, District Court, The Hague, N.J. 1985, no. 709; *Postma*, District Court, Leeuwarden, 21 Feb. 1973, N.J. 1973, no. 183, 560, translated by Walter Lagerwey, 'Euthanasia Case Leeuwarden–1973' (1987–1988) 3 *Issues in Law & Med.* 439, 440; *Pols*, Supreme Court, 21 Oct. 1986, N.J. 1987, no. 607, 2124. See also, Sneiderman & Verhoef, above n. 15, text accompanying n. 51. Although whether the patient is suffering from a terminal illness will affect 'the extent to which the patient's life is shortened by euthanasia [and thereby] the extent, for example, to which [the doctor] should insist on exploring treatment alternatives or should engage in more than the minimum consultation.' Griffiths, Bood & Weyers, above n. 4, 104.

non-somatic.[21] The latter 'can include . . . the prospect of inhuman deterioration and the possibility of not being able to die in a "dignified" way.'[22]

The lack of a reasonable alternative to the patient's unbearable and hopeless suffering gives rise to the defendant's conflict of duties once the patient makes a considered and voluntary request for euthanasia or assisted suicide.[23] 'If the consideration leads to the unavoidable conclusion that euthanasia is the only realistic option, under the current legal context, the physician will have entered into a conflict of duties once the patient requests euthanasia.'[24] The requirements associated with the patient's request are discussed in Chapter 6.[25]

It should be noted that only a doctor can be faced with this conflict of duties.[26] Neither lay-persons (including relatives) nor nurses are thought to be faced with a

---

[21] *Chabot*, Supreme Court, 21 June 1994, N.J. 1994, no. 656, translated in John Griffiths, 'Assisted suicide in the Netherlands: the *Chabot* case' (1995) 58 *Mod. L. Rev.* 232. The translation is reproduced in Griffiths, Bood & Weyers, above n. 4, App. II-2. See also, John Griffiths, Heleen Weyers & Maurice Adams, *Euthanasia and the Law in Europe: With Special Reference to the Netherlands and Belgium* (Oxford: Hart Publishing, 2007 (forthcoming)) [3.2.3.3]; B.A. van der Veer & A. Sennef, 'Case Descriptions' in M. Malsch & J.F. Nijboer, *Complex Cases: Perspectives on the Netherlands criminal justice system* (Amsterdam: Thela Thesis, 1999) 123, 141–7; Gene Kaufmann, '*State v. Chabot*: A Euthanasia Case from the Netherlands' (1994) 20 *Ohio N.U. L. Rev.* 815; Ubaldus de Vries, 'Psychological Suffering and Physician-Assisted Suicide: *Chabot* (1994)' in Eoin O'Dell, ed., *Leading cases of the twentieth century* (Dublin: Round Hall Sweet & Maxwell, 2000) 496; H.J.J. Leenen, 'Dutch Supreme Court about Assistance to Suicide in the Case of Severe Mental Suffering' (1994) *Eur. J. Health L.* 377; Raphael Cohen-Almagor, 'The Chabot Case: Analysis and Account of Dutch Perspectives' (2001) 5 *Med. L. Int'l* 141; Sjef Gevers & Johan Legemaate, 'Physician assisted suicide in psychiatry: an analysis of case law and professional opinions' in Thomasma, above n. 2, 71; 'Arlene Judith Klotzko and Dr. Boudewijn Chabot Discuss Assisted Suicide in the Absence of Somatic Illness' in Thomasma, ibid. 373; J.K.M. Gevers, 'Physician-Assisted Suicide and the Dutch Courts' (1996) 5(1) *Camb. Q. Healthcare Ethics* 93, 94–6.

In cases of non-somatic suffering there is an additional requirement that the independent consulting physician *must* examine the patient herself. *Chabot*, above n. 21, 337–8. Although, even in cases of suffering of somatic origin, the consultant should examine the patient herself. Griffiths, Bood & Weyers, above n. 4, 105; Bregje D. Onwuteaka-Philipsen et al., 'Consultation with another Physician on Euthanasia and Assisted Suicide in the Netherlands' (2000) 51 *Social Science & Med.* 429, 430. Griffiths, Weyers & Adams suggest that the difference between the examination requirement in cases of somatically- and non-somatically-based suffering is that in the former case failure to have the consultant examine the patient is a procedural failing for which the doctor may be pursued in disciplinary proceedings, whereas in the latter case such failure will render the defence of necessity unavailable. 'The different treatment of the consultation requirement in the situation of non-somatic suffering follows, in the view of the Supreme Court, from the "extraordinary care" required in such cases.' Griffiths, Weyers & Adams, ibid. [3.2.3.3]. The status of the consultation requirement has changed following codification. See below, text accompanying nn. 35–38. Finally, there was some suggestion in the disciplinary decision in *Chabot* that *two* independent consulting physicians must be involved (with one a psychiatrist). See the summary of the disciplinary decision in *Chabot* in John Griffiths, 'Assisted suicide in the Netherlands: postscript to *Chabot*' (1995) 58 *Mod. L. Rev.* 895. See also, Netherlands Ministry of Foreign Affairs, *A Guide to the Dutch Termination of Life on Request and Assisted Suicide (Review Procedures) Act* (2001) § 12, www.minbuza.nl/binaries/minbuza_core_pictures/pdf/c/c_56513.pdf, accessed 24 Sept. 2006.   [22] Weyers, above n. 1, 21.

[23] Ubaldus de Vries, 'A Dutch perspective: the limits of lawful euthanasia' (2004) 13 *Annals Health L.* 365, 372, 374.

[24] Ibid. 374. The 'no reasonable alternative' requirement is discussed in greater depth in Chapter 6, Sections III.A.3. and III.B.4.   [25] See Chapter 6, Section III.A.1.

[26] The doctor must be acting in her capacity as the patient's physician. District Court, Rotterdam, 7 Dec. 1992 (denying the defence of necessity to a physician working for the Dutch Society for

professional duty to relieve suffering which may conflict with their duty to preserve life and to abide by the criminal prohibition against killing.[27]

Once the conflict of duties exists, and there is no reasonable alternative to relieve the requesting patient's unbearable and hopeless suffering, the doctor will be found to have acted proportionately[28] and the defence of necessity will be available.[29] The act itself must have been carried out with due care. Procedural requirements must also be met.[30] Prior to codification, 'deviation from [some of] these requirements [did] not necessarily stand in the way of an appeal to the justification of necessity.'[31]

C. Codification

The Termination of Life on Request and Assisted Suicide (Review Procedures) Act 2001 did not change the substantive elements of the defence of necessity in euthanasia cases.[32] Article 293 of the Criminal Code was amended to read:

1. Any person who terminates another person's life at that person's express and earnest request shall be liable to a term of imprisonment not exceeding twelve years or a fifth-category fine.

Voluntary Euthanasia who had assisted in the suicide of a patient whose own doctors had refused to help him), discussed in Gevers, above n. 21, 94.

[27] Belian, above n. 15, 265–6; Tony Sheldon, 'Dutch court rules on nurses' role in euthanasia' (1995) 311 *Br. Med. J.* 895. Griffiths, Bood & Weyers cite a number of lower court decisions in support of the proposition that neither laypersons nor nurses may avail themselves of the defence of necessity. Griffiths, Bood & Weyers, above n. 4, 103, n. 40. See also, the comments of Attorney General Remmelink on *Pols*, Supreme Court, 21 Oct. 1986, N.J. 1987, no. 607, 2124, 2131, translated in Bostrom & Lagerwey, above n. 16, 450 (rejecting the use of the defence of duress as this would 'open [ ] the way to "euthanatic actions" by other experts, in particular nursing personnel'). Duress can include a 'psychological external constraint' which compels the defendant to violate the law. De Vries, above n. 23, 370, n. 20. Doctors may not use the defence of duress as they are expected 'to be able to resist this sort of pressure from patients'. Griffiths, Bood & Weyers, above n. 4, 99. See also, Welie, above n. 16, 433.

[28] De Vries, above n. 23, 374–6; J.F. Nijboer, 'Criminal Justice System' in J.M.J. Chorus et al., *Introduction to Dutch Law* (3rd rev. edn.) (The Hague: Kluwer Law International, 1999) 383, 410–11 (Nijboer's chapter was based on L.H.C. Hulsman et al., 'The Dutch Criminal Justice System From a Comparative Legal Perspective' in D.C. Fokkema et al., eds., *Introduction to Dutch Law for Foreign Lawyers* (Deventer: Kluwer, 1978) 289, 339). See also, *Chabot*, Supreme Court, 21 June 1994, N.J. 1994, no. 656, translated in Griffiths, Bood & Weyers, above n. 4, App. II-2, 336 ('the trial court must decide whether the defense of necessity is compatible with the requirement that the course of conduct chosen be proportional to the harm to be avoided and also the least harmful choice available').

[29] Griffiths, Bood & Weyers, ibid.

[30] These include reporting and consultation requirements. The main requirements are now codified in the new law. See Termination of Life on Request and Assisted Suicide (Review Procedures) Act 2001, s. 2(1). The pre-codification requirements are discussed in Griffiths, Bood & Weyers, above n. 4, 104–7. On the reporting requirement, see also, J.K.M. Gevers, 'Legislation on euthanasia: recent developments in The Netherlands' (1992) 18 *J. Med. Ethics* 138.

[31] Griffiths, Bood & Weyers, above n. 4, 107.

[32] See Weyers, above n. 1, 26; Rob Schwitters, 'Slipping into normality? Some Reflections on Slippery Slopes' in Klijn, above n. 1, 93, 99 ('Most of the steps towards legalisation in Holland of euthanasia were taken by the judiciary, and the recent legislation can be seen primarily as an ex-post ratification.'). The new law is further discussed in Chapter 6, Section III.A. See also, Gerrit K. Kimsma & Evert van Leeuwen, 'The New Dutch Law on Legalizing Physician-Assisted Death' (2001) 10 *Camb. Q. Healthcare Ethics* 445; de Haan, above n. 7.

2. The act referred to in the first paragraph shall not be an offence if it is committed by a physician who fulfils the due care criteria set out in section 2 of the Termination of Life on Request and Assisted Suicide (Review Procedures) Act, and if the physician notifies the municipal pathologist of this act in accordance with the provisions of section 7, subsection 2 of the Burial and Cremation Act.[33]

The due care criteria are set out in section 2(1) of the 2001 Act. The substantive and procedural requirements are, unfortunately, jumbled together:[34]

In order to comply with the due care criteria referred to in article 293, paragraph 2, of the Criminal Code, the attending physician must:

a. be satisfied that the patient has made a voluntary and carefully considered request;
b. be satisfied that the patient's suffering was unbearable, and that there was no prospect of improvement;
c. have informed the patient about his situation and his prospects;
d. have come to the conclusion, together with the patient, that there is no reasonable alternative in the light of the patient's situation;
e. have consulted at least one other, independent physician, who must have seen the patient and given a written opinion on the due care criteria referred to in a. to d. above; and
f. have terminated the patient's life or provided assistance with suicide with due medical care and attention.

Although the substantive requirements remain the same, the Act involves two major procedural changes. The consultation[35] and reporting[36] requirements are included as conditions which must be satisfied in order for the new statutory defence in Article 293(2) of the Criminal Code to apply.[37] This means, in theory at least, that failure to meet one or both of these conditions could result in the defendant being convicted of termination of life upon request under Article 293(1).[38] The other major procedural change was to the role of review committees which act

---

[33] Termination of Life on Request and Assisted Suicide (Review Procedures) Act 2001, s. 20A. The provision on assisted suicide (Art. 294) was similarly amended by s. 20B of the 2001 Act. The Burial and Cremation Act 1991 is often referred to by its more literal translation as the Law on Disposal of Corpses (Wet op de Lijkbezorging). In this work I use the former translation as this is the one used in the official translation of the Termination of Life on Request and Assisted Suicide (Review Procedures) Act 2001 which amends the Burial and Cremation Act 1991. See below, n. 36.

[34] The distinction between substantive and procedural requirements is not mine. See, e.g., Griffiths, Bood & Weyers, above n. 4, 98–107; Bregje D. Onwuteaka-Philipsen et al., 'Dutch experience of monitoring euthanasia' (2005) 331 *Br. Med. J.* 691.

[35] Termination of Life on Request and Assisted Suicide (Review Procedures) Act 2001, ss. 2(1)(e), 20A.

[36] Termination of Life on Request and Assisted Suicide (Review Procedures) Act 2001, ss. 20A, 21A (amending s. 7 of the Burial and Cremation Act 1991).

[37] See above, text accompanying n. 33.

[38] Although it is more likely that the defendant would be prosecuted for issuing a false death certificate under Article 228(1) of the Criminal Code. See, e.g., the discussion of *Van Oijen*, Supreme Court, 9 Nov. 2004, N.J. 2005, no. 217 in Chapter 6, Section III.B.3; Tony Sheldon, 'Two test cases in Holland clarify law on murder and palliative care' (2004) 329 *Br. Med. J.* 1206; Tony Sheldon, 'Dutch GP Found Guilty of Murder Faces No Penalty' (2001) 322 *Br. Med. J.* 509 and see also, Griffiths, Weyers & Adams, above n. 21, [3.2.3.3].

as a buffer between the physician and the prosecutor.[39] These committees were first introduced in 1998, but the new law now provides that cases which are approved by a review committee are no longer to be reported to the prosecutorial authorities.[40] This change has not yet produced the hoped for resulting upward effect on reporting rates,[41] although the evidence on this point is presently unclear.[42]

II. Necessity at Common Law

Why has the Dutch approach not found favour with judges in common law jurisdictions? The opportunities afforded to common law judges to accept or reject the

[39] Marta van Dijk, Guy A.M. Widdershoven & Agnes M. Meershoek, 'Reporting Euthanasia: Physicians' Experiences with a Dutch Regional Evaluation Committee' in Schotsmans & Meulenbergs, above n. 11, 71, 71–2.

[40] See Tony Sheldon, 'Dutch reporting of euthanasia cases falls – despite legal reporting requirements' (2004) 328 *Br. Med. J.* 1336; Tony Sheldon, 'New penalties proposed for Dutch doctors who flout euthanasia law' (2004) 329 *Br. Med. J.* 131; Onwuteaka-Philipsen, above n. 34, 692, 693. The provisions regulating the committees are found in Termination of Life on Request and Assisted Suicide (Review Procedures) Act 2001, ss. 3–19.

[41] The hope was that reporting to a committee rather than the police would be easier as doctors would feel less like criminals, which had apparently been one of the inhibiting factors. See Herman Nys, 'Physician Involvement in a Patient's Death: A Continental European Perspective' (1999) 7 *Med. L. Rev.* 208, 241–3; de Haan, above n. 7, 61–2, 66; Guy Widdershoven, 'Beyond Autonomy and Beneficence: The Moral Basis of Euthanasia in the Netherlands' in Schotsmans & Meulenbergs, above n. 11, 83, 85; van Dijk, Widdershoven & Meershoek, above n. 39, 71–2; Netherlands Ministry of Foreign Affairs, above n. 21, § 7. On reluctance to report, see also, Griffiths, above n. 1, 189.

[42] 'The drop in reported cases since 2000 . . . raises questions about the effectiveness of the review committees. Until a new notification rate can be calculated, we cannot tell whether the drop reflects a fall in notification rate or a decrease in euthanasia and physician assisted suicide. The rise in reported cases in 2004 might, if it is not coincidental, indicate that the further shift in the focus of the review process from repressive (by the public prosecutor) to educative (through review committees) has been effective. If the total cases of euthanasia and physician assisted suicide has fallen rather than notification it shows that the review procedure has not increased the practice of euthanasia. Euthanasia might have fallen because of improvements in palliative care in the Netherlands in recent years and the introduction of terminal sedation, which could sometimes be used as an alternative for euthanasia and physician assisted suicide.' Onwuteaka-Philipsen, above n. 34, 693. The rise in 2004 continued in 2005. Regionale toetsingscommissies euthanasie (Regional Euthanasia Review Committees), *Jaarverslag (Annual Report) 2005* (Apr. 2006) 8.

John Griffiths has argued that the reporting rate – which is based on the classification by researchers (rather than doctors) of particular cases as euthanasia – would be significantly higher if it reflected only those cases which doctors consider to be euthanasia. Changes in reporting procedure, therefore, were unlikely to affect the rate as 'knowingly false reporting' constitutes only a small fraction of the 'unreported' cases. John Griffiths, 'Criminal Law is the Problem, Not the Solution' in Charles A. Erin & Suzanne Ost, *The Criminal Justice System and Health Care* (Oxford: Oxford Univ. Press, 2007 (forthcoming)), relying on the work of Govert den Hartogh, 'Mysterieuze cijfers' ('Mysterious numbers') (2003) 58 *Medisch Contact (Medical Contact)* 1063 and Donald van Tol, *Grensgeschillen. Een rechtssociologische onderzoek naar het classificeren van euthanasie en ander medisch handelen rond het levenseinde (Boundary Disputes. A Legal-Sociological Study of the Classification of Euthanasia and other Medical Behavior that Shortens Life)* (Groningen: Facilitair Bedrijf/GrafiMedia, 2005) (for an English summary, see (2005) *Newsletter RSPMB (Special Issue)* 17, 23 and http://irs.ub.rug.nl/ppn/290674735, accessed 11 July 2006) (reporting '*systematic difference* in the way general practitioners, coroners and public prosecutors classify' various cases of medical behaviour that shortens life (emphasis in original)).

defence of necessity have not included the kind of voluntary euthanasia cases which have been prosecuted in the Netherlands. This could be due to a reluctance to prosecute such cases in common law jurisdictions, to defence lawyers' preferences for other defences,[43] or to the 'seemingly greater willingness of Dutch doctors to risk prosecution in court for their principles, though this may be a reflection of the more lenient attitude of Dutch law towards doctors than individual medical altruism.'[44]

Although there have been some opportunities to accept the defence of necessity afforded to the English and Canadian courts, judges have been unwilling or unable to follow the course taken by the judiciary in the Netherlands. These courts have been reluctant to establish a wide defence of necessity.[45] The proposal by Glanville Williams to use the defence of necessity in cases of euthanasia has not been taken up.[46] Indeed, prior to the decision of the English Court of Appeal in the recent conjoined twins case,[47] 'no court in a common law jurisdiction ha[d] ever allowed the defence of necessity to a charge of murder'.[48] The common law courts have remained implacably hostile to necessity as a defence in a case of murder.[49]

A. England: cannibals and conjoined twins

In England and Wales, the defence of necessity has developed at common law with no statutory intervention. The Law Commission has been reluctant to intervene.[50] In *Dudley and Stephens*, two sailors who had been shipwrecked were

---

[43] Perhaps because the defence of necessity is simply seen as inapplicable to euthanasia cases. See Wayne R. LaFave, *Substantive Criminal Law* (2nd edn.) (St. Paul, Minn.: West Publishing, 2003) § 5.3. See, e.g., *Roberts* (1920) 211 Mich. 187 (Mich. S.C.).

[44] Diana Brahams, 'The reluctant survivor: Part 2' (1990) 140(6454) *New L.J.* 639.

[45] *Latimer* [2001] 1 S.C.R. 3, [28] ('It is well established that the defence of necessity must be of a limited application'); *Perka* [1984] 2 S.C.R. 232, 250 (Dickson J.) ('If the defence of necessity is to form a valid and consistent part of our criminal law it must, as has been universally recognized, be strictly controlled and scrupulously limited to situations that correspond to its underlying rationale').

[46] Glanville Williams, *The Sanctity of Life and the Criminal Law* (London: Faber, 1958) 286–8. For later proposals, see, e.g., Derrick Augustus Carter, 'Knight in the Duel with Death: Physician Assisted Suicide and the Medical Necessity Defense' (1996) 41 *Vill. L. Rev.* 663; Robin Isenberg, 'Medical Necessity as a Defense to Criminal Liability: *United States v. Randall*' (1978) 46 *Geo. Wash. L. Rev.* 273, 297; Suzanne Ost, 'Euthanasia and the defence of necessity: advocating a more appropriate legal response' [2005] *Crim. L.R.* 355.   [47] See below, text accompanying nn. 61–70.

[48] Barney Sneiderman, 'The *Latimer* Mercy-Killing Case: A Rumination on Crime and Punishment' (1997) 5 *Health L.J.* 1, [45], n. 43.

[49] George Fletcher, 'The Individualization of Excusing Conditions' (1974) 47 *So. Cal. L. Rev.* 1269, 1279.

[50] Law Commission of England and Wales (L.C.E.W.), *Defences of General Application*, Report No. 83 (1977) 25–32, rejecting the recommendations contained in L.C.E.W., *Defences of General Application*, Working Paper No. 55 (1974) 20–42. For criticism, see Glanville Williams, 'Necessity' [1978] *Crim. L.R.* 128; P.H.J. Huxley, 'Proposals and Counter Proposals on the Defence of Necessity' [1978] *Crim. L.R.* 141. See also, L.C.E.W., *A New Homicide Act for England and Wales*, Consultation Paper No. 177 (2005) [1.1(3)], [1.3(1)], [8.3] (exempting the issues surrounding necessity and euthanasia from the most recent proposals on homicide).

convicted of the murder of a cabin boy whom they had killed and eaten. It was held that necessity was unavailable as a defence to murder.[51]

Over a century after the decision in *Dudley and Stephens*, the House of Lords held in *Howe* that neither duress nor necessity were available as defences to a murder charge.[52] Although only duress was argued on the facts of the case, the decision addressed the availability of both duress and necessity.[53] The House of Lords refused to accept the choice apparently made by the defendants to prefer their own lives over those of their victims. 'The primary reason for the[ ] decision [in *Howe*] was that the law should not recognize that any individual has the liberty to choose that one innocent citizen should die rather than another.'[54] This reasoning could also be applied to the choice made by the defendants in *Dudley and Stephens* a century earlier.[55]

In *obiter* in *Howe*, Lord Hailsham considered 'mercy killing' to be an 'almost venial, if objectively immoral' kind of murder.[56] The House of Lords thus failed to distinguish the different choices involved in cannibalism, duress, and euthanasia. The choice in cannibalism and duress cases is between the life of the defendant and the life of the victim, while in euthanasia cases the choice is between the duty to preserve life and the duty to relieve suffering.[57] Nevertheless, it is clear from the court's absolute refusal to allow duress and necessity in murder cases that despite the different choices involved, no difference in the availability of necessity exists.

Necessity had been allowed as a defence to the crime of procuring a miscarriage in the earlier case of *Bourne*.[58] The defendant obstetric surgeon was charged with procuring a miscarriage of a fourteen year old girl who had been violently raped. The defendant and two medical experts had testified that the continuance of the pregnancy would probably cause serious injury to the girl resulting in her becoming a 'mental wreck'.

While *Dudley and Stephens* involved a choice between the life of the defendant and that of the victim, this scenario can be distinguished from *Bourne*, which

---

[51] (1884) 14 Q.B.D. 273. See A.W. Brian Simpson, *Cannibalism and the Common Law: The Story of the Tragic Last Voyage of the Mignonette and the Strange Legal Proceedings to Which It Gave Rise* (Chicago: Univ. of Chicago Press, 1984). See also, *United States v. Holmes* (1842) 26 F.Cas. 360, No. 15383 (C.C.E.D. Pa.) (affirming guilty verdict on manslaughter charge of a sailor who threw male passengers overboard to die from an overcrowded lifeboat and approving the trial judge's charge to the jury that selection in such circumstances must be made by drawing lots).

[52] *Howe* [1987] A.C. 417. See also, *Pommell* [1995] Cr. App. R. 607; *Rodger* [1998] 1 Cr. App. R. 143. [53] *Howe* [1987] A.C. 417, 429, 439, 453.

[54] Andrew Ashworth, *Principles of Criminal Law* (4th edn.) (Oxford: Oxford Univ. Press, 2003) 229.

[55] *Howe* [1987] A.C. 417, 432 (Lord Hailsham), 439 (Lord Griffiths), 453 (Lord Mackay).

[56] Ibid., 433.

[57] The suffering would have to be severe as necessity is only available where there is a danger of death or serious injury. *Conway* [1989] 3 All E.R. 1025 (Eng. C.A.).

[58] *Bourne* [1939] 1 K.B. 687, [1938] 3 All E.R. 615 (Eng. C.C.A.) (the two reports are different in substantial respects). See Williams, above n. 46, 152: 'The only legal principle on which the exception could be based … [and] the only principle indicating the extent of legality is the defence of necessity.'

involved a choice between the lives of a girl and her foetus.[59] Both of these situations are different from the case of euthanasia, in which the choice that gives rise to a claim of necessity is not between two lives, but rather between conflicting duties to preserve life and relieve suffering. Indeed, one could argue that the choice between the lives of the woman and foetus involved in abortion has closer parallels to the choice between the defendant and victim in *Dudley and Stephens* than to the conflicting duties in a euthanasia case. Thus if necessity is available in cases of abortion, *Dudley and Stephens* would not appear to stand in the way of its use in cases of euthanasia, although the weight of precedent is clearly against this possibility.[60]

In *Re A (Children) (Conjoined Twins: Surgical Separation)*, the English Court of Appeal allowed the use of the defence of necessity in a case involving a choice between two lives, although the case can be distinguished from *Dudley and Stephens* as the choice would not be one made by the potential defendant, but rather determined by the poor prognosis of one of the twins.[61] Without the operation to separate them, both infant twins would die within a few months. If the operation were performed, the weaker twin would die immediately, but it was hoped that the stronger twin would survive to lead a 'relatively normal life'.[62]

Lord Justice Brooke adopted Sir James Stephen's formulation of the defence of necessity:

there are three necessary requirements for the application of the doctrine of necessity: (i) the act is needed to avoid inevitable and irreparable evil; (ii) no more should be done

---

[59] In *Bourne*, the defence in s. 1(1) of the Infant Life Preservation Act 1929 permitting abortion where essential to preserve the life of the mother was incorporated into s. 58 of the Offences Against the Person Act 1861, and this defence was interpreted 'in an extended sense to include preserving the longevity of the mother.' Williams, above n. 46, 151. It is in this extended sense that the choice involved is between the 'life' of the mother and that of her foetus.

[60] *Dudley and Stephens* (1884) 14 Q.B.D. 273, 287–8; *Howe* [1987] A.C. 417, 433.

[61] [2001] Fam. 147, 239 (Brooke L.J.) (describing the weaker twin as 'self-designated for a very early death'). See also, the commentary by J.C. Smith on this case at [2001] *Crim. L.R.* 400, 404. For further discussion of this case, see Elizabeth Wicks, 'The Greater Good? Issues of Proportionality and Democracy in the Doctrine of Necessity as Applied in *Re A*' (2003) 32 *Common L. World Rev.* 115; Jonathan Rogers, 'Necessity, Private Defence and the Killing of Mary' [2001] *Crim. L.R.* 515; Sabine Michalowski, 'Sanctity of life – are some lives more sacred than others?' (2002) 22 *Legal Stud.* 377; Richard Huxtable, 'Logical Separation? Conjoined Twins, Slippery Slopes and Resource Allocation' (2001) 23(4) *J. Social Welfare & Family Law* 459. One could argue that the victim in *Dudley and Stephens* was also 'self-designated for death' as he had drunk salt-water and was, according to the defendants, extremely unwell at the time that they decided to kill him. *Dudley and Stephens* (1884) 14 Q.B.D. 273, 274. See Winnie Chan & A.P. Simester, 'Duress, Necessity: How Many Defences?' (2005) *King's Coll. L.J.* 121, 130. Chan & Simester also identify another distinction between *Dudley and Stephens* and *Re A*: 'In *Dudley and Stephens*, the cabin boy's death was directly intended: the defendants aimed to kill him, in order then to eat him. In *Re A*, [the weaker twin's] death was no part of the doctors' aim or purpose, although it was an inevitable consequence of what they sought to achieve.' This distinction was not one relied upon by the court in *Re A*. As death is directly intended in cases of euthanasia, such a limitation on the defence of necessity would prevent the application of the defence to euthanasia cases.

[62] *Re A* [2001] Fam. 147, 197 (Eng C.A.). See Sandra Laville, 'Surviving Siamese twin Gracie goes home to Gozo' *Daily Telegraph*, 16 June 2001.

than is reasonably necessary for the purpose to be achieved; (iii) the evil inflicted must not be disproportionate to the evil avoided.[63]

In *Re A*, the court limited its holding carefully, and Lord Justice Ward specifically excluded the possibility that the defence of necessity could be used to justify or excuse euthanasia.[64] Lord Justice Brooke described the availability of the defence of necessity as 'unique' to the circumstances of the present case. He also observed that '[s]uccessive governments, and Parliaments, have set their face against euthanasia.'[65]

In the narrow sense, the issues in *Re A* and the case of euthanasia are different. However, to borrow Stephen's phrase, if the 'inevitable and irreparable evil'[66] is the unbearable suffering of the patient which cannot be assuaged by other means than euthanasia, then this formulation could in theory allow for euthanasia provided it is seen as proportionate to the avoidance of unbearable suffering.[67]

Doubts have been raised about the effectiveness of the limitations proposed in *Re A*, coupled with suggestions that the decision might be used to justify euthanasia. For example, Elizabeth Wicks writes:

Although the Court of Appeal went to great efforts to emphasize the unique nature of the case and the fact that it provided no general authority for doctors to kill their patients if the patient cannot survive, there remains a lingering fear that, in the absence of stronger authority, *Re A* could be used in the future as persuasive authority for voluntary active euthanasia. For the first time in *Re A* the courts permitted a doctor to take active steps to cause the death of his patient largely on the basis that the patient's quality of life was poor and that her ability to exercise her continuing right to life was greatly diminished. There is a danger that the existence of conflicting rights to life, although essential to this judgment, could be overlooked in future cases if a judge were predisposed to permit a mercy killing.[68]

Jenny McEwan also raises the spectre of the legalization of euthanasia via the defence of necessity, although she does not recognize Lord Justice Ward's attempt to avoid the very scenario she envisions:[69]

The Court of Appeal did not consider whether it is now the case that a trial judge would have to allow the jury to return a verdict of not guilty where they are persuaded that death was 'necessary' as euthanasia. The Court of Appeal has opened the door to lawful acquittal where euthanasia is the reason for a killing, and it can be only a matter of time before such cases are before the courts.[70]

---

[63] *Re A* [2001] Fam. 147, 240 (Eng C.A.), derived from Sir James Fitzjames Stephen, *A Digest of the Criminal Law (Crimes and Punishments)* (4th edn.) (London: Macmillan, 1887) 24.

[64] *Re A* [2001] Fam. 147, 204–5 (Eng C.A.).   [65] Ibid., 239, 211 (Eng C.A.).

[66] Above, text accompanying n. 63.

[67] See below, the discussion of the proportionality requirement in the Canadian case of *Latimer*, text accompanying nn. 79, 85.

[68] Wicks, above n. 61, 22. See also, Richard Huxtable, 'Separation of Conjoined Twins: Where Next for English Law' [2002] *Crim. L.R.* 459, 468. Huxtable posits that faced with a different factual scenario, a later court might utilize the defence of consent coupled with the doctrine of necessity from *Re A* to legitimize active voluntary euthanasia. But there is no indication in *Re A* that consent could be used in this way.   [69] See above, text accompanying n. 70.

[70] Jenny McEwan, 'Murder by Design: the "Feel-Good Factor" and the Criminal Law' (2001) 9 *Med. L. Rev.* 246, 248. Jonathan Rogers makes a different argument based on Robert Walker L.J.'s

Both of these analyses of the court's holding in *Re A* are unconvincing as they fail to incorporate the reality of the choice facing the judges in *Re A*: either both twins would die in a few months, or the stronger twin might be saved if the weaker twin were killed by the operation to separate them. This is not the same choice faced by either the defendant or the judge in a euthanasia case. That choice is between the duty to preserve life and the duty to relieve suffering.

B. Canada: non-voluntary euthanasia of a disabled child

The Supreme Court of Canada has had more direct experience of the defence of necessity in the context of euthanasia, as the most recent case on point is the non-voluntary euthanasia case of *Latimer*.[71] Twelve year old Tracy Latimer suffered from severe cerebral palsy caused by brain damage during her birth or gestation. She was confined to a wheelchair with no use of her limbs, could not talk and had great difficulty swallowing. On a daily basis she suffered five or six seizures. She was incontinent, and according to her parents, she was in constant pain. The evidence established that Robert Latimer had been a caring and nurturing father, actively involved in Tracy's daily care. During a temporary stay in a group home while her mother was in the later stages of her fourth pregnancy, Tracy lost a significant amount of weight and dislocated her hip. She was scheduled for hip surgery, the latest operation in a long line of surgical interventions to correct muscular and skeletal problems caused by Tracy's violent muscle spasms, a common problem associated with severe cerebral palsy. Effective pain control was extremely difficult in Tracy's case owing to the prospect of drug interactions with her anti-convulsant medication and the risk of respiratory distress. Two weeks before the surgery, Robert Latimer apparently decided that Tracy had suffered enough. While the rest of the family was at church, he placed Tracy in the cab of his pickup truck, rigged up a hose from the exhaust, and poisoned his daughter with carbon monoxide fumes. During the investigation into Tracy's death, and consistently thereafter, Latimer maintained that he was motivated solely by a desire to halt Tracy's constant pain. 'My priority was to put her out of her pain. She was in

holding in *Re A* that the operation which would cause the weaker twin's death was in her best interests and presumably could be justified using the doctrine of necessity used to justify medical intervention for incompetent persons described by the House of Lords in *Re F (Mental Patient: Sterilisation)* [1990] 2 A.C. 1. See *Re A* [2001] Fam. 147, 258 (Eng C.A.). Rogers argues that this 'confuses the utilitarian doctrine of necessity which Brooke L.J. preferred with the more limited doctrine of necessity which has already been recognised by the common law, and in so doing, his Lordship (presumably inadvertently) condones what can only be described as euthanasia.' Rogers, above n. 61, 517. He continues: 'It does seem that Walker L.J. (in the minority) might have considered himself to be applying *Re F*, since his Lordship thought that the operation would be in [the weaker twin's] best interests; but with respect, such analysis must be wrong. If it is lawful to kill someone deliberately for his or her own benefit, then euthanasia must already be lawful after all, and I know of no one who holds this view.' Ibid. 519.

71 [2001] 1 S.C.R. 3.

'pain constantly,' he told the police. Latimer was originally convicted of second degree murder, but this conviction was overturned on the grounds of prosecutorial misconduct.[72] Latimer was again convicted at a second trial and the Supreme Court upheld the trial judge's decision not to leave the defence of necessity to the jury.[73]

The decision of the Supreme Court in *Latimer* built on its earlier decision in *Perka*. In that case, the defendants were transporting cannabis from Colombia to Alaska by sea. Owing to bad weather and mechanical problems they were forced to land in Canada to make repairs and the cargo was off-loaded in case the ship capsized. The defendants were acquitted at trial on the grounds that they had been forced to bring the cargo onto Canadian soil by necessity. The prosecution appealed in part on the basis that the trial judge had made errors in his charge to the jury on the defence of necessity. At the Supreme Court, Mr. Justice Dickson (as he then was) adopted a test similar to the Dutch approach in some respects:

First, there is the requirement of imminent peril or danger. Second, the accused must have had no reasonable legal alternative to the course of action he or she undertook. Third, there must be proportionality between the harm inflicted and the harm avoided.[74]

The *Latimer* court considered three possible standards by which the first two components could be assessed. Rejecting both the subjective[75] and objective[76] standards, the court chose a 'modified objective standard'.[77] This is 'an objective evaluation, but one that takes into account the situation and characteristics of the particular accused person.'[78]

The key element of the Canadian test is the proportionality requirement.[79] *Perka* required that the 'harm inflicted must be less than the harm sought to be avoided'.[80] The proportionality test was relaxed somewhat in *Latimer*. Rather

---

[72] *Latimer* [1997] 1 S.C.R. 217, reversing *Latimer* (1995) 126 D.L.R. (4th) 203, 232–5 (Sask. C.A.). The prosecutor was subsequently acquitted of wilful obstruction of justice. *Kirkham* (1998) 17 Crim. Rep. (5th) 250 (Sask. Q.B.).

[73] See *Latimer* [2001] 1 S.C.R. 3, [42], upholding *Latimer* (1998) 131 C.C.C. (3d) 191, [36] (Sask. C.A.). The medical evidence in *Latimer* is discussed by Barney Sneiderman, '*Latimer* in the Supreme Court: Necessity, Compassionate Homicide, and Mandatory Sentencing' (2001) 64 *Sask. L. Rev.* 511, 514–27.

[74] *Latimer* [2001] 1 S.C.R. 3, [28], describing the test adopted in *Perka* [1984] 2 S.C.R. 232.

[75] 'A subjective test would be met if the person believed he or she was in imminent peril with no reasonable legal alternative to committing the offence.' *Latimer* [2001] 1 S.C.R. 3, [32].

[76] 'Conversely, an objective test would not assess what the accused believed; it would consider whether in fact the person *was* in peril with no reasonable legal alternative.' *Latimer* [2001] 1 S.C.R. 3, [32] (emphasis in original).   [77] Ibid., [32]–[33], citing *Hibbert* [1995] 2 S.C.R. 973.

[78] *Latimer* [2001] 1 S.C.R. 3, [32]. See Paul Guy, '*R. v. Latimer* and the Defence of Necessity: One Step Forward, Two Steps Back' (2003) 66 *Sask. L. Rev.* 485, 496–9 (criticizing the court's failure to explain which of the defendant's characteristics (for example, his age or education) can be included in the modified objective test).

[79] 'This criterion will subsume or overtake the others that are material to the defence.' 'Editorial' (2001) 6 *Can. Crim. L. Rev.* 129.   [80] *Perka* [1984] 2 S.C.R. 232, 251.

than requiring the 'harm sought to be avoided'[81] to outweigh the 'harm inflicted', instead the two harms must be 'seriously comparable' or 'proportionate'.[82]

In *Latimer*, the Supreme Court decided that proportionality is to be assessed on a 'purely objective standard':

Evaluating the nature of an act is fundamentally a determination reflecting society's values as to what is appropriate and what represents a transgression.... The evaluation of the seriousness of the harms must be objective. A subjective evaluation of the competing harms would, by definition, look at the matter from the perspective of the accused person who seeks to avoid harm, usually to himself. The proper perspective, however, is an objective one, since evaluating the gravity of the act is a matter of community standards infused with constitutional considerations (such as, in this case, the s. 15(1) equality rights of the disabled).[83]

Although not excluding the possibility that necessity could be a defence to murder in the future, the Supreme Court in *Latimer* found such a possibility 'difficult... to imagine'.[84] Nonetheless trying to imagine it, the court stated that '[k]illing a person – in order to relieve the suffering produced by a medically manageable physical or mental condition – is not a proportionate response to the harm represented by the non-life-threatening suffering resulting from that condition.'[85] The phraseology here is unusual. The court mentions the manageability of the condition producing the suffering, but not the manageability of the suffering itself (that is, palliative care). The reference to the 'non-life-threatening' nature of the suffering is also puzzling. It is rare for the suffering produced by a condition to be life-threatening. Rather, the more likely scenario is that the condition itself is life-threatening, and it produces suffering which may be more or less medically manageable. Quibbles with the wording aside, for the Supreme Court of Canada it appears that in order for the possibility of necessity as a defence to murder to exist, the key factors would be whether the condition (or suffering) was life-threatening and whether it was medically unmanageable. Thus in the classic voluntary euthanasia scenario, the existence of reasonable options such as palliative care, or perhaps terminal sedation,[86] would be fatal to the defence of necessity.

---

[81] See Guy, above n. 78, 505–7 (criticizing the Supreme Court of Canada's careless interchanging of the terms 'harm avoided' and 'harm the accused sought to avoid' and arguing that *Perka* mandates the latter formulation).

[82] *Latimer* [2001] 1 S.C.R. 3, [40]–[41]. See Gary T. Trotter, 'Necessity and Death: Lessons from *Latimer* and the Case of the Conjoined Twins' (2003) 40 *Alta. L. Rev.* 817, 821.

[83] *Latimer* [2001] 1 S.C.R. 3, [34]. The use of an objective test is criticized in 'Editorial', above n. 79, 129. Section 15(1) of the Canadian Charter of Rights and Freedoms provides: 'Every individual is equal before and under the law and has the right to the equal protection and equal benefit of the law without discrimination and, in particular, without discrimination based on race, national or ethnic origin, colour, religion, sex, age or mental or physical disability.'

[84] *Latimer* [2001] 1 S.C.R. 3, [40]. The Law Reform Commission of Canada (L.R.C.C.) had excluded the possibility in *Recodifying Criminal Law*, Report No. 31 (1987) 36 (recommending an extension of the unavailability of the defence to anyone who purposely causes death or serious harm to another).   [85] *Latimer* [2001] 1 S.C.R. 3, [41].

[86] Terminal sedation is discussed in Chapter 6, n. 105.

C. The elements of the defence of necessity explored

Although there are distinct differences between the test of necessity set out by the Canadian and English courts, the structure of the defence is substantially similar. The test is bi-partite. The first part tests the reasonableness of the defendant's actions, while the second part is a test of proportionality.[87] These elements are discussed in reverse order in the next two sections.

1. Proportionality

Before assessing the role of the proportionality test, the question whether the defence of necessity is a justification or an excuse must be addressed.

a. Justification or excuse?

'In the case of justification the wrongfulness of the alleged offensive act is challenged; in the case of excuse the wrongfulness is acknowledged but a ground for the exercise of judicial compassion for the actor is asserted.'[88] Thus self-defence is an example of a justification, while duress is an example of an excuse.

As a justification, the utilitarian logic of the defence of necessity is that 'within certain limits, it is justifiable in an emergency to break the letter of the law if breaking the law will avoid a greater harm than obeying it.'[89] As an excuse, the defence recognizes human frailty so that 'again within limits, it is excusable in an emergency to break the law if compliance would impose an intolerable burden on the accused.'[90] Necessity as an excuse is known in English law as 'duress of circumstances'.[91]

b. Classification of necessity in the presence of a proportionality requirement

The presence of the proportionality element of the necessity test causes problems for the Supreme Court of Canada, which appears to be wedded to the premise that the defence of necessity is an excuse rather than a justification. The inclusion of a requirement of proportionality in both the Canadian and English tests suggests that the defence of necessity is seen as a justification.[92] The Dutch

---

[87] Stephen G. Coughlan, 'Duress, Necessity, Self-Defence and Provocation: Implications of Radical Change?' (2002) 7 *Can. Crim. L. Rev.* 147, 152.

[88] *Perka* [1984] 2 S.C.R. 232, 268 (Wilson J., concurring). See Fletcher, above n. 49, 1274; George Fletcher, *Rethinking Criminal Law* (Oxford: Oxford Univ. Press, 1978) 819.

[89] L.R.C.C., *Criminal Law: The General Part – Liability and Defences*, Working Paper No. 29 (1982) 93. See, e.g., Model Penal Code (U.S.), § 3.02.

[90] L.R.C.C., above n. 89, describing this as a 'humanitarian principle'.

[91] *Re A* [2001] Fam. 147, 236 (Eng C.A., Brooke J.A.). See also, *Shayler* [2001] 1 W.L.R. 2206, [52]–[56] (Eng. C.A.).

[92] See Don Stuart, *Canadian Criminal Law* (4th edn.) (Toronto: Carswell, 2001) 514; Jeremy Horder, 'Self-Defence, Necessity and Duress: Understanding the Relationship' (1998) 11 *Can. J. L. & Juris.* 143, 160; Trotter, above n. 82, 821; Wicks, above n. 61, 27.

defence is clearly conceptualized as a justification rather than as an excuse.[93] The Supreme Court of Canada, though, has preferred to describe it as an excuse. For example, in *Perka*, Mr. Justice Dickson (as he then was) observed:

[the defence] rests on a realistic assessment of human weakness, recognizing that a liberal and humane criminal law cannot hold people to the strict obedience of laws in emergency situations where normal human instincts, whether of self-preservation or of altruism, overwhelmingly impel disobedience. The objectivity of the criminal law is preserved; such acts are still wrongful, but in the circumstances they are excusable. Praise is indeed not bestowed, but pardon is . . .[94]

Indeed, it was the vision of necessity as an excuse rather than a justification which distinguished the majority reasons (written by Dickson J.) from the concurring reasons of Madam Justice Wilson.[95] In her reasons, Wilson J. argued that both formulations of the defence of necessity should be included in the canon of defences.[96] The English Court of Appeal in *Re A* commented favourably on this part of her judgment.[97] Lord Justice Brooke explicitly grounded his judgment on a justificatory defence of necessity:

In cases of pure necessity the actor's mind is not irresistibly overborne by external pressures. The claim is that his or her conduct was not harmful because on a choice of two evils the choice of avoiding the greater harm was justified.[98]

However, justificatory necessity has been limited by the English Court of Appeal. As we have already seen, in *Re A* it was restricted to the conjoined twins scenario, and its use as a defence to murder in euthanasia cases was explicitly repudiated.[99]

2. *Reasonableness*

Both the English and Canadian courts have split this requirement into two, but there is some divergence between the two approaches. The Canadian test includes an element of imminent peril which derives from the Canadian refusal to abandon

---

[93] See *Schoonheim*, Supreme Court, 27 Nov. 1984, N.J. 1985, no. 106, translated in Griffiths, Bood & Weyers, above n. 4, App. II-1, 327. See also, below, text accompanying n. 107.

[94] *Perka* [1984] 2 S.C.R. 232, 248. Dickson J. explicitly rejected a justificatory approach, although he seems to have based this rejection on concern that it would be too subjective – a complaint which seems inappropriate if the proportionality test is assessed on the basis of an objective test.

[95] Ibid., 268. See Guy, above n. 78, n. 4.

[96] *Perka* [1984] 2 S.C.R. 232, 278–9.

[97] *Re A* [2001] Fam. 147, 202 (Ward L.J.), 236 (Brooke L.J.) (Eng C.A.).

[98] Ibid. See also, ibid. 239 (emphasis added): 'I turn finally to the question whether [the defence of necessity] is, *uniquely*, available in the present case to provide a lawful *justification* for what would otherwise be an offence of murder.'

[99] See above, text accompanying nn. 64–68. In subsequent cases it has been restricted to the medical context, although this may reflect the confusion discussed by Rogers, see above n. 70. See, e.g., *Shayler* [2001] 1 W.L.R. 2206, [52]–[56] (Eng C.A.); *Pommell* [1995] Cr. App. R. 607, 614; *Jones* [2004] 3 W.L.R. 1362, [53]–[54] (Eng. C.A.), citing *Re A* [2001] Fam. 147 (Eng C.A.) and *Re F (Mental Patient: Sterilisation)* [1990] 2 A.C. 1. *Jones* and *Shayler* are discussed by Simon Gardner, 'Direct action and the defence of necessity' [2005] *Crim. L.R.* 371.

the excuse formulation of necessity. Before reaching this requirement, the less controversial requirement that the defendant have no reasonable alternative is considered.

a. No reasonable alternative

The test of no reasonable alternative is a stringent one according to the Canadian cases. For example, in *Perka*, Dickson J. (as he then was) stated that 'the wrongful act [must] truly [have been] the only realistic reaction open to the actor'.[100] He concluded that the act must have been 'inevitable, unavoidable, and afford[ed] no reasonable opportunity for an alternative course of action that [did] not involve a breach of the law'.[101] Interpreting this requirement in *Latimer*, the court held that while 'the accused need not be placed in the last resort imaginable, ... he must have no reasonable legal alternative.'[102]

In *Re A*, Brooke L.J. applied Sir James Stephen's test: 'the act is needed to avoid inevitable and irreparable evil [and] no more should be done than is reasonably necessary for the purpose to be achieved'.[103] In the context of euthanasia, surely this test could only be met if there were no reasonable alternative way of ending the patient's suffering other than terminating her life. Thus any apparent distinction between the English and Canadian courts on this requirement is without a difference.

b. Imminent peril or inevitable evil

The wholly excusatory Canadian approach requires that 'disaster must be imminent, or harm unavoidable and near. It is not enough that the peril is foreseeable or likely; it must be on the verge of transpiring and virtually certain to occur.'[104] A justificatory approach, though, is free to abandon the requirement of immediacy or urgency which has persisted in the Canadian jurisprudence. As Brooke L.J. observed in *Re A*:

There are sound reasons for holding that the existence of an emergency in the normal sense of the word is not an essential prerequisite for the application of the doctrine of necessity. The principle is one of necessity, not emergency ...[105]

---

[100] *Perka* [1984] 2 S.C.R. 232, 251. Dickson J. distinguished this scenario from one in which the defendant 'was in fact making ... a choice'.

[101] *Perka* [1984] 2 S.C.R. 232, 259. Even this stringent test could be seen as a relaxation of the *Morgentaler* requirement that compliance with the law be 'demonstrably impossible'. Tim Quigley, '*R. v. Latimer*: Hard Cases Make Interesting Law' (1995) 41 Crim. Rep. (4th) 89, 96–8. See *Morgentaler* [1976] 1 S.C.R. 616, 678; *Perka* [1984] 2 S.C.R. 232, 251–2.

[102] 'It may be noted that the requirement involves a realistic appreciation of the alternatives open to a person.' *Latimer* [2001] 1 S.C.R. 3, [30].

[103] *Re A* [2001] Fam. 147, 240 (Eng C.A.), derived from Stephen, above n. 63, 24. For the full quotation, see above, text accompanying n. 63.

[104] *Latimer* [2001] 1 S.C.R. 3, [29]. See also, *Perka* [1984] 2 S.C.R. 232, 273–4 (Wilson J.); Horder, above n. 92, 161; Trotter, above n. 82, 824. For further examples of this requirement, see *Morgentaler* [1976] 1 S.C.R. 616, 678; *Perka*, above, 251 (Dickson J.).

[105] *Re A* [2001] Fam. 147, 239 (Eng C.A.), citing *Re F (Mental Patient: Sterilisation)* [1990] 2 A.C. 1, 75d; L.C.E.W., *Report on Criminal Law: Legislating the Criminal Code: Offences against the*

Indeed, as George Fletcher has observed, in cases in which the actor is a third party, such as a doctor, 'the only relevant doctrine of necessity is that of justification. A finding of involuntary conduct is precluded because the actor's personal interests are not at stake.'[106] It is precisely for this reason that the Dutch courts have rejected duress, the excusatory form of the defence of *overmacht*, in euthanasia cases involving doctors.[107]

c. Personal limitation

Whether as part of the Canadian excusatory imminent peril requirement, or within the English 'inevitable' evil component of the 'no reasonable alternative' test, the possible existence of a 'personal limitation' on the operation of the defence is of importance in the euthanasia context. The facts of the decided cases make clear that there is no such limitation in either the English or Canadian cases.[108] That is, it is not necessary that the defendant himself be in peril.[109] In neither the abortion cases,[110] nor *Latimer*, nor *Re A* was the defendant or prospective defendant himself in peril. Rather it was the patient (or in *Latimer*, the defendant's daughter) who faced peril. In *Perka*, the Supreme Court of Canada expressly recognized that altruism, as well as self-preservation, could compel the defendant to break the law.[111]

III. Explaining the Different Roads Taken

Why was the defence of necessity the mechanism of legal change used by the Dutch courts? In part, the answer is that courts can only respond to the cases before them. Rather than bringing judicial proceedings in an attempt to secure legal euthanasia or assisted suicide in advance – using constitutionally entrenched human rights – the Dutch courts responded instead to criminal cases involving individual physicians. The question of the *duties* owed by Dutch physicians to their patients (including the duty to relieve suffering), rather than the *rights* of those patients, was therefore at the forefront of Dutch developments.[112]

Person and General Principles, No. 218 (1993) 63–64, [35.5]–[35.6]; *Perka* [1984] 2 S.C.R. 232, 273–4 (Wilson J.). See also, Simon Gardner, 'Necessity's Newest Inventions' (1991) 11 *Ox. J. Legal Studies* 125, 134.

106 Fletcher, above n. 49, 1278.   107 See above n. 27.

108 Guy, above n. 78, 501–2; Barney Sneiderman & Raymond Deutscher, 'Dr. Nancy Morrison and Her Dying Patient: A Case of Medical Necessity' (2002) 10 *Health L.J.* 1, [49], n. 57.

109 Guy, above n. 78, (although noting that the court's language in *Latimer* [2001] 1 S.C.R. 3, [32], [33], [38] is less than helpful in clarifying this point); Sneiderman & Deutscher, above n. 108.

110 See *Bourne* [1939] 1 K.B. 687, [1938] 3 All E.R. 615 (Eng. C.C.A.); *Morgentaler* [1976] 1 S.C.R. 616. On whether *Morgentaler* explicitly decides this point, see Guy, above n. 78, 503–4, n. 66.

111 *Perka* [1984] 2 S.C.R. 232, 249.

112 See Kimsma & Van Leeuwen, above n. 2, 37 (comparing the 'domination of a moral and legal discussion on rights' in the United States with the ethical debate in the Netherlands).

But how might one explain the varying interpretations of the Dutch and common law defences of necessity in the context of euthanasia? And why were there no Dutch parallels to the challenges to criminal prohibitions on assisted suicide which were brought by patients using constitutionally entrenched human rights in Canada, the United States, and the United Kingdom?[113] This section attempts to provide some answers to these difficult questions.

A. Why has the common law defence of necessity excluded euthanasia?

1. Alternatives to the use of necessity at common law

The existence of alternative methods of exonerating doctors charged with murder or assisting suicide could provide a pragmatic answer to the question why the common law defence of necessity has excluded euthanasia. In place of reliance on the defence of necessity, common law judges have preferred to use covert tools, holding or suggesting that a doctor performing euthanasia did not *intend* the death of her patient, or did not *cause* the death.[114] Such escape routes are only available when the medication used can be used to relieve pain, in addition to causing death. When a euthanaticum is used,[115] such as potassium chloride, these covert tools are unavailable,[116] and convictions have ensued.[117] The use of these covert

---

[113] *Rodriguez v. British Columbia (Attorney-General)* [1993] 3 S.C.R. 519; *Washington v. Glucksberg* (1997) 521 U.S. 702; *Vacco v. Quill* (1997) 521 U.S. 793; *R. (on the application of Pretty) v. D.P.P.* [2002] 1 A.C. 800; *Pretty v. U.K.* (2002) 35 E.H.R.R. 1 (Eur. Ct. H.R.). See Chapter 2, Section I.B.

[114] See, e.g., *Kansas v. Naramore* (1998) 965 P.2d 211, 213–14 (Kansas C.A.); *Compassion in Dying v. Washington* (1996) 79 F.3d 790, 822 (9th Cir. en banc); *Adams (Bodkin)* [1957] Crim. L.R. 365 (Central Crim. Ct. (Eng.)); *Airedale NHS Trust v. Bland* [1993] A.C. 789, 867 (Lord Goff); *Re A* [2001] Fam. 147, 251, 259 (Eng C.A., Robert Walker L.J.); Anthony Arlidge, 'The Trial of Dr David Moor' [2000] *Crim. L.R.* 31, 38–9; *Rodriguez v. British Columbia (Attorney-General)* [1993] 3 S.C.R. 519, [57]; *Auckland Area Health Board v. Attorney-General* [1993] 1 N.Z.L.R. 235, 252, 253 (N.Z.H.C.). See generally, Alister Browne, 'Causation, Intention, and Active Euthanasia' (2006) 15 *Camb. Q. Healthcare Ethics* 71; David Price, 'Euthanasia, Pain Relief and Double Effect' (1997) 17 *Legal Stud.* 323; Williams, above n. 46, 322; Margaret Otlowski, *Voluntary Euthanasia and the Common Law* (Oxford: Oxford Univ. Press, 1997) 170–84. The trial judge in *Adams*, Devlin J. (later Lord Devlin) wrote of his experiences in Patrick Devlin, *Easing the Passing: The Trial of Dr. John Bodkin Adams* (London: Bodley Head, 1985). See also, Henry Palmer, 'Dr Adams' Trial for Murder' [1957] *Crim. L.R.* 365, 375; A.W. Brian Simpson, 'Euthanasia for Sale?' (1986) 84 *Mich. L. Rev.* 807. On *Moor*, see also, J.C. Smith, 'A Comment on Moor's case' [2000] *Crim. L.R.* 41; James Goss, 'A Postscript to the Trial of Dr David Moor' [2000] *Crim. L.R.* 568.

[115] A drug 'whose only medical purpose in the circumstances is to cause death'. Griffiths, Weyers & Adams, above n. 21, [3.2.3].

[116] Although Robert Walker L.J. did make some attempt to bend the concept of intention in *Re A*, a case when the outcome was certain death for the weaker twin. *Re A* [2001] Fam. 147, 251, 259 (Eng C.A.).

[117] See, e.g., *Cox* (1992) 12 B.M.L.R. 38 (Winchester (Eng.) Crown Ct.); Dirk Johnson, 'Kevorkian Sentenced to 10 to 25 Years in Prison' *N.Y. Times*, 14 Apr. 1999, A1. This is not invariably the case, however. For example, in 1990, the prosecution discontinued its case against Dr. Lodwig, an English doctor who had reportedly injected his patient, who was suffering from terminal cancer, with potassium chloride. See Diana Brahams, 'The reluctant survivor: Part 1' (1990) 140(6453) *New L.J.* 586, 586–7 (both causation and intention were apparently doubted).

tools has a lamentable distorting effect on the criminal law governing intention and causation.[118]

Another covert tool which may play a role in this context is jury nullification, that is, 'the jury's power to acquit on compassionate grounds, even if instructed that the accused has no defence in law'.[119] Perhaps because of the risk of jury nullification, prosecutors have been willing to accept guilty pleas to lesser offences, thus avoiding the prospect of a jury trial.[120] Selective charging decisions may also make convictions unlikely.[121] In some cases prosecutors may decide not

---

[118] See Otlowski, above n. 114, 174; Ian Kennedy & Andrew Grubb, *Medical Law* (3rd edn.) (London: Butterworths, 2000) 1961–3; Williams, above n. 46, 286, 289–90; Andrew Ashworth, 'Criminal Liability in a Medical Context' in A.P. Simester & A.T.H. Smith, eds., *Harm and Culpability* (Oxford: Oxford Univ. Press, 1996) 173.

[119] Barney Sneiderman, John C. Irvine & Philip H. Osborne, *Canadian Medical Law: An Introduction for Physicians, Nurses and other Health Care Professionals* (3rd edn.) (Scarborough, Ont.: Carswell, 2003) 637. See also, Walter W. Steele & Bill B. Hill, 'A Plea for A Legal Right to Die' (1976) 29 *Okla. L. Rev.* 328, 337–8; Kent Roach, 'Crime and Punishment in the Latimer Case' (2001) 64 *Sask. L. Rev.* 469, 473–6. See, e.g., the cases listed by Clay S. Conrad, 'Jury Nullification as a Defense Strategy' (1995) 2 *Tex. Forum on Civ. Lib. & Civ. Rts.* 1, 30–1; Margaret Otlowski, 'The Effectiveness of Legal Control of Euthanasia: Lessons from Comparative Law' in Klijn, above n. 1, 137, 144, n. 28; Margaret Otlowski, 'Mercy Killing Cases in the Australian Criminal Justice System' (1993) 17 *Crim. L.J.* 10, 13–28; Kenneth R. Thomas, 'Confronting End-of-Life Decisions: Should We Expand the Right to Die?' (May 1997) 44 *Fed. Law.* 30, 34 (describing 'indications that the juries that have acquitted Dr. Kevorkian have engaged in jury nullification, finding that all the elements of the crime had been established, but failing to convict anyway'). See also, Irwin A. Horowitz et al., 'Jury Nullification: Legal and Psychological Perspectives' (2001) 66 *Brooklyn L. Rev.* 1207, 1232–7 (discussing earlier studies by Horowitz demonstrating that mock jurors in a euthanasia case were more likely to acquit if given a strong instruction on jury nullification powers). See Irwin A. Horowitz, 'The Effect of Jury Nullification Instruction on Verdicts and Jury Functioning in Criminal Trials' (1985) 9 *Law & Hum. Behav.* 25; Irwin A. Horowitz, 'Jury Nullification: The Impact of Judicial Instructions, Arguments, and Challenges on Jury Decision Making' (1988) 12 *Law & Hum. Behav.* 439.

[120] See House of Lords Select Committee on Medical Ethics, *Report*, HL Paper 21-I (Session 1993–1994) [128] (in 22 'mercy-killing' cases between 1982 and 1991, only one defendant was convicted of murder (which carries a mandatory life sentence), charges were downgraded to lesser offences in the other cases, resulting in probation or suspended sentences; all of the defendants were family members or acquaintances); Julia Pugliese, 'Don't Ask – Don't Tell: The Secret Practice of Physician-Assisted Suicide' (1993) 44 *Hastings L.J.* 1291, 1299, n. 49 (describing 6 cases in which charges were downgraded or dropped). In Canada, see, e.g., the unreported cases of *Mataya* 24 Aug. 1992 (Ont. Ct. of Justice) (guilty plea accepted to administering a noxious thing with intent to endanger the life of the victim on first degree murder charge) and *de la Rocha* 2 Apr. 1993 (Ont. Gen. Div.) (second degree murder charge withdrawn, defendant doctor pleaded guilty to administering a noxious thing with intent to endanger the life of the victim), both discussed in *Latimer* (1995) 126 D.L.R. (4th) 203, [126]–[131] (Sask. C.A., Bayda C.J.S., dissenting) and Sneiderman & Deutscher, above n. 108, [42]–[46]; *Brush* [1995] O.J. No. 656 (Ont. (Prov. Div.) Hamilton) (guilty plea to manslaughter accepted on second degree murder charge); *Myers* 23 Dec. 1994, C.R. 110506 (N.S.S.C.) (guilty plea to manslaughter accepted on second degree murder charge). A similar trend has been noted in France. See Gérard Mémeteau, 'La mort aux trousses' ('Death on your heels') (2000) 3 *Revue de Recherche Juridique et de droit prospectif (J. of Juridical Research and Prospective Law)* 914, 919.

[121] In *Morrison* (1998) 174 N.S.R. (2d) 201 (N.S.S.C.), the patient's doctor injected him with potassium chloride to end horrific terminal suffering which had not been assuaged by huge doses of narcotics and sedatives. There was some evidence that the potassium chloride was not the cause of death (owing to displacement of a catheter), nevertheless the prosecution did not proceed with a

to go forward with a prosecution or bring an indictment, or in the United States the grand jury may refuse to indict.[122]

The existence of alternatives for judges does not really explain the divergence between the common law and Dutch approaches to necessity in the context of euthanasia and assisted suicide. Dutch judges also could have found alternative routes,[123] and Dutch prosecutors could have avoided prosecutions in euthanasia cases as has been done in other jurisdictions. Instead,

perhaps surprisingly, Dutch judges appeared to be receptive to new issues.... Dutch prosecuting authorities did use the prosecution of doctors to explore the boundaries of the law.... [and] subject to directions of the Minister of Justice, have actively sought to accomplish legal developments and clarification by bringing prosecutions.[124]

Many other factors have undoubtedly operated to cause the divergence between the common law and Dutch interpretations of necessity.[125] The next section considers one important factor: the existence of consensus.

2. The role of consensus

What import has the question whether necessity is an excuse, a justification, or possibly both? However the defence is described, all agree that there is a requirement that the defendant had 'no reasonable alternative'.[126] Stephen Coughlan

---

charge of attempted murder, which is what had occurred in *Cox* (1992) 12 B.M.L.R. 38 (Winchester (Eng.) Crown Ct.). The case is discussed in Sneiderman, above n. 73, 530–3; Sneiderman & Deutscher, above n. 108; Jocelyn Downie & Karen Anthony, 'The Push-Me/Pull-You of Euthanasia in Canada: A Chronology of the Nancy Morrison Case' (1998) 7(2) *Health L. Rev.* 16.

[122] See the case involving Timothy Quill, described in *Quill v. Koppell* (1994) 870 F. Supp. 78, 80 (S.D.N.Y.), discussed in Chapter 2, Section I.A; *Dr. X* (1990) (Qué.), discussed in Sneiderman & Deutscher, above n. 108, [81]; Mustafa D. Sayid, 'Euthanasia: A Comparison of the Criminal Laws of Germany, Switzerland and the United States' (1983) 6 *Boston Coll. Int'l & Comp. L. Rev.* 533, 541–2; Otlowski, above n. 114, 146–7. Interestingly, the presence of prosecutorial and judicial 'flexibility' in assisted suicide and euthanasia cases was considered favourably by the European Court of Human Rights in support of the proportionality of a blanket ban on assisted suicide under Article 8(2) of the European Convention. *Pretty v. U.K.* (2002) 35 E.H.R.R. 1, [76]. In France, such cases are often diverted into the disciplinary arena. See Penney Lewis, 'The evolution of assisted dying in France: A third way?' (2005) 13(4) *Med. L. Rev.* 44.

[123] See, e.g., above n. 16 and Griffiths, Bood & Weyers, above n. 4, 162–6, 270–1.

[124] Heleen Weyers, 'Legal recognition of the right to die' in Austen Garwood-Gowers et al., eds., *Contemporary Issues in Healthcare Law and Ethics* (Edinburgh: Elsevier Butterworth-Heinemann, 2005) 253, 264. See also, Griffiths, above n. 1, 186. On prosecutorial decision-making in Dutch euthanasia cases, see Jacqueline M. Cuperus-Bosma et al., 'Physician-assisted Death: Policy-making by the Assembly of Prosecutors General in the Netherlands' (1997) 4 *Eur. J. Health L.* 225; Jacqueline M. Cuperus-Bosma et al., 'Assessment of physician-assisted death by members of the public prosecution in the Netherlands' (1999) 25(1) *J. Med. Ethics* 8; Gerrit van der Wal et al., 'Evaluation of the notification procedure for physician-assisted death in the Netherlands' (1996) 335(22) *New Eng. J. Med.* 1706; Gerrit van der Wal & P.J. van der Maas, 'Empirical Research on Euthanasia and Other Medical End-of-Life Decisions and the Euthanasia Notification Procedure' in Thomasma, above n. 2, 149, 155, 163, 175, 177.

[125] Another possibility may be the suppressive effect of rights discourse on the legalization debate. The political and popular power of rights often partially or wholly eliminates other forms of moral discourse, particularly arguments about duties. See Chapter 3, Section II.A.2.

[126] See above, Section II.C.2.a.

argues that any defendant who can meet this requirement will simultaneously meet the proportionality requirement inherent in necessity as a justification:

Situations where it can plausibly be asserted that the accused had no other reasonable choice are likely to be precisely those where there is near-universal agreement about which social good is greater. If that were not so, the accused's actions would not be seen as the only reasonable way to behave.[127]

Coughlan asserts that this is particularly likely to be true when the defendant acts out of altruism for another person in peril rather than out of fear for himself.[128] Applying this argument to a case of euthanasia, the common law necessity defence in its current guise (whether excuse or justification) will not succeed in the absence of 'near-universal agreement' that relieving severe suffering is more important than respecting the prohibition on actively terminating the patient's life. That is, such agreement is required in order for there to be a plausible assertion that the defendant had no reasonable alternative in such circumstances. One key distinction between the contexts in which the apparently similar[129] Dutch and common law defences of necessity operate is the presence of far greater agreement in Dutch society that the proportionality requirement may, in some circumstances at least, be met in cases of euthanasia. Although agreement is far from universal, the extent of the Dutch consensus is notable[130] and can be contrasted with judicial descriptions of a consensus against legalization in some common law jurisdictions. For example, in *Rodriguez*, Mr. Justice Sopinka stated that 'no new consensus has emerged in society opposing the right of the state to regulate the involvement of others in exercising power over individuals ending their lives', further asserting that there is a 'substantial consensus among western countries, medical organizations

---

[127] Coughlan, above n. 87, 158–9.   [128] Ibid. 159.

[129] The historical evolution of the Dutch and common law defences of necessity may suggest that this similarity is more apparent than real. See George Fletcher, *Basic Concepts of Criminal Law* (Oxford: Oxford Univ. Press, 1998) 138–42. Nevertheless, having evolved similar contours, it is interesting to examine why modern common law judges did not take the route taken in the Netherlands.

[130] Dutch public opinion is strongly in favour of the permissibility of euthanasia. See, e.g., Margo Trappenburg & Joop van Holsteyn, 'The Quest for Limits: Law and Public Opinion on Euthanasia in the Netherlands' in Klijn, above n. 1, 109, 113, nn. 13–14, remarking that '[o]nly a small minority of Dutch citizens of 12 percent opposes euthanasia' in cases of terminal illness. However, this is also true of many common law jurisdictions. See, e.g., House of Lords Select Committee on the Assisted Dying for the Terminally Ill Bill, *Report*, HL Paper 86-I (2005) [215]–[233], App. 7, www.publications. parliament.uk/pa/ld200405/ldselect/ldasdy/86/86i.pdf, accessed 27 July 2006. On the Netherlands, see also, the comments of Leenen [in a personal communication to Cohen-Almagor] 'that gradually a kind of consensus has grown "within a majority"' in Cohen-Almagor, above n. 15, 54, n. 7; Sneiderman & Verhoef, above n. 15, Section VII; de Vries, above n. 23, 368. On the difficulties associated with comparing surveys of attitudes across jurisdictions, see Tore Nilstun et al., 'Surveys on attitudes to active euthanasia and the difficulty of drawing normative conclusions' (2000) 28(2) *Scandinavian J. of Public Health* 111, 111–14; Agnes van der Heide et al., 'End-of-life Decisions in Six European Countries: A research note' in Klijn, above n. 1, 129, 132. On moral consensus in the Netherlands more generally, see James Kennedy, 'The Moral State: How Much Do the Americans and the Dutch Differ?' in Krabbendam & ten Napel, above n. 1, 9, 19, 21.

and our own Law Reform Commission' that the protection of life and the vulnerable requires a prohibition on assisted suicide.[131]

The absence of consensus within the Dutch medical profession precluded the use of the 'medical exception' as a defence to euthanasia.[132] However, in relation to the conflict of duties embedded in the defence of necessity, consensus has played an important role. '[T]he Supreme Court [has] stated more than once that it could not rule on the lawfulness of euthanasia in general in the absence of broad societal consensus.'[133] It may be this consensus, then, that explains why Dutch judges, unlike their common law counterparts, were 'willing to use the legal room for manoeuvre offered by' the defence of necessity.[134]

a. An example of the importance of consensus: existential suffering

The importance of consensus was illustrated in the recent existential suffering or 'tired of life' case *Brongersma*, in which absence of consensus appeared to be a determining factor.[135] Edward Brongersma was an elderly retired Senator whose suicide was assisted by his physician on the grounds of his ' "existential suffering," which was defined by one of the experts at the [subsequent] trial as the unbearable suffering of life in the absence of any clinical cause and without hope of any improvement.'[136] Brongersma's general practitioner, Sutorius, believed that his patient 'was suffering unbearably because of his obsession with his physical decline and hopeless existence'.[137]

The prosecution appealed against the doctor's acquittal[138] on the ground that since the patient's suffering had no clinical origin, the doctor had acted outside of his professional domain.[139] If this were the case, the defence of necessity would be unavailable: 'if there is no disease, there is no patient and, it would seem, no

---

[131] *Rodriguez v. British Columbia (Attorney-General)* [1993] 3 S.C.R. 519, [15], [74]. See also, ibid. [40], [59]–[60]; *R. (on the application of Pretty) v. D.P.P.* [2002] 1 A.C. 800, [28], [101].

[132] See above n. 16.

[133] De Vries, above n. 23, n. 17, citing *Schoonheim*, Supreme Court, 27 Nov. 1984, N.J. 1985, no. 106 and *Pols*, Supreme Court, 21 Oct. 1986, N.J. 1987, no. 607.

[134] Weyers, above n. 124, 265.

[135] Dutch cases are not formally referred to by name, although within the euthanasia literature it is common to discuss *Schoonheim* or *Pols*, for example. Following this convention, the *Brongersma* case should really be called *Sutorius* as this is the defendant's name. But as the most well-known defence lawyer in the euthanasia cases has the same name, this would be confusing, and the case is almost universally referred to as the *Brongersma* case.

[136] De Vries, above n. 23, 384. See also, Maike Möller & Richard Huxtable, 'Euthanasia in the Netherlands: the case of "life fatigue"' (2001) 151(7006) *New L.J.* 1600; Tony Sheldon, ' "Existential" suffering not a justification for euthanasia' (2001) 323 *Br. Med. J.* 1384; Tony Sheldon, 'Doctor convicted of helping patient to commit suicide may be retried' (2002) 325 *Br. Med. J.* 924; Trappenburg & van Holsteyn, above n. 130, 115; Gerrit K. Kimsma & Evert van Leeuwen, 'Shifts in the Direction of Dutch Bioethics: Forward or Backward?' (2005) 14 *Camb. Q. Healthcare Ethics* 292, 294–6.

[137] Tony Sheldon, 'Being "tired of life" is not grounds for euthanasia' (2003) 326 *Br. Med. J.* 71.

[138] *Brongersma*, District Court, Haarlem, 30 Oct. 2000, *Tijdschrift voor Gezondheidsrecht (J. of Health Law)* 2001, no. 21.

[139] Donald van Tol, 'Physician-Assisted Suicide: The Brongersma Case' (2001) 5 *Newsletter MBPSL* 3.

medical duty to alleviate suffering such as to place a physician in a potential conflict of duties'.[140] The Appeals Court commissioned two expert witnesses to answer three questions:

(1) whether a doctor could legitimately honor a request for euthanasia in the absence of any physical or psychological illness; (2) whether it is part of a doctor's function to assist people, whose suffering is primarily characterized by psychological factors, such as the daily experience of an empty and lonely existence and the fear that it may continue for many years; and (3) whether there is a consensus among doctors about the answer to these [two] questions.[141]

As we have already seen, the necessity defence is restricted to doctors as only they are faced with the relevant conflict of duties.[142] Thus only if there is consensus that existential suffering forms part of the remit of doctors will the defence of necessity be available. In other words, the doctor, by virtue of her professional role, has a duty to relieve only certain kinds of suffering. Prior to *Brongersma*, it was clear that this duty included suffering of non-somatic origin.[143] But in the absence of consensus that the doctor's duty to relieve suffering includes a duty to relieve *existential* suffering, the necessity defence cannot be used in cases of existential suffering.[144] As the experts agreed that no such consensus existed among doctors, the doctor was convicted.[145] Were such a consensus to develop, the position could be revisited.[146] This prospect came closer in 2005 with the

---

[140] Gevers, above n. 21, 97.

[141] De Vries, above n. 23, 386–7, citing *Brongersma*, Court of Appeals, Amsterdam, 6 Dec. 2001, *Tijdschrift voor Gezondheidsrecht (J. of Health Law)* 2002, no. 17.

[142] See above, text accompanying nn. 26–27.

[143] See above, text accompanying n. 21. In *Brongersma*, the Supreme Court held that the defence only applies if the patient is suffering as a result of a 'classifiable physical or mental condition'. *Brongersma*, Supreme Court, 24 Dec. 2002, N.J. 2003, no. 167, discussed in Tony Sheldon, 'Dutch euthanasia law should apply to patients "suffering through living," report says' (2005) 330 *Br. Med. J.* 61.

[144] The distinction between existential and other types of psychological suffering may be exceedingly hard to draw. Rob Schwitters, 'Medical Competence as a restriction on physician-assisted suicide: the Brongersma case' (2003) 7 *Newsletter MBPSL* 2. The distinction may also be easily manipulable. Schwitters argues that 'in the case of elderly people, it is almost always possible to identify a medical cause to their suffering. Some have suggested that if Brongersma's doctor had emphasized the various medical problems the elderly man experienced, he would have had no difficulty in securing legal acceptance of his decision.' See also, Sheldon, above n. 137 ('Doctors and ethicists have already attacked the judgment...GPs, they argue, treat patients every day whose complaints cannot be linked to a classifiable disorder.').

[145] The experts in the trial court had also reported a lack of such consensus. See van Tol, above n. 139, 4; Tony Sheldon, 'Dutch GP cleared after helping to end man's "hopeless existence"' (2000) 321 *Br. Med. J.* 1174. In the research carried out by Trappenburg & van Holsteyn, above n. 130, 120–1, public opinion was clearly against the permissibility of euthanasia or assisted suicide in cases of existential suffering.

[146] 'The court appears to keep the door open for lawful euthanasia if and when there is a consensus among doctors as to whether existential suffering is suffering of a medical or clinical nature. If so, it may well be that the necessity defense could extend to such cases.' De Vries, above n. 23, n. 126. For the situation in practice, see Mette L. Rurup et al., 'When being "tired of living" plays an important role in a request for euthanasia or physician-assisted suicide: patient characteristics and the physician's

publication of a report by the Royal Dutch Medical Association entitled *Suffering Through Living*, which stated that 'no reason can be given to exclude situations of such suffering from a doctor's area of competence'.[147]

Not only does *Brongersma* illustrate the importance of consensus in relation to types of suffering for which euthanasia may be permitted, but it also illustrates the significance of the Dutch consensus that only doctors should be allowed to perform euthanasia.[148] Having decided that the doctor's duty to relieve suffering does not extend to the relief of existential suffering, the courts could have revisited the rule that doctors are the sole providers of euthanasia.[149] If existential suffering could constitute unbearable and hopeless suffering (but not suffering that doctors have a duty to relieve) might some other professional have a duty to relieve existential suffering? A social worker perhaps, if diagnosis does not require clinical expertise?[150]

b. The democracy problem

Could the presence of consensus in the Netherlands also explain the relative lack of Dutch judicial concern over 'the democracy problem'?[151] In common law jurisdictions, both academic commentators[152] and, to a lesser extent, judges[153] have raised concerns over 'the democracy problem' in relation to the justificatory defence of necessity. The problem is that by determining whether illegal conduct is morally justified as part of their evaluation of the availability of the defence of

decision' (2005) 74(2) *Health Policy* 157; Mette L. Rurup et al., 'Requests for euthanasia or physician-assisted suicide from older persons who do not have a severe disease: an interview study' (2005) 35(5) *Psychol. Med.* 665.

[147] Royal Dutch Medical Association, *Op zoek naar normen voor het handelen van artsen bij vragen om hulp bij levensbeëindiging in geval van lijden aan het leven (In search of standards for the treatment by doctors of requests for help in ending life because of suffering through living)* (2005), discussed in Sheldon, above n. 143. The report does not suggest that consensus has already been achieved. '[The] report recommends caution, saying that doctors currently lack sufficient expertise and that their roles remain unclear. It recommends drawing up protocols by which to judge "suffering through living" cases and collecting and analysing further data. In the meantime it recommends an "extra phase" to treatment, where therapeutic and social solutions can first be sought.' Sheldon, ibid.

[148] 'The consensus in the Netherlands, beginning in the 1980s and continuing through today, sees the doctor as the only suitable person to whom euthanasia and decisions about life and death can be trusted.' De Vries, above n. 23, 389, citing James Kennedy, *Een Weloverwogen Dood – Euthanasie in Nederland (A Well-Considered Death: Euthanasia in the Netherlands)* (Amsterdam: Uitgeverij Bert Bakker, 2002) 128–35. See above, text accompanying nn. 26–27.

[149] However, this was unlikely given the limited powers of the Supreme Court in cassation. The court can only review questions of law. Judicial Organization Act 1827, Art. 99. See also, Nijboer, above n. 28, 428–9.

[150] 'The Supreme Court reasoned that a physician has no expertise to assess the un-bearable nature of a person's existential suffering; therefore, a physician who ends the life of such an individual cannot be exonerated.' G.K. Kimsma, 'Euthanasia for existential reasons' (2006) 13(1) *Lahey Clinic Med. Ethics* 1, 2.   [151] The term is from Gardner, above n. 105, 132.

[152] See, e.g., Gardner, ibid. 132–5; Wicks, above n. 61, 27–32; Rogers, above n. 61, 522–4; Trotter, above n. 82, 840.

[153] See, e.g., *Perka* [1984] 2 S.C.R. 232, 248 (Dickson J.), citing *Morgentaler* [1976] 1 S.C.R. 616, 678 (Dickson J.); *Southwark London Borough Council v. Williams* [1971] Ch. 734, 746 (Eng. C.A., Edmund Davies L.J.).

necessity, 'the courts are making (rather than interpreting) law and thus are adopting the legislative role of Parliament'.[154] In the context of euthanasia in common law jurisdictions, it is quite clear that '[s]uccessive governments, and Parliaments, have set their face against euthanasia.'[155] The democracy problem is therefore more acute in this context than it was, for example, in relation to abortion in *Bourne*, as Parliament had already decided that an exception to the crime of child destruction existed when the mother's life was in danger.[156] The democracy problem, then, may provide a further reason for the divergence between the judicial approaches in the Netherlands and the common law world.

B. Why did the Dutch not use constitutionally entrenched rights as the mechanism of legalization?

Critics of the Dutch system wrongly describe the process of legal change as rights-based, perhaps in an attempt to make its perceived failings more relevant to the debate surrounding the unsuccessful use of constitutionally entrenched rights to overturn criminal prohibitions on assisted suicide in Canada, the United States, and the United Kingdom, which was discussed in Chapters 2 and 3.[157] For example, a 1998 Report to the U.S. House of Representatives Judiciary Subcommittee on the Constitution entitled *Physician-Assisted Suicide and Euthanasia in the Netherlands* stated:

The acceptance in the Netherlands of a right to physician-assisted suicide for terminally-ill, competent patients has led the Dutch to embrace physician-assisted suicide for the chronically-ill, the elderly and those who are suffering mentally.[158]

---

[154] Wicks, above n. 61, 28.

[155] *Re A* [2001] Fam. 147, 211 (Eng C.A., Brooke L.J.). See, e.g., the reaction of the federal Parliament in Australia to the Northern Territory's legislation permitting voluntary active euthanasia. Euthanasia Laws Act 1997 (Cth.), repealing Rights of the Terminally Ill Act 1995 (N.Terr.), discussed in Chapter 6, Section VI.C.

[156] See above n. 59 and Gardner, above n. 105, 133, applying to *Bourne* [1939] 1 K.B. 687, [1938] 3 All E.R. 615 (Eng. C.C.A.) the first limb of Fletcher's bi-partite test for overcoming the democracy problem: 'The first test is whether the rule shows signs of being the product of detailed modern reflection by the legislature. If it does, the democracy problem will lead to justification being denied; but otherwise, it may be allowed. As an observation about actual judicial practice, there is almost certainly some truth in this analysis.' Gardner, ibid., citing Fletcher, *Rethinking Criminal Law*, above n. 88, 792–8. The second test is the requirement of imminent peril. Gardner, ibid. 134. This requirement is discussed above, Section II.C.2.b, and is similarly fatal in the context of euthanasia.

[157] See above n. 113.

[158] A report of Chairman Charles T. Canady to the House Judiciary Subcommittee on the Constitution, of the Committee on the Judiciary, House of Representatives, 104th Congress, 2nd Session, Sept. 1996; Executive Summary published as 'Physician-Assisted Suicide and Euthanasia in the Netherlands: A Report to the House Judiciary Subcommittee on the Constitution' (1998) 14 *Issues in Law & Med.* 301, 302–3. See also, Neil M. Gorsuch, 'The Legalization of Assisted Suicide and the Law of Unintended Consequences: A Review of the Dutch and Oregon Experiments and Leading Utilitarian Arguments For Legal Change' [2004] *Wis. L. Rev.* 1347, 1368. Critics are not the only ones to describe the Dutch system as rights-based. See, e.g., Gerrit K. Kimsma & B.J. van Duin, 'Teaching Euthanasia: The Integration of the Practice of Euthanasia into Grief, Death and Dying Curricula of Post-Graduate Family Medicine Training' in Thomasma, above n. 2, 105, 106.

Less explicitly, but with similar effect, Ira Byock asserts that:

Unless society with the medical profession can effectively respond to suffering within [those groups of patients who would not be eligible for physician-assisted suicide (PAS) under current proposals] in alternative ways, it will become mandatory to extend the service of PAS or euthanasia to them. Indeed, once PAS is made available to one group, the social ethics based on rights will necessitate such extensions and they can be predicted from the Netherlands experience.[159]

This is an argument based on the difficulty of limiting a right to assisted suicide once it is recognized. Legalization in the Netherlands was not achieved using the mechanism of constitutionally entrenched rights, and the Dutch experience can tell us little about the difficulties associated with placing such limits on rights.[160] Why, though, were rights not used as a mechanism of legal change in the Netherlands? The next two sections suggest some possible legal, strategic, and cultural answers to this question.

1. Legal and strategic arguments

Constitutionally entrenched rights were not used as the mechanism of legalization in the Netherlands, despite the presence of relevant rights in the Netherlands Constitution,[161] and the entrenchment of both the European Convention on Human Rights[162] and the International Covenant on Civil and Political Rights.[163] In relation to the Netherlands Constitution, Article 120 provides that 'the constitutionality of Acts of Parliament and treaties shall not be reviewed by the courts.'[164] This unavailability of 'constitutional judicial review'[165] means that a patient cannot bring a claim under the Constitution that prohibitions on euthanasia or assisted suicide violate her constitutional rights.[166]

In theory, such a challenge could have been brought using the European Convention on Human Rights (ECHR). On the contrary, the ECHR seems to have been seen as a potential restriction on legalization, rather than as a mechanism

---

[159] Ira Byock, 'Physician-Assisted Suicide Is *Not* an Acceptable Practice for Physicians' in Robert Weir, ed., *Physician-Assisted Suicide* (Bloomington: Indiana Univ. Press, 1997) 107, 127.

[160] See, instead, Chapter 3, Section II.A.4.b and Chapter 6, Sections II and V.

[161] Constitution of the Kingdom of the Netherlands of 24 August 1815, Stb. 45, as amended by the law of 29 March 1996, Stb. 218. For an English translation, see www.minbzk.nl/contents/pages/6156/grondwet_UK_6–02.pdf, accessed 29 July 2006. Ch. I of the Constitution contains a broad right to equal treatment (Art. 1), a right to free manifestation of religion or belief (Art. 6), a right to privacy (Art. 10) and a right to inviolability of the person (Art. 11).

[162] The Netherlands was one of the original signatories to the European Convention on Human Rights on 4 Nov. 1950. Ratification occurred on 31 Aug. 1954. See http://conventions.coe.int/Treaty/Commun/ChercheSig.asp?NT=005&CM=8&DF=6/27/2006&CL=ENG, accessed 27 June 2006.

[163] Signed by the Netherlands on 25 June 1969 and ratified on 11 Dec. 1978. See www.ohchr.org/english/law/ccpr-ratify.htm, accessed 27 June 2006.

[164] Constitution of the Kingdom of the Netherlands, above n. 161, Art. 120. See E.A. Alkema, 'Constitutional Law' in Chorus, above n. 28, 291, 322–3.   [165] De Vries, above n. 23, 366.

[166] Ibid. 368–9.

of legalization. Both Dutch[167] and foreign[168] commentators have examined the issue of the compatibility of Dutch law and practice with the right to life found in Article 2 of the ECHR.[169] The Dutch government also addressed this issue during the passage of the Termination of Life on Request and Assisted Suicide (Review Procedures) Act 2001.[170] However, the use of other ECHR rights to *achieve* legal change was not attempted, nor has it been at the forefront of debate. The reasons for this are unclear, but one might speculate that success using this mechanism was seen as unlikely.[171] In addition, the preoccupation with Article 2 suggests that the choice not to use the ECHR as a mechanism to achieve legal change might have been influenced by the possibility that any such attempt might not only have been unsuccessful, but that the European Court of Human Rights might have taken the opportunity to declare that legalization would violate Article 2. Finally, the medical profession, which played a 'very active role . . . in the process of legalization'[172] using the mechanism of the duty-based defence of necessity, might have been unwilling to support legalization founded on the rights of the patient.

[167] Griffiths, Bood & Weyers, above n. 4, 169–70, 174–76; Leenen, above n. 16, 130; H.J.J. Leenen, 'Dying with Dignity: Developments in the Field of Euthanasia in the Netherlands' (1989) 8 *Med. Law* 517, 519; Henk Jochemsen, 'Why euthanasia should not be legalized: A reflection on the Dutch experiment' in David N. Weisstub et al., eds., *Aging: Decisions at the End of Life* (Dordrecht: Kluwer Academic Publishers, 2001) 67, 86, n. 1; Wöretshofer & Borgers, above n. 6, 15–17; Jozef H.H.M. Dorscheidt, 'Assessment Procedures Regarding End-of-Life Decisions in Neonatology in the Netherlands' (2005) 24 *Med. & L.* 803, 812–24.

[168] Smies, above n. 15, 45–63; John Keown, *Euthanasia, Ethics, and Public Policy* (Cambridge: Cambridge Univ. Press, 2002) 192; J. Velaers, 'Het leven, de dood en de grondrechten – juridische beschowing over zelfdoding en euthanasia' ('Life, death and fundamental rights – juridical discourse on suicide and euthanasia') in J. Velaers, ed., *Over zichzelf beschikken? Juridische en ethische bijdragen over het leven, het lichaam en de dood (Self determination? Juridical and ethical essays on life, the body and death)* (Antwerp: Maklu, 1996) 469, 573, discussed briefly by Jochemsen, above n. 167, 86, n. 1.

[169] One other ECHR right is relevant to the Dutch debate over euthanasia, but again it is as a limitation on Dutch law and practice: the privilege against self-incrimination found in the fair trial guarantee in Article 6 of the ECHR, and its impact on the requirements that deaths caused by euthanasia must be reported to the authorities. Griffiths, Bood & Weyers, above n. 4, 116–17, 344–5 (discussing the *Kadijk* case which is examined in detail in Chapter 6, Section III.B.1). See also, Wöretshofer & Borgers, above n. 6, 17–20. On this issue, see *Zoon v. the Netherlands*, Application No. 29202/95, 14 Jan. 1998 (Eur. Comm. H.R.) (application arguing that the reporting obligation violated the applicant's right not to incriminate himself was declared inadmissible as the applicant had failed to exhaust domestic remedies).

[170] Kim Goossens, 'The ECHR Rejects the "Right to Die"' (2002) 6 *Newsletter MBPSL* 2 ('In the Netherlands, the government argued during the legislative process that the proposed law was not at odds with the Convention Rights; it assumed that article 2 of the Convention, which guarantees the right to life, includes a right to die.'). See also, Netherlands Ministry of Foreign Affairs, above n. 21, § 17 ('Performing euthanasia in response to a voluntary request from a patient does not constitute intentional deprivation of life within the meaning of [Article 2 of the ECHR]'); Herman Nys, 'Physician Involvement in a Patient's Death: A Continental European Perspective' (1999) 7 *Med. L. Rev.* 208, 214–16.   [171] De Vries, above n. 23, n. 8.

[172] John Griffiths, 'Comparative Reflections: Is the Dutch Case Unique?' in Klijn, above n. 1, 197, 203.

2. Cultural arguments

Perhaps cultural arguments may assist in explaining why the Dutch declined to use constitutionally entrenched rights as the mechanism of legalization? John Griffiths, Alex Bood, and Heleen Weyers emphasize the Dutch tactics of depoliticization of contentious issues and the Dutch distaste for confrontation.[173] In reflections on the significance of the Dutch experience for other jurisdictions, they observe:

A[n] important characteristic of Dutch society concerns the level of confidence in public institutions and in professions. It seems no accident that legalization of euthanasia is conceived in the United States, for example, in terms of the rights of *patients* (with doctors' organizations often prominent in opposition) whereas in the Netherlands the public discussion concerns the scope of the professional discretion of *doctors* (doctors having from the beginning been prominent in the movement for legalization). On the whole, the Dutch seem comfortable with the idea that doctors can be trusted with the discretion to perform euthanasia, so that the public debate concerns the boundaries of this professional discretion and the sorts of procedural controls to which it should be subjected.[174]

This prominent role of doctors and the medical profession in the process of legal change[175] also helps explain the centrality of the doctor's duty to relieve suffering in the process of legal change: 'The issue was legally formulated not so much in terms of what patients have a right to demand as in terms of what doctors are authorized to do.'[176]

3. The role of other arguments in the Dutch debate

Most Dutch doctors are undoubtedly sensitive to and respectful of the rights of their patients,[177] and the rights debate over euthanasia certainly exists in the Netherlands, but as we have already seen, rights were not the primary mechanism of legalization. Instead, the rights debate over euthanasia is 'a political debate, taking place in all forums but the judicial forum.'[178] Although rights were not used as the mechanism for legal change in the Netherlands, it would be a mistake to assume that they are not relevant to the legal debate in the Netherlands and to the shape of the Dutch regulation of assisted dying.

---

[173] Griffiths, Bood & Weyers, above n. 4, 86–8.   [174] Ibid. 304 (emphasis in original).

[175] See above, text accompanying n. 1.

[176] Griffiths, Weyers & Adams, above n. 21, [3.2.3.3]. See also, Govert den Hartogh, 'Euthanasia: Reflections on the Dutch Discussion' in Raphael Cohen-Almagor, ed., *Medical Ethics at the Dawn of the 21st Century* (New York: New York Academy of Sciences, 2000) 174, 177.

[177] Patients' rights are generally well-protected in Dutch law. See the discussion of the Law on Contracts for Medical Care (Wet op de geneeskundige behandelingsovereenkomst) in L.F. Markenstein, 'The Codification in the Netherlands of the Principal Rights of Patients: A Critical Review' (1995) 2(1) *Eur. J. Health L.* 33. According to anthropologist Robert Pool, the importance of the right to self-determination in Dutch culture helps explain the desire for control over the time and manner of death which provokes many euthanasia requests. Robert Pool, *Negotiating a Good Death: Euthanasia in the Netherlands* (Binghamton, N.Y.: The Haworth Press, 2000) 210.

[178] De Vries, above n. 23, 369.

Rights, then, are relevant in the Dutch euthanasia context, but not as mechanisms for changing the law. For example, when discussing the principle of autonomy, Griffiths, Bood, and Weyers state:

Appeal to the principle of autonomy is not meant as an appeal to an existing legal right. Those who make use of the argument use it either as a moral principle considered to be of such heavy weight that it must be taken as a starting point for the regulation of euthanasia, or as a legal principle already implicit in the law as a whole.[179]

a. Autonomy

Despite impassioned reliance on autonomy in the Dutch academic literature and public debate and also as a basis for proposed (but ultimately unsuccessful) legislative reform, '[i]n the case law, the principle of autonomy plays a more limited role that it does in the public debate.'[180] Govert den Hartogh observes that 'the dominant view on the morality of euthanasia [based on the patient's autonomy] has never been accepted by the law or by medical practice'.[181]

Dutch courts have been unwilling to override the criminal prohibition against killing on request on the grounds of patient autonomy. The conflict of duties which forms the basis of the defence of necessity is a conflict between the duty to preserve life and the duty to relieve suffering, rather than a duty to respect the patient's autonomous choice.[182] Although the right to autonomy received some attention in the lower courts, in *Schoonheim*, the Supreme Court rejected the defence of substantial violation of the law which relied on a right to autonomy.[183] In his commentary on the *Pols* case, Attorney General Remmelink stated that '[t]he urgent wish of the patient taken by itself definitely is not a justification in these matters.'[184]

The decision of the Supreme Court in the existential suffering case of *Brongersma* confirms the non-dominant role played by autonomy.[185] If autonomy were the

---

[179] Griffiths, Bood & Weyers, above n. 4, 168–9.

[180] Griffiths, Bood & Weyers, ibid. 170. See also, Jurriaan de Haan, 'The Ethics of Euthanasia: Advocates' Perspectives' (2002) 16(2) *Bioethics* 154, 156 (describing the pure autonomy view 'held by some very influential advocates of euthanasia in the Netherlands... [including] health care lawyers like Leenen and patients' organizations such as the Dutch Society for Voluntary Euthanasia'); Loes Kater et al., 'Health care ethics and health law in the Dutch discussion on end-of-life decisions: a historical analysis of the dynamics and development of both disciplines' (2003) 34 *Stud. Hist. Phil. Biol. & Biomed. Sci.* 669, 679–80.   [181] Den Hartogh, above n. 176, 176.

[182] Den Hartogh, ibid. 177; Griffiths, Bood & Weyers, above n. 4, 170–1, citing *Chabot*, Supreme Court, 21 June 1994, N.J. 1994, no. 656, translated in Griffiths, Bood & Weyers, ibid., App. II-2, 333 ('a doctor may be in a situation of necessity if he has to choose between the duty to preserve life and the duty as a doctor to do everything possible to relieve the unbearable and hopeless suffering of a patient committed to his care'). See also, Griffiths, 'Assisted suicide in the Netherlands', above n. 21, 236. There are Dutch scholars who disagree with this characterization of the conflict of duties. See Griffiths, Bood & Weyers, above n. 4, 171, n. 41.   [183] See above n. 16.

[184] *Pols*, Supreme Court, 21 Oct. 1986, N.J. 1987, no. 607, 2124, 2129, translated in Bostrom & Lagerwey, above n. 16, 448.

[185] *Brongersma*, Supreme Court, 24 Dec. 2002, N.J. 2003, no. 167, discussed above, Section III.A.2.a. See Möller & Huxtable, above n. 134, describing the trial court's (subsequently overturned)

key, the patient's autonomous decision that life is no longer worth living should have carried greater weight for the court.[186] It is clear, though, that the principle of autonomy does play a part in the Dutch cases. For example, Rob Schwitters points out that the patient's role in determining whether suffering is hopeless and unbearable, in particular by rejecting available treatments,[187] is evidence 'that in the appraisal of euthanasia practices, the principle of autonomy is gaining increasing significance.'[188]

However, the role played by autonomy is not a defining one, and whether conceived as a right or principle, autonomy clearly was not the mechanism of legal change in the Netherlands. It should be added, though, that in the euthanasia cases, there was no need for autonomy to function as a mechanism of legal change, since the offence with which the defendants were charged was the termination of life *upon request*.[189] The presence of an autonomous request was a necessary - pre-requisite – otherwise the defendant would have been charged with murder. In contrast, Chapter 6 examines the use of the defence of necessity as the mechanism of legal change in cases involving neonates and other incompetent patients who are unable to make a request.[190]

b. Respect for life

An alternative explanation for autonomy's non-dominant role in the Dutch debate is based on the concept of respect for life. Griffiths, Bood, and Weyers argue that 'the Dutch euthanasia controversy is influenced to an important extent by what one might call concern for *respect for life*'.[191] Griffiths, Bood, and Weyers suggest that this concept has been under-developed and yet is implicit in the Dutch debate.[192] Briefly, the argument is that the limits which have been placed on autonomous choice in the Netherlands (such as the requirement of 'unbearable and hopeless suffering') cannot wholly be explained by reference to the liberal harm principle,[193] and are better accounted for using the concept of respect for life.[194] 'Where according to the liberal paradigm every form of shortening of life that does not cause harm to others must be tolerated, the principle of respect for

acquittal of Sutorius 'as a profound manifestation of the greater prominence of patient autonomy within medical practice as reflected by the greater role of autonomy within society as a whole.'

[186] Although if the court's holding is restricted to the medical context, it is conceivable that autonomy might play a greater role in existential suffering cases if non-medical euthanasia were permitted. Both of these possibilities seem extremely unlikely. See above, text accompanying nn. 148–150.

[187] See Chapter 6, Section III.A.3.

[188] Schwitters, above n. 32, 106. See also, Welie, above n. 16, 421.

[189] Criminal Code, Art. 293. See above, Section I.A.

[190] See Chapter 6, Section III.B and III.C, and in particular, text accompanying nn. 111–112.

[191] See Griffiths, Bood & Weyers, above n. 4, 189 (emphasis in original). The concept is also discussed in Gerrit van der Wal, 'Unrequested Termination of Life: Is It Permissible?' (1993) 7 *Bioethics* 330, 336.

[192] Griffiths, Bood & Weyers, above n. 4, 192, 195 (acknowledging that greater explicitness would be desirable).   [193] See Chapter 2, Section II.C.1.

[194] See the detailed account of this argument in Griffiths, Bood & Weyers, above n. 4, 189–95.

life allows only those sorts of shortening of life that show respect for life.'[195] In his commentary on the *Pols* case, Attorney General Remmelink suggested that the separate (and lesser) criminal offences of termination of life on request and assisting in suicide[196] protect respect for life rather than the life of the individual: 'assistance in self-killing violates the respect commanded toward life, even though the personal right of life is not violated.'[197]

While it is true that the requirement of unbearable and hopeless suffering provides further confirmation of autonomy's non-dominant position, from a legal perspective the requirement can also be explained as implicit in the use as a mechanism of legal change of the justification of necessity based on the doctor's conflicting duties to preserve life and relieve suffering. Unless the patient's suffering is unbearable and hopeless and no reasonable alternative to relieve her suffering exists, the conflict of duties will not be triggered.[198]

IV. Conclusion

Adoption of the Dutch approach using the defence of necessity seems unlikely in common law jurisdictions. The Dutch either through choice or happenstance have avoided the use of constitutionally entrenched rights as the mechanism of legal change. Although the debate in the Netherlands may reflect similar arguments to those made in terms of rights in other jurisdictions, given that the process of legal change has not, for the most part, reflected such arguments, this would suggest caution with regard to the exportability of the Dutch experience into the rights debate over assisted dying.

---

[195] Griffiths, Bood & Weyers, above n. 4, 192.   [196] See above, Section I.A.

[197] *Pols*, Supreme Court, 21 Oct. 1986, N.J. 1987, no. 607, 2124, 2129, translated in Bostrom & Lagerwey, above n. 16, 448. See also de Vries, above n. 23, 369 ('In cases of euthanasia, the intent of the person carrying through with the action may be regarded as being directed toward life, or the sanctity of life, as compared to murder where the person carrying through with the action has malicious intent toward the individual he seeks to kill and, by implication, has a complete disregard for the sanctity of life').   [198] See above, Section I.B.

5

Compassion

I. Introduction

Jurisprudentially, the main drivers of legal change or attempts at legal change on assisted dying have been rights and the duty-based defence of necessity. An alternative proposal has been made in France, based on the virtue of compassion. This would be a novel basis for legal change which has little precedent. Nonetheless, it warrants some consideration, particularly in light of its proposal in a jurisdiction in which neither rights nor duties are available as drivers of legal change on assisted dying. This chapter will first examine the proposal for legalization on the basis of compassion. The reasons why neither rights nor necessity are likely candidates to drive forward legal change on assisted dying in France will also be considered.

II. CCNE Opinion Number 63

In 1991 the French National Bioethics Advisory Committee (le Comité Consultatif National d'Éthique or CCNE) issued a short opinion concerning a draft resolution on assistance to the dying which had been adopted by a committee of the European Parliament (the Schwartzenberg resolution).[1] In this opinion, the CCNE strongly disapproved of any proposal to legitimize euthanasia, citing the fundamental principle of respect for human dignity as its basis for this unequivocal stance.[2] In January 2000, however, the CCNE reversed its position in a lengthy opinion entitled *End of life, ending life, euthanasia*.[3] Euthanasia could be permissible in certain exceptional circumstances.

[1] Resolution on assistance to the dying, adopted 25 April 1991 by the Commission on the Environment, Public Health and Consumer Protection, European Parliament.

[2] CCNE, *Avis concernant la proposition de résolution sur l'assistance aux mourants, adoptée le 25 avril 1991 au Parlement européen par la Commission de l'environnement, de la santé publique et de la protection des consommateurs (Opinion on the proposed resolution on assistance to the dying, adopted 25 April 1991 at the European Parliament by the Commission on the Environment, Public Health and Consumer Protection)*, no. 26, 24 June 1991.

[3] CCNE, *Fin de vie, arrêt de vie, euthanasie (End of life, ending life, euthanasia)*, no. 63, 27 Jan. 2000. All translations from CCNE opinions are from the official translations.

The CCNE appears at the forefront of change, and to have a significant impact on public opinion. The government and both chambers of the legislature (the Sénat and the Assemblée Nationale) all have the power to request advice from the CCNE. Many CCNE members are former members of the judiciary.[4]

The CCNE advocated a change in the way euthanasia is currently dealt with by the criminal and disciplinary authorities. Although the CCNE did not countenance a positive right to euthanasia, they identified some cases in which palliative care, accompaniment, and the rejection of futile and aggressive therapy (l'acharnement thérapeutique) would be inadequate to provide 'a tolerable end of life'.[5] In these cases, they recommended that 'human solidarity and compassion' and a 'joint commitment' made 'to face the inevitable' should allow for an exceptional approach.[6]

While rejecting the possibility of a change in the substantive criminal law, the CCNE suggested that a change in criminal procedure could provide an appropriate solution. At the beginning of the criminal investigation, the suspect/defendant could raise a 'plea of defence of euthanasia' which would then be subject to scrutiny by an interdisciplinary commission 'whose task would be to evaluate the probity of the claims made by those concerned, not so much regarding their guilt in fact and in law, but as regards their motivation, i.e. concern to end suffering, respect for a request made by the patient, compassion in the face of the inevitable.'[7] The judge would remain the sole decision-maker as to whether the charge should progress, although presumably the advice of the commission would be taken into account in making this decision. The CCNE sought to restrict this approach to 'borderline or extreme cases' and would impose certain evidentiary requirements on the patient's consent.

A. Incorporating the CCNE's proposal into the criminal law

The CCNE was keen to avoid a change to the substantive criminal law, and favoured instead an amendment to the Code of Penal Procedure (Code de procédure pénale). It is unclear, however, whether such a procedural approach is possible. If it were to be attempted, it appears that the CCNE's proposal would establish a new legal exception alongside existing exceptions for illegality, incompetence, and minority.[8] Two types of procedural exception exist in French criminal procedure: exceptions

---

[4] In a preliminary meeting to discuss this project with M. Jean Michaud, former Vice-President of the CCNE and Conseiller Honoraire at the Cour de Cassation in September 2000, M. Michaud described the close, informal links between the CCNE and the legislature.

[5] CCNE, no. 63, above n. 3, § 4. One of the principal authors of the report has stated that those doctors who appeared as witnesses before the CCNE had admitted that these three approaches could only resolve 95–98% of cases. Jean-François Collange, 'L'Avis 63 et l'éthique protestante' ('Opinion 63 and Protestant Ethics') Chaire Benjamin Edmond de Rothschild pour l'éthique bio-médicale, *Fin de vie, arrêt de vie, euthanasie: avis 63 du CCNE (End of life, ending life, euthanasia: opinion 63 of the CCNE)*, 16ème Entretiens consacrés à l'éthique bio-médicale, Palais du Luxembourg, 18 & 19 Nov. 2000, 4.   [6] CCNE, no. 63, above n. 3, § 4.

[7] Ibid.

[8] Jean Michaud, 'A propos d'un avis du CCNE' ('About a CCNE opinion') (2000) 43 *Méd. & Droit (Med. & Law)* 1.

to judgment and exceptions to action. The operation of an exception to action prevents the initiation of the judicial investigation, while an exception to judgment operates later in an existing investigation, preventing the judgment from occurring. Although the CCNE gave no indication of the type of exception it proposed, the fact that a judge would already have initiated the investigation and remain in charge of the decision-making appears to make it likely that an exception to judgment would be involved.[9]

Along the same lines, Pascale Boucaud proposes another approach which is similar to the system that existed in the Netherlands prior to the establishment of the regional review committees.[10] A decision would be made by the prosecutor prior to the commencement of criminal proceedings not to pursue them, which already happens informally in many cases. Boucaud contends however that 'the systematic character of the decision to discontinue prosecution would shortly lead to the decriminalization of the act'[11] which would not be in line with the intentions of the CCNE.

Alternatively, some commentators argue that the substantive nature of the inquiry to be undertaken by the interdisciplinary commission and the decision to be taken by the judge make a preliminary procedural exception unsuitable. Thus the only way to take forward the CCNE's proposal would be to insert a new defence (un fait justificatif) into the Penal Code, that is, into the substantive criminal law.[12] This defence would run along existing defences such as necessity and duress which are not available to the defendant in a case of euthanasia.[13]

B. The basis of the CCNE's proposal

The CCNE admitted itself that its position is based on 'human solidarity' and compassion, rather than on principles or logical analysis.[14] Moreover, on a pragmatic basis the CCNE recognized that the practice of euthanasia exists in France and is practised in silence, in order to avoid the effect of the harsh provisions of the criminal law. Although a recent estimate puts the annual number of cases of active euthanasia at 2000,[15] there are very few reported

---

[9] Elisabeth Fortis, 'Exception d'euthanasie et droit pénal: A propos de l'avis no 63 rendu par le comité national consultatif d'éthique le 3 mars 2000' ('The euthanasia exception and the criminal law: CCNE Opinion no. 63 of 3 Mar. 2000') (2000) 48(7) *Laennec* 3, 4–5.

[10] See Chapter 4, text accompanying nn. 30, 39–42.

[11] Pascale Boucaud, 'Commentaire de l'avis du comité national consultatif d'éthique du 27 janvier 2000, intitulé "fin de vie, arrêt de vie, euthanasie" ' ('Commentary on the opinion of the CCNE of 27 Jan. 2000 entitled "end of life, ending life, euthanasia" ') (2000) 48(6) *Laennec* 10, 15.

[12] Boucaud, ibid. 13–15; Gérard Mémeteau, 'La mort aux trousses' ('Death on your heels') (2000) 3 *Revue de Recherche Juridique et de droit prospectif (J. of Juridical Research and Prospective Law)* 914, 927; Fortis, above n. 9, 5. [13] See below, Section III.B.

[14] CCNE, no. 63, above n. 3, § 4.

[15] J.-P. Wagner, 'Table ronde – Droits des malades et fin de vie – L'accompagnement de la fin de vie' ('Round table – Rights of patients and the end of life – Accompaniment at the end of life'), Sénat, Travaux de la commission des affaires sociales (Work by the Social Affairs Commission), 2 Feb. 2005, 2, www.senat.fr/commission/soc/soc050207.html, accessed 20 July 2006. See also, Chapter 6, n. 79 (on the rate of neonatal euthanasia in France).

French cases[16] of active euthanasia, despite widespread use of the 'lethal cocktail' ('cocktail lytique')[17] or potassium chloride.[18] Most probably many such charges are diverted away from the criminal courts through the operation of prosecutorial discretion,[19] or downgraded by prosecutors anxious to avoid a jury trial and possible acquittal.[20]

The CCNE was keen to avoid the hypocrisy of the underground practice of euthanasia, and yet unwilling to allow for a right to assisted dying.[21] Despite the cautious approach, numerous concerns have been raised about this proposal, which the CCNE was careful to term only a 'suggestion' which may 'contribute to reflection on the subject'.[22]

The basis for the CCNE's proposal is not altogether clear. Arguably, though, it is the concept of compassion. When the alternatives have been exhausted,[23] compassion mandates an exceptional approach. The 'joint commitment' embodied in the concept of 'human solidarity' then permits euthanasia with the consent of all parties.[24] Thus a helpful starting point in considering the basis of the CCNE's proposal is to attempt to define compassion. Lawrence Blum states:

Compassion is not a simple feeling-state but a complex emotional attitude toward another, characteristically involving imaginative dwelling on the condition of the other person, an active regard for his good, a view of him as a fellow human being, and an emotional response of a certain degree of intensity....[Compassion] involves a sense of shared humanity... [in which] the other person's suffering... is seen as the kind of thing that could happen to anyone, including oneself insofar as one is a human being.[25]

An advantage of using compassion as the mechanism of legal change lies in its direct focus on the patient. 'At the basis of compassion lies an identification with the sufferer as a fellow human being, a recognition that similar misfortunes may also befall one, insofar as one is human.'[26]

---

[16] A few prosecutions have been reported. See Penney Lewis, 'The evolution of assisted dying in France: A third way?' (2005) 13(4) *Med. L. Rev.* 44, 46.

[17] 'A combination of three sedative drugs, Dolosal, Largactyl and Phenergan, given intravenously in a high dose.' Nicolas Aumonier et al., *L'euthanasie* (Paris: Presses Universitaires de France, 2001) 19.

[18] Aumonier, ibid. 19–20; M.S. Husson, 'Infirmièr(e) et Cocktails Lytiques' (The nurse and lethal cocktails') (1996), www.admd.net/dossier1.htm, accessed 20 July 2006.

[19] See Code of Penal Procedure, Art. 40; Aumonier, above n. 17, 107; R. Merle & A. Vitu, *Traité de Droit Criminel (Treatise on Criminal Law)* (7th edn.) (Paris: Cujas, 1997) vol. 1, [477], [602]. Merle and Vitu suggest that such prosecutorial discretion is exercised particularly in cases where there is no 'partie civile' ('civil party', usually the victim or the victim's heirs). See generally, Catherine Elliott & Catherine Vernon, *French Legal System* (Harlow, Eng.: Longman, 2000) 158–60, 173. See also, Hearing of M. B. Beignier (Minutes of the meeting of 24 Feb. 2004), Assemblée Nationale, *Hearings (Leonetti Report)*, No. 1708, 30 June 2004, vol. 2, 797, 804, www.assemblee-nat.fr/12/rap-info/i1708-t2.asp, accessed 20 July 2006.   [20] Mémeteau, above n. 12, 919.

[21] CCNE, no. 63, above n. 3, § 4.   [22] Ibid.

[23] See above, text accompanying n. 5.   [24] CCNE, no. 63, above n. 3, § 4.

[25] Lawrence Blum, 'Compassion' in Amélie Oksenberg Rorty, ed., *Explaining Emotions* (Berkeley: Univ. of Cal. Press, 1980) 507, 509.

[26] Liezl van Zyl, *Death and compassion: A virtue-based approach to euthanasia* (Aldershot, U.K.: Ashgate, 2000) 165.

Within the law, the focus has been on the role of compassion in judicial reasoning.[27] There has been little discussion of the role of compassion as the basis of legal change. Indeed, in the assisted dying context, its role has been denigrated. In the first Ninth Circuit decision in *Compassion in Dying v. Washington*, Noonan J., writing for the majority, stated:

Compassion is a proper, desirable, even necessary component of judicial character; but compassion is not the most important, certainly not the sole law of human existence. Unrestrained by other virtues ... it leads to catastrophe. Justice, prudence, and fortitude are necessary too. Compassion cannot be the compass of a federal judge. That compass is the Constitution of the United States. Where, as here in the case of Washington, the statute of a state comports with that compass, the validity of the statute must be upheld.[28]

Compassion as a driver for legal change has no legal status in either common law or civilian legal systems. It does not fit neatly alongside 'the positive legal entities of rights, duties, and liberties' and could perhaps instead be viewed as 'a curious kind of legal anti-matter.'[29]

C. Future developments

Political changes in France mean that the CCNE proposal is unlikely to be taken forward at this time. In June 2004 the Leonetti Report was issued, rejecting the possibility of legalizing euthanasia and specifically setting aside the CCNE proposal of a euthanasia exception.[30] Following this, the legislature passed a new law in 2005 which strengthens the right to refuse treatment, particularly for the terminally ill. Proxy decision-making and advance refusals of medical treatment will also be available to those who are terminally ill.[31] In theory such changes

[27] See, e.g., Martha Nussbaum, 'Compassion: The Basic Social Emotion' (1996) 13 *Soc. Phil. & Pol'y* 27; Laurence Tribe, 'Revisiting the Rule of Law' (1989) 64 *N.Y.U. L. Rev.* 726, 729–30; Benjamin Zipursky, '*Deshaney* and the Jurisprudence of Compassion' (1990) 65 *N.Y.U. L. Rev.* 1101; Robin West, *Caring for Justice* (New York: N.Y.U. Press, 1997).

[28] *Compassion in Dying v. Washington* (1995) 49 F.3d 586, 594 (9th Cir.).

[29] Antje Pedain, 'The Human Rights Dimension of the Diane Pretty Case' (2003) 62(1) *Camb. L.J.* 181, 185, n. 9, describing Hohfeld's 'no-right'. See Wesley Newcomb Hohfeld, *Fundamental Legal Conceptions As Applied in Judicial Reasoning* (New Haven, Conn.: Yale Univ. Press, 1919).

[30] Assemblée Nationale, *Rapport au nom de la mission d'information sur l'accompagnement de la fin de vie (Rapport Leonetti) (Report in the name of the inquiry into accompaniment at the end of life (Leonetti Report))*, No. 1708, 30 June 2004, vol. 1, 192–201, www.assemblee-nat.fr/12/rap-info/i1708-t1.asp, accessed 20 July 2006. See also, Sénat, *Rapport fait au nom de la commission des Affaires sociales sur la proposition de loi, adoptée par L'Assemblée Nationale, relative aux droits des malades et à la fin de vie (Rapport Dériot) (Report in the name of the Social Affairs Commission on the Bill adopted by the National Assembly on the rights of patients and at the end of life (Dériot Report))*, No. 281, 6 Apr. 2005, www.senat.fr/rap/l04–281/l04–281.html, accessed 20 July 2006.

[31] Loi no. 2005–370 du 22 avril 2005 relative aux droits des malades et à la fin de vie (Law no. 2005-370 of 22 Apr. 2005 on the rights of patients and the end of life), www.senat.fr/dossierleg/ppl04-090.html, accessed 20 July 2006. Regulations setting out the conditions of validity and provisions governing confidentiality and safe-keeping were issued in 2006. See Décret no. 2006-119 du 6 fév. 2006 (Decree no. 2006-119 of 6 Feb. 2006), *Journal officiel*, 7 Feb. 2006, www.admi.net/jo/20060207/SANP0620219D.html, accessed 20 July 2006.

should not be necessary given the very strong provisions on refusal of treatment already in place; however, court decisions have weakened the effect of these provisions.[32] By restricting the changes predominantly to the terminally ill, and explicitly rejecting the decriminalization of euthanasia, the government has ensured that the changes cannot be used by the judiciary or activist groups to argue for a right to assisted dying.

III. The Unavailability of Other Mechanisms of Legal Change

A. A right to assisted dying in France?

The decision of the European Court of Human Rights in *Pretty v. U.K.* means that challenges to criminal prohibitions on assisted suicide (or more serious offences) on the basis of the patient's rights under the European Convention on Human Rights are doomed to failure in Strasbourg.[33] But long before any challenge at that level, French courts are unlikely to vindicate any rights-based challenge. Numerous legislative enunciations of a patient's right to refuse treatment have not persuaded the French judiciary to respect such a right.[34] A patient who has no right to refuse life-saving or life-sustaining treatment cannot argue that the courts should recognize her right to assisted dying. Whatever the proposed basis for the latter right (autonomy, equality, privacy, liberty, etc.) it would have to apply equally to the refusal scenario.

In the 1973 case of *Gatineau*, the Cour de Cassation[35] held that a doctor who respected his patient's obstinate and aggressive refusal of life-saving treatment could not be prosecuted for wilfully failing to assist a person in danger.[36] The offence of wilfully failing to assist a person in danger was then found in Article 63(2) of

---

[32] See below, Section III.A.

[33] *Pretty v. U.K.* (2002) 35 E.H.R.R. 1 (Eur. Ct. H.R.), discussed in Chapter 2, Section I.B.

[34] See Loi no. 94-653 du 29 juillet 1994 (Law no. 94-653 of 29 July 1994), Art. 3, amending Art. 16(3) of the Code civil; Code de déontologie médicale (Code of Medical Ethics), Décret no. 95-1000 du 6 sept. 1995 (Decree no. 95-1000 of 6 Sept. 1995), *Journal officiel*, 8 Sept. 1995, [13305], Art. 36; Code de la santé publique (Public Health Code), Art. L1111-4, introduced by Loi no. 2002-303 du 4 mars 2002 (Law no. 2002-303 of 4 Mar. 2002), Arts. 9 & 11, *Journal officiel*, 5 Mar. 2002; Loi no. 2005-370 du 22 avril 2005 relative aux droits des malades et à la fin de vie (Law no. 2005-370 of 22 Apr. 2005 on the rights of patients and the end of life).

[35] The Cour de Cassation is the highest appeal court for matters of civil and criminal law. Appeals from suits involving private medical facilities are also heard by the Cour de Cassation. In matters of public or administrative law including medical disciplinary law and suits involving public hospitals, the highest appeal court is the Conseil d'État (Council of State). See generally, Elliott & Vernon, above n. 19, chs. 5 and 6.

[36] *Gatineau*, Cour de Cassation, Criminal Chamber, 3 Jan. 1973, (1973) *Dalloz* I.R. 13; (1973) *Dalloz* Jur. 220; (1973) *Rev. Sci. Crim. (J. of Criminal Sciences)* 693, obs. Levasseur; (1974) *Rev. Sci. Crim.* 591, obs. Levasseur. The CCNE suggests that a written refusal may be necessary to avoid criminal liability for failing to assist a person in danger, despite the failure of the court in *Gatineau* to mention any such requirement. CCNE, *Refus de traitement et autonomie de la personne (Refusal of treatment and autonomy of the person)*, no. 87, 14 Apr. 2005, 32, § VII, recommendation 3.

the Penal Code and is now Article 223-6: 'Anyone who wilfully fails to render to a person in danger any assistance which, without risk to himself or to third parties, he could render him either by his own action, or by initiating rescue operations . . . is punished by five years' imprisonment and a fine of €75,000'.[37]

Disciplinary action may nevertheless be taken in such circumstances. In *Garnier*, the national disciplinary tribunal, supported by the highest administrative court, the Conseil d'État (Council of State),[38] preferred the doctor's obligation to use all of the therapeutic means at his disposal to save the patient's life over the doctor's duty to respect her refusal.[39] The patient's right to refuse treatment is limited: although her doctor may not be criminally prosecuted or civilly liable[40] for respecting it, he may be guilty of a disciplinary fault (faute disciplinaire), the knowledge of which may render the patient's right illusory.[41]

The patient's right to refuse treatment is further limited by the failure of the law to hold doctors liable for breaches of this right. In the context of private medical treatment, a doctor who fails to obtain the consent of his patient to a surgical procedure is liable in damages for the consequences of that procedure,[42] unless the situation was one of 'evident necessity or immediate danger'.[43] However, the exception described is wide, and has serious implications for patients seeking to refuse life-saving or life-sustaining treatment. While there is much debate in the doctrine

---

[37] All translations of statutory provisions are official and all other translations are mine unless otherwise indicated.

[38] The Conseil d'État rejected the Conclusions of its Commissaire du gouvernement recommending that in cases of conflict between these duties, the will of the patient must prevail. *Garnier*, Conseil d'État, 29 July 1994, no. 146.978; (1995) 31(1) *Rev. Dr. Sanit. Soc.* 57, 60, note Dubouis (the Commissaire du gouvernement). The Commissaire du gouvernement is an impartial and independent judge who publicly advises the deciding judges on the facts and the law and provides an opinion as to how the case should conclude. See www.conseil-etat.fr/ce/outils/index_ou02_c.shtml, accessed 20 July 2006. The conclusions of the Commissaire du gouvernement are often published in academic journals, as is the case here.

[39] Other comments on the decision of the Conseil d'État are found at (13 July 1995) *Gaz. Pal.* Juris. 366, note Garay; (1994) *J.C.P.* IV [1361], note Roualt. See also, *B.*, Court of Appeal, Nancy, Special Chamber, 3 Dec. 1982, (1984) 1 *Gaz. Pal.* 132, 134, note Dorsner-Dolivet. It may be possible to distinguish *Garnier* on the basis that it was decided prior to the coming into force of the legislative provisions reinforcing the right to refuse treatment listed above n. 34. See *Mme. X.*, Conseil d'État, 26 Oct. 2001, no. 198546, (15 Jan. 2002) 11 *Petites Affiches* 18, 21, note Clément; Emmanuel Dunet-Larousse, 'L'euthanasie: signification et qualification au regard du droit pénal' ('Euthanasia: significance and description in relation to the criminal law') (1998) 34(2) *Rev. Dr. Sanit. Soc.* 265, 272.

[40] *Vignalou*, Cour de Cassation, 1st Civil Chamber, 7 Nov. 1961, *Bull.* I, no. 508, 401, 402.

[41] See *Mme. X.*, Court of Administrative Appeal, Paris, 9 June 1998, no. 95 PA03104 & 95 PA0365, (1999) *Dalloz* Juris. 277, note Péllissier.

[42] *B.*, Court of Appeal, Angers, 1st Chamber, 4 Mar. 1947, (1947) 1 *Gaz. Pal.* 168; (1948) *Dalloz* 298, note Savatier (doctor failed to obtain consent for an amputation).

[43] *Mme. D.*, Cour de Cassation, 1st Civil Chamber, 11 Oct. 1988, (1989) *J.C.P. G.* II [21358], note Dorsner-Dolivet (patient sterilized by tubal ligation without her consent could recover); *Leseurre c. Dr. Couturier et S.A. Abeille Assurances*, Court of Appeal, Paris, 12 Jan. 1996, (16 July 1996) *Gaz. Pal.* 407, 409, note Bonneau (patient who did not consent to a partial hysterectomy could recover).

about the ambit of 'evident necessity',[44] in the context of refusal of life-sustaining or life-saving treatment, the refusal is likely to fall into the rubric of 'immediate danger'.

A similar approach is taken in cases involving public hospitals.[45] In a case in which the refusal of blood transfusions by two of Jehovah's Witnesses was over-ridden by their doctors, the Conseil d'État held that the court below had committed an error of law in holding as a general principle that the doctor's obligation to save life should prevail over his obligation to respect the patient's will. Nevertheless, in the 'extreme situation' in which the doctor intended to save the patient's life, and performed an act indispensable to that goal and proportionate to the patient's condition, no finding of fault was made.[46]

Although the doctor appears safe from criminal prosecution and civil proceedings if she respects her patient's refusal of life-saving or life-sustaining treatment, the case of *Garnier* suggests that the threat of disciplinary proceedings still remains. The doctor who chooses not to respect her patient's refusal is unlikely to be the subject of criminal, civil, administrative, or disciplinary proceedings if the refusal placed the patient's life in danger.[47] In these circumstances, a right to assistance in dying seems an extremely remote possibility.

B. The defence of necessity in France

Many continental European systems allow necessity as justification but its scope may be so limited as to exclude the possibility of euthanasia.[48] In contrast to the broad defence of necessity found in the Dutch Criminal Code,[49] the defence of necessity in the French Penal Code provides that: 'A person is not criminally liable if confronted with a present or imminent danger to himself, another person or property, he performs an act necessary to ensure the safety of the person or property, except where the means used are disproportionate to the seriousness of

[44] Dorsner-Dolivet, above n. 43.

[45] These cases are dealt with by the administrative courts while cases involving private hospitals are dealt with by the civil courts. See above n. 35.

[46] *Mme. X.*, Conseil d'État, 26 Oct. 2001, no. 198546, (15 Jan. 2002) 11 *Petites Affiches* 18, 21, note Clément. This exception was made contrary to the recommendations of the Commissaire du gouvernement, Chauvaux, who had argued that when confronted with a competent, conscious patient who maintains a clear and firm refusal of treatment, the duty of the doctor is to respect that refusal. Clément, ibid. 21. The decision survived the enactment of the refusal provision in the Code de la santé public (Public Health Code), Art. L1111-4. The Conseil d'État repeated again the criteria that the act performed must be indispensable to the patient's survival and proportional to her condition. The only effect of Art. L1111-4 appeared to be the explicit requirement that the medical team do all in their power to convince the patient to accept the vital treatment.

[47] The refusal jurisprudence is discussed in greater depth in Lewis, above n. 16, 53–66.

[48] See the discussion of the French and German approaches in Benjamin L. Berger, 'A Choice Among Values: Theoretical and Historical Perspectives on the Defence of Necessity' (2002) 39 *Alta. L. Rev.* 848, [28]–[32]. The Belgian jurisprudential approach which has not been codified in the Penal Code is much broader than the approaches discussed here. See Chapter 6, Section VI.B.

[49] See Chapter 4, Section I.A.

the threat.'[50] There is no appellate jurisprudence regarding the availability of necessity as a defence to euthanasia. It seems unlikely that the defence would be considered applicable by the judiciary, given the specificity of the statutory language. It is difficult to see how killing someone could be an act necessary to ensure his *safety*.[51] Thus, the statutory defence of necessity provides little or no room for the argument that the doctor has a duty to relieve his patient's suffering which can override his duty to preserve the patient's life. The duty to rescue embodied in Article 223-6 of the Penal Code makes even more remote the prospect of the legalization of assisted dying based on the doctor's duty to relieve suffering.[52] Even in the civil, administrative, and disciplinary contexts there is no recognition of the doctor's duty to relieve suffering as a justification for either the active termination of life, or for the withdrawal or withholding of treatment.[53]

IV. Conclusion

Legalization of assisted dying in France is unlikely using either the rights of patients or the defence of necessity. Legislative change may have to await a change of government. However, there are some interesting aspects of the proposal to legalize euthanasia on the basis of compassion, which will be further considered in Chapter 6.[54] Although compassion is an unlikely driver for legal change on assisted dying in any jurisdiction, particularly in light of its lack of legal status in either common law or civilian legal systems, concerns which have been raised about compassion are relevant to issues surrounding proxy decision-making in the assisted dying context.[55]

---

[50] Penal Code, Art. 122-7. A similar provision is found in the German Penal Code, Art. 35.

[51] Mémeteau, above n. 12, 928; Fortis, above n. 9, 3–5; Alain Prothais, 'Accompagnement de la fin de vie et droit pénal' ('Accompaniment at the end of life and the criminal law') (2004) *J.C.P. G.* I 130 [12].   [52] Penal Code, Art. 223-6. See above, text accompanying n. 37.

[53] See Lewis, above n. 16, 46–53.   [54] See Chapter 6, Section IV.

[55] See Chapter 6, Section V.A.3.

6

Comparing the Mechanisms of
Legal Change

I. Introduction

The first half of this chapter examines the contours of the legal regulation of assisted dying resulting from the use of the three mechanisms of legal change which were canvassed in Chapters 2, 4, and 5: constitutionally entrenched rights; the defence of necessity based on the conflicting duties to preserve life and relieve suffering; and compassion. While the shape of the regimes produced by legalization using necessity and compassion are both relatively easy to define (and fairly similar) the problems associated with rights discourse which were discussed in Chapter 3 mean that numerous different formulations could result from legalization using one or more rights as the mechanism of legal change. Four of these possible formulations are described in the next section.

The second half of this chapter brings the three types of regime together, contrasting their contours in relation to their key features. Legislative approaches are also introduced to see if they mirror, in any significant respect, the results of the three mechanisms of legal change.

II. Rights as the Mechanism of Legal Change

In addition to the problems posed by rights discourse, the shape of a regime resulting from the use of one or more rights as the mechanism of legal change is also difficult to describe with certainty owing to the lack of success of any rights-based claims. No legislature has been forced to draft legislation legalizing assisted dying in direct response to a judgment striking down a criminal prohibition on assisted suicide, murder, or any lesser offence on the grounds of a violation of one or more constitutionally entrenched human rights.[1] In contrast, there has been substantial judicial and legislative input into the Dutch defence of necessity which was introduced in

---

[1] See the discussion of this possibility in Michael Freeman, 'Denying Death its Dominion: Thoughts on the Dianne Pretty Case' (2002) 10(3) *Med. L. Rev.* 245, 265–7.

Chapter 4 and is discussed in Section III, below. However, some help may be found by looking at the rulings made by those judges who were sympathetic to the rights-based claims brought in Canada, the United States, and England. Although they did not prevail (either because they were overruled on appeal, or writing in dissent), nevertheless their judgments do provide some guidance.

A. The dissenting reasons of McEachern C.J.B.C.[2] in *Rodriguez*

In the Canadian case of *Rodriguez*, one of the judges of the British Columbia Court of Appeal found in favour of the appellant, who was suffering from amyotrophic lateral sclerosis, or motor neurone disease.[3] McEachern C.J.B.C. held that the criminal prohibition against assisted suicide violated the appellant's constitutional 'right to life, liberty and security of the person and the right not to be deprived thereof except in accordance with the principles of fundamental justice' which is found in section 7 of the Canadian Charter of Rights and Freedoms. Relying on the earlier abortion case of *Morgentaler*,[4] McEachern C.J.B.C. held that 'a person suffering a terminal illness wishing to end her life when death is near would ... be *prima facie* entitled to protection against state-imposed prohibitions which have the effect of imposing continued physical and psychological suffering upon her.'[5] Therefore, the appellant was entitled to rely on both the liberty and security of the person elements of section 7.[6] The criminal prohibition on assisted suicide was not in accordance with the principles of fundamental justice, as

s. 7 was enacted for the purpose of ensuring human dignity and individual control, so long as it harms no one else. When one considers the nobility of such purpose, it must follow as a matter of logic as much as of law, that any provision which imposes an indeterminate period of senseless physical and psychological suffering upon someone who is shortly to die anyway cannot conform with any principle of fundamental justice. Such a provision, by any measure, must clearly be characterized as the opposite of fundamental justice.[7]

McEachern C.J.B.C. thus concluded that the operation of the criminal prohibition on assisted suicide violated the appellant's rights guaranteed under section 7 of the Charter and set out six conditions with which the appellant and her physician would have to comply in order to avoid criminal liability:

First, the Appellant must be mentally competent to make a decision to end her own life, such competence to be certified in writing by a treating physician and by an independent psychiatrist who has examined her not more than 24 hours before arrangements are put in place which will permit the Appellant to actually terminate her life and such arrangements must only be operative while one of such physicians is actually present with the Appellant.

---

² Chief Justice of British Columbia.
³ *Rodriguez v. British Columbia (Attorney-General)* (1993) 76 B.C.L.R. (2d) 145 (B.C.C.A.). For a brief discussion of the facts of *Rodriguez*, see Chapter 2, Section I.B.
⁴ *Morgentaler* [1988] 1 S.C.R. 30.
⁵ *Rodriguez v. British Columbia (Attorney-General)* (1993) 76 B.C.L.R. (2d) 145, [60] (B.C.C.A.).
⁶ Ibid.   ⁷ Ibid. [75].

Such certificate must include the professional opinion of the physicians not just that she is competent, but also that, in the opinion of such physicians, she truly desires to end her life and that, in their opinion, she has reached such decision of her own free will without pressure or influence from any source other than her circumstances.

The fact that the Appellant has made her intentions known by bringing these proceedings, and in many other ways, may be taken into consideration by the physicians in reaching their opinions, but they will of course be careful to ensure that the Appellant has not changed her mind since making her earlier declarations.

Secondly, in addition to being mentally competent, the physicians must certify that, in their opinion, (1) the Appellant is terminally ill and near death, and that there is no hope of her recovering; (2) that she is, or but for medication would be, suffering unbearable physical pain or severe psychological distress; (3) that they have informed her, and that she understands, that she has a continuing right to change her mind about terminating her life; and, (4) when, in their opinion, the Appellant would likely die (a) if palliative care is being or would be administered to her, and (b) if palliative care should not be administered to her.

Thirdly, not less than three clear days before any psychiatrist examines the Appellant for the purposes of preparing a certificate for the purposes aforesaid, notice must be given to the Regional Coroner for the area or district where the Appellant is to be examined, and the Regional Coroner or his nominee, who must be a physician, may be present at the examination of the Appellant by a psychiatrist in order to be satisfied that the Appellant does indeed have mental competence to decide, and does in fact decide, to terminate her life.

Fourthly, one of the physicians giving any certificate as aforesaid must re-examine the Appellant each day after the above-mentioned arrangements are put in place to ensure she does not evidence any change in her intention to end her life. If she commits suicide, such physician must furnish a further certificate to the Coroner confirming that, in his or her opinion, the Appellant did not change her mind.

Fifthly, no one may assist the Appellant to attempt to commit suicide or to commit suicide after the expiration of thirty-one days from the date of the first mentioned certificate, and, upon the expiration of that period, any arrangements made to assist the Appellant to end her life must immediately be made inoperative and discontinued. I include this condition to ensure, to the extent it can be ensured, that the Appellant has not changed her mind since the time she was examined by a psychiatrist.

This limitation troubles me greatly as I would prefer that the Appellant be permitted a free choice about the time when she wishes to end her life. I am, however, unwilling to leave it open for a longer period because of the concern I have that the Appellant might change her mind. She is able to proceed at her preferred pace by delaying the time for her psychiatric examination until the time she thinks she is close to the time when she wishes to end her ordeal. If she delays causing her death for more than thirty-one days after such examination then there is a risk either that she had not finally made up her mind, or that, as is everyone's right, she has changed it, or possibly that she is no longer competent to make such a decision.

Lastly, the act actually causing the death of the Appellant must be the unassisted act of the Appellant herself, and not of anyone else.[8]

---

[8] Ibid. [100]–[108]. The judge added a cautionary note: 'These conditions have been prepared in some haste because of the urgency of the Appellant's circumstances, and I would not wish judges in subsequent applications to regard them other than as guidelines.' Ibid. [109].

The substantive criteria articulated by McEachern C.J.B.C. were those of terminal illness, a competent, voluntary, and enduring request, and 'unbearable physical pain or severe psychological distress'.

B. The dissenting reasons of Lamer C.J.C.[9] in *Rodriguez*

On appeal to the Supreme Court of Canada, one of the dissenting judges also fashioned a remedy for the appellant. The Chief Justice found that the appellant's right to equality under section 15(1) of the Charter[10] was infringed by the criminal prohibition on assisted suicide which

creates an inequality since it prevents persons physically unable to end their lives unassisted from choosing suicide when that option is in principle available to other members of the public. This inequality is moreover imposed on persons unable to end their lives unassisted solely because of a physical disability, a personal characteristic which is among the grounds of discrimination listed in s. 15(1) of the *Charter*. Furthermore, in my opinion the inequality may be characterized as a burden or disadvantage, since it limits the ability of those who are subject to this inequality to take and act upon fundamental decisions regarding their lives and persons. For them, the principle of self-determination has been limited.[11]

Unable to justify the infringement under the saving provision in section 1 of the Charter,[12] the Chief Justice fashioned a remedy similar to the constitutional exemption created by McEachern C.J.B.C.:

(1) the constitutional exemption may only be sought by way of application to a superior court;
(2) the applicant must be certified by a treating physician and independent psychiatrist, in the manner and at the time suggested by McEachern C.J.B.C., to be competent to make the decision to end her own life, and the physicians must certify that the applicant's decision has been made freely and voluntarily, and at least one of the physicians must be present with the applicant at the time the applicant commits assisted suicide;
(3) the physicians must also certify:
    (i) that the applicant is or will become physically incapable of committing suicide unassisted, and
    (ii) that they have informed him or her, and that he or she understands, that he or she has a continuing right to change his or her mind about terminating his or her life;
(4) notice and access must be given to the Regional Coroner at the time and in the manner described by McEachern C.J.B.C.;

---

[9] Chief Justice of Canada.

[10] Section 15(1) provides: 'Every individual is equal before and under the law and has the right to the equal protection and equal benefit of the law without discrimination and, in particular, without discrimination based on race, national or ethnic origin, colour, religion, sex, age or mental or physical disability.'

[11] *Rodriguez v. British Columbia (Attorney-General)* [1993] 3 S.C.R. 519, [167]. This argument was discussed in Chapter 2, Section II.C.5.a.

[12] Ibid. [190]–[215]. Section 1 provides: 'The *Canadian Charter of Rights and Freedoms* guarantees the rights and freedoms set out in it subject only to such reasonable limits prescribed by law as can be demonstrably justified in a free and democratic society.'

(5) the applicant must be examined daily by one of the certifying physicians at the time and in the manner outlined by McEachern C.J.B.C.;

(6) the constitutional exemption will expire according to the time limits set by McEachern C.J.B.C.; and

(7) the act causing the death of the applicant must be that of the applicant him or herself, and not of anyone else.[13]

The substantive criteria articulated by Lamer C.J.C. were those of physical incapacity to commit suicide unaided and a competent, voluntary, and enduring request. McEachern C.J.B.C.'s requirements of terminal illness and 'unbearable physical pain or severe psychological distress' were dropped. The criterion of terminal illness was no longer relevant given that Lamer C.J.C. had found a violation of the right to equality for all those incapable of committing suicide unaided.[14] To restrict the exemption to the terminally ill, therefore, might violate the rights of those who are unable to commit suicide unaided but are not terminally ill.[15]

Lamer C.J.C. also suggested that the restriction of the exemption to assisted suicide might have to be reconsidered.

While I believe this to be appropriate in [the appellant's] current circumstances as a mechanism can be put in place allowing her to cause her own death with her limited physical capabilities, why should she be prevented the option of choosing suicide should her physical condition degenerate to the point where she is no longer even physically able to press a button or blow into a tube? Surely it is in such circumstances that assistance is required most.[16]

As the appellant had not requested an order exempting her assister from the criminal prohibition on first degree murder, the Chief Justice decided that it was not necessary to address this issue.[17]

C. The Second Circuit Decision in *Quill v. Vacco*

Thus far we have observed variance in the substantive criteria articulated by McEachern C.J.B.C. and Lamer C.J.C. This variance could be explained, however, on the basis that each judge found that a different right had been violated by the criminal prohibition on assisted suicide. However, even similar rights violations may result in the enunciation of different criteria. In *Quill v. Vacco*,[18] as we have already seen in Chapter 2, the Second Circuit accepted an argument that the appellants' right to equal protection found in the Fourteenth

---

[13] Ibid. [236]–[244]. Lamer C.J.C. also added a note of caution: 'I wish to emphasize that these conditions have been tailored to the particular circumstances of Ms. Rodriguez. While they may be used as guidelines for future petitioners in a similar position, each application must be considered in its own individual context.' Ibid. [245].   [14] Ibid. [234].

[15] Ibid.   [16] Ibid.

[17] Ibid. Indeed, the Chief Justice did not even advert to the fact that his suggestion might have required an exemption to the law on first degree murder.

[18] Subsequently overruled by *Vacco v. Quill* (1997) 521 U.S. 793, 799.

Amendment[19] was infringed by the inequality between terminally ill patients dependent on life-sustaining medical treatment, who may refuse such treatment and thereby end their lives; and terminally ill patients who do not require life-sustaining treatment and therefore are prevented by the criminal prohibition on assisted suicide from deciding to end their lives.[20] The relevant comparison, therefore, was not between those who are physically able to end their lives without assistance and those who are not, but rather between two groups of terminally ill patients: those dependent on life-sustaining treatment and those who are not. The substantive criteria for legalization based on this argument presumably would be terminal illness and a competent, voluntary, and enduring request.[21]

The requirement of terminal illness was sustained not only on the basis of the pleadings,[22] but also as the violation of the right to equal protection could not be justified by the state interest in preserving life in cases of terminal illness. '[W]hat interest can the state possibly have in requiring the prolongation of a life that is all but ended? Surely, the state's interest lessens as the potential for life diminishes.'[23] Although not addressed by the court, the state's interest in preserving life might well have been considered to be stronger if the individual were unable to end her life without assistance but was not terminally ill.

The status of a suffering requirement in this context is less clear. Although suffering is mentioned in *Quill v. Vacco*,[24] it is not articulated as one of the requirements. In the District Court decision in *Compassion in Dying*, which also followed this course,[25] the absence of a suffering requirement is clearer.[26] Logically, the absence of a suffering requirement is consistent with the comparison to a group of people who do not have to demonstrate that their suffering is unbearable or intolerable before deciding to end their lives by refusing life-sustaining treatment.[27]

---

[19] The first clause of the Fourteenth Amendment provides: 'No State shall make or enforce any law which shall abridge the privileges or immunities of citizens of the United States; nor shall any State deprive any person of life, liberty, or property, without due process of law; nor deny to any person within its jurisdiction the equal protection of the laws.'

[20] See Chapter 2, Section II.C.5.b. Although the court was concerned only with the effect of the criminal prohibition on assisted suicide, a similar argument to that made by Lamer C.J.C. would allow *any* assistance in dying needed in order to overcome this inequality. See above, text accompanying nn. 16–17.

[21] See *Quill v. Vacco* (1996) 80 F.3d 716, 731 (2nd Cir.). This argument was also accepted in *Compassion in Dying v. Washington* (1994) 850 F. Supp. 1454, 1467 (W.D. Wash.) and by Wright J., dissenting, in *Compassion in Dying v. Washington* (1995) 49 F.3d 586, 597 (9th Cir.).

[22] That is, what kind of remedy had been requested.

[23] *Quill v. Vacco* (1996) 80 F.3d 716, 729–30 (2nd Cir.), citing *In re Quinlan* (1976) 355 A.2d 647, 664 (N.J.S.C.), *certiorari* denied, (1976) 429 U.S. 922.

[24] See, e.g., *Quill v. Vacco* (1996) 80 F.3d 716, 720–2, 730 (2nd Cir.).

[25] See Chapter 2, Section II.C.5.b.

[26] *Compassion in Dying v. Washington* (1994) 850 F. Supp. 1454, 1467 (W.D. Wash.). Dissenting in the Ninth Circuit, Wright J. adopted the analysis of the District Court on this point. *Compassion in Dying v. Washington* (1995) 49 F.3d 586, 597.

[27] A similar explanation can be given for Lamer C.J.C.'s abandonment of McEachern C.J.B.C.'s suffering requirement (above, text accompanying n. 14) as those who are physically able to commit suicide do not have to meet a requirement that they are suffering.

D. The En Banc Ninth Circuit Decision in *Compassion in Dying v. Washington*

A similar result was reached in the Ninth Circuit,[28] although based on an entirely different foundation. The court relied on the liberty interest protected by the Due Process clause of the Fourteenth Amendment.[29] In the case of the terminally ill, the individual's liberty interest 'in choosing the time and manner of death' outweighed the state's interests in preserving life; preventing suicide; 'avoiding the involvement of third parties and...precluding the use of arbitrary, unfair, or undue influence'; 'protecting the integrity of the medical profession'; and 'avoiding adverse consequences that might ensue'.[30] Those state interests were attenuated in the context of the terminally ill.[31] The resulting substantive criteria were terminal illness, a competent request, and that the medication used be prescribed by the patients' physicians.[32] This latter requirement was necessary in order to address the

strong [state] interest in avoiding undue influence and other forms of abuse. Here, that concern is ameliorated in large measure because of the mandatory involvement in the decision-making process of physicians, who have a strong bias in favor of preserving life, and because the process itself can be carefully regulated and rigorous safeguards adopted. Under these circumstances, we believe that the possibility of abuse, even when considered along with the other state interests, does not outweigh the liberty interest at issue.[33]

Although the liberty basis of the court's reasoning was close to that of McEachern C.J.B.C. (as distinct from the equality-based reasoning of Lamer C.J.C. and the Second Circuit), nevertheless the criteria set out by McEachern C.J.B.C. and the Ninth Circuit vary as the latter do not contain a suffering requirement.

III. Necessity as the Mechanism of Legal Change

A. (Active voluntary) euthanasia or termination of life on request

The legalization of assisted dying in the Netherlands through the defence of necessity was discussed in Chapter 4.[34] In order to rely on the defence of necessity in euthanasia cases, in addition to the presence of the patient's competent request,[35]

---

[28] Subsequently overruled by *Washington v. Glucksberg* (1997) 521 U.S. 702.

[29] See above n. 19.

[30] *Compassion in Dying v. Washington* (1996) 79 F.3d 790, 816–17 (9th Cir. en banc).

[31] Ibid. 837. See also, *Compassion in Dying v. Washington* (1995) 49 F.3d 586, 596–7 (9th Cir., Wright J., dissenting).

[32] *Compassion in Dying v. Washington* (1996) 79 F.3d 790, 837 (9th Cir. en banc). See also, *Compassion in Dying v. Washington* (1995) 49 F.3d 586, 597 (9th Cir., Wright J., dissenting).

[33] *Compassion in Dying v. Washington* (1996) 79 F.3d 790, 837 (9th Cir. en banc).

[34] See Chapter 4, Section I.

[35] Recall that in the Dutch context, euthanasia refers only to the termination of life on request. See Chapter 4, text accompanying n. 6.

the defendant doctor[36] must be faced with a conflict between the duties to preserve life and relieve suffering. This conflict of duties only arises if the patient is experiencing unbearable and hopeless suffering and there is no reasonable alternative to relieve that suffering.

1. *The patient's request*

Under the new Dutch legislation, the patient's request must be 'voluntary and carefully considered'.[37] '[T]he problem of competence of patients suffering from a somatic disorder has received relatively little attention.'[38] The Dutch Association for Psychiatry guidelines require that the attending physician consult a psychiatrist if she suspects the patient is incompetent 'or suffering from psychiatric (co)morbidity.'[39] The consulted psychiatrist may also assess transference and counter-transference issues,[40] and will check voluntariness and whether there has been undue pressure from others.[41] Psychiatric consultation is rare, particularly if the patient's primary physician is not a psychiatrist.[42]

---

[36] Recall that prior to codification, judicial decisions had held that only a doctor can be faced with this conflict of duties, as only a doctor has a professional duty to relieve suffering which may conflict with her duty to abide by the criminal prohibition against killing. Julia Belian, 'Deference to Doctors in Dutch Euthanasia Law' (1996) 10 *Emory Int'l L. Rev.* 255, 265. See Chapter 4, Section I.B. The new defence in the Criminal Code, Art. 293(2), inserted by the Termination of Life on Request and Assisted Suicide (Review Procedures) Act 2001, s.20A, applies only to physicians. See Chapter 4, Section I.C. English translations of the new law can be found at (2001) 8 *Eur. J. Health L.* 183 and as an appendix to Jurriaan de Haan, 'The New Dutch Law on Euthanasia' (2002) 10 *Med. L. Rev.* 57, 68–75.

[37] Termination of Life on Request and Assisted Suicide (Review Procedures) Act 2001, s. 2(1)(a).

[38] John Griffiths, Alex Bood & Heleen Weyers, *Euthanasia and Law in the Netherlands* (Amsterdam: Amsterdam Univ. Press, 1998) 101, n. 31.

[39] Johanna H. Groenewoud et al., 'Psychiatric consultation with regard to requests for euthanasia or physician-assisted suicide' (2004) 26 *Gen'l Hosp. Psychiatry* 323, 324, citing Nederlandse Vereniging voor Psychiatrie (Dutch Association for Psychiatry), *Hulp bij zelfdoding door patiënten met een psychiatrische stoornis: richtlijnen voor de psychiater (Assisted suicide by patients with a mental disorder: guidelines for the psychiatrist)* (1998). An English translation of this report was published in 2000.

[40] Groenewoud, above n. 39, 326. Psychiatrists are more often asked to evaluate transference and counter-transference issues in cases where the patient's primary physician is herself a psychiatrist (asked in 41% of cases) than in cases where the primary physician is a non-psychiatrist (asked in 18% of cases). Ibid. Table 2.

[41] Marjolein Bannink et al., 'Psychiatric consultation and quality of decision making in euthanasia' (2000) 356 *Lancet* 2067. However, Bannink concludes that the 'benefits of [mandatory psychiatric] consultation should be balanced against the disadvantages of pushing the psychiatrist to the fore as the final gatekeeper.' Ibid. 2068.

[42] Groenewoud, above n. 39, 325, Table 1, 328 (estimating that the rate of psychiatric consultation is about 4% of all requests for euthanasia and assisted suicide and reporting almost twice as many requests for psychiatric consultation from psychiatrists than from non-psychiatrists). See also, Johanna H. Groenewoud et al., 'Physician-assisted death in psychiatric practice in the Netherlands' (1997) 336(25) *New Eng. J. Med.* 1795. Groenewoud et al. point out that rates of psychiatric consultation in the Netherlands are comparable with those in Oregon. Groenewoud, above n. 39, 328. The rate of psychiatric referral in Oregon is currently 5% (2003–2005), which is indeed comparable to the Dutch rate. However, the rate was significantly higher in the early years of the Oregon Act: 31% in 1998; 37% in 1999; 19% in 2000; 14% in 2001; and 13% in 2002. See the Annual Reports produced by the Oregon Department of Human Services, available at http://egov.oregon.gov/DHS/ph/pas/ar-index.shtml, accessed 25 July 2006.

2. Unbearable and hopeless suffering

The original requirement that the patient be experiencing unbearable and hopeless suffering enunciated in the jurisprudence discussed in Chapter 4 has now been codified by the 2001 statute which requires that the 'attending physician ... must have been satisfied that the patient's suffering was unbearable, and that there was no prospect of improvement'.[43] The source of the patient's suffering may be either somatic (that is, stemming from a physiological disorder which may or may not be a terminal illness) or non-somatic.[44] The latter 'can include ... the prospect of inhuman deterioration and the possibility of not being able to die in a ' "dignified" way'.[45]

3. No reasonable alternative

The 2001 legislation codifies the jurisprudential development discussed in Chapter 4, requiring that the attending physician must 'have come to the conclusion, together with the patient, that there is no reasonable alternative in light of the patient's situation'.[46] It is the lack of another reasonable alternative which causes the defendant's conflict of duties once the patient makes a considered and voluntary request for euthanasia or assisted suicide.[47] In cases where the source of the suffering is somatic, the courts have held that the patient's decision to refuse treatment which might ease her suffering 'does not preclude a request for euthanasia based on the resulting suffering'.[48] However, where the source of the suffering is non-somatic, resort to the necessity defence is prohibited if the patient has rejected 'a realistic alternative to relieve the suffering'.[49] Once the conflict of duties

---

[43] Termination of Life on Request and Assisted Suicide (Review Procedures) Act 2001, s. 2(1)(b).

[44] *Chabot*, Supreme Court, 21 June 1994, N.J. 1994, no. 656, translated in John Griffiths, 'Assisted suicide in the Netherlands: the *Chabot* case' (1995) 58 *Mod. L. Rev.* 232, 238, 243. The translation is also found in Griffiths, Bood & Weyers, above n. 38, App. II-2. See Chapter 4, Section I.B.

[45] Heleen Weyers, 'Euthanasia: The process of legal change in the Netherlands' in Albert Klijn et al., eds., *Regulating Physician-Negotiated Death* (Amsterdam: Elsevier, 2001) 11, 21.

[46] Termination of Life on Request and Assisted Suicide (Review Procedures) Act 2001, s. 2(1)(d). See Chapter 4, Section I.B.

[47] Ubaldus de Vries, 'A Dutch perspective: the limits of lawful euthanasia' (2004) 13 *Annals Health L.* 365, 372, 374.

[48] Griffiths, Bood & Weyers, above n. 38, 102, n. 38, citing *Schoonheim*, Supreme Court, 27 Nov. 1984, N.J. 1985, no. 106 (translated in Griffiths, Bood & Weyers, ibid. App. II-1); *Schoonheim*, Court of Appeals, The Hague, 10 June & 11 Sept. 1986, N.J. 1987, no. 608 (patient had refused psychopharmaca). There may be some lack of knowledge of this position amongst the medical community. See, e.g., Anonymous Family Physician, 'In Death He Achieved a Stature that He Never Had in Life' in David C. Thomasma et al., eds., *Asking to Die: Inside the Dutch Debate about Euthanasia* (Dordrecht: Kluwer, 1998) 281, 291. See also, John Griffiths, Heleen Weyers & Maurice Adams, *Euthanasia and the Law in Europe: With Special Reference to the Netherlands and Belgium* (Oxford: Hart Publishing, 2007 (forthcoming)) [3.2.3.2] (raising the possibility that an unreasonable refusal of a relatively minor treatment might prevent access to euthanasia).

[49] *Chabot*, Supreme Court, 21 June 1994, N.J. 1994, no. 656 (translations listed above n. 44). The difficulties of this formulation are discussed in Griffiths, Bood & Weyers, above n. 38, 337, n. 37, 147, n. 179. Moreover, the somatic/non-somatic distinction is not always clear. See Griffiths, Bood & Weyers, ibid. 150, n. 193, discussing District Court, Haarlem, *Tijdschrift voor*

exists, and there is no reasonable alternative to relieve the patient's unbearable suffering, the doctor will be found to have acted proportionately[50] and the defence of necessity will be available.[51]

4. The doctor–patient relationship

In principle there should be a close relationship between the doctor and patient (where the doctor has treated the patient for some time) as the doctor must know the patient well enough to be able to assess whether his request is both voluntary and well-considered, and whether his suffering is unbearable and without prospect of improvement.[52] Cases in which there is no pre-existing doctor–patient relationship are likely to be closely investigated.[53]

B. Non-voluntary euthanasia or termination of life without request[54]

The shape of a regime resulting from necessity as the mechanism of legal change is not limited, however, to cases involving the patient's request. In the Netherlands, despite criticism from parliamentarians, lawyers, and philosophers,[55] the regulatory reporting scheme established in 1993 included cases of termination of life

---

Gezondheidsrecht (J. of Health Law) 1994, no. 48 (characterizing the patient's suffering stemming from paralysis caused by strokes as non-somatic and holding that the doctor 'had too readily accepted the patient's refusal of any alternative to assistance with suicide'). See also, Griffiths, Weyers & Adams, above n. 48, [3.2.3.3].

[50] De Vries, above n. 47, 374–6. J.F. Nijboer, 'Criminal Justice System' in J.M.J. Chorus et al., *Introduction to Dutch Law* (3rd rev. edn.) (The Hague: Kluwer Law International, 1999) 383, 410–11 (Nijboer's chapter was based on L.H.C. Hulsman et al., 'The Dutch Criminal Justice System From a Comparative Legal Perspective' in D.C. Fokkema et al., eds., *Introduction to Dutch Law for Foreign Lawyers* (Deventer: Kluwer, 1978) 289, 339).

[51] Griffiths, Bood & Weyers, above n. 38, 107. The procedural requirements are discussed in Chapter 4, text accompanying nn. 30–31, 34–42.

[52] See Griffiths, Bood & Weyers, ibid. 103, n. 41; Griffiths, Weyers & Adams, above n. 48, [3.2.3.2]; Netherlands Ministry of Foreign Affairs, *A Guide to the Dutch Termination of Life on Request and Assisted Suicide (Review Procedures) Act* (2001), § 15, www.minbuza.nl/binaries/minbuza_core_pictures/pdf/c/c_56513.pdf, accessed 24 Sept. 2006.

[53] See, e.g., Regionale toetsingscommissies euthanasie (Regional Euthanasia Review Committees), *Jaarverslag (Annual Report) 2005* (Apr. 2006) 30–31 (describing a case which was reported to the prosecutorial authorities on the grounds that the doctor, an acquaintance of the patient, did not have a sufficiently strong treatment relationship with the patient). See also, Griffiths, Bood & Weyers, above n. 38, 103, n. 41; Jacqueline M. Cuperus-Bosma et al., 'Physician-assisted Death: Policy-making by the Assembly of Prosecutors General in the Netherlands' (1997) 4 *Eur. J. Health L.* 225, 233.

[54] 'By unrequested termination of life is meant; *the intentionally and active termination of the life of a patient without the latter having requested this explicitly.*' Gerrit van der Wal, 'Unrequested Termination of Life: Is It Permissible?' (1993) 7 *Bioethics* 330, 333 (emphasis in original).

[55] See van der Wal, ibid. 331; Henk Jochemsen, 'Dutch Court Decisions on Nonvoluntary Euthanasia Critically Reviewed' (1998) 13 *Issues in Law & Med.* 447, 448; Griffiths, Weyers & Adams, above n. 48, [6.2.1].

without request.[56] Changing the reporting scheme, though, does not change the legal status of what is reported. More significantly, there were a small number of judicial decisions allowing the use of the defence of necessity in cases of termination of life without request, predominantly in cases involving neonates. This use of the defence of necessity had been anticipated by commentators.[57]

By definition, these cases are not regarded as 'euthanasia' and are therefore prosecuted as murder rather than the lesser offence of termination of life on request.[58] This case law is unaltered by the recent legislation which covers *only* termination of life on request.[59] In addition to the small number of judicial decisions, there is also considerable empirical evidence of termination of life without request for incompetent patients.[60]

---

[56] Burial and Cremation Act 1991, s. 10. This Act is often referred to by its more literal translation as the Law on Disposal of Corpses (Wet op de Lijkbezorging). In this work I use the former translation as this is the one used in the official translation of the Termination of Life on Request and Assisted Suicide (Review Procedures) Act 2001 which amends the Burial and Cremation Act 1991. See Chapter 4, Section I.C. The 1993 amendments to this provision and the Order in Council issued pursuant to it are set out in Griffiths, Bood & Weyers, above n. 38, 309. The new provisions formalized an agreement reached between the Ministry of Justice and the Royal Dutch Medical Association in 1990. See Gerrit van der Wal et al., 'Evaluation of the notification procedure for physician-assisted death in the Netherlands' (1996) 335(22) *New Eng. J. Med.* 1706; Robert J.M. Dillmann & Johan Legemaate, 'Euthanasia in The Netherlands: The state of the legal debate' (1994) 1 *Eur. J. Health L.* 81, 84–6.

[57] See, e.g., J.K.M. Gevers, 'Legislation on euthanasia: recent developments in The Netherlands' (1992) 18(3) *J. Med. Ethics* 138, 139; Dillmann & Legemaate, above n. 56, 85–6; Johannes J.M. van Delden et al., 'The Remmelink Study: Two Years Later' (1993) 23(6) *Hastings Center Rep.* 24, 25.

[58] See above n. 35.

[59] Termination of Life on Request and Assisted Suicide (Review Procedures) Act 2001. It should be noted that the statute does allow termination of life on *advance* request, if a competent person becomes incompetent after having made a 'written declaration requesting that his life be terminated' (s. 2(2)) which complies with the due care criteria in s. 2(1). See also, Mette L. Rurup et al., 'Frequency and determinants of advance directives concerning end-of-life care in The Netherlands' (2006) 62(6) *Social Science & Med.* 1552. The moral justifiability and practical feasibility of such requests is doubted by J.J.M. van Delden, 'The unfeasibility of requests for euthanasia in advance directives' (2004) 30 *J. Med. Ethics* 447. Prior to codification, the legal validity of an advance request for euthanasia had been questioned. Contrast John Griffiths & Albert Klijn, 'Can Doctors' Hands Be Bound? Advance Directives under Current Dutch Law' in Roberta Dameno, ed., *Autodeterminarsi nonostante. Atti del Convegno: Verso il riconoscimento giuridico della carta di autodeterminazione, un confronto europeo (Self-Determination notwithstanding. Conference proceedings: Towards judicial recognition of the self-determination charter, a European comparison)* (Milan: Guerini, 2002) 153 with Maurice A.M. de Wachter, 'Euthanasia in the Netherlands' (1992) 22(2) *Hastings Center Rep.* 23, 24 (stating that advance requests for euthanasia made by now incompetent patients are considered valid). This Section considers only those individuals who could not make or have not made such a declaration.

[60] See, e.g., Astrid M. Vrakking et al., 'Medical End-Of-Life Decisions for Children in the Netherlands' (2005) 159(9) *Arch. Pediat. Adol. Med.* 802, 804, Table 1 (2.7% of all reported deaths of children (aged 1 to 17) during the four-month period studied in 2001 involved the use of drugs with the explicit intention of hastening death (95% confidence interval (CI) 1.2%–6.1%); the decision was made at the child's request in 0.7% of cases (95% CI 0.1%–3.6%) (although this would not have been a legally valid request) and at the request of the family in 2% of cases (95% CI 0.8%–5.2%)); Bregje D. Onwuteaka-Philipsen et al., 'Euthanasia and other end-of-life decisions in the Netherlands in 1990, 1995, and 2001' (2003) 362 *Lancet* 395 (reporting rates of termination of life without explicit request in the range of 0.6%–0.7% of all deaths in 2001). The empirical evidence in relation to

1. The neonate cases

The termination of life of severely disabled neonates (new-born infants) was a matter of societal and academic discussion in the Netherlands in the 1980s and 1990s.[61] Both the Royal Dutch Medical Association and the Dutch Paediatrics Association published reports dealing with neonatal end of life issues.[62] In the mid-1990s, two doctors were prosecuted for murder after terminating the lives of severely disabled neonates.[63] In both *Prins* and *Kadijk* the defendant doctors were acquitted.[64] Neither case was heard by the Supreme Court (Hoge Raad),[65] so the jurisprudence is limited to the decisions of two trial courts and two Courts of Appeals (Amsterdam in *Prins*,[66] and Leeuwarden in *Kadijk*).[67] In both cases

neonates is discussed below, text accompanying nn. 78–79. For adults, see van der Wal, above n. 54, 331 (estimating that Dutch family doctors perform termination of life without request about 100 times per year). The detail of the Dutch evidence of termination of life without request and the comparability of this evidence with rates in other jurisdictions is discussed in Chapter 7, Section III.B.1.

[61] Loes Kater et al., 'Health care ethics and health law in the Dutch discussion on end-of-life decisions: a historical analysis of the dynamics and development of both disciplines' (2003) 34 *Stud. Hist. Phil. Biol. & Biomed. Sci.* 669, 679–80; Griffiths, Bood & Weyers, above n. 38, 82–4, 123–6, 229–32. In English, see, e.g., H.J.J. Leenen & Chris Ciesielski-Carlucci, 'Force Majeure (Legal Necessity): Justification for Active Termination of Life in the Case of Severely Handicapped Newborns after Forgoing Treatment' (1993) 2(3) *Camb. Q. Healthcare Ethics* 271; E. van Leeuwen & G.K. Kimsma, 'Acting or Letting Go: Medical Decision Making in Neonatology in The Netherlands' (1993) 2(3) *Camb. Q. Healthcare Ethics* 265; CQ *Interview* with Heleen M. Dupuis, 'Actively Ending the Life of a Severely Handicapped Newborn: A Dutch Ethicist's Perspective' (1993) 2(3) *Camb. Q. Healthcare Ethics* 275.

[62] Commissie Aanvaardbaarheid Levensbeëindigend Handelen (Commission on the Acceptability of Termination of Life of the Royal Dutch Medical Association), *Discussienota Levensbeëindigend handelen bij wilsonbekwame patiënten: I. Zwaar-defecte pasgeborenen (Discussion Papers on Life Ending Treatment with Incompetent Patients: Part I. Severely Defective Neonates)* (1990); Nederlandse Vereniging voor Kindergeneeskunde (Dutch Paediatrics Association), *Doen of laten? Grenzen van het medisch handelen in de neonatologie (Acting or Deciding to Forgo? Limits of Medical Treatment in Neonatology)* (1992).

[63] Criminal Code, Art. 289. See Louise Rayar & Stafford Wadsworth, trans., *The Dutch Penal Code* (Littleton, Colo.: Fred B. Rothman & Co., 1997) 199, reproduced in Griffiths, Bood & Weyers, above n. 38, 308. See above, text accompanying n. 58.

[64] These decisions have been condemned by two United Nations committees. See U.N. International Covenant on Civil and Political Rights Human Rights Committee, *Concluding Observations: Netherlands,* 27 Aug. 2001, CCPR/CO/72/NET, [6], www.unhchr.ch/tbs/doc.nsf/0/dbab71d01e02db11c1256a950041d732?Opendocument, accessed 29 July 2006; U.N. Committee on the Rights of the Child, *Concluding Observations: The Kingdom of the Netherlands (Netherlands and Aruba),* 26 Feb. 2004, CRC/C/15/Add.227, [33]–[34], www.unhchr.ch/tbs/doc.nsf/0/91e3134842f2024cc1256e76002b5ff8?Opendocument, accessed 29 July 2006.

[65] In both cases '[t]he responsible prosecutorial officials saw no grounds for an appeal to the Supreme Court.' Griffiths, Bood & Weyers, above n. 38, 126.

[66] *Prins*, Court of Appeals, Amsterdam, 7 Nov. 1995, N.J. 1996, no. 113, summarized in Jochemsen, above n. 55, 451–3. See also, Arlene Judith Klotzko, 'What Kind of Life? What Kind of Death? An Interview with Dr. Henk Prins' in Thomasma, above n. 48, 389; Griffiths, Bood & Weyers, above n. 38, 83; Jozef H.H.M. Dorscheidt, 'Assessment Procedures Regarding End-of-Life Decisions in Neonatology in the Netherlands' (2005) 24 *Med. & L.* 803, 804–6.

[67] *Kadijk*, Court of Appeals, Leeuwarden, 4 Apr. 1996, *Tijdschrift voor Gezondheidsrecht (J. of Health Law)* 1996, no. 35, translated in Griffiths, Bood & Weyers, above n. 38, App. II-3, 341. See also, Jochemsen, above n. 55, 451–4; Dorscheidt, above n. 66.

alternative defences were rejected,[68] but the defence of necessity was held to be applicable. The doctors had been faced with conflicting duties to preserve life and relieve unbearable and hopeless suffering.[69] In both cases a decision had already been taken that continued treatment was medically futile, and all parties had accepted that this decision would result in the child's death.[70] The unbearable suffering experienced by both children was therefore hopeless. In *Kadijk*, the Appeal Court concluded that in these circumstances, the doctor was faced with 'two options: to treat the manifest pain and the discomfort of the baby as adequately as possible until she gave up the struggle, or actively to terminate the child's life in accordance with the parents' request.'[71]

Both doctors had consulted colleagues and had reported the deaths as unnatural. These procedural requirements were considered important by the courts,[72] and are analogous to the judicially imposed procedural requirements in cases of euthanasia.[73] In the absence of any further governmental intervention to regulate the procedural requirements, and in particular, to set up a review committee to advise the prosecutorial authorities (as had been done prior to codification in the euthanasia context),[74] the University Medical Center Groningen recently developed a protocol setting out both the substantive requirements derived from *Prins* and *Kadijk* and a lengthy list of procedural and documentary requirements.[75] The Groningen Protocol was subsequently adopted by the Dutch Paediatrics Association for national use.[76] Finally, at the end of 2005, the government

---

[68] See *Kadijk*, above n. 67, 346–7 and Jochemsen, above n. 66, 452. These alternative defences (that life had not been 'taken' within the meaning of the Criminal Code and the medical exception) had earlier been rejected in the context of euthanasia (termination of life on request). See Chapter 4, n. 16.   [69] *Kadijk*, above n. 67, 348.

[70] See Dorscheidt, above n. 66, 806.

[71] *Kadijk*, above n. 67, 349. See also, *Prins*, discussed in Jochemsen, above n. 55, 452–3.

[72] See amendment to the Burial and Cremation Act, above n. 56, discussed in Jonathan T. Smies, 'The Legalization of Euthanasia in the Netherlands' (2003–04) 7 *Gonz. J. Int'l L.* 1, 32–35; Griffiths, Bood & Weyers, above n. 38, 79–80; Griffiths, Weyers & Adams, above n. 48, [6.2.2.2]; *Kadijk*, above n. 67, 350; *Prins*, District Court, Alkmaar, 26 Apr. 1995, N.J. 1995, no. 602, 2878, summarized in Griffiths, Bood & Weyers, above, 83 and Tony Sheldon, 'Dutch Court Convicts Doctor of Murder' (1995) 310 *Br. Med. J.* 1028.

[73] The procedural requirements are discussed in Chapter 4, text accompanying nn. 30–31, 34–42.

[74] The government 'promised repeatedly, since 1997, to do [this]'. Eduard Verhagen & Pieter J.J. Sauer, 'The Groningen Protocol – Euthanasia in Severely Ill Newborns' (2005) 352(10) *New Eng. J. Med.* 959, 961. The establishment of a review committee was recommended by the Consultative Committee set up in 1996 by the Ministers of Health and Justice. *Toetsing als Spiegel van de Medische Praktijk: Rapport van de overleggroep toetsing zorgvuldig medisch handelen rond het levenseinde bij pasgeborenen* (*Assessment as a mirror of medical practice: Report by the consultative committee concerned with examining careful medical treatment in relation to neonatal deaths)* (Rijswijk: Ministerie van VWS, 1997), discussed by Griffiths, Weyers & Adams, above n. 48, [6.2.2.4]. See also, Tony Sheldon, 'Dutch doctors call for new approach to reporting "mercy killings"' (2004) 329 *Br. Med. J.* 591.

[75] Verhagen & Sauer, above n. 74, 961. The protocol was developed in collaboration with the local prosecutor. See also, Eduard Verhagen & Pieter J.J. Sauer, 'End-of-life decisions in newborns: An approach from the Netherlands' (2005) 116(3) *Pediatrics* 736. See the critical discussion of some of the ambiguities in the protocol in Griffiths, Weyers & Adams, above n. 48, [6.2.2.5]. See also, the interview with Eduard Verhagen in Tony Sheldon, 'Killing or caring?' (2005) 330 *Br. Med. J.* 560.

[76] Nederlandse Vereniging voor Kindergeneeskunde (NVK) (Dutch Paediatrics Association), 'NVK neemt "Gronings Protocol" over' ('NVK adopts "Groningen Protocol"') 1 July 2005,

incorporated the essence of the protocol into an Order in Council creating a national Review Committee for these cases.[77]

Although only *Prins* and *Kadijk* have been prosecuted, other cases of the termination of life of a neonate have been reported. During the period from 1997 to 2004, 22 such cases were reported. 'In all cases the Public Prosecutor decided not to prosecute the physicians in charge, as they were believed to have acted in an emergency situation in which the termination of the child's life was considered to be the last remaining humane option.'[78] Legal uncertainty probably contributes to a low reporting rate – it is estimated that 90–100 such cases occur annually.[79]

---

www.nvk.pedianet.nl/pdfs/persbericht_nvk_010705.pdf, accessed 23 June 2006. See also, NVK, 'Point of view NVK on "Procedure active life-ending treatment newborns"' 10 Mar. 2005, www.nvk.pedianet.nl/index.htm?/standpunt_le_en.htm, accessed 23 June 2006; Tony Sheldon, 'Dutch doctors adopt guidelines on mercy killing of newborns' (2005) 331 *Br. Med. J.* 126; Griffiths, Weyers & Adams, above n. 48, [6.2.2.5].

[77] Clémence Ross-van Dorp, State Secretary for Health, Welfare and Sport & Piet Hein Donner, Minister of Justice, *Termination of life (neonates)*, Parliamentary document, 29 Nov. 2005, IBE/E-2637467, www.minvws.nl/en/kamerstukken/ibe/2005/termination-of-life-neonates.asp, accessed 29 July 2006, establishing a review procedure including an expert committee to make recommendations to the public prosecutor. See also, Tony Sheldon, 'The Netherlands regulates ending the lives of severely ill neonates' (2005) 331 *Br. Med. J.* 1357.

[78] Dorscheidt, above n. 66, 829, citing A.A.E. Verhagen et al., 'Actieve levensbeëindiging bij pasgeborenen in Nederland, Een analyse van alle 22 meldingen van 1997–2004' ('Deliberate ending of life in newborns in the Netherlands, an analysis of all reported cases 1997–2004') (2005) 149(4) *Nederlands Tijdschrift voor Geneeskunde (Dutch J. of Med.)* 183. 'Almost all reported cases involved children with severe spina bifida.' Dorscheidt, ibid. See also, Ian Traynor, 'Secret Killings of Newborn Babies Trap Dutch Doctors in Moral Maze' *Guardian*, 21 Dec. 2004.

[79] The evidence on the total number of cases is unclear. See Agnes van der Heide et al., 'Medical end-of-life decisions made for neonates and infants in the Netherlands' (1997) 350 *Lancet* 251, 253 (in a study of 299 neonatal deaths in 1995 (total number of neonatal deaths in 1995 was 1041), 8% of deaths studied involved decision to forgo life-sustaining treatment combined with drugs given explicitly to hasten death (95% CI 5%–12%); 1% of cases involved administration of drug explicitly to hasten death to an infant not preceded by a decision to withhold or withdraw life-sustaining treatment (95% CI 0.5%–4%)). In the 2001 follow-up to Van der Heide et al.'s 1995 study, ibid., the authors concluded that '[t]he frequency of the active ending of life has not risen despite the new, more liberal, regulatory system of such actions in the Netherlands.' Astrid M. Vrakking et al., 'Medical end-of-life decisions made for neonates and infants in the Netherlands, 1995–2001' (2005) 365 *Lancet* 1329, Table 1, 1331 (in a study of 233 neonatal deaths in 2001 (the total number of neonatal deaths in 2001 was 1088), 8% of deaths studied involved a decision to forgo life-sustaining treatment combined with drugs given explicitly to hasten death (95% CI 5%–12%); 1% of cases involved administration of a drug explicitly to hasten death to an infant not preceded by a decision to withhold or withdraw life-sustaining treatment (95% CI 0.5%–4%)). Lower numbers reported by Verhagen & Sauer, above n. 74, 961 (estimating 15–20 deaths per year) and Eduard Verhagen, 'Developments with regard to end-of-life decisions concerning newborns in The Netherlands' (2005) 9 *Newsletter RSPMB* 3, 5 (estimating 10–20 deaths per year) involve a 'much more limited category than that of active termination [of life]. In their view, the Protocol applies only to the situation in which, after treatment has been withdrawn, the baby does not die immediately; its medical situation becomes (temporarily) stable, and the use of euthanatica is the only reasonable way of putting an end to its suffering.' Griffiths, Weyers & Adams, above n. 48, [6.2.3], n. 75.

Although these numbers are high in comparison to many other European jurisdictions, the numbers are comparable in Flanders, Belgium and probably higher in France (both jurisdictions in which such actions are unlawful). See Veerle Provoost et al., 'Medical end-of-life decisions in neonates and infants in Flanders' (2005) 365 *Lancet* 1315, Table 2 (lethal dose of drugs administered in 7% of

When the defence of necessity is the mechanism of legal change in cases of termination of life, the inclusion of those who are not able to consent for themselves is unsurprising. After all, an incompetent person may also experience unbearable and hopeless suffering,[80] with the result that her doctor may be faced with conflicting duties to preserve life and relieve suffering.[81] In both *Prins* and *Kadijk*, the requirement of unbearable and hopeless suffering was met as a consequence of an agreed decision that continued treatment was medically futile; a decision which would inevitably result in the child's death.[82] The unbearable suffering experienced by both children was therefore hopeless. It seems unlikely, however, that this is the only way in which unbearable and hopeless suffering can be demonstrated in neonate cases.[83]

The defence of necessity is predominantly used in cases involving a request, when the defendant is prosecuted for the termination of life on request.[84] But it is also used in cases where there is no possibility of a request, and the defendant is prosecuted for murder. A regime resulting from necessity as the mechanism of legal change, therefore, does not *require* a competent request if the patient is incompetent.

2. Proxy consent

Could proxy consent be considered a substitute for the request of the individual who is unable to make one?[85] In both of the lower court decisions in *Prins* and

cases); Marina Cuttini et al., 'End-of-life decisions in neonatal intensive care: physicians' self-reported practices in seven European countries' (2000) 355 *Lancet* 2112, 2114, Table 6 (73% of French neonatologists and 47% of Dutch neonatologists surveyed reported having made decisions to administer drugs 'with the purpose of ending the patient's life'; adjusted figures show an even greater disparity of 86% and 45% respectively).

[80] See Gerrit K. Kimsma & Evert van Leeuwen, 'Euthanasia and Assisted Suicide in the Netherlands and the USA: Comparing Practices, Justifications and Key Concepts in Bioethics and Law' in Thomasma, above n. 48, 35, 50 ('if the definition of [euthanasia] is narrowed down to the accepted termination of life only when a request is present, patients who cannot communicate run the risk of abandonment if the legal definition is taken *strictu sensu*'); Harry Kuitert with Evert van Leeuwen, 'A Religious Argument in Favor of Euthanasia and Assisted Suicide' in Thomasma, above n. 48, 221, 225 ('Is it the bitter privilege of patients who are beyond asking for euthanasia, not to be helped out of their agony, just because they cannot . . . articulate their wish to die?'); Martien A.M. Pijnenburg, 'Catholic Healthcare and the Dutch National Character' in Thomasma, ibid. 241, 246, 247–8.

[81] See Leenen & Ciesielski-Carlucci, above n. 61, 273–4 (anticipating the application of the defence of necessity to severely disabled neonates prior to the decisions in *Prins* and *Kadijk*).

[82] See Dorscheidt, above n. 66, 806.

[83] See Ross-van Dorp & Donner, above n. 77, § 2(a): 'Termination of life is only at issue when the life of a newborn infant is intentionally shortened because of the extreme nature of its suffering. In some cases the child would have died anyway. In other cases, the child might be able to survive but there is no possibility of any improvement in its health, resulting in constant, unbearable suffering with no prospect of improvement. There is also no prospect of an independent life. In these cases palliative care will also be given.' See also, the evidence that 1% of cases studied in 1995 and 2001 involved the administration of a drug explicitly to hasten death to an infant which was not preceded by a decision to withhold or withdraw life-sustaining treatment (95% CI 0.5%–4%). Vrakking, above n. 79, Table 1, 1331; van der Heide, above n. 79, 253.

[84] Criminal Code, Art. 293. See Chapter 4, Section I.

[85] In the District Court in *Kadijk*, the court 'explicitly rejected the idea that the termination of a baby's life at the request of the parents could legally be seen as a case of euthanasia by proxy request

Kadijk, and in the decision of the Court of Appeals in *Kadijk*, 'the fact that there was no doubt at all as to the well-considered consent of the parents to the termination of life'[86] was an important factor in the courts' decisions. However, in the decision of the Court of Appeals in *Prins*, '[t]he parents' request disappeared as a crucial legal determinant,'[87] although it was nonetheless present. There is little empirical evidence available on the presence or absence of parental consent in such cases,[88] though parental consent was obtained in all of the 22 cases which were reported to the prosecutorial authorities from 1997 to 2004.[89]

Arguably, while a requirement of parental consent can be considered to be 'good as a matter of medical ethics',[90] and is required under the Groningen protocol and its government-created successor,[91] it is not mandated by a focus on the conflicting duties to preserve life and relieve suffering. That conflict of duties could be present in circumstances where the parents have either refused consent or have not been asked for their consent.[92] It could, however, be seen as further evidence of the role of the principle of autonomy in Dutch law and practice.[93]

3. Incompetent persons generally

Nothing in *Kadijk* or *Prins* suggests that the applicability of the defence of necessity outside of the euthanasia context is restricted to neonates. Indeed, the defence could be available if an incompetent person, whether child or adult, is experiencing unbearable and hopeless suffering, most likely following a decision

[and thereby fall under Article 293 of the Criminal Code]. Life and death are not matters in which a proxy could decide on behalf of the patient himself.' Jochemsen, above n. 55, 453, citing *Kadijk*, District Court, Groningen, 13 Nov. 1995.

86 *Kadijk*, above n. 67, 350.

87 Klotzko, above n. 66, 390. See also, Griffiths, Bood & Weyers, above n. 38, 83, n. 129.

88 On physicians' attitudes, see van der Heide, above n. 79, Table 3, 254 (while 100% of the 31 neonatologists and paediatric intensive care specialists interviewed thought that the decision to administer a drug with the explicit intention of ending life was inconceivable without parental approval, '23% of the [35] general paediatricians, however, thought that the . . . administration of a drug explicitly to end life can very occasionally, occur without the parents' approval'). On parental involvement more generally, see Vrakking, above n. 79, 1330, reporting that in all end of life decision-making, discussion with parents increased by 6% in 2001 (from 1995, see van der Heide, above), although a large majority of end of life decisions are not made at the explicit request of parents. In 2001, 29% of end of life decisions were made at the explicit request of parents (95% CI 23%–37%). In 1995, 28% of end of life decisions were made at the explicit request of parents (95% CI 22%–34%). Vrakking, above, Table 2.
Once again, this phenomenon is not restricted to the Netherlands. Parents were not consulted in 3 of the 17 cases of the administration of a lethal dose of drugs reported in Provoost, above n. 79, Table 2. See Veerle Provoost, *End-of-life Decisions in Neonates and Infants in Flanders, Belgium* (Dissertation: Vrije Universiteit Brussels, 2005) ch. 4, discussed in Griffiths, Weyers & Adams, above n. 48, [6.3.2].

89 See above, text accompanying n. 78; Verhagen & Sauer, above n. 74, 961.

90 *Kadijk*, above n. 67, 348.

91 See Verhagen & Sauer, above n. 74, 961, Table 2; Ross-van Dorp & Donner, above n. 77, § 4.

92 For an anecdotal example of the reverse scenario, in which a neonatologist refused to honour the parents' request for the termination of life of a child the doctor did not believe was suffering, see Anonymous Neonatologist, 'Just What Are We Doing?' in Thomasma, above n. 48, 355, 359.

93 See Chapter 4, Section III.B.3.a.

that the continuation of life-sustaining treatment is medically futile. At least one such case has been reported to prosecutorial authorities who declined to prosecute on the grounds that the circumstances of the case 'would have led to a successful defence of [necessity]'.[94] In another case, a doctor who had terminated the life of an unconscious terminal cancer patient whose suffering was unbearable and hopeless was acquitted of manslaughter on the grounds of necessity.[95]

More recently, in *Van Oijen*, a doctor who terminated the life of his incompetent patient was found guilty of murder.[96] The patient suffered from a heart condition and osteoporosis. She was bedridden and developed necrotic bedsores. Palliative pain relief was provided and the patient eventually became unconscious. With the consent of her daughters, the defendant injected the patient with a euthanaticum and she died almost immediately.[97]

The Supreme Court accepted that the defence of necessity could be available, in principle, in cases of termination of life without request. As in the euthanasia cases, the defendant must face conflicting duties. In *Van Oijen*, the court found that '[t]his threshold ... had not been met by the case put forward by the defendant.'[98] The patient was comatose and therefore not suffering unbearably, and her death was imminent. As a reasonable alternative, the defendant could have given the patient a further injection of the sedative phenobarbital, as he himself had recognized. Thus the defendant had not found himself in a situation of necessity.[99]

The Supreme Court agreed with the reasons of the Court of Appeals which had held that in cases of termination of life without request, in addition to the substantive requirements of unbearable and hopeless suffering with no reasonable alternative to relieve that suffering, the doctor must also abide by the procedural rules established in the euthanasia cases.[100] The defendant had failed to comply with the procedural due care criteria in several respects, including the requirement of consultation with another doctor.[101] In addition, he was found guilty of failing to report the event.[102]

---

[94] Griffiths, Bood & Weyers, above n. 38, 130–1, quoting the Minister of Justice, Second Chamber of Parliament 1991–1992, appendix, no. 394.

[95] District Court, Almelo, 28 Jan. 1997, discussed in Griffiths, Bood & Weyers, above n. 38, 132–3. Increasingly large doses of morphine had not eased the patient's pain. Terminal sedation had been attempted but had failed, and the doctor was concerned that the patient might wake up with brain damage before another anaesthetic dose could be obtained.

[96] Supreme Court, 9 Nov. 2004, N.J. 2005, no. 217. The court upheld the sentence imposed by the Court of Appeals, Amsterdam of one week's imprisonment, suspended for two years. See the case comment by Michael Bohlander at (2005) 69(5) *J. Crim. L.* 401. Van Oijen's patient had, when competent, expressed a desire to be kept alive. Bohlander, ibid.   [97] Bohlander, ibid.

[98] Ibid.   [99] Ibid.

[100] Ibid. The procedural requirements are discussed in Chapter 4, text accompanying nn. 30–31, 34–42.

[101] Tony Sheldon, 'Dutch GP Found Guilty of Murder Faces No Penalty' (2001) 322 *Br. Med. J.* 509.

[102] A violation of Article 228(1) of the Dutch Criminal Code: 'A physician ... who intentionally issues a false certificate ... of the cause of death ... is liable to a term of imprisonment of not more than three years or a fine of the fourth category.' Rayar & Wadsworth, above n. 63, 176. A suspended fine of ƒ5,000 was imposed (this was a fine of the second category (now €2,250)). A fine of the fourth category would have been ƒ25,000 and is now €11,250. Van Oijen also faced a medical disciplinary

4. No reasonable alternative

In cases of suffering caused by a somatic condition, the 'no reasonable alternative' requirement may still be met if a competent person refuses treatment which might ease the suffering.[103] What if the individual is not competent? An advance (competent) refusal of palliative care would presumably be unlikely.[104] Thus the medical team will need to examine carefully the prospect of easing the patient's dying using palliative care techniques, although palliative care may not always be effective.[105] Indeed, in all of the cases discussed above, palliative care was given and the decision to terminate life was only taken after an assessment that the patient was suffering despite the use of palliative care.[106] For example, in *Kadijk*, the baby

board and received a warning. See Tony Sheldon, 'Two test cases in Holland clarify law on murder and palliative care' (2004) 329 *Br. Med. J.* 1206; Tony Sheldon, 'Court upholds murder verdict on doctor who ended woman's life' (2003) 326 *Br. Med. J.* 1351.

[103] See above, text accompanying n. 48.

[104] Although in rare cases, such a refusal might be coupled with a declaration requesting euthanasia. See above n. 59.

[105] Even terminal sedation may not always be effective. See Susan Chater et al., 'Sedation for intractable distress in the dying – a survey of experts' (1998) 12 *Palliative Med.* 255, 260 (reporting terminal sedation unsuccessful in 10 out of 100 cases). For other examples of unsuccessful terminal sedation, see above n. 95 and *Morrison* (1998) 174 N.S.R. (2d) 201 (N.S.S.C.), discussed in Barney Sneiderman & Raymond Deutscher, 'Dr. Nancy Morrison and Her Dying Patient: A Case of Medical Necessity' (2002) 10 *Health L.J.* 1, [62]. In their concurrences in *Vacco v. Quill* (1997) 521 U.S. 793 and *Washington v. Glucksberg* (1997) 521 U.S. 702, 736–7, 791–2, O'Connor, Breyer, and Ginsburg JJ. stated that palliative care, including terminal sedation if necessary, could alleviate the pain of *all* terminally ill patients. Terminal sedation is 'defined as the *intention* of deliberately inducing and maintaining deep sleep, but *not* deliberately causing death . . . for the relief of one or more intractable symptoms when all other possible interventions have failed and the patient is perceived to be close to death, or . . . for the relief of profound anguish (possibly spiritual) that is not amenable to spiritual, psychological, or other interventions, and the patient is perceived to be close to death.' Chater, above, 257–8 (emphasis in original). The Royal Dutch Medical Association (KNMG) has recently published guidelines on 'palliative sedation' which it defines as 'the deliberate lowering of a patient's level of consciousness in the last stages of life.' KNMG Committee on National Guidelines for Palliative Sedation, *Guidelines for Palliative Sedation* (2005), http://knmg.artsennet.nl/uri/?uri= AMGATE_6059_100_TICH_R171322439726668, accessed 30 July 2006. See also, Judith A.C. Rietjens et al., 'Physician Reports of Terminal Sedation without Hydration or Nutrition for Patients Nearing Death in the Netherlands' (2004) 141(3) *Annals Internal Med.* 178; Muriel R. Gillick, 'Terminal Sedation: An Acceptable Exit Strategy?' (2004) 141(3) *Annals Internal Med.* 236, 237. The legality of terminal sedation in the Netherlands was the subject of a recent prosecution which resulted in acquittal at both the trial and appeal levels. *Vencken*, District Court, Breda, Nov. 2004; Court of Appeals, Den Bosch, 29 July 2005, discussed in Sheldon, 'Two test cases in Holland', above n. 102; Tony Sheldon, 'Dutch murder case leads to talks with attorney general' (2005) 331 *Br. Med. J.* 473; Tony Sheldon, 'Doctor who was remanded for murder wins record damages' (2006) 332 *Br. Med. J.* 443. See also, Tony Sheldon ' "Terminal sedation" different from euthanasia, Dutch ministers agree' (2003) 327 *Br. Med. J.* 465; Tony Sheldon, 'Dutch doctors choose sedation rather than euthanasia' (2004) 329 *Br. Med. J.* 368.

[106] In *Prins*, Court of Appeals, Amsterdam, 7 Nov. 1995, N.J. 1996, no. 113, 'the baby had spina bifida, hydrocephalus, a spinal cord lesion and brain damage. The specialists decided not to operate on the spina bifida, because of the bad prognosis. From her behavior it was concluded that the baby was suffering severe pain which was difficult to treat.' Jochemsen, above n. 55, 451. See also, Griffiths, Bood & Weyers, above n. 38, 83. In the case of the adult terminal cancer patient discussed above, text accompanying n. 95, various forms of pain relief and terminal sedation had been unsuccessful at the time the decision was taken.

suffered from serious congenital defects due to the chromosomal condition trisomy-13.[107] Some time after a decision had been made that aggressive treatment would be medically futile, she developed a complication.[108] Despite the administration of pain relief and a sedative, she appeared to be experiencing worsening pain and suffering as the severity of the complication increased.[109] It was at this point that the parents made a formal request for the doctor to terminate the child's life.

C. Conclusion

The key elements of the regime resulting from the defence of necessity as the mechanism of legal change in the Netherlands are the requirement that the patient be experiencing unbearable and hopeless suffering and the unavailability of any reasonable alternative to relieve that suffering. If the patient is competent, she must make a considered and voluntary request for euthanasia or assisted suicide. Although there have been no prosecutions for murder in circumstances of involuntary euthanasia,[110] it is clear that this would not be permissible from the competent patient's role in determining whether her suffering is hopeless and unbearable, and in rejecting available treatments.[111] The emphasis on the principle of autonomy provides further confirmation of the impermissibility of involuntary euthanasia.[112]

If the patient is incompetent and receiving life-sustaining treatment, a decision should be made whether the continuation of that treatment is medically futile. If so, it can be withdrawn, and active termination of life may be justifiable under the defence of necessity if she then experiences unbearable and hopeless suffering and no reasonable alternative is available to relieve that suffering.

Finally, if the patient is incompetent but is not receiving any life-sustaining treatment (for example, a terminal cancer patient who is incompetent for reasons which may or may not be related to the cancer), the decision in *Van Oijen* suggests that the defence of necessity may also be available, provided that the patient is suffering unbearably and hopelessly, and there is no reasonable alternative to relieve the suffering. In some (perhaps many) cases, the alternative of palliative care (possibly including terminal sedation if this is a viable option) may preclude the use of necessity in this context. One can nonetheless conclude, from both the neonate and incompetent adult cases, that non-voluntary euthanasia is permissible in certain limited circumstances.[113]

---

[107] The baby had 'deformities of skull, face and hands, heart and kidney malfunction and brain damage'. Jochemsen, above n. 55, 451.

[108] Cerebral membrane was bulging through an opening in the baby's skull. *Kadijk*, above n. 67, 342–3.   [109] *Kadijk*, ibid. 343.

[110] There is some limited evidence of involuntary euthanasia in the Netherlands, although it is not legally accepted. See, e.g., van der Wal, above n. 54, 337.

[111] See Rob Schwitters, 'Slipping into normality? Some Reflections on Slippery Slopes' in Klijn, above n. 45, 93, 106.   [112] See Chapter 4, Section III.B.3.a.

[113] Questions have been raised about the compatibility of this position with the right to life found in Article 2 of the European Convention on Human Rights. See, e.g., Dorscheidt, above n. 66,

IV. Compassion as the Mechanism of Legal Change

The regime resulting from the proposal by the French National Bioethics Advisory Committee (Comité Consultatif National d'Éthique or CCNE) to use compassion as the mechanism of legal change would apply only in a small minority of cases, when palliative care, accompaniment, and the rejection of futile and aggressive therapy (l'acharnement thérapeutique) would be inadequate to provide 'a tolerable end of life'.[114] In these cases, the CCNE recommended that 'human solidarity and compassion' and a 'joint commitment' made 'to face the inevitable' should allow for an exceptional approach permitting active euthanasia.[115] Retrospective assessment would examine the defendant's 'motivation, i.e. concern to end suffering,' whether the defendant had acted upon a request made by the patient, and whether the defendant had acted with compassion in the face of the inevitable.[116]

Discerning the shape of this regime is not straightforward. The substantive requirements apparently include terminal illness, as this is presumably what is meant by the repeated references to 'the inevitable'.[117] There is also a suffering requirement, as the patient's suffering must be 'intolerable', 'unbearable', and 'intractable'.[118] The prerequisite that euthanasia is only available in the exceptional cases where palliative care, accompaniment, and the rejection of futile and aggressive therapy would be inadequate may constitute a 'no reasonable alternative' requirement.[119]

Critics of the CCNE proposal have raised the problem of vagueness in relation to these criteria. How would these exceptional or extreme cases be defined?[120] If euthanasia is only to be used in the exceptional cases where palliative care, accompaniment, and the rejection of futile and aggressive therapy would be inadequate, then how will a legal standard be fixed which will ensure that adequate efforts have been made in all of these three areas and who will decide

---

812–24; Griffiths, Weyers & Adams, above n. 48, [6.2.2.6]. Van der Wal points out that it may be difficult to distinguish non-voluntary from involuntary euthanasia in some cases. Van der Wal, above n. 54, 339 ('in principle it will never be possible to draw a clear dividing line between unrequested and unwanted termination of life'). This would only be relevant, though, in cases where the now incompetent individual was once competent to express her views.

[114] CCNE, *Fin de vie, arrêt de vie, euthanasie (End of life, ending life, euthanasia)*, no. 63, 27 Jan. 2000. All translations from CCNE opinions are from the official translations.

[115] CCNE, no. 63, ibid. § 4. Boitte et al. question whether the notion of 'joint commitment' can have meaning in a legal context. P. Boitte et al., 'Point de vue sur le rapport n° 63 du Comité Consultatif National d'Éthique: "Fin de vie – Arrêt de vie – Euthanasie" ' ('Point of view on CCNE Report no. 63: "End of life, ending life, euthanasia" ' (2000) 24 *Les Cahiers du CCNE* 11, 12–13.

[116] CCNE, no. 63, above n. 114, § 4.

[117] See, e.g., ibid.: 'In the face of imminent death, at the end of life, when the battle is done, there is surely more dignity in facing up to inevitable fatality and thereby consenting to it, than in seeking to disguise it and run away from it.'   [118] Ibid. § 3.

[119] Ibid. § 4.

[120] Patrick Verspieren, 'L'exception d'euthanasie' ('The euthanasia exception') (2000) 392(5) *Études* 581, 582.

when suffering becomes intolerable?[121] In the Netherlands it is clear that both the patient and the doctor play a role in this assessment.[122]

Finally, the opinion states that the individual's request for euthanasia must be 'lucid, repeated, and freely given'.[123] However, although the opinion mentions repeatedly the need to obtain consent, there is no discussion of the need for the *request* for euthanasia to come from the patient.[124] Indeed, the CCNE would allow for the possibility of euthanasia to be consented to by a health care proxy: either one who had obtained the patient's consent prior to her incompetence or the parents of a severely disabled neonate.[125] Once this latter category is permitted, it would be illogical not to allow the inclusion of incompetent children of any age whose parents consent. Certainly it is hard to reconcile the emphasis on consent with the CCNE's identification of severely disabled neonates as one example of persons who might qualify for euthanasia.

At first glance, the contours of regimes using either compassion or the defence of necessity as the mechanisms of legal change look similar, with the addition of a terminal illness requirement in the former. More detailed comparison is undertaken in the next section.

V. Summarizing the Boundaries

This section considers the main substantive and procedural components of the three regimes canvassed above. The overall aim is to assess the extent to which the three mechanisms of legal change produce outcomes which are different in any respects, and in particular relevant to the slippery slope arguments which are discussed in Chapter 7.

One specific question to be addressed here is whether regimes resulting from necessity and compassion as mechanisms of legal change can be distinguished or

---

[121] Jacques Ricot, 'Un avis controversé sur l'euthanasie' ('A controversial opinion on euthanasia') (2000) 11 *Esprit* 98, 109; National Assembly, Hearing of Dr. J.-M. Gomas on 6 Jan. 2004, *Hearings (Leonetti Report)*, No. 1708, 30 June 2004, vol. 2, 413, 418, www.assemblee-nat.fr/12/rap-info/i1708-t2.asp, accessed 20 July 2006. These objections could also be levelled against the Dutch regime resulting from necessity as the mechanism of legal change, although in cases of suffering stemming from a somatic condition, the patient's right to refuse other alternatives gives her some control over the judgment as to whether there is a reasonable alternative, which reduces the problem of vagueness. See above, Section III.A.3.   [122] See above, Section III.A.2.

[123] CCNE, no. 63, above n. 114, § 3.

[124] Pascale Boucaud, 'Commentaire de l'avis du comité national consultatif d'éthique du 27 janvier 2000, intitulé "fin de vie, arrêt de vie, euthanasie" ' ('Commentary on the CCNE opinion of 27 Jan. 2000 entitled "end of life, ending life, euthanasia" ' (2000) 48(6) *Laennec* 10, 12. Although one of the members of the CCNE has referred extensively to the need for a request from the patient in writings intended to explain the opinion. See Jean-François Collange, 'Editorial' (2000) 23 *Cahiers du CCNE* 2 and also Jean-François Collange, 'L'Avis 63 et l'éthique protestante' ('Opinion 63 and protestant ethics') Chaire Benjamin Edmond de Rothschild pour l'éthique bio-médicale, *Fin de vie, arrêt de vie, euthanasie: avis 63 du CCNE*, 16ème Entretiens consacrés à l'éthique bio-médicale, Palais du Luxembourg, 18 & 19 Nov. 2000, 4.   [125] CCNE, no. 63, above n. 114, § 4.

rather should be considered together. Three aspects of the CCNE proposal could serve to distinguish it from the position in the Netherlands: the requirement of the patient's consent or request; the requirement of terminal illness; and the question whether the performance of assisted dying would be restricted to doctors. The role of the suffering criterion; whether the regime necessarily encompasses assisted dying or can be restricted to assisted suicide; and the role of prospective versus retrospective assessment are also examined.

A. Request

Although euthanasia in the Netherlands is restricted to cases of competent request, termination of life without request is also permissible when necessity is the mechanism of legal change.[126] Proxy consent is encompassed within the CCNE proposal which would use compassion as the mechanism of legal change. In this respect, therefore, the contours of regimes using either compassion or necessity as the mechanisms of legal change look similar: when the patient is incompetent, termination of life without the patient's request may be permissible, though only in certain limited circumstances.[127]

Given that the use of rights as a mechanism of legal change has been unsuccessful where it has been attempted, drawing out the contours of the potential regimes is far more difficult than for the defence of necessity in the Netherlands, for example. What if the constitutional challenges brought in Canada, the United States, and England had been successful? These three jurisdictions are the only ones in which this mechanism of legal change was attempted, albeit unsuccessfully. They provide an appropriate legal context, therefore, to attempt to answer this hypothetical question and will be referred to as the test jurisdictions.

All of the regimes described in Section II as potential outcomes of the use of rights as a mechanism of legal change require a competent request. As we saw in Chapter 3, some commentators have argued that the extension of the right to refuse life-sustaining treatment to incompetent persons suggests that any right to assistance in dying could be similarly extended.[128] How realistic might this be? Different basic rights may underlie the right to refuse treatment and the right to assistance in dying.[129] Nevertheless, the issue here is whether an extension to incompetent persons can be predicted *once* a right to assistance in dying has been recognized.

Three decision-making approaches must be distinguished. First, an advance request for assistance in dying made prior to incompetence can most easily be considered an exercise of the right to assistance in dying. Anticipatory refusals of

---

126 See above, Section III.B.
127 See above, Section III.C and text accompanying nn. 123–125.
128 See Chapter 3, text accompanying nn. 92–100.
129 See Chapter 3, Section II.B.1.

life-sustaining treatment are legally valid across the test jurisdictions.[130] However, the conceptual problems traditionally associated with advance refusals of life-sustaining treatment would also operate here.[131]

The more difficult scenarios arise when there is neither a contemporaneous nor an anticipatory request. All of the test jurisdictions allow decision-making on behalf of an incompetent individual by a proxy or surrogate, whether the proxy was appointed by the individual when still competent,[132] judicially

---

[130] See, e.g., Mental Capacity Act 2005 (Eng.), ss. 24–26 (expected to come into force in April 2007); Patient Self-Determination Act (U.S.), Omnibus Budget Reconciliation Act of 1990, Pub. L. No. 101-508, 4206, 4751, 104 Stat. § 1388, 1388–115, 1388–204 (codified at 42 USC § 1395cc(f) (Medicare), 1396a(w) (Medicaid) (1994)) (requiring health care facilities that receive federal funding (including any facility participating in Medicare or Medicaid) to inform patients upon admission of their rights under state law 'to make decisions concerning [their] medical care, including the right to accept or refuse medical or surgical treatment and the right to formulate advance directives . . . such as a living will or durable power of attorney for health care' if these are recognized under state law). For a list of U.S. state provisions, see Karl A. Menninger, II, 'Proof of Basis for Refusal or Discontinuance of Life-Sustaining Treatment on Behalf of Incapacitated Person' (2005) 40 *Am. Jur. Proof of Facts* 3d 287, § 17, n. 62. In Canada, see *Malette v. Shulman* (1990) 72 O.R. (2d) 417 (Ont. C.A.); Personal Directives Act (Alta.) R.S.A. 2000, c. P-6, s. 14(2); Health Care (Consent) and Care Facility (Admission) Act (B.C.) R.S.B.C. 1996, c. 181, s. 12.1; Health Care Directives Act (Man.) S.M. 1992, c. 33, C.C.S.M. c. H-27, ss. 5, 7, 13(1), (3); Advance Health Care Directives Act (Nfld.) S.N.L. 1995, c. A-4.1, s. 5(1); Health Care Consent Act (Ont.) S.O. 1996, c. 2, Sch. A, s. 26; Consent to Treatment and Health Care Directives Act (P.E.I.) R.S.P.E.I. 1998, c. C-17.2, ss. 17(2), 20; Civil Code of Québec S.Q. 1991, c. 64, s. 10; Health Care Directives and Substitute Health Care Decision Maker Act (Sask.) S.S. 1997, c. H-0.001, s. 5.

[131] Two themes appear in the literature on advance refusals, which may have even greater impact when an advance directive contains a *consent* to a procedure that may not be in its creator's best interests. First, the 'personal identity problem' raises doubts about the validity of the autonomy rationale supporting the projection of autonomous choice into the future, which will bind the incompetent. See Penney Lewis, 'Procedures that are against the medical interests of incompetent adults' (2002) 22(4) *Ox. J. Legal Studies* 575, 578–82; Penney Lewis, 'Medical Treatment of Dementia Patients at the End of Life: Can the Law Accommodate the Personal Identity and Welfare Problems?' (2006) 13 *Eur. J. Health L.* 219, 221–2, 229–34; Derek Parfit, *Reasons and Persons* (Oxford: Oxford Univ. Press, 1986) 204–9; Rebecca Dresser, 'Life, Death, and Incompetent Patients: Conceptual Infirmities and Hidden Values in the Law' (1986) 28(3) *Ariz. L. Rev.* 373, 379–81; Ronald Dworkin, *Life's Dominion: An argument about abortion and euthanasia* (New York: Vintage, 1994) 180–8, 210–16; Allen Buchanan, 'Advance directives and the personal identity problem' (1988) 17 *Phil. & Pub. Aff.* 277. Secondly, with regard to the duties owed to incompetent persons, '[c]urrent legal doctrine . . . fails to address the possibility of conflict between a competent person's exercise of future-oriented autonomy and her welfare as an incompetent individual.' Rebecca Dresser, 'Missing Persons: Legal Perceptions of Incompetent Patients' (1994) 46 *Rutgers L. Rev.* 609, 635. Dresser discusses at length the problems associated with implementing advance directives when they appear to conflict with present experiential interests of the incompetent person. Ibid. 624–32. See also, Lewis, 'Procedures that are against the medical interests of incompetent adults, above, 582–3; Lewis, 'Medical Treatment of Dementia Patients', above, 222–3, 229, 234; Dworkin, above. The new Dutch legislation also allows for such advance requests. See above n. 59.

[132] In England and Wales, see Mental Capacity Act 2005, ss. 9–14, 22–23 (expected to come into force in April 2007, allowing a competent person to appoint a donee of a lasting power of attorney to make medical decisions on her behalf after the onset of incompetence). U.S. state provisions allowing for the appointment of a health care proxy or durable power of attorney for health care are listed in Menninger, above n. 130, § 17, n. 63. In Canada, see Personal Directives Act (Alta.) R.S.A. 2000, c. P-6; Representation Agreement Act (B.C.) R.S.B.C. 1996, c. 405; Health Care Directives Act (Man.) S.M. 1992, c. 33, C.C.S.M. c. H-27; Advance Health Care Directives Act (Nfld.) S.N.L.

appointed,[133] presumed by virtue of a relationship to the individual,[134] or is the patient's physician.[135] Such decisions can be made either on the basis of the substituted judgment or best interests tests.

The subjective[136] substituted judgment approach requires decisions to conform with those which evidence dictates that the incompetent individual would have made were she competent, and is based on respect for the individual's autonomy interests.[137] The requirement that there be evidence that the incompetent individual would have made a particular decision means that the doctrine is only available for those incompetent persons who were previously competent and whose wishes were known or whose value system could be applied to the present situation of incompetence.[138]

1995, c. A-4.1; Medical Consent Act (N.S.) R.S.N.S. 1989, c. 279; Substitute Decisions Act (Ont.) S.O. 1992, c. 30, ss. 46–53; Consent to Treatment and Health Care Directives Act (P.E.I.) R.S.P.E.I. 1998, c. C-17.2, s. 20; Civil Code of Québec S.Q. 1991, c. 64, s. 15; Health Care Directives and Substitute Health Care Decision Maker Act (Sask.) S.S. 1997, c. H-0.001, s. 5(3); Health Act (Yuk.) R.S.Y. 2002, c. 106, s. 45(1)(a).

[133] In England and Wales, see Mental Capacity Act 2005, ss. 16–20 (expected to come into force in April 2007, allowing a court to appoint a deputy to make medical decisions on behalf of an incompetent person who has not made a lasting power of attorney). In Canada, see, e.g., Substitute Decisions Act (Ont.) S.O. 1992, c. 30, ss. 55–61; Civil Code of Québec S.Q. 1991, c. 64, s. 15; Health Act (Yuk.) R.S.Y. 2002, c. 106, s. 45(1)(b).

[134] Surrogate or family consent statutes allow for a surrogate to be appointed by default (either long-term or to make a particular decision) without the prior involvement of the now incompetent person. The U.S. provisions are listed in A. Kimberley Dayton et al., 'Surrogate consent statutes' (2005) 3 *Advising the Elderly Client* § 33:43. In Canada, see Advance Health Care Directives Act (Nfld.) S.N.L. 1995, c. A-4.1, s. 10; Health Care Consent Act (Ont.) S.O. 1996, c. 2, Sch. A, s. 20; Consent to Treatment and Health Care Directives Act (P.E.I.) R.S.P.E.I. 1998, c. C-17.2, s. 11; Civil Code of Québec S.Q. 1991, c. 64, s.15; Health Care Directives and Substitute Health Care Decision Maker Act (Sask.) S.S. 1997, c. H-0.001, ss. 15–16; Health Act (Yuk.) R.S.Y. 2002, c. 106, s. 45(1)(c)–(f).

[135] In the absence of jurisprudence or statutory intervention allowing the appointment of a surrogate, the medical professional is effectively the proxy decision-maker, unless the court's intervention is sought. See, e.g., *Re F (mental patient: sterilisation)* [1990] 2 A.C. 1.

[136] There is also an objective form of this approach, focusing on the decision a reasonable person would make in the circumstances. However, this test is hard to reconcile with the autonomy rationale which purports to render legitimate the substituted judgment approach. If there is insufficient *evidence* to support the ascription of a particular type of moral reasoning to the incompetent person, then it is impossible to argue that such a substituted judgment is a morally sound approximation of the autonomous choice that the incompetent would have made if competent. The objective substituted judgment approach is more consistent with the best interests test than the truly subjective substituted judgment approach, although it must be noted that there is no bright-line distinction between the objective and subjective versions of substituted judgment, particularly when there is little subjective evidence of the incompetent's wishes. See Louise Harmon, 'Falling Off the Vine: Legal Fictions and the Doctrine of Substituted Judgment' (1990) 100 *Yale L.J.* 1, 63–5.

[137] Allen E. Buchanan & Dan W. Brock, *Deciding for Others: The Ethics of Surrogate Decision-Making* (Cambridge: Cambridge Univ. Press, 1990) 112–14.

[138] See Buchanan and Brock, ibid. 112–17; Harmon, above n. 136, 63–5; U.S. President's Commission for the Study of Ethical Problems in Medicine and Biomedical and Behavioral Research, *Deciding to Forego Life-Sustaining Treatment* (1983) 132–3, 136. For an influential counter-example in which the subjective substituted judgment approach was applied to someone who had never been competent, see *Superintendent of Belchertown State Sch. v. Saikewicz* (1977) 370 N.E.2d 417, 430–1 (Mass. S.J.C.). Subsequent U.S. courts have recognized that 'the best interests standard

Many U.S. states[139] and Canadian provinces[140] require surrogate decision-makers to use this approach when evidence is available, although it is not used in England and Wales.[141]

The best interests test is based on the protection of the incompetent individual's welfare interests, and can be used regardless of whether the individual was previously competent. In England and Wales, decisions on medical treatment for incompetent individuals are made using this test which requires the weighing of

applies when the patient has never been competent or has not expressed her wishes concerning medical treatment.' *In re A.M.B.* (2001) 248 Mich. App. 144, 200 (Mich. C.A.). See also, *In re K.I.* (1999) 735 A.2d 448, 455–6 (D.C.C.A.); *In re Christopher I.* (2003) 131 Cal.Rptr.2d 122, 133 (Cal. C.A.) ('The substituted judgment test is . . . an inappropriate tool for making medical decisions for patients like Christopher, who has never been competent to make his own decisions or express his emotions and feelings on the subject.'). Similarly, in Canada, see *Re Eve* [1986] 2 S.C.R. 388 (applying the best interests test when the incompetent person was never competent).

139 The substituted judgment doctrine is widely used in the United States. See, e.g., *Conroy* (1985) 486 A.2d 1209 (N.J.S.C.); *Cruzan v. Harmon* (1988) 760 S.W.2d 408, 425 (Missouri S.C.), affirmed *sub nom Cruzan v. Director, Mo. Dep't of Health* (1990) 497 U.S. 261. A high standard of 'clear and convincing evidence' has been required by some U.S. courts dealing with decisions to withdraw or withhold life-sustaining or life-saving treatment. See *In re Storar* (1981) 420 N.E.2d 64, 72 (N.Y.C.A.) (requiring 'clear and convincing evidence' of the incompetent person's previous competent intent); *Cruzan v. Director, Mo. Dep't of Health*, above, 283 (holding that a state may require clear and convincing evidence in proceedings where a guardian wishes to withdraw artificial nutrition and hydration from a person in a persistent vegetative state); *Conroy*, above, 1229–31 (requiring a clear expression of the person's former preferences regarding treatment); *In re Martin* (1995) 450 Mich. 204 (Mich. S.C.). Most states, however, use a less stringent standard when applying the substituted judgment test. See 'Developments in the Law – Medical Technology and the Law' (1990) 103 *Harv. L. Rev.* 1519, 1646–51; Dresser, above n. 131, 374–9; *Schiavo ex rel. Schindler v. Schiavo* (2005) 403 F.3d 1289 (11th Cir.) (clear and convincing evidence standard not mandated by the Due Process Clause of the Fourteenth Amendment); *Matter of Edna M.F.* (1997) 210 Wis. 2d 557 (Wis. S.C.) (requiring guardian to demonstrate incompetent's prior wishes by a preponderance of the evidence). Rebecca Dresser has argued in favour of an even higher standard: 'To apply the autonomy principle in this context necessarily "requires evidence of an actual past decision contemplating the circumstances the patient is now in."' Dresser, above n. 131, 622–3, citing Ronald Dworkin, 'Autonomy and the Demented Self' (1986) 64 *Milbank Q.* 4, 14 (Supp. 2). This would conflate the substituted judgment test into the standard required for an advance decision.

140 Personal Directives Act (Alta.) R.S.A. 2000, c. P-6, s. 14(3); Representation Agreement Act (B.C.) R.S.B.C. 1996, c. 405, s. 16 (although s. 7(2.1) provides that 'A representative may not be authorized . . . to help make, or to make on the adult's behalf, a decision to refuse life-supporting care or treatment'); Health Care Directives Act (Man.) S.M. 1992, c. 33, C.C.S.M. c. H-27, s. 13(2), (4); Advance Health Care Directives Act (Nfld.) S.N.L. 1995, c. A-4.1, s. 12(1); Substitute Decisions Act (Ont.) S.O. 1992, c. 30, ss. 66(3), 67; Health Care Consent Act (Ont.) S.O. 1996, c. 2, Sch. A, s. 21; Consent to Treatment and Health Care Directives Act (P.E.I.) R.S.P.E.I. 1998, c. C-17.2, s. 13; Civil Code of Québec S.Q. 1991, c. 64, s. 12; Health Care Directives and Substitute Health Care Decision Maker Act (Sask.) S.S. 1997, c. H-0.001, s. 12; Health Act (Yuk.) R.S.Y. 2002, c. 106, ss. 45(5), (6).

141 See *Airedale NHS Trust v. Bland* [1993] A.C. 789, 895 (Lord Mustill), 872 (Lord Goff)(rejecting substituted judgment as 'simply a fiction'); *Re A (Children) (Conjoined Twins: Surgical Separation)* [2001] Fam. 147, 185 (Eng. C.A., Ward L.J.); Law Commission of England and Wales (L.C.E.W.), *Mentally Incapacitated Adults and Decision-Making: An Overview*, Consultation Paper No. 119 (1991) [4.22]–[4.23]. The Law Commission did recommend that the incompetent's views, wishes and feelings should be considered as a component of the best interests test. L.C.E.W., *Mental Incapacity*, Report No. 231 (1995) [3.25]–[3.31]. This proposal was accepted by the Government in Lord Chancellor's Department, *Making Decisions*, Cm 4465 (1999) [1.11] and subsequently enacted in the Mental Capacity Act 2005, s. 4(6) (expected to come into force in April 2007).

benefit and detriment that will flow from the proposed procedure.[142] Some U.S. states also use this approach.[143]

Can the decision of a proxy be considered the exercise of a right on behalf of the individual? In some U.S. states, the answer appears to be that it can. In the other test jurisdictions, however, proxy decision-making is viewed differently.

1. Jurisdictions which accept proxy exercise of the incompetent person's rights

Although the concept of surrogate exercise of a right to assisted suicide or euthanasia may seem unconvincing, the analogous concept of a right to refuse medical treatment which can be exercised on behalf of an incompetent person by a proxy or surrogate has been accepted in many U.S. jurisdictions.[144] To the consternation of the United States Supreme Court in *Washington v. Glucksberg*, the Ninth Circuit (the court below) in *Compassion in Dying v. Washington* certainly thought that a decision by a surrogate on behalf of an incompetent patient could constitute an exercise of that patient's right to assisted suicide:

We view the critical line in right-to-die cases as the one between the voluntary and involuntary termination of an individual's life. In the first case – volitional death – the physician is aiding or assisting a patient who wishes to exercise a liberty interest, and in the other – involuntary death – another person acting on his own behalf, or, in some instances society's, is determining that an individual's life should no longer continue . . . *we should make it clear that a decision of a duly appointed surrogate decision maker is for all legal purposes the decision of the patient himself.*[145]

---

[142] *Re F (Mental Patient: Sterilisation)* [1990] 2 A.C. 1. The best interests approach will remain the operative test once the Mental Capacity Act 2005, s. 4 comes into force (expected in April 2007).

[143] See, e.g., *In re K.I.* (1999) 735 A.2d 448 (D.C.C.A.) (requiring clear and convincing evidence that terminating life-sustaining treatment is in the incompetent person's best interests); *Woods v. Com.* (2004) 142 S.W.3d 24 (Ky. S.C.); *In re Guardianship of L.W.* (1992) 167 Wis. 2d 53 (Wis. S.C.). Some states use the substituted judgment and best interests tests in the alternative. See, e.g., *Conservatorship of Wendland* (2001) 26 Cal. 4th 519 (Cal. S.C.) (requiring clear and convincing evidence either that the incompetent person wished to refuse life-sustaining treatment or that to withhold such treatment would be in her best interests).

[144] Such a right may be either constitutional or derived from a state patients' rights statute. See, e.g., *Cruzan v. Director, Mo. Dep't of Health* (1990) 497 U.S. 261, 278, 280, (recognizing that 'a competent person has a constitutionally protected liberty interest in refusing unwanted medical treatment' and extending that principle to incompetent patients in certain circumstances); *In re Quinlan* (1976) 355 A.2d 647, 672 (N.J.S.C.) (holding that a comatose individual has a constitutional privacy right to be free from bodily invasion, that such right is not diminished by the individual's incompetence and could be exercised by a parent on her behalf); *Matter of Conservatorship of Torres* (1984) 357 N.W.2d 332 (Minn. S.C.) (Minnesota Patients' Bill of Rights (Minn. Stat. § 144.651) allowed a proxy to seek enforcement of a patient's rights to participate in health care planning and to refuse treatment on the patient's behalf). Detailed discussion of the relevant U.S. authorities is found in Thomas J. Marzen et al., ' "Suicide: A Constitutional Right?" – Reflections Eleven Years Later' (1996) 35 *Duq. L. Rev.* 261, 279–84; John D. Hodson, 'Judicial power to order discontinuance of life-sustaining treatment' (1986, updated weekly) 48 A.L.R.4th 67, § 8[a].

[145] *Compassion in Dying v. Washington* (1996) 79 F.3d 790, 832, n. 120 (9th Cir. en banc) (emphasis added), quoted disapprovingly by the majority of the Supreme Court in *Washington v. Glucksberg* (1997) 521 U.S. 702, 733, overturning the decision of the Ninth Circuit. See also,

Commentators have also argued that the decision of the Second Circuit in *Quill v. Vacco*[146] implicitly accepts the same position as the Ninth Circuit. For example, Thomas Marzen et al. argue that:

in states which permit surrogates or guardians to direct the withholding or withdrawal of life support from an incompetent patient who has never expressed any views on the subject, the Second Circuit's reasoning logically requires that surrogates or guardians be equally empowered to direct the active killing of such patients, or nonvoluntary euthanasia.[147]

In short, in jurisdictions which have accepted that a proxy may exercise rights on behalf of an incompetent individual, it would be difficult to rule out the possibility that a regime resulting from the use of rights as the mechanism of legal change on assisted dying might eventually dispense with the requirement of a competent request.

2. Jurisdictions which do not accept proxy exercise of the incompetent person's rights

In jurisdictions in which the concept of a proxy exercising rights on behalf of an incompetent individual is an alien one, the requirement of a competent request is more easily sustained. Limits on the decision-making power of a proxy are not considered to be limits on the rights of the incompetent person. The objects of rights possessed by the competent individual are often excluded from or not included in the categories of decisions which may be made by a proxy on the now incompetent individual's behalf. The right to marry is one example of many.[148] In these jurisdictions, although an anticipatory request by the individual when competent may be considered to be the exercise of that individual's right to assistance in dying,[149] the requirement of a competent request (whether contemporaneous or advance) is likely to be maintained.

3. Concerns about proxy decision-making

In regimes resulting from either necessity or compassion as the mechanism of legal change, the individual's request is not a necessary criterion. This may also be the case if legal change occurs as a result of a successful rights claim in a jurisdiction which has accepted that a proxy may exercise rights on behalf of an incompetent individual. This section briefly critiques the use of proxy decision-makers in the assisted dying context.

Marzen, above n. 144, 275 ('the court is declaring the right of a guardian/surrogate to authorize the killing of an incompetent patient who has never expressed a desire to be killed').

[146] *Quill v. Vacco* (1996) 80 F.3d 716, 727–30 (2nd Cir.).

[147] Marzen, above n. 144, 277–8. A similar conclusion is reached by Richard M. Doerflinger, 'Conclusion: Shaky Foundations and Slippery Slopes' (1996) 35 *Duq. L. Rev.* 523, 526–7.

[148] See, e.g., Mental Capacity Act 2005 (Eng.), s. 27(1)(a) (expected to come into force in April 2007).   [149] See above, text accompanying nn. 130–131.

Concerns have been raised about the role of compassion in relation to judicial reasoning, many of which may be relevant to its use as an agent for legal change[150] and more generally when proxy decision-making is motivated by compassion when necessity or rights are the mechanisms of legal change. Lois Shepherd raises the danger of presumptuousness, or the assumption that we can know how another feels, suggesting that 'we may inaccurately judge the degree and nature of the suffering of another person'.[151] Martha Nussbaum identifies a further danger of projection: 'we have great difficulty seeing the lives of those who are different from ourselves. We easily imagine the other in our own image.'[152] Finally, concerns are raised that compassion may tend towards over-expansiveness – it may be difficult to focus on the interests of the subject of compassion when others are also worthy of our compassion.

Approaches to assisted dying which would permit proxy decision-making may be vulnerable to presumptuousness, projection, and over-expansiveness. When decisions are made on behalf of another, the decision-maker may presume to know the nature of the other's suffering. Similarly, when deciding for another, we may project how we would feel in similar circumstances rather than focusing on how the suffering person feels. Finally, proxy decision-makers (or those responsible for scrutinizing their decisions) may include in their assessments their own interests and/or the interests of those close to the patient, who are also worthy of compassion.[153]

B. Terminal illness

1. If necessity or compassion are the mechanisms of legal change

A regime resulting from necessity as the mechanism of legal change cannot sustain a terminal illness requirement.[154] The conflict of duties may be present in cases where the patient does not suffer from a terminal illness.[155] Nonetheless, '[i]f for legal purposes, within the context of the defence of justification to a criminal charge, the requirement of a "terminal phase" plays no role, it does not follow that it is irrelevant as a matter of legal policy.'[156] In the Dutch cases, the patient's life expectancy is a relevant factor in assessing whether there is a conflict between the duties to preserve life and relieve suffering. Under the new law, whether the patient has a terminal illness will be relevant to assessments of whether 'the patient's

---

[150] The unusual use of compassion as an agent for legal change was discussed in Chapter 5, Section II.B.

[151] Lois Shepherd, 'Face to Face: A Call for Radical Responsibility in Place of Compassion' (2003) 77 *St. John's L. Rev.* 445, 461.

[152] Martha Nussbaum, 'Compassion: The Basic Social Emotion' (1996) 13 *Soc. Phil. & Pol'y* 27, 28.

[153] See Edmund D. Pellegrino, 'Compassion Needs Reason Too' (1993) 270(7) *J. Am. Med. Ass'n* 874, 874–5.   [154] See above, text accompanying n. 44 and Chapter 4, Section I.B.

[155] See, e.g., *Chabot*, Supreme Court, 21 June 1994, N.J. 1994, no. 656 (translations listed above n. 44).   [156] Griffiths, Bood & Weyers, above n. 38, 103.

suffering was unbearable, and that there was no prospect of improvement;... [and whether] there is no reasonable alternative in the light of the patient's situation'.[157]

Can a regime resulting from compassion as the mechanism of legal change sustain a terminal illness requirement? The inclusion of this requirement in the CCNE proposal results from the opinion's focus on the dying patient. However, the opinion also includes as an example of an exceptional circumstance, 'the case of... new-born infants suffering from extreme and incurable neurologic sequelae of which the parents have been informed.'[158] Such infants may not, however, be likely to die in the short or medium term if aggressive treatment is provided, thus it is difficult to see how they could, as a group, be regarded as terminally ill.

What if we abandon the attempt at a legalistic interpretation of the CCNE's opinion (which, after all, is not a legal text) and think about compassion as an agent of legal change more generally? Those who are not terminally ill are also worthy of compassion. Indeed, the description of this approach by the CCNE bears out this reasoning:

When the existential, psychological, and sentimental sufferings of someone are unbearable and intractable and that person requests a termination, the act of interruption of life by a third party should not be punishable... [159]

Thus terminal illness is likely to fall away as a criterion for the same reasons as it does when necessity is the mechanism of legal change. If a person who is not terminally ill is suffering and there is no other reasonable alternative available to relieve that suffering, then compassion would allow for assistance in dying.

2. If rights are the mechanism of legal change

Regimes resulting from legal change based on the rights to liberty, privacy, security of the person, and even equality can be restricted to those suffering from a terminal illness on the basis that any violation of those rights cannot be justified by the state interest in preserving life in cases of terminal illness, but could be in non-terminal cases.[160] However, if the equality violation is as described by Lamer C.J.C., then the terminal illness requirement must be abandoned,[161] as is also evidenced by its abandonment in the refusal of treatment cases discussed in Chapter 3.[162]

C. Suffering and the 'no reasonable alternative' requirement

When necessity or compassion is the mechanism of legal change, the essential criteria are hopeless and unbearable suffering with no reasonable alternative to relieve it.[163] In contrast, if the right to equality is the mechanism of legal change,

---

[157] Termination of Life on Request and Assisted Suicide (Review Procedures) Act 2001, ss. 2(1)(b), (d).   [158] CCNE, no. 63, above n. 114, § 4.
[159] Ibid.   [160] See above, text accompanying nn. 22–23, 31.
[161] See above, text accompanying nn. 14–15.   [162] See Chapter 3, Section II.A.4.b.
[163] See above, Section III.A.2 and text accompanying nn. 118–119.

a suffering requirement cannot be sustained as there is no such requirement imposed on the relevant comparator class. Those who are physically able to commit suicide or those who choose to refuse life-sustaining treatment need not prove that they are suffering before doing so.[164] A suffering requirement may be sustainable if the rights to security of the person or dignity are the mechanisms of legal change,[165] but not if the rights to autonomy or liberty are used.[166]

As regimes resulting from rights as the mechanism of legal change may dispense with a suffering requirement, clearly a 'no reasonable alternative' requirement is not mandated either, although one could be included if the rights to security of the person or dignity are used.[167]

D. Assisted suicide or assisted dying?

When necessity or compassion is the mechanism of legal change, both assisted suicide and euthanasia are permissible providing that the suffering and no reasonable alternative requirements are met. Under either of the two hypothetical regimes resulting from the right to equality as the mechanism of legal change, assistance in dying cannot be restricted to assisted suicide but must include the possibility of termination of life upon request if the individual is unable to commit suicide with assistance.[168] In fact, whichever right is used as the mechanism of legal change, the right to equality could be used in complement with that right. Thus if the individual is unable to commit suicide with assistance, the right to equality could be used to challenge any limitation to assisted suicide.[169] For example, the majority of the Ninth Circuit in *Compassion in Dying v. Washington* accepted an argument based on the right to liberty but nevertheless 'recognize[d] that in some instances, the patient may be unable to self-administer the drugs and that administration by the physician, or a person acting under his direction or control, may be the only way the patient may be able to receive them.'[170]

E. Prospective approval

If rights are the mechanism of legal change is prospective approval required prior to the act of assistance in dying? The examples of the McEachern C.J.B.C. and Lamer C.J.C. proposals suggest that prospective approval *could* be consistent with such regimes, provided that the approval process does not place any undue burden on the patient's rights.[171] While prospective approval may be a cautionary

---

[164] See above, text accompanying n. 27.   [165] See above, text accompanying nn. 5–7.
[166] See above, Section II.D.   [167] See above, text accompanying nn. 5–7.
[168] See above, text accompanying nn. 16–17 and n. 20.
[169] See, e.g., *R. (on the application of Pretty) v. D.P.P.* [2002] 1 A.C. 800, [5] (accepting the logic of such an extension though without mentioning the right to equality).
[170] *Compassion in Dying v. Washington* (1996) 79 F.3d 790, 832 (9th Cir. en banc). See Chapter 3, Section II.A.1.d.   [171] In the abortion context, see *Morgentaler* [1988] 1 S.C.R. 30.

approach adopted by judges setting out interim measures which will operate only until the legislature responds to a judicial decision that individuals have a right to assistance in dying, prospective approval is not mandated under such regimes.

Both the Dutch system and the CCNE proposal involve retrospective assessment rather than prospective approval, although the Dutch due care criteria do provide significant prospective guidance to doctors,[172] particularly the requirement of consultation.[173] Indeed, it is difficult to see how a formal prospective approval requirement could be consistent when either necessity or compassion are the mechanism of legal change – even if a doctor had not obtained prospective approval, she would still be able to claim retrospectively that she had faced a conflict of duties, or that she was acting out of compassion.

F. Restriction to doctors

The Dutch regime resulting from necessity as the mechanism of legal change applies only to doctors, as only a doctor has a professional duty to relieve suffering which may conflict with her duty to preserve life.[174] Arguably, however, the inevitability of this restriction is less clear if compassion is used as the mechanism of legal change. While a medical assessment that the patient's suffering is intolerable and there is no reasonable alternative may be required,[175] the act of termination of life could be performed by any individual motivated by the need to relieve the patient's suffering.[176] Thus one distinguishing feature between regimes resulting from necessity and compassion as the mechanism of legal change is that the latter may not be restricted to doctors.

As with prospective approval requirements, when rights are used as the mechanism of legal change, a rule that only doctors can perform assisted dying could be imposed, provided that such a requirement did not unduly burden the exercise of the chosen right.[177] Unlike the regime resulting from necessity as the mechanism of legal change, there is no *necessary* requirement that only doctors may provide

---

[172] See Chapter 4, Section I.C.

[173] Moreover, a form of informal prospective approval is provided by the growing use of a network of euthanasia consultants (the 'Support and Consultation on Euthanasia in the Netherlands' (SCEN) initiative). See Bregde Onwuteaka-Philipsen & Gerrit van der Wal, 'Support and Consultation for General Practitioners Concerning Euthanasia: The SCEA Project' (2001) 56 *Health Policy* 33 (discussing the predecessor project in Amsterdam); M.C. Jansen-van der Weide et al., 'Implementation of the project "Support and Consultation on Euthanasia in the Netherlands" (SCEN)' (2004) 69 *Health Policy* 365; Tony Sheldon, 'Netherlands sets up euthanasia advisory body' (1999) 318 *Br. Med. J.* 348.

[174] See above n. 36.

[175] CCNE, no. 63, above n. 114, § 3 ('The intolerable nature of the suffering endured and the lack of other reasonable solutions to relieve that suffering would need corroborating by the attending physician and by another health care provider').

[176] Recall that the defendant's motivation is one of the factors to be examined in the retrospective review proposed by the CCNE. See CCNE, ibid. § 4.

[177] See above, text accompanying n. 171.

assisted dying. For example, the Ninth Circuit decision in *Compassion in Dying v. Washington* explicitly included all those who might provide assistance with suicide:

We hold that a liberty interest exists in the choice of how and when one dies, and that the provision of the Washington statute banning assisted suicide, as applied to competent, terminally ill adults who wish to hasten their deaths by obtaining medication prescribed by their doctors, violates the Due Process Clause.... We would add that those whose services are essential to help the terminally ill patient obtain and take that medication and who act under the supervision or direction of a physician are necessarily covered by our ruling. That includes the pharmacist who fills the prescription; the health care worker who facilitates the process; the family member or loved one who opens the bottle, places the pills in the patient's hand, advises him how many pills to take, and provides the necessary tea, water or other liquids; or the persons who help the patient to his death bed and provide the love and comfort so essential to a peaceful death.[178]

G. Moving forward

Compassion is an unlikely mechanism of legal change on assisted dying, in light of its lack of legal status in either common law or civilian legal systems.[179] What of the prospects for the other two mechanisms of legal change considered here? The failure of claims to legalize assisted dying using constitutionally entrenched rights[180] has left the defence of necessity as the sole alternative mechanism of legal change in common law jurisdictions which lack the political will for legislative change, as is frequently the case. Yet common law hostility to the use of the defence of necessity in this context appears to rule out this alternative.[181] Although the prospect of legislative change seems remote, it is interesting to examine the legislative regimes which have been enacted against the background of the contours of the regimes produced by the three mechanisms of legal change already considered.

VI. Legislative Change

Thus far we have concentrated predominantly on mechanisms of legal change which involve the courts rather than the legislature. In this section the legislative regimes in Oregon, Belgium, and the Northern Territory of Australia are assessed. Although they are not the only jurisdictions in which assisted dying has been legalized by statute,[182] these jurisdictions have been selected as they have undergone a relatively recent, clear, and extensive process of legal change.

---

[178] *Compassion in Dying v. Washington* (1996) 79 F.3d 790, 838, n. 140 (9th Cir. en banc).
[179] See Chapter 5, text accompanying nn. 27–29.
[180] See Chapter 2, Section I.B.   [181] See Chapter 4, Sections II and III.A.
[182] See Chapter 1, Sections III.A.2, III.B.2 and III.B.3.

In contrast, in Switzerland, for example, although assisted suicide is criminalized only where the assister's motive was selfish rather than compassionate,[183] there has been no legal change since 1942 despite 'recent extensive reform of Swiss penal law'.[184] Moreover, when it was originally drafted, medically-assisted suicide for the terminally ill was not envisaged as a possible use of the relevant article of the Penal Code:

the whole discussion did not envisage assisted suicide from a medical perspective. Instead, it was inspired by romantic stories about people committing suicide in defence of their own, or their family's, honour and about suicides committed by rejected lovers.[185]

The process of legal change in Switzerland, therefore, is less relevant to the assisted dying debate than the process in those jurisdictions in which assisted dying in the medical context was at the heart of legal change.

A. Oregon

1. A brief history

Following two narrowly unsuccessful attempts to enact dignified death provisions by referenda in Washington[186] and California,[187] Oregon voters passed the first of such proposed laws in November 1994 by a majority of fifty-two per cent, providing for physician-assisted suicide under certain specified conditions.[188] The Oregon Death with Dignity Act allows terminally ill persons with less than six months to live to request a prescription of a lethal dose of drugs to end unbearable suffering. Two doctors must concur in the determination that the patient's condition is terminal, the request must be made at least three times, and the third time must be in writing before witnesses. The Oregon measure differs from the California and Washington proposals in that the administration of the lethal dose must be by the patient, and not the doctor. As required under the Act, the Oregon Department of Human Services monitors compliance, collects data on those who use the Act,

---

[183] Penal Code, Art. 115. See Olivier Guillod & Aline Schmidt, 'Assisted suicide under Swiss law' (2005) 12 *Eur. J. Health L.* 25; Samia A. Hurst & Alex Mauron, 'Assisted suicide and euthanasia in Switzerland: allowing a role for non-physicians' (2003) 326 *Br. Med. J.* 271.

[184] Guillod & Schmidt, above n. 183, 29.   [185] Ibid.

[186] The Death with Dignity ballot proposal was introduced through the initiative process for the November 1991 elections. Initiative 119 would have legalized physician 'aid in dying' for terminally-ill competent patients. Despite favourable advance polls, the measure was defeated by 54% to 46%. See Jane Gross, 'The 1991 Election: Euthanasia; Voters Turn Down Mercy Killing Idea' *N.Y. Times*, 7 Nov. 1991, B16; Rob Carson, 'Washington's I-119' (1992) 22(2) *Hastings Center Rep.* 7. Subsequently, Washington's Natural Death Act was amended to expressly exclude physician-assisted suicide. Wash. Laws, ch. 98, § 10 (1992); Wash. Rev. Code § 70.122.100 (1994).

[187] California's Proposition 161 was also defeated in November 1992 by a majority of 54% to 46%. The law would have allowed terminally ill adults with less than 6 months to live to request medical assistance in dying. See Ben Macintyre, 'Voters Hold Sway on Life and Death' *The Times*, 3 Nov. 1992, 10.

[188] Death with Dignity Act, Ore. Rev. Stat. § 127.800 – § 127.995 (1996); 'Voters in Oregon Allow Doctors To Help the Terminally Ill Die' *N.Y. Times*, 11 Nov. 1994, A28.

and publishes annual reports detailing such use.[189] The Task Force to Improve the Care of Terminally Ill Oregonians publishes a guidebook to the Act for health care providers which is updated on a continuous basis.[190]

The Oregon Act has been controversial from the moment the ballot measure was passed. Immediately prior to its implementation, an injunction was issued enjoining its operation.[191] This injuction was later vacated,[192] and the U.S. Supreme Court subsequently denied *certiorari*.[193] The measure was again placed on the ballot in 1997 and affirmed by a sixty per cent majority.[194]

After the Act was brought into force, there were unsuccessful attempts by members of Congress to amend the federal Controlled Substances Act[195] to prevent doctors 'intentionally dispensing, distributing or administering a controlled substance for the purpose of causing death or assisting another person in causing death.'[196] This measure would have prevented Oregon doctors from using federally controlled drugs in assisted suicide cases, but would not have prevented alternative methods of assistance with suicide (although only assistance using prescription medication is currently covered under the Oregon statute).[197] Congress did

---

[189] The Annual Reports are available at http://egov.oregon.gov/DHS/ph/pas/ar-index.shtml, accessed 25 July 2006. The first five were summarized in the *New England Journal of Medicine*: Katrina Hedberg et al., 'Five Years of Legalized Physician-Assisted Suicide in Oregon' (2003) 348(10) *New Eng. J. Med.* 961; Katrina Hedberg et al., 'Legalized Physician-Assisted Suicide in Oregon, 2001' (2002) 346(6) *New Eng. J. Med.* 450; Amy D. Sullivan et al., 'Legalized Physician-Assisted Suicide in Oregon 1998–2000' (2001) 344(8) *New Eng. J. Med.* 605; Amy D. Sullivan et al., 'Legalized Physician-Assisted Suicide in Oregon – The Second Year' (2000) 342(8) *New Eng. J. Med.* 598; Arthur E. Chin et al., 'Legalized Physician-Assisted Suicide in Oregon – The First Year's Experience' (1999) 340(7) *New Eng. J. Med.* 577. See also, Susan R. Martyn & Henry J. Bourguignon, 'Now is the Moment to Reflect: Two Years of Experience with Oregon's Physician-Assisted Suicide Law' (2000) 8 *Elder L.J.* 1; Linda Ganzini et al., 'Physicians' Experiences with the Oregon Death with Dignity Act' (2000) 342(8) *New Eng. J. Med.* 557.

[190] Task Force to Improve the Care of Terminally Ill Oregonians, *The Oregon Death with Dignity Act: A Guidebook for Health Care Providers* (1998, revised on a continuous basis). See www.ohsu.edu/ethics/guidebook.pdf, accessed 29 July 2006.

[191] *Lee v. Oregon* (1995) 891 F. Supp. 1429, 1437 (D. Or.) (holding that the statute violates the Equal Protection Clause of the Fourteenth Amendment (see above n. 19)).

[192] *Lee v. Oregon* (1997) 107 F.3d 1382, 1392 (9th Cir.) (concluding that plaintiffs lacked standing under Article III of the United States Constitution).

[193] *Lee v. Harcleroad* (1997) 522 U.S. 927.

[194] 'In November 1997, a measure asking Oregon voters to repeal the Death with Dignity Act was placed on the general election ballot (Measure 51, authorized by Oregon House Bill 2954). Voters rejected this measure by a margin of 60% to 40%, retaining the Death with Dignity Act.' Oregon Department of Human Services, *Eighth Annual Report on Oregon's Death with Dignity Act*, 9 Mar. 2006, 6, http://oregon.gov/DHS/ph/pas/docs/year8.pdf, accessed 24 July 2006. See Oregon Constitution, Art. IV, s. 1. See also, David Garrow, 'The Oregon Trail' *N.Y. Times*, 6 Nov. 1997, A31; Kim Murphy, 'Voters in Oregon Soundly Endorse Assisted Suicide' *L.A. Times*, 5 Nov. 1997, A1.

[195] 21 U.S.C.A. § 801 et seq.

[196] The Pain Relief Promotion Act of 2000, S. 2607, § 201(a)(1), 106th Cong. The Act failed to gain passage in the Senate. See August Gribbin, 'Hill Measure Would OK Illicit Drugs for Palliation' *Wash. Times*, 7 Jan. 2001, A7. See generally, Robert A. Klinck, 'Pain Relief Promotion Act' (2001) 38 *Harv. J. on Legis.* 249; Joy Fallek, 'The Pain Relief Promotion Act: Will it spell death to "death with dignity" or is it unconstitutional?' (2000) 27 *Fordham Urb. L.J.* 1739.

[197] Jim Barnett, 'Assisted Suicide Has September Showdown' *Oregonian*, 28 July 2000, A1.

successfully pass a measure in 1997 which prevents federal funds from being used for assisted suicide.[198]

The United States Supreme Court has recently confirmed a decision by the Ninth Circuit Court of Appeals[199] that the Attorney General acted outside his authority under the federal Controlled Substances Act when he issued a directive stating that assistance in suicide is not a 'legitimate medical purpose' under the Act, and thus that prescribing, dispensing, or administering federally controlled substances to assist suicide violated the Act.[200] The directive ordered the Drug Enforcement Agency to enforce and apply the Attorney General's determination that the registration of a physician who assists a suicide (including one permitted under Oregon law) may be 'inconsistent with the public interest' and could therefore be suspended or revoked under the Controlled Substances Act.[201]

2. An examination of the Oregon provisions

It is possible to conceive of the legislative approach adopted by ballot measure in Oregon as resembling one using rights as the mechanism of legal change, without prospective approval. Indeed, the substantive requirements of the Oregon statute are similar to those proposed by the Second and Ninth Circuits:[202] terminal illness[203] and a competent,[204] voluntary request.[205] No suffering requirement obtains in Oregon. Only assisted suicide is available through the provision of medication to end life.[206]

---

[198] Assisted Suicide Funding Restriction Act of 1997, 42 U.S.C. §§ 14401–14408 (2000).

[199] *Gonzales v. Oregon* (2006) 126 S.Ct. 904, confirming *Oregon v. Ashcroft* (2004) 368 F.3d 1118 (9th Cir.). See Charles H. Baron, 'Not DEA'd Yet: *Gonzales v. Oregon*' (2006) 36(2) *Hastings Center Rep.* 8.

[200] Office of the Attorney General, 'Dispensing of Controlled Substances to Assist Suicide' 21 CFR Part 1306 [AG Order No. 2534-2001] 2001 WL 1385910.

[201] Ibid. See Controlled Substances Act, 21 U.S.C.A. § 824(a)(4).

[202] See above, Sections II.C and II.D.

[203] Death with Dignity Act, Ore. Rev. Stat. § 127.800–§ 127.995 (1996), § 2.01, defined as 'an incurable and irreversible disease that has been medically confirmed and will, within reasonable medical judgment, produce death within six months'. Ibid. § 1.01(12).

[204] The patient must be capable, which is defined as having 'the ability to make and communicate health care decisions to health care providers, including communication through persons familiar with the patient's manner of communicating if those persons are available.' Death with Dignity Act, Ore. Rev. Stat. § 127.800 – § 127.995 (1996), § 1.01(3). A counselling referral must be made if either the attending or consulting physician suspects that the patient may be suffering from a psychiatric or psychological disorder or depression causing impaired judgment. Physician-assisted suicide is not available unless the counsellor determines that the patient is not suffering from a psychiatric or psychological disorder or depression causing impaired judgment. Ibid. § 3.03. The Guidebook recommends that all requesting patients be referred for counselling. Task Force to Improve the Care of Terminally Ill Oregonians, *The Oregon Death with Dignity Act: A Guidebook for Health Care Providers* (1998, revised on a continuous basis) Ch. 9, Guideline 9.1, www.ohsu.edu/ethics/guidebook.pdf, accessed 29 July 2006. The rate of psychiatric referral in Oregon is discussed above n. 42.

[205] The two witnesses must attest that the patient is acting voluntarily and is not being coerced to sign the request. Death with Dignity Act, Ore. Rev. Stat. § 127.800 – § 127.995 (1996), § 2.02. Concerns have been raised about the quality of voluntariness assessments in Oregon. See Martyn & Bourguignon, above n. 189, 23–30.

[206] Death with Dignity Act, Ore. Rev. Stat. § 127.800 – § 127.995 (1996), § 2.01.

However, the similarity between the contours of the Oregon law and the proposed regimes canvassed above in Section II may be more apparent than real. The Oregon legislature was not forced to draft legislation legalizing assisted suicide in response to the striking down of criminal prohibitions on assisted suicide by a court on the grounds of a violation of one or more constitutionally entrenched rights. Indeed, no right to assisted suicide has been recognized by the Oregon courts. Thus it is unlikely that claims using rights could be used to expand the contours of the Oregon law to dispense with, for example, the requirement of terminal illness or the limitation to assisted suicide.[207] Moreover, the law could be repealed with no replacement by a further ballot measure.[208] This would not be the case if the law were a response to a judicial decision vindicating one or more constitutional rights, as further court challenges would undoubtedly ensue.

B. Belgium

1. A brief history

In a 1997 opinion on euthanasia, the Belgian National Bioethics Advisory Committee (Comité Consultatif de Bioéthique de Belgique or CCBB) was unable to reach a position, but recommended continuing broad societal debate.[209] In the 1980s and 1990s, a series of legislative moves to allow euthanasia had been unsuccessful.[210] Following intensive debate in 2001, the Belgian Senate voted to legalize euthanasia on 25 October 2001, followed by the Chamber of Representatives on 16 May 2002.[211]

---

[207] See above, Sections V.B.2 and V.D.

[208] Indeed, one such attempt was unsuccessful. See above, text accompanying n. 194.

[209] CCBB, *Opinion on the opportunity of the legal regulation of euthanasia*, no. 1, 12 May 1997. An English translation is provided by Herman Nys, 'Advice of the Federal Advisory Committee on Bioethics Concerning Legalisation of Euthanasia' (1997) 4 *Eur. J. Health L.* 389. The Belgian debate is discussed by M. Botbol-Baum, 'L'originalité du débat belge sur l'euthanasie: analyser et discuter les valeurs en question' ('The originality of the Belgian debate on euthanasia: an analysis and discussion of the values in question') (1999/2000) 9–10-11 *Espace éthique: la lettre (Ethical space: the letter)* 92; Bert Broeckaert, 'Belgium: Towards a Legal Recognition of Euthanasia' (2001) 8 *Eur. J. Health L.* 95 (pointing out that the 'divided' advice of the CCBB is partly explained by the fact that 'the agreement between the federal and regional governments as a result of which the [CCBB] was established, stipulates . . . that the advices [sic] adopted . . . should always represent the different opinions that would be offered'); Paul Schotsmans, 'Debating Euthanasia in Belgium' (1997) 27(5) *Hastings Center Rep.* 46; Ph. Mahoux, 'La Loi Relative à l'Euthanasie: Concilier les Éthiques' ('The Law on Euthanasia: Reconciling Ethics') (2002) 102(6) *Acta Chirurgica Belgica* 379; E. Vermeersch, 'The Belgian Law on Euthanasia: The Historical and Ethical Background' (2002) 102(6) *Acta Chirurgica Belgica* 394.

[210] See Broeckaert, above n. 209, 95; Maurice Adams, 'Euthanasia: the Process of Legal Change in Belgium' in Klijn, above n. 45, 29, 33–4; Paul Schotsmans, 'The Belgian Euthanasia Debate: Some New Developments since December 1999' (2000) 160 *Bull. Med. Ethics* E4.

[211] Act on Euthanasia of 28 May 2002. English translations can be found at (2003) 10 *Eur. J. Health L.* 329; (2002) 9(2–3) *Ethical Perspectives* 182; Appendix I in Paul Schotsmans & Tom Meulenbergs, eds., *Euthanasia and Palliative Care in the Low Countries* (Leuven: Peeters, 2005) 245 and www.kuleuven.ac.be/cbmer/viewpic.php?LAN=E&TABLE=DOCS&ID=23, accessed 24 July 2006. See also, Herman Nys, 'A Presentation of the Belgian Act on Euthanasia Against the Background of Dutch Euthanasia Law' (2003) 10 *Eur. J. Health L.* 239; Maurice Adams & Herman

Prior to the proposals that led to the Belgian law, there had been no criminal prosecutions in cases of termination of life upon request.[212] It is unclear whether the defence of necessity lay behind the apparent reluctance to prosecute doctors.[213]

2. An examination of the Belgian provisions

Similarly to the Dutch law,[214] the Belgian law defines euthanasia as termination of life upon request,[215] although assisted suicide is not explicitly included.[216] Thus

---

Nys, 'Comparative Reflections on the Belgian Euthanasia Act 2002' (2003) 11 *Med. L. Rev.* 353. A later version of the article by Adams & Nys is 'Euthanasia in the Low Countries: Comparative Reflections on the Belgian and Dutch Euthanasia Act' in Schotsmans & Meulenbergs, above, 5. All references to the Adams & Nys article are to this later version.

[212] Unlike its Dutch counterpart, the Belgian Penal Code does not contain a separate provision for termination of life on request. Instead, a defendant who terminated the life of another on her request could be charged with murder, manslaughter, or poisoning. Broeckaert, above n. 209, 95. A few recent investigations are described by Freddy Mortier & Luc Deliens, 'The Prospects of Effective Legal Control on Euthanasia in Belgium: Implications of recent end-of-life studies' in Klijn, above n. 45, 179, 181. See also, Heleen Weyers, 'Legal recognition of the right to die' in Austen Garwood-Gowers et al., eds., *Contemporary Issues in Healthcare Law and Ethics* (Edinburgh: Elsevier Butterworth-Heinemann, 2005) 253, 256, n. xi ('In Belgium ... there were a few prosecutions of family members of the patient for killing on request or out of compassion').

[213] Compare Adams & Nys, above n. 211, 5–6 (suggesting that the failure to prosecute means that 'it was not known ... whether the concept of the so-called "state of necessity" ... would ... be applicable to Belgium') with Ludovic Hennebel, 'La dépénalisation de l'euthanasie en Belgique' ('The decriminalization of euthanasia in Belgium') (2002) 2 *J. de l'Institut Int'l des Droits de l'Homme (J. of the Int'l Human Rights Institute)* 1, 2, 5 (arguing that the use of the judicially created justification of necessity explains the absence of prosecutions of doctors for the termination of life on request, citing Cour de Cassation, 13 May 1987, *R.C.J.B.*, 1989, 588; C. Hennau & J. Verhaegen, *Droit Pénal Général* (Bruxelles: Bruylant, 1995) 178). See also, Belgian Senate, Bill on Euthanasia, *Annex to the Report of the Joint Commissions of Justice and Social Affairs by Mmes Laloy & Van Riet: Hearings*, No. 2–244/24, 9 July 2001, Hearing of Jules Messinne on 2 May 2000, 849–53, www.senat.be/wwwcgi get_pdf?33576763, accessed 29 July 2006.   [214] See above n. 35.

[215] Act on Euthanasia of 28 May 2002, s. 2.

[216] Although neither suicide itself nor assisting suicide are criminal offences, anyone who intentionally provides assistance could be prosecuted for failing to assist a person in danger (Penal Code, Art. 422bis) or even involuntary homicide. See Adams & Nys, above n. 211, 8–10; Sénat de France, *Legislation Comparé: Euthanasie (Comparative Legislation: Euthanasia)*, No. LC 109 (2002) 4, www.senat.fr/lc/lc109/lc109.html, accessed 26 July 2006; Herman Nys, 'Physician assisted suicide in Belgian law' (2005) 12(1) *Eur. J. Health L.* 39. See also, Chapter 1, Section III.B.3. In its first biannual report, the Federal Control and Evaluation Commission on Euthanasia accepted cases of assisted suicide as falling under the euthanasia law. See Belgian Senate and House of Representatives, 2003–2004 Session, Federal Control and Evaluation Commission on Euthanasia, *First Report to the Legislative Chambers (22 Sept. 2002–31 Dec. 2003)* No. 3–860/1 (Senate), DOC 51 1374/001 (House) 16 Sept. 2004, 13–14, 21, www.senat.be/wwwcgi/get_pdf?50333038, accessed 29 July 2006. See also, Belgian Chamber of Representatives, *Report by the Commission on Public Health, Environment and Societal Renewal on Federal Control and Evaluation Commission on Euthanasia, First Report to the Legislative Chambers (22 Sept. 2002–31 Dec. 2003)*, DOC 51 1374/002, 22 Nov. 2004, 13, www.lachambre.be/FLWB/pdf/51/1374/51K1374002.pdf, accessed 29 July 2006. The correctness of this view may soon be tested by a case involving a physician who assisted in the suicide of his demented patient. See Jane Burgermeister, 'Doctor reignites euthanasia row in Belgium after mercy killing' (2006) 332 *Br. Med. J.* 382; 'Le suicide assisté d'une vieille dame' ('The assisted suicide of an elderly woman') *La libre Belgique*, 10 Feb. 2006.

termination of life without request remains murder.[217] The statute does not use the phrase 'defence of necessity', although the term was used in some of the predecessor bills.[218] The defence of necessity was much discussed during the legislative hearings and had provided the basis for the legalization options canvassed by the CCBB.[219] The result is uncertainty as to whether the defence of necessity continues to be available in cases which fall outside of the new law.[220] Some legislators argued during the hearings that by omitting this phrase, the defence of necessity would remain available for facts outside of the definition of 'euthanasia'.[221]

The main contours of the Belgian law are fairly similar to the Dutch law on which the Belgian proposals were based.[222] The patient must be 'legally competent'[223] and the request must be *both* 'completely voluntary' and 'not the result of any external pressure'.[224] There is a suffering requirement: the 'patient [must be] in a medically futile condition of constant and unbearable physical or mental suffering that

---

[217] Hennebel, above n. 213, 2. See CCBB, *Opinion on the active ending of life of persons incapable of expressing their will*, no. 9, 22 Feb. 1999. The opinion is discussed in English in Broeckaert, above n. 209, 98; Paul Schotsmans & Bert Broeckaert, 'Debating Euthanasia in Belgium: Part Two' (1999) 29(5) *Hastings Center Rep.* 47; Eva Strubbe, 'Toward Legal Recognition for Termination of Life without Request? Remarks on Advice No 9 of the Belgian Advisory Committee on Bioethics Concerning Termination of Life of Incompetent Patients' (2000) 7(1) *Eur. J. Health L.* 57.

[218] See Broeckaert, above n. 209, 99.

[219] Belgian Senate, *Hearings*, above n. 213; CCBB, no. 1, above n. 209, § III.2, § III.3. Option 2 was modelled on the Dutch approach.

[220] See Hennebel, above n. 213, 6–7; Hearing of Jules Messinne, above n. 213, 853, 868–9 (arguing that once necessity is particularly available as a defence to 'euthanasia', it will be unavailable in all other cases of termination of life); Hearing of Christian Panier on 2 May 2000 in Belgian Senate, *Hearings*, above n. 213, 939–40 (recommending the insertion of a form of words indicating that the legalization of 'euthanasia' does not prejudice the applicability of other defences to facts outside of the definition of 'euthanasia'). See also, CCBB, above n. 217, no. 9, § III.1, § III.2.

[221] See the comments of Philippe Monfils and the President during the Hearing of Christian Panier, above n. 220, 941.

[222] See, e.g., Loes Kater, 'The Dutch Model for Legalizing End-of-life Decisions' (2003) 22 *Med. & L.* 543, 544: 'Initiatives like that in Belgium ... whereby several elements of the Dutch debate are imitated and inserted into their own debate on the practice of end-life-decisions, raise questions about the Dutch model as an export product.' There are other differences which do not affect the characterization of the Belgian law as resembling one resulting from the defence of necessity as the mechanism of legal change. For example, the Belgian law does not apply to minors unless they are 'emancipated', while the Dutch law may be used by children as young as twelve with parental consent. The provisions are compared in Nys, above n. 211, 244. Another difference is structural: the Dutch law inserts defences into the provisions of the Criminal Code dealing with termination of life on request and assisted suicide (see Chapter 4, Section I.C). In contrast, the Belgian law simply states that the doctor 'commits no criminal offence' if she complies with the statutory requirements. Act on Euthanasia of 28 May 2002, s. 3§1. See Vermeersch, above n. 209, 397 (describing 'the undesirable side-effect that every breach of the rules is to be prosecuted as murder').

[223] Act on Euthanasia of 28 May 2002, s. 3§1.

[224] Ibid., ss. 3§1, 3§2(1). A request may be made in advance, but as the triggering condition is unconsciousness, advance directives will not be applicable to many scenarios of future incompetence, including dementia. Act on Euthanasia of 28 May 2002, s. 4. A recent proposition in the Senate would change the triggering condition from unconsciousness to 'loss of awareness of one's person, one's mental and physical state and one's social and physical environment'. Belgian Senate, Bill modifying article 4 of the law on euthanasia of 28 May 2002, No. 3–1485/1, 14 Dec. 2005, www.senat.be/wwwcgi/get_pdf?50334399, accessed 29 July 2006.

cannot be alleviated, resulting from a serious and incurable disorder caused by illness or accident'.[225] While there is a clear analogy here to the Dutch 'no reasonable alternative' requirement, it appears that a patient's refusal of potentially *curative* treatment will prevent access to euthanasia.[226] However, the refusal of treatment which may assuage suffering will not have this effect, even if the patient's suffering is due to a non-somatic cause.[227]

There is no terminal illness requirement, although additional procedural requirements are imposed in cases of somatic non-terminal illness.[228] These additional protections would also apply in cases of non-somatic non-terminal illness, although there is some disagreement as to whether a psychiatric patient could meet the condition of voluntariness.[229] As is the case in the Netherlands, euthanasia is not available in cases of existential suffering.[230] Only a doctor may perform euthanasia.[231]

Although there are differences between the Dutch and Belgian regimes, the Dutch influence on the Belgian law and their similarities in most important respects suggests that the Belgian regime resembles one resulting from necessity as the mechanism of legal change. Aside from a number of procedural differences, the Belgian law diverges from the Dutch in two main respects. The first clear distinction is in relation to the legal status of assisted suicide, although the significance of this distinction may be more apparent than real.[232] The second distinction is less clear.

---

[225] Act on Euthanasia of 28 May 2002, s. 3§1. Broeckaert suggests that 'this last requirement [makes] the scope of [the Act] significantly narrower than the Dutch [Act], in which this additional medical and objective requirement is not present.' Broeckaert, above n. 209, n. 29. However, it is not clear how this narrows the scope of the Act beyond excluding existential suffering, which is also excluded in the Netherlands. See Chapter 4, Section III.A.2.a.

[226] Nys, above n. 211, 247.

[227] Nys, ibid. Compare the Dutch position, discussed above, Section III.A.3. This point may be moot if euthanasia is unavailable to psychiatric patients for other reasons. See below, text accompanying n. 229.

[228] If the patient 'is clearly not expected to die in the near future', a second consultation with either a psychiatrist or a relevant specialist is required and there is a waiting period of at least one month. See Act on Euthanasia of 28 May 2002, s. 3§3.

[229] Nys, above n. 211, 248. In the first two years of operation of the Act, all of the persons who obtained euthanasia or assisted suicide were suffering from somatic disorders (cancer, progressive neurological disorders, neurological deficits, lung disease, heart disease, kidney disease, or multiple pathologies). See Federal Control and Evaluation Commission on Euthanasia, *First Report to the Legislative Chambers*, above n. 216, 4, Table VII.

[230] As s. 3§1 requires a 'serious and incurable disorder'. See above n. 225.

[231] Act on Euthanasia of 28 May 2002, ss. 3§1, 4§2. Adams and Nys, above n. 211, 11–12, suggest that the requirement of a long-standing or pre-existing physician-patient relationship could possibly be derived from s. 3§2(2) of the Act, which requires that the physician has 'several conversations with the patient spread out over a reasonable period of time' in order to be certain that the patient's suffering is constant and that his request is a durable one. The Dutch argument (that in order to assess whether the requirements of the statute are met, the doctor must have some familiarity with the patient) might also be used (see above, Section III.A.4). However, Adams and Nys note that the legislative history makes clear that the patient should be able to completely exclude his attending physician if so desired – from which one might infer that there is no requirement of a pre-existing physician–patient relationship.   [232] See above n. 216 and accompanying text.

As discussed above, unless and until Belgian prosecutors begin to proceed in relation to cases falling outside of the new law, it is not obvious whether its enactment will be judicially interpreted as precluding the application of the defence of necessity in cases involving the termination of life without request.[233]

C. The Northern Territory of Australia

In 1995, the Northern Territory of Australia passed the Rights of the Terminally Ill Act, which legalized physician-assisted suicide and physician-performed voluntary active euthanasia.[234] The Act was overturned by the Australian Parliament in 1997, having been in force for less than a year.[235] The substantive requirements of the Northern Territory statute were similar to those now in force in Oregon: terminal illness[236] and a competent, voluntary request.[237] However, unlike Oregon, there was a suffering requirement.[238] This was coupled with a subjective 'no reasonable alternative' constraint. The doctor could not proceed if there were 'palliative care options reasonably available to the patient to alleviate the patient's pain and suffering to levels acceptable to the patient.'[239] Numerous procedural safeguards were also included.[240]

---

[233] The president of the CCBB argued during the Hearings that the state of necessity could not be limited to cases of termination of life on request as once necessity is the basis for permissible euthanasia, it cannot be restricted to those conditions set down in the law, but will be available more generally. Belgian Senate, *Hearings*, above n. 213, Hearing of Prof. Etienne Vermeersch on 15 Feb. 2000, 34. The difficulty with this argument is that the Act makes no reference to the defence of necessity, nor has the defence ever been judicially recognized in cases of termination of life on request. See above, text accompanying nn. 218–221.   [234] Rights of the Terminally Ill Act 1995 (N.Terr.), s. 3.

[235] Euthanasia Laws Act 1997 (Cth.), Sched. 1. The Act further provides that 'the power of the Legislative Assembly... in relation to the making of laws does not extend to the making of laws which permit or have the effect of permitting (whether subject to conditions or not) the form of intentional killing of another called euthanasia (which includes mercy killing) or the assisting of a person to terminate his or her life.' The Northern Territory experience is discussed by Simon Chesterman, 'Last Rights: Euthanasia, the Sanctity of Life, and the Law in the Netherlands and the Northern Territory of Australia' (1998) 47 *Int'l Comparative L.Q.* 362, 384–5; Kumar Amarasekara, 'Euthanasia and the Quality of Legislative Safeguards' (1997) 23 *Monash U. L. Rev.* 1; Danuta Mendelson, 'The Northern Territory's Euthanasia Legislation in Historical Perspective' (1995) 3(1) *J. Law & Med.* 136; Grant Gillett, 'Ethical Aspects of the Northern Territory Euthanasia Legislation' (1995) 3(1) *J. Law & Med.* 145; Andrew L. Plattner, 'Australia's Northern Territory: The First Jurisdiction to Legislate Voluntary Euthanasia, and the First to Repeal it' (1997) 1 *DePaul J. Health Care L.* 645; Lara L. Manzione, 'Is there a Right to Die?: A Comparative Study of Three Societies (Australia, Netherlands, United States)' (2002) 30 *Ga. J. Int'l. & Comp. L.* 443.

[236] Rights of the Terminally Ill Act 1995, ss. 4, 7(1)(b).   [237] Ibid., s. 7(1)(h).

[238] The patient could make a request if she '[were] experiencing pain, suffering and/or distress to an extent unacceptable to the patient'. The medical practitioner could assist only if 'the illness [was] causing the patient severe pain or suffering'. Ibid., ss. 4, 7(1)(d).

[239] Ibid., s. 8(1). Although as Simon Chesterman points out, '[t]his is ... not the same as ensuring that such palliative care options are in fact available.' Chesterman, above n. 235, 386.

[240] See, e.g., the requirement of consultation with another physician (who had to examine the patient) in ss. 7(1)(c)(i), (iii); the requirement of a psychiatric assessment in ss. 7(1)(c)(ii), (iv); and the two-stage cooling off period in ss. 7(1)(i), (n). For information on the use of the law during the

Unlike the Oregon and Belgian statutes, the Northern Territory law does not resemble even superficially a regime resulting from the use of either rights or necessity as the mechanism of legal change. Instead, the law combines elements from both types of regime. The terminal illness requirement could be consistent with a regime resulting from rights as the mechanism of legal change.[241] The coupling of a suffering requirement with a 'no reasonable alternative' constraint is closely associated with necessity as a mechanism of legal change.[242] The statute is an example of the greater freedom possessed by legislators in comparison to judges, who may be constrained by the way in which a claim has been brought using constitutionally entrenched human rights, or, in the case of common law judges, the need to develop the substantive law incrementally in a consistent and principled fashion with due regard to precedent.[243]

VII. Conclusion

The length of Section V, above, entitled 'Summarizing the Boundaries', confirms the impossibility of summing up the key distinctions between regimes resulting from rights, necessity or compassion as mechanisms of legal change. In this conclusion I highlight only two of the most important distinctions. Regimes resulting from necessity or compassion as mechanisms of legal change are not restricted to cases of an autonomous request but will include termination of life without request where necessary to relieve suffering (although the crimes involved will be different in jurisdictions which have a separate provision for termination of life upon request). Regimes resulting from rights as the mechanism of legal change require a competent request unless the relevant jurisdiction allows proxies to exercise rights on behalf of incompetent individuals, in which case it would be difficult to rule out the possibility of dispensing with the requirement of a competent request.

Regimes resulting from necessity or compassion as mechanisms of legal change will always maintain a suffering requirement, however, which is not necessarily the case with regimes resulting from rights as the mechanism of legal change. In the next chapter, the significance of the differences between the various regimes will be considered in the context of slippery slope arguments.

---

brief period of its operation, see David W. Kissane et al., 'Seven deaths in Darwin: case studies under the Rights of the Terminally Ill Act, Northern Territory, Australia' (1998) 352 *Lancet* 1097.

[241] See above, Section V.B.2.   [242] See above, Sections V.C, V.D.

[243] This distinction is discussed further in Chapter 7, Section II.B.

7

The Slippery Slope

I. Introduction

Slippery slope arguments appear regularly whenever morally contested social change is proposed.[1] Such arguments assume that all or some of the consequences which will flow from permitting a particular practice are morally unacceptable.

Typically, 'slippery slope' arguments claim that endorsing some premise, doing some action or adopting some policy will lead to some definite outcome that is generally judged to be wrong or bad. The 'slope' is 'slippery' because there are claimed to be no plausible halting points between the initial commitment to a premise, action, or policy and the resultant bad outcome. The desire to avoid such projected future consequences provides adequate reasons for not taking the first step.[2]

Thus the legalization of abortion in limited circumstances is asserted to lead down the slippery slope towards abortion on demand[3] and even infanticide;[4] and the legalization of assisted suicide to lead inexorably to the acceptance of voluntary euthanasia,[5]

---

[1] On slippery slopes generally, see Frederick Shauer, 'Slippery Slopes' (1985) 99 *Harv. L. Rev.* 361; Wilbren van der Burg, 'The Slippery-Slope Argument' (1991) 102 *Ethics* 42, 42–3 (noting that the slippery slope argument has been invoked against the legalization of abortion, euthanasia, in vitro fertilization, and DNA research); Benjamin Freedman, 'The Slippery-Slope Argument Reconstructed: Response to Van der Burg' (1992) 3 *J. Clinical Ethics* 293. See also, Bernard Williams, 'Which Slopes Are Slippery?' in Michael Lockwood, ed., *Moral Dilemmas in Modern Medicine* (Oxford: Oxford Univ. Press, 1985) 126, 126–7 (pointing out that slippery slope arguments are often applied to matters of medical practice); Douglas Walton, *Slippery Slope Arguments* (Oxford: Clarendon Press, 1992); David J. Mayo, 'The Role of Slippery Slope Arguments in Public Policy Debates' (1990–91) 21–22 *Phil. Exchange* 81; Jeffrey P Whitman, 'The Many Guises of the Slippery Slope Argument' (1994) 20 *Soc. Theory & Prac.* 85; Eric Lode, 'Slippery Slope Arguments and Legal Reasoning' (1999) 87 *Cal. L. Rev.* 1469.

[2] Walter Wright, 'Historical Analogies, Slippery Slopes, and the Question of Euthanasia' (2000) 28 *J. L. Med. & Ethics* 176, 177.

[3] See, e.g., John Keown, 'Euthanasia in the Netherlands: sliding down the slippery slope?' in John Keown, ed., *Euthanasia Examined: Ethical, Clinical and Legal Perspectives* (Cambridge: Cambridge Univ. Press, 1995) 261, 262, 287–8.

[4] See Chenyang Li, 'The Fallacy of the Slippery Slope Argument on Abortion' (1992) 9(2) *J. Applied Philosophy* 233; John D. Arras, 'The Right to Die on the Slippery Slope' (1982) 8(3) *Soc. Theory & Prac.* 285, 288; Lorraine Eisenstat Weinrib, 'The Body and the Body Politic: Assisted Suicide under the *Canadian Charter of Rights and Freedoms*' (1994) 39 *McGill L.J.* 619, 637.

[5] See, e.g., *Krischer v. McIver* (1997) 697 So. 2d 97, 109 (Fla. S.C., Harding J., concurring); Yale Kamisar, 'Physician-Assisted Suicide: The Last Bridge to Active Voluntary Euthanasia' in Keown, *Euthanasia Examined*, above n. 3, 225, 245; Herbert Hendin, 'Scared To Death of Dying' *N.Y. Times*,

and subsequently to the sanctioning of the practice of non-voluntary euthanasia and even involuntary euthanasia of 'undesirable' individuals.[6]

This chapter concentrates on the slippery slope argument which is most widely employed in the context of discussion about the legalization of assisted dying: the argument that the legalization of voluntary active euthanasia will lead to acceptance of non-voluntary active euthanasia.[7] The slippery slope argument that legalization of assisted suicide will lead to acceptance of euthanasia will not be discussed.[8] The historical and empirical evidence in the Netherlands does not reflect a move from assisted suicide to voluntary euthanasia.[9] Moreover, other jurisdictions which

---

16 Dec. 1994, A39 ('The Netherlands has moved from assisted suicide to euthanasia, from euthanasia for the terminally ill to euthanasia for the chronically ill, from euthanasia for physical illness to euthanasia for psychological distress and from voluntary euthanasia to involuntary euthanasia.').

[6] See, e.g., Yale Kamisar, 'Some Non-Religious Views Against Proposed "Mercy Killing" Legislation' (1958) 42 *Minn. L. Rev.* 969, 1030–41 (discussing the 'parade of horrors' that could occur following the legalization of euthanasia); Canadian Law Reform Commission, *Euthanasia, Aiding Suicide and Cessation of Treatment*, Working Paper No. 28 (1982) 46; Gregory Gelfand, 'Euthanasia and the Terminally Ill' (1984) 63 *Neb. L. Rev.* 741, 764–5; J. Gay-Williams, 'The Wrongfulness of Euthanasia' in Ronald Munson, ed., *Intervention and Reflection: Basic Issues in Medical Ethics* (Belmont, Calif.: Wadsworth, 1983) 156; Joseph V. Sullivan, 'The Immorality of Euthanasia' in Marvin Kohl, ed., *Beneficent Euthanasia* (Buffalo, N.Y.: Prometheus, 1975) 12, 23–6; Germain Grisez, 'Suicide and Euthanasia' in Dennis J. Horan & David Mall, eds., *Death, Dying and Euthanasia* (Washington: Univ. Publications of America, 1980) 742, 811 (comparing the possible future legal stance on euthanasia in the United States and other western societies to the experience of Nazi Germany); Alexander Morgan Capron, 'Euthanasia in the Netherlands: American Observations' (1992) 22(2) *Hastings Center Rep.* 30, 32–3 (drawing a comparison with the euthanasia programme in Nazi Germany); Kumar Amarasekara & Mirko Bagaric, 'The Legalisation of Euthanasia in the Netherlands: Lessons to be Learnt' (2001) 27 *Monash U. L. Rev.* 179, 181; Daniel Callahan, 'When Self-Determination Runs Amok' (1992) 22(2) *Hastings Center Rep.* 52, 54.

[7] Other examples of slippery slope arguments made in this context include the fears that legalization will legitimize the horrors of the Nazi genocide; erode the rights of the disabled; or promote the idea that only some lives are inherently worthwhile. For an example of the latter argument, see Richard Sherlock, 'Liberalism, Public Policy and the Life Not Worth Living: Abraham Lincoln on Beneficent Euthanasia' (1981) 26 *Am. J. Juris.* 47, 49–50 (arguing that the decision to allow euthanasia requires an answer to the question of when a life is not worth living; even to discuss such an answer poses a threat to the fundamental principle of equality before the law and the principles derived therefrom). See generally, Carl Schneider, 'Rights Discourse and Neonatal Euthanasia' (1988) 76 *Cal. L. Rev.* 151, 167–71; David A.J. Richards, 'Constitutional Privacy, The Right to Die and The Meaning of Life: A Moral Analysis' (1981) 22 *Wm. & Mary L. Rev.* 327, 398.

[8] For examples of this argument, see above n. 5.

[9] See Heleen Weyers, 'Euthanasia: The process of legal change in the Netherlands' in Albert Klijn et al., eds., *Regulating Physician-Negotiated Death* (Amsterdam: Elsevier, 2001) 11. According to the 1990, 1995 and 2001 Dutch studies of 'medical behaviour which shortens life', assisted suicide is 'relatively uncommon' in the Netherlands, occurring in 0.2% (95% confidence interval (CI) 0.1%–0.3%) of all deaths in 1990, 1995 and 2001 (based on death certificate studies (or 0.3% (1990, 95% CI 0.2%–0.4%), 0.4% (1995, 95% CI 0.2%–0.5%) and 0.1% (2001, 95% CI 0–0.1%) of all deaths (based on interviews))), while voluntary euthanasia took place in 1.7% (1990, 95% CI 1.4%–2.1%), 2.4% (1995, 95% CI 2.1%–2.6%) and 2.6% (2001, 95% CI 2.3%–2.8%) of all deaths (based on death certificate studies (or 1.9% (1990, 95% CI 1.6%–2.2%), 2.3% (1995, 95% CI 1.9%–2.7%) and 2.2% (2001, 95% CI 1.8%–2.5%) (based on interviews))). Bregje D. Onwuteaka-Philipsen et al., 'Euthanasia and other end-of-life decisions in the Netherlands in 1990, 1995, and 2001' (2003) 362 *Lancet* 395, Table 1, drawing on P.J. van der Maas et al., 'Euthanasia, Physician-Assisted Suicide, and Other Medical Practices Involving the End of Life in the Netherlands, 1990–1995' (1996) 335(22)

have legalized assisted dying have either included both assisted suicide and euthanasia from the outset (for example, the Northern Territory of Australia),[10] or have legalized only assisted suicide and have shown no signs of legalizing euthanasia (for example, Oregon).[11]

Agreement on the slippery slope problems surrounding the legalization of assisted dying is clearly unlikely.[12] For some, slippery slope arguments are a powerful warning of the dangers portended by change which might otherwise remain unrecognized until it is too late.[13] For others, slippery slope arguments are simply a tactic designed to divert attention away from the topic at hand, and are moreover often singularly unconvincing.[14] This chapter will evaluate comparatively how slippery slope arguments work in the context of the different mechanisms of legal change discussed in Chapter Six. An argument which might be thought persuasive in relation to the defence of necessity may be ineffective if legal change occurs using the mechanism of constitutionally entrenched rights, for example.

A. The legal significance of the slippery slope argument

This book closes with a chapter on the slippery slope, a topic which could be seen as ethical or philosophical rather than legal. Yet slippery slope arguments are used extensively in the legal context.[15] Frederick Shauer suggests an explanation for this:

Legal decisionmaking concentrates on the future more than does decisionmaking in other arenas... [T]oday's decisionmakers [are called upon] to consider the behavior of others who tomorrow will have to apply or interpret today's decisions. The prevalence of slippery slope arguments in law may reflect a societal understanding that proceeding through law rather than in some other fashion involves being bound in some important way to the past, and responsible in some equally important way to the future.[16]

In the assisted dying context, the legal significance of the dispute over the slippery slope argument is enormous. In *Rodriguez*, the 1993 decision of the Supreme

---

New Eng. J. Med. 1699; P.J. van der Maas et al., 'Euthanasia and other medical decisions concerning the end of life' (1991) 338 *Lancet* 669. See also, Marvin E. Newman, 'Active Euthanasia in the Netherlands' in Arthur S. Berger & Joyce Berger, eds., *To Die Or Not To Die? Cross-Disciplinary, Cultural and Legal Perspectives on The Right to Choose Death* (New York: Praeger, 1990) 117.

[10] See Chapter Six, Section VI.C.

[11] See Chapter Six, Section VI.A. Belgium has explicitly legalized only euthanasia, although assisted suicide may be folded into the regulatory regime. See Chapter Six, n. 216.

[12] For rebuttal of slippery slope arguments in this context, see, e.g., Richards, above n. 7, 398–403; Glanville Williams, *The Sanctity of Life and the Criminal Law* (New York: A.A. Knopf, 1957) 339–46; Glanville Williams, 'Euthanasia Legislation: A Rejoinder to the Non-Religious Objections' in A.B. Downing, ed., *Euthanasia and the Right to Death* (London: Owen, 1969) 134, 134–47; Alister Browne, 'Assisted Suicide and Active Voluntary Euthanasia' (1989) 2 *Can. J. L. & Juris.* 35, 46–7.   [13] See Schneider, above n. 7, 170–4.

[14] Mary Anne Warren, 'The Ethics of Sex Preselection' in Kenneth D. Alpern, ed., *The Ethics of Reproductive Technology* (New York: Oxford Univ. Press, 1992) 232.   [15] See Lode, above n. 1.

[16] Shauer, above n. 1, 382–3.

Court of Canada holding that the criminal prohibition against assisted suicide was not unconstitutional, the perspective of critics of Dutch practice who rely on the slippery slope argument was accepted unquestioningly by Mr. Justice Sopinka (writing for the majority). Without providing sources, Sopinka J. wrote that:

Critics of the Dutch approach point to evidence suggesting that involuntary active euthanasia (which is not permitted by the guidelines) is being practised to an increasing degree. This worrisome trend supports the view that a relaxation of the absolute prohibition takes us down 'the slippery slope'.[17]

In 1997, in *Washington v. Glucksberg* and *Vacco v. Quill*, the United States Supreme Court similarly held that state bans on assisted suicide were constitutional.[18] Chief Justice Rehnquist relied on an almost identical argument to that of Sopinka J., although he did buttress it with sources, citing critics[19] whose use of the Dutch experience has been heavily criticized by Dutch researchers.[20] The Chief Justice simply stated that 'regulation of the practice may not have prevented abuses in cases involving vulnerable persons, including severely disabled neonates and

---

[17] *Rodriguez v. British Columbia (Attorney-General)* [1993] 3 S.C.R. 519, 603. The case is discussed in Chapter 2, Section I.B and Chapter Six, Sections II.A and B.

[18] *Washington v. Glucksberg* (1997) 521 U.S. 702; *Vacco v. Quill* (1997) 521 U.S. 793, both discussed in Chapter 2, Section I.B.

[19] *Washington v. Glucksberg* (1997) 521 U.S. 702, 734–5, citing Carlos Gomez, *Regulating Death: Euthanasia and the Case of the Netherlands* (New York: The Free Press, 1991) 104–13; Herbert Hendin, *Seduced by Death: Doctors, Patients and the Dutch Cure* (New York: W.W. Norton & Co., 1997) 75–84; Keown, above n. 3, 289; A report of Chairman Charles T. Canady to the House Judiciary Subcommittee on the Constitution, of the Committee on the Judiciary, House of Representatives, *Physician-Assisted Suicide and Euthanasia in the Netherlands*, 104th Congress, 2nd Session, Sept. 1996; Executive Summary published as 'Physician-Assisted Suicide and Euthanasia in the Netherlands: A Report to the House Judiciary Subcommittee on the Constitution' (1998) 14 *Issues in Law & Med.* 301 (heavily reliant on the work of Hendin and Gomez).

[20] See John Griffiths, Alex Bood & Heleen Weyers, *Euthanasia and Law in the Netherlands* (Amsterdam: Amsterdam Univ. Press, 1998) 23, n. 15. The authors' comments on Herbert Hendin (one of the most vociferous critics of the Dutch approach) are that his research methods are inadequate, and that his analysis is 'so filled with mistakes of law, of fact, and of interpretation, mostly tendentious, that it is hard to be charitable and regard them as merely negligent.' See also, Griffiths, Bood & Weyers, ibid. 217, n. 54 discussing one of the 'irresponsible claim[s]' made by Hendin; Heleen Weyers, 'Herbert Hendin: de dood als verleider. Weinig overtuigende verwoording van een bekend standpunt tegen liberalisering van euthanasie' ('Herbert Hendin: death as temptress. An unconvincing presentation of a well-known objection to the liberalization of euthanasia policy') (1997) 52 *Medisch Contact (Medical Contact (Official Journal of the Royal Dutch Medical Association))* 173; John Griffiths, 'Een Amerikaan over euthanasie in Nederland' ('An American's view of euthanasia in the Netherlands – review of C.F. Gomez, *Regulating Death: Euthanasia and the Case of the Netherlands*, 1991') (1993) 48 *Medisch Contact* 1208. Researchers outside of the Netherlands have also criticized these critics. See, e.g., Jocelyn Downie, 'The Contested Lessons of Euthanasia in the Netherlands' (2000) 8 *Health L.J.* 119, 132–5; Timothy E. Quill, 'Book Review: Linda L. Emanuel, ed. *Regulating How We Die: The Ethical, Medical, and Legal Issues Surrounding Physician-Assisted Suicide*' (2000) 25 *J. Health Pol'y & L.* 391, 393 (describing 'the glib and biased accounting of the Dutch experience in the U.S. literature', citing Hendin, above n. 19); Ronald Dworkin, 'Assisted Suicide: What the Court Really Said' (1997) 44(14) *N.Y. Review of Books* 40, 43, n. 13. An exchange between Hendin and Dworkin is found at 'Assisted Suicide and Euthanasia: An Exchange' (1997) 44(17) *N.Y. Review of Books* 68, 69–70.

elderly persons suffering from dementia.'[21] No attempt was made to investigate whether regulation is related to the incidence of abuse, or whether abuse occurs more frequently in the Netherlands than in other jurisdictions, questions which will be addressed here in Section III. The use of the slippery slope argument in the context of legal disputes over assisted dying mandates its evaluation here, fortified with the knowledge of the diversity of mechanisms of legal change considered in Chapter Six.

B. Terminology

There is much dispute over the appropriate terminology for these kinds of arguments, nevertheless, as they are commonly termed 'slippery slope arguments' in the assisted dying literature, this terminology is used here 'in deference to the rhetoric'.[22] Many varieties of slippery slope argument have been described. The distinction encountered most frequently is between the logical and empirical forms of argument. James Rachels explains this distinction:

The logical [or conceptual] form of the argument goes like this. Once a certain practice is accepted, from a logical point of view we are committed to accepting certain other practices as well, since there are no good reasons for not going on to accept the additional practices once we have taken the all-important first step. But, the argument continues, the additional practices are plainly unacceptable, therefore, the first step had better not be taken . . . . The [empirical or psychological] form of the argument is very different. It claims that once certain practices are accepted, people shall in fact go on to accept other, more questionable practices. This is simply a claim about what people will do and not a claim about what they are logically committed to.[23]

As we shall see in the next two sections, there are also subcategories within these two broad strands of argument.

---

[21] *Washington v. Glucksberg* (1997) 521 U.S. 702, 734. See also, the concurring opinion of Souter J., ibid. 785–6 (recognizing that the Dutch 'evidence is contested'); *Vacco v. Quill* (1997) 521 U.S. 793, 809. The Dutch experience was also mentioned briefly in the earlier decision of the Second Circuit in *Quill v. Vacco* (1996) 80 F.3d 716, 730, citing New York State Task Force on Life and the Law, *When Death Is Sought: Assisted Suicide and Euthanasia in the Medical Context* (1994) 133–4 ('As to the interest in avoiding abuse similar to that occurring in the Netherlands, it seems clear that some physicians there practice nonvoluntary euthanasia, although it is not legal to do so.'). The first decision in the Ninth Circuit in *Compassion in Dying v. Washington* (1995) 49 F.3d 586, 593 identified a state interest in 'preventing abuse similar to what has occurred in the Netherlands'. See also, *R. (on the application of Pretty) v. D.P.P.* [2002] 1 A.C. 800, [55], citing Keown, above n. 3, 261–96.

[22] Simon Chesterman, 'Last Rights: Euthanasia, the Sanctity of Life, and the Law in the Netherlands and the Northern Territory of Australia' (1998) 47 *Int'l Comparative L.Q.* 362, 363.

[23] James Rachels, *The End of Life: Euthanasia and Morality* (Oxford: Oxford Univ. Press, 1986) 172–3. See also, van der Burg, above n. 1, 43; Williams, above n. 1, 126; Arras, above n. 4, 288–9; Jonathan Glover, *Causing Death and Saving Lives* (London: Penguin Books, 1977) 165–8; David Lamb, *Down the Slippery Slope: Arguing in Applied Ethics* (London: Croom Helm, 1988) 61; Lode, above n. 1, 1477, 1483; Keown, above n. 3, 261–2.

II. The Logical Slippery Slope Argument

A. Two versions

Wilbren van der Burg has distinguished two separate versions of the logical slippery slope argument:

> The first one . . . says that there is either no relevant conceptual difference between A and B, or that the justification for A also applies to B, and therefore acceptance of A will logically imply acceptance of B . . . . The second version . . . holds that there is a difference between A and B but that there is no such difference between A and *m*, *m* and *n*, . . . *y* and *z*, *z* and B, and that therefore allowing A will in the end imply the acceptance of B.[24]

Although the debate over terminology is not of huge import, most commentators describe an argument in the first category as an argument 'from precedent'[25] or 'from consistency'.[26] The second version is also known as a 'sorites-type argument'.[27]

1. *An argument from consistency*

Both Hallvard Lillehammer and Stephen Smith have classified the logical slippery slope argument made by John Keown in his criticism of Dutch law and practice as an example of the first version.[28] Keown argues that in cases of voluntary active euthanasia (VAE), the doctor's power to accede to or refuse the patient's request for euthanasia based on an assessment of the applicable requirements[29] carries all of the moral weight:

> The real, rather than the rhetorical, justification for VAE is not the patient's autonomous request *but the doctor's judgment that the request is justified because death would benefit the patient*. True, in the proposals currently advanced by campaigners for VAE, this judgment would not be made without a prior, autonomous request by the patient. But even under such proposals the autonomous request is not decisive. It serves merely to trigger the *doctor's* judgment about the merits of the request.[30]

---

[24] Van der Burg, above n. 1, 44.

[25] David Enoch, 'Once You Start Using Slippery Slope Arguments, You're On A Very Slippery Slope' (2001) 211 *Ox. J. Legal Studies* 629, 644–5. In fact, Enoch argues that neither type of argument described here by van der Burg should be viewed as a slippery slope argument, reserving that term for the empirical argument only. Ibid. 644–6.

[26] Stephen W. Smith, 'Fallacies of the Logical Slippery Slope in the Debate on Physician-Assisted Suicide and Euthanasia' (2005) 13 *Med. L. Rev.* 224, 229.

[27] See Enoch, above n. 25, 643–4; Trudy Govier, 'What's Wrong with Slippery Slope Arguments?' (1982) 12(2) *Cdn. J. Philosophy* 303, 307–9; Walton, above n. 1, 38–9. 'According to this paradox, taking a grain of sand away from a heap of sand makes no significant difference: What we are left with will still be a heap of sand.' Lode, above n. 1, 1485.

[28] Hallvard Lillehammer, 'Voluntary Euthanasia and the Logical Slippery Slope Argument' (2002) 61(3) *Camb. L.J.* 545, 546–7; Smith, above n. 26, 229–31.

[29] For example, a requirement that the patient's suffering is hopeless and unbearable.

[30] John Keown, *Euthanasia, Ethics, and Public Policy* (Cambridge: Cambridge Univ. Press, 2002) 77 (emphasis in original). A similar argument is made by Amarasekara & Bagaric, above n. 6, 181. See also, the comments of Daniel Callahan reported in Maurice A.M. de Wachter, 'Euthanasia in the Netherlands' (1992) 22(2) *Hastings Center Rep.* 23, 29.

By dismissing the role of the autonomous request, Keown highlights the conceptual comparability of voluntary and non-voluntary euthanasia. If the key is the doctor's judgment that the patient is suffering hopelessly and unbearably, for example, then this could apply both to situations involving an autonomous request and those in which the patient is incapable of making such a request. However, the flaw in this argument is that the position that *both* the autonomous request *and* the doctor's assessment are necessary criteria for the permissibility of voluntary euthanasia is not precluded by the temporal reality that the patient's request precedes the doctor's assessment.[31]

2. A sorites-type argument

What of the second type? Here the argument is that although there is a distinction between voluntary and non-voluntary euthanasia (the two are not conceptually equivalent), there is a logical connection between the two. This argument is often summarily dismissed by proponents of the legalization of assisted dying simply by emphasizing the distinction or asserting that a logical line can be and has been drawn. Alister Browne, for example, argues:

This argument is singularly implausible if one who makes it means that there is a *logical* connection between the killings in question such that one who endorses the first cannot without inconsistency refuse to endorse the last. The fact that in one case a person is killed in his own interest because he requests it, whereas in the other a person is killed in the interest of others without (or contrary to) his consent, is surely a morally relevant difference. Since this is so, the question 'How can we draw the line?' should not perplex one for long. No one thinks that making killing in self defence an exception to criminal homicide starts one on a slippery slope which logically must end in the abolition of the crime of murder; no one should think the same about legalizing active voluntary euthanasia.[32]

---

[31] Lillehammer, above n. 28, 548–50; Smith, above n. 26, 231–3, citing Gerald Dworkin 'The Nature of Medicine' in Gerald Dworkin et al., eds., *Euthanasia and Physician-Assisted Suicide* (Cambridge: Cambridge Univ. Press, 1998) 6, 10; Margaret Pabst Battin, 'Is a Physician Ever Obligated to Help a Patient Die?' in Linda L. Emanuel, ed., *Regulating How We Die. The Ethical, Medical, and Legal Issues Surrounding Physician-Assisted Suicide* (Cambridge, Mass.: Harvard Univ. Press, 1998) 21, 26. Keown also makes an alternative argument, that the only relevant criterion is the patient's autonomous request, which must therefore be granted regardless of the doctor's assessment of her suffering: 'If the core justification for VAE is thought to be respect for patient autonomy, this is surely inconsistent with the requirement that the patient be suffering unbearably, bearably, or at all.' Keown, above n. 30, 79. This argument can be disposed of in a similar fashion. See Lillehammer, above; Smith, ibid. 232–3.

[32] Browne, above n. 12, 47 (emphasis in original). See also, Joel Feinberg, *Harm to Self* (New York: Oxford Univ. Press, 1986) 346; Margaret Otlowski, *Voluntary Euthanasia and the Common Law* (Oxford: Oxford Univ. Press, 1997) 221; G. Steven Neeley, 'The Constitutional Right to Suicide, the Quality of Life, and the "Slippery-Slope": An Explicit Reply to Lingering Concerns' (1994) 28 *Akron L. Rev.* 53, 59–60; Ronald Dworkin et al., 'Assisted Suicide: The Philosophers' Brief' 1996 WL 708956, *16-*17 (brief of *amici curiae* filed in the U.S. Supreme Court by a group of moral philosophers prior to the hearing of *Vacco v. Quill* (1997) 521 U.S. 793 and *Washington v. Glucksberg* (1997) 521 U.S. 702).

Similarly, John Griffiths, responding to criticism of the Dutch experience, remarks that '[t]here is nothing to be said for the conceptual thesis since no "logic" can prohibit us from making relevant moral distinctions.'[33] In her chapter on slippery slopes, Jocelyn Downie devotes a single paragraph to dismissing the logical argument:

If a logically sustainable distinction can be drawn between the evaluation of life at the top of the slope [voluntary active euthanasia] and the evaluation of life at the bottom of the slope [involuntary euthanasia], then we have sufficient materials to erect a barrier on the slope. In other words, if reasons for allowing the activities at the top do not logically entail reasons for allowing activities at the bottom, then the descent is not logically necessary. Since we can distinguish between different evaluations (e.g., evaluations of the value of life made by the subject and evaluations of the value of life made by another person), we can avoid the logical slippery slope even if we allow assisted suicide and voluntary euthanasia. So long as we retain a firm criterion of free and informed consent, the logical slide to involuntary assisted death will not be a problem.[34]

B. The legal context

It is surely true that the presence of an autonomous request by the individual constitutes a logical distinction between voluntary active euthanasia and non-voluntary or involuntary euthanasia. However, while this rebuttal may be effective against the second version of the logical slippery slope argument in an ethical or moral context, it is less convincing in a legal one. Wilbren van der Burg has argued that:

In law, there is . . . a legitimate place for the . . . logical version of the slippery slope . . . When there is a decision of a court allowing A, then this is a new element in the body of legal norms from which courts must make their own theory of law. It may make one decision in a related case much stronger in the 'dimension of fit' than it would have been without this precedent, and this may tip the scales.[35]

The fact that one can identify a distinction between two scenarios does not necessarily make that distinction legally relevant. In order to rebut the logical argument in a legal context, the requirement of an autonomous request must be a necessary condition of legality. Based on the analysis in Chapter Six, this does not appear to be the case for incompetent persons if necessity or compassion are used as mechanisms of legal change (that is, in relation to non-voluntary euthanasia). However, it may be so if rights are used as the mechanism of legal change.

---

[33] John Griffiths, 'Comparative Reflections: Is the Dutch Case Unique?' in Klijn, above n. 9, 197, 201. See also, Rob Schwitters, 'Slipping into normality? Some Reflections on Slippery Slopes' in Klijn, above, 93, 94: 'How can two cases be conceptually alike, while at the same time be different in terms of one being morally right and the other morally objectionable? Do moral discriminations not demand conceptual discriminations?'

[34] Jocelyn Downie, *Dying Justice: A Case for Decriminalizing Euthanasia and Assisted Suicide in Canada* (Toronto: Univ. of Toronto Press, 2004) 106–7. See also, Warren, above n. 14, 241.

[35] Van der Burg, above n. 1, 62.

1. Necessity and compassion as mechanisms of legal change

'Euthanasia' in the Netherlands is, by definition, restricted to cases of competent request, consistent with the principle of autonomy.[36] Nevertheless, termination of life without request is also permitted for incompetent persons under a regime in which legal change is based on the potentially conflicting duties to preserve life and relieve suffering. The Dutch neonate cases discussed in Chapter Six demonstrated the logic of this position: if an incompetent person experiences unbearable and hopeless suffering, her doctor may be faced with this conflict of duties.[37] A regime resulting from necessity as the mechanism of legal change, therefore, does not necessarily require a competent request in cases where a patient is incompetent. A similar argument applies to the use of compassion as a mechanism of legal change.[38]

2. Rights as the mechanism of legal change

If rights are used as the mechanism of legal change, a competent request is required. Such regimes would therefore appear to be less open to the legality of non-voluntary euthanasia than regimes resulting from the use of necessity or compassion as mechanisms of legal change. The exception to this general rule was discussed in Chapter Six. If rights are used as the mechanism of legal change in a jurisdiction which has accepted that a proxy may exercise rights on behalf of an incompetent individual, it would be difficult to rule out the possibility of dispensing with the requirement of a competent request.[39]

3. Conclusion on the logical arguments in a legal context

Relevant moral distinctions exist between voluntary, non-voluntary, and involuntary euthanasia. Those distinctions could be adopted by a legislature in a jurisdiction with no judicial history of legalization based on either rights or necessity, and therefore become legally determinative.[40] In such (rare) cases, logical slippery slope arguments would have little force. Margaret Otlowski makes this point in her discussion of the logical slippery slope argument in a legal context. She disputes that 'the extension from voluntary to non-voluntary euthanasia . . . is so logically linked with the legalization of active voluntary euthanasia that it would necessarily occur: to suggest as much amounts to a denial of capacity of reasoned and balanced judgment on the part of the State's law-making bodies.'[41] This is true as far as it goes: the logical slippery slope arguments are unconvincing in the context of legislation in a jurisdiction with no judicial history of legalization based on either rights or necessity.[42] 'Legislatures can make compromises which, even if

---

[36] See Chapter 4, Section III.B.2 and the discussion of Articles 293 and 294 of the Dutch Criminal Code in Chapter 4, Section I.A.   [37] See Chapter Six, Section III.B.1.

[38] See Chapter Six, Section V.A.

[39] See Chapter Six, Section V.A. See also, Otlowski, above n. 32, 224.

[40] See, e.g., Oregon and the Northern Territory of Australia, discussed in Chapter Six, Sections VI.A, VI.C.   [41] Otlowski, above n. 32, 224–5.

[42] Van der Burg, above n. 1, 48.

they "illogically" limit the availability of assisted death, can do so in an explicit attempt to balance the competing moral frameworks of our pluralist society.'[43]

Yet what if legalization has occurred through judicial intervention based on either rights or necessity?[44] Van der Burg has argued that the importance of principle and consistency in judicial reasoning adds force to the first category of logical slippery slope arguments.[45] The binding nature of precedent and the judicial preference for making changes which are 'incremental developments of existing principle'[46] lend strength to the second category of logical slippery slope arguments.[47] Van der Burg's arguments may be more persuasive in common law than in civilian jurisdictions.[48] Bearing in mind this caveat, how might these arguments be applied to assisted dying?

As the analysis here and in the previous chapter demonstrates, if the defence of necessity is the mechanism of legal change for termination of life on request, the courts may find it difficult to conclude that termination of life without request is never legally justified for incompetent persons.[49] The reasoning behind the original decision may be applied to the new facts: the duties to relieve suffering and preserve life may conflict in both scenarios. In common law jurisdictions, van der Burg's argument suggests that such a move could also be based on consistency and precedent or on a logical connection. Much depends on the significance attributed to the requirement of an autonomous request in the initial application of the defence of necessity to a case of termination of life on request. If the request requirement is seen merely as an artefact of the initial case – because the defendant terminated the life of a competent, requesting patient and was prosecuted for consensual homicide rather than murder – then an argument from consistency could be used to apply the defence of necessity to permit termination of life without request in the case of an incompetent patient. Alternatively, reasoning based on a logical connection (rather than an identity) between voluntary and

---

[43] Roger S. Magnusson, *Angels of Death - Exploring the Euthanasia Underground* (New Haven, Conn.: Yale Univ. Press, 2002) 277.   [44] See Chapter Six, Sections II and III.

[45] Van der Burg, above n. 1, 49, 56. See also, Lode, above n. 1, 1494.

[46] *Cuerrier* [1998] 2 S.C.R. 371, [43], [58], [65] ('The basic precondition of [court-made] change is that it is required to bring the law into step with the changing needs of society. This established, the change must meet the condition of being an incremental development of the common law that does not possess unforeseeable and complex ramifications.'). See also, *Watkins v. Olafson* [1989] 2 S.C.R. 750; *Salituro* [1991] 3 S.C.R. 654, 670; *Seaboyer* [1991] 2 S.C.R. 577; *Winnipeg Child and Family Services (Northwest Area) v. G.(D.F.)* [1997] 3 S.C.R. 925; *Bow Valley Husky (Bermuda) Ltd. v. Saint John Shipbuilding Ltd.* [1997] 3 S.C.R. 1210; *Hynes* [2001] 3 S.C.R. 623, [114]–[115]. In his discussion of the Dutch experience, Chesterman describes 'the incremental nature of the law-making process'. Chesterman, above n. 22, 383, 389.

[47] Van der Burg, above n. 1, 49–50. See also, Shauer, above n. 1, 383.

[48] Van der Burg's reliance on the work of Ronald Dworkin in this section of his article might explain the greater relevance of his analysis to common law jurisdictions. Van der Burg, above n. 1, 48–51, citing Ronald Dworkin, *A Matter of Principle?* (Cambridge, Mass.: Harvard Univ. Press, 1985); Ronald Dworkin, *Taking Rights Seriously* (Cambridge, Mass.: Harvard Univ. Press, 1977) 113.

[49] As has proved the case in the Netherlands and may well do so in Belgium in the coming years. See Chapter Six, Sections III.B and VI.B respectively.

non-voluntary euthanasia might substitute proxy or parental consent for the patient's request.

In conclusion, the mechanism of legal change used affects whether a distinction is legally relevant, or more importantly, legally determinative. For example, in the Netherlands, the presence of a competent request is legally *relevant*: whether such a request was made determines the applicable provision of the Criminal Code (taking life on request or murder) and thus whether the doctor is covered by the new law or must rely on the judicial defence of necessity. However, the neonate and incompetent adult cases discussed in Chapter Six demonstrate that the presence of a competent request is not *determinative* of legality. Even in the absence of a competent request, the termination of life of an incompetent person may be legally justified.[50] In contrast, if rights are used as the mechanism of legal change, the presence of a competent request would be both legally relevant and (in most of the test jurisdictions)[51] necessary.[52] Finally, a legislature acting in a jurisdiction with no judicial history of legalization based on either rights or necessity could make the presence of a competent request legally determinative without fear of the logical slippery slope.

III. The Empirical Slippery Slope Argument

The empirical slippery slope argument allows that there is a relevant moral and/or legal distinction between, for example, voluntary and non-voluntary or involuntary euthanasia, but that 'we are bad at abiding by [that] distinction':

Once we allow voluntary euthanasia... we may (or will) fail to make the crucial distinction, and then we will reach the morally unacceptable outcome of allowing involuntary euthanasia; or perhaps even though we will make the relevant distinction, we will not act accordingly for some reason (perhaps a political reason, or a reason that has to do with weakness of will, or some other reason).[53]

Whether this failure to abide by the relevant distinction will occur is often difficult to resolve if the social change is new and innovative and evidence from other jurisdictions is unavailable. The Netherlands has become the primary battleground of empirical slippery slope arguments in the debate outside the Netherlands over the legalization of euthanasia and assisted suicide.[54] This status

---

[50] See Chapter Six, Section III.B.   [51] See Chapter Six, Section V.A.

[52] That is, in jurisdictions which have not accepted that a proxy may exercise rights on behalf of an incompetent individual such as England and Wales and all Canadian jurisdictions. See Chapter Six, Section V.A and above, text accompanying n. 39.

[53] Enoch, above n. 25, 631 (describing rather than supporting this argument).

[54] See, e.g., Hendin, above n. 19, 163–5; Richard Fenigsen, 'A Case Against Dutch Euthanasia' (1989) 19(1) *Hastings Center Rep*. S22, S24–S26; John Keown, 'The Law and Practice of Euthanasia in the Netherlands' (1992) 108 *Law Q. Rev*. 51, 61–78; John Keown, 'Further Reflections on Euthanasia in The Netherlands in the Light of The Remmelink Report and The Van Der Maas

'as the world's best "test case" for disputes about physician-assisted suicide and euthanasia' has given 'the experience of the Netherlands ... paramount importance [in] the debates over dying in the rest of the world.'[55] A brief examination of the empirical evidence will suffice to illustrate the difficulties associated with resolving the competing arguments.

Most critics rely predominantly on Dutch evidence of cases of 'termination of life without an explicit request' as evidence for the slide from voluntary euthanasia to non-voluntary euthanasia.[56] According to the three national surveys of 'medical behaviour which shortens life',[57] the cases in this category represent less than one per cent of all deaths.[58] The figure from the 1990 Remmelink survey[59] of one

Survey' in Luke Gormally, ed., *Euthanasia, Clinical Practice and the Law* (London: The Linacre Centre, 1994) 219; Keown, above n. 3.

55 Margaret P. Battin, 'The Euthanasia Debate in the United States: Conflicting Claims about the Netherlands' in Hans Krabbendam & Hans-Martien ten Napel, eds., *Regulating Morality: A Comparison of The Role of the State in Mastering the Mores in the Netherlands and the United States* (Antwerp: Maklu, 2000) 151, 156–7.

56 See, e.g., Fenigsen, above n. 54, 24–6 ('Those who contend that it is possible to accept and practice "voluntary" euthanasia and not allow involuntary [euthanasia] totally disregard the Dutch reality'); Richard Fenigsen, 'Dutch euthanasia revisited' (1997) 13 *Issues in Law & Med.* 301, 310–11; Keown, 'The Law and Practice of Euthanasia in the Netherlands', above n. 54, 61–78; Keown, 'Further Reflections', above n. 54, 219; Amarasekara & Bagaric, above n. 6, 189; Henk Jochemsen & John Keown, 'Voluntary euthanasia under control? Further empirical evidence from the Netherlands' (1999) 25(1) *J. Med. Ethics* 16, 17–18, 20; *Pretty v. U.K.* (2002) 35 E.H.R.R. 1, [31] (Eur. Ct. H.R.) (summarizing the intervention of the Catholic Bishops' Conference of England and Wales). For the counter-argument, see Henk Rigter, 'Euthanasia in the Netherlands: distinguishing facts from fiction' (1989) 19(1) *Hastings Center Rep.* S31, S31–2 (arguing that there is no evidence of involuntary euthanasia in the Netherlands); G.M. Aartsen et al., 'Letter to the Editor' (1989) 19(5) *Hastings Center Rep.* 47 (agreeing with Rigter's assessment of euthanasia in the Netherlands and describing Fenigsen's article (above n. 54) as 'completely misplaced'); van der Maas, 'Euthanasia and other medical decisions concerning the end of life', above n. 9, 669 (criticizing 'ill-founded speculation' by Fenigsen (above n. 54) on the number of cases of euthanasia in the Netherlands).

57 The Remmelink Commission was appointed to carry out research into the practice of euthanasia in 1990. The research was published in full in English as Paul J. van der Maas et al., 'Euthanasia and other Medical Decisions Concerning the End of Life: An Investigation Performed upon Request of the Commission of Inquiry into the Medical Practice Concerning Euthanasia' (1992) 22(1/2) *Health Policy* 1 and Paul J. van der Maas et al., *Euthanasia and other Medical Decisions Concerning the End of Life* (Amsterdam: Elsevier, Health Policy Monographs, 1992). A summary of the report was also published in the *Lancet*. See van der Maas, 'Euthanasia and other medical decisions concerning the end of life', above n. 9. Some of the results of the 1995 follow-up study were published in English in van der Maas, 'Euthanasia, Physician-Assisted Suicide, and Other Medical Practices Involving the End of Life in the Netherlands, 1990–1995', above n. 9 and Gerrit van der Wal et al., 'Evaluation of the notification procedure for physician-assisted death in the Netherlands' (1996) 335(22) *New Eng. J. Med.* 1706. A summary of the third follow-up study in 2001 was published in English in Onwuteaka-Philipsen, above n. 9.   58 Ibid., Table 1.

59 See above n. 57. The evidence is that the cases in this category are 'quite heterogeneous,' including severely handicapped neonates, coma patients, and terminal cancer patients. In over half of the cases, there is evidence of some earlier discussion with the patient regarding euthanasia or a previously expressed wish. Loes Pijnenborg et al., 'Life terminating acts without explicit request of the patient' (1993) 341 *Lancet* 1196, 1197; Griffiths, Bood & Weyers, above n. 20, 226–7. This may account for the conclusion reached by Margaret Otlowski that 'there is some basis for suggesting that the incidence of active termination of life without the patient's request reported in the Remmelink survey

thousand deaths in this category is often cited by those who use the slippery slope argument.[60]

The critics who rely on this slippery slope argument often omit two important elements, thereby using flawed logic. First, the argument is only effective against legalization if it is legalization which *causes* the slippery slope.[61] Second, it is only effective if it is used *comparatively*, to show that the slope is *more* slippery in the Netherlands than it is in jurisdictions which have not legalized assisted suicide or euthanasia.[62] Since these questions have not been addressed by critics, not much attention has been paid to available evidence on causation and comparability.

A. The causal argument

In order to show that legalization causes a slippery slope from voluntary to non-voluntary euthanasia, one must show that (1) there has been an increase in the rate of non-voluntary euthanasia following the legalization of voluntary euthanasia,[63] and (2) that increase was caused by the legalization of voluntary euthanasia.

may be disproportionately high.' Otlowski, above n. 32, 438. The category represents non-voluntary rather than involuntary euthanasia. 'In all situations in which there had been no discussion with the patient and in which no wish of the patient was known, the patients were incompetent.' Johannes J.M. van Delden et al., 'The Remmelink Study: Two Years Later' (1993) 23(6) *Hastings Center Rep.* 24, 25. Significantly, 'most of these cases resemble death due to administration of pain relief more than they do euthanasia.' Griffiths, Bood & Weyers, above n. 20, 228 ('In 65% of the cases only morphine or the like was used, and in only 8% were muscle relaxants used, whereas in the case of euthanasia muscle relaxants are now used 90% of the time'). See also, van Delden, above, 25. A further indication that at least some of these cases would be better classified as due to the administration of pain relief is that '[a]lmost all [of them] involve patients with only a few hours or days to live.' Pijnenborg, above, 1198.

60   See Edmund D. Pellegrino, 'The False Promise of Beneficent Killing' in Emanuel, above n. 31, 71, 88; *Washington v. Glucksberg* (1997) 521 U.S. 702, 734; Keown, 'Further Reflections', above n. 54; John I. Fleming, 'Euthanasia, the Netherlands, and Slippery Slopes' (1992) *Bioethics Research Notes (Occasional Paper No. 1)* 1, 6-7; Terry Cipriani, 'Give Me Liberty and Give Me Death' (1995) 3(1) *J. Law & Med.* 177, 190.

61   Johannes J.M. van Delden et al., 'Dances with Data' (1993) 7 *Bioethics* 323, 327, citing van der Burg, above n. 1, 57. See also, Enoch, above n. 25, 631; Griffiths, Bood & Weyers, above n. 20, 300; Otlowski, above n. 32, 439.

62   See van Delden, above n. 61, 327; Helga Kuhse & Peter Singer, 'Active Voluntary Euthanasia, Morality and the Law' (1995) 3(1) *J. Law & Med.* 129, 132; Griffiths, Bood & Weyers, above n. 20, 300–1. Raphael Cohen-Almagor views the comparative argument with scepticism, arguing that its use by the Dutch is a form of defensiveness: 'Many Dutch scientists suggest that physicians in many countries are secretly doing what Dutch physicians are doing openly. However, this suggestion is dubious. There are not enough data to either support or refute this suggestion.' Raphael Cohen-Almagor, *Euthanasia in the Netherlands: The Policy and Practice of Mercy Killing* (Dordrecht: Kluwer, 2004) 147–8 (citing only one source for his first sentence: Loes Pijnenborg, 'The Dutch Euthanasia Debate in International Perspective' in *End-of-Life Decisions in Dutch Medical Practice* (Rotterdam: Thesis, 1995) 119–31). Section III.B below examines the comparative evidence.

63   'To demonstrate a slippery slope one would need to show that something changed after introducing a certain practice and for this at least two investigations would be required.' van Delden, above n. 61, See also, Kuhse & Singer, above n. 62; Otlowski, above n. 32, 439.

1. A post-legalization increase in non-voluntary euthanasia

Although there have been three major Dutch investigations, unfortunately the Dutch empirical evidence does not cover the period prior to effective legalization.[64] The first comprehensive Dutch survey took place in 1990. We do not know, therefore, whether the rate of non-voluntary euthanasia was lower or higher prior to effective legalization, or whether it has remained relatively stable.[65] While conceding this point, John Keown argues that the inference that non-voluntary euthanasia has in fact increased is more plausible than the inference that it has decreased or remained stable:

There is good reason to think that NVAE [non-voluntary active euthanasia] has indeed increased since 1984. Breach of the guideline requiring a request is more likely to occur in a situation in which some VAE is allowed than when none is allowed, if only because of the greater problems in policing a practice allowed according to professional guidelines than a practice which is legally prohibited. Moreover, the *official endorsement* of NVAE by, for example, the Remmelink Commission can only have served to lessen doctors' inhibitions against it. Despite the absence of prior statistics it is, therefore, more plausible to conclude that NVAE has increased since 1984 rather than remained static.[66]

The evidence of 'underground euthanasia' described below casts doubt on Keown's claim that it is easier to police a prohibitive regime than a regulatory one.[67] The argument that doctors' inhibitions against non-voluntary euthanasia will have been lessened by legalization is even less persuasive, as if this were the case one would expect to see a gradual rise in the rate of non-voluntary euthanasia in the post-legalization period. Instead, the Dutch surveys of 1990, 1995, and 2001 reveal that the rate of non-voluntary euthanasia or 'ending of life without explicit request' has remained stable since 1990 at 0.8% of all deaths in 1990 and 0.7% of all deaths in 1995 and 2001.[68] Paul van der Maas and Linda Emanuel therefore conclude that 'neither the argument that such cases increase in number over time, nor the argument that open regulation lowers the rate, is well supported by the data.'[69]

Neil Gorsuch makes a more moderate argument, contending that in the absence of evidence to the contrary, one would expect that the legalization of voluntary

[64] M.A.M. de Wachter, 'Active Euthanasia in the Netherlands' (1989) 262(23) *J. Am. Med. Ass'n* 3316, 3316–17; van Delden, above n. 59, 26. For a discussion of the relevant judicial decisions, see Chapter 4, Section I.

[65] See Griffiths, above n. 33, 202 ('there is no evidence that...termination of life without a request has become more frequent since legalisation in 1984').

[66] Keown, above n. 30, 146 (emphasis in original). John Griffiths suggests on the contrary that 'it seems pretty clear that many of the things to which opponents of euthanasia point as the horribles to which legalisation will lead, in fact pre-existed legalisation of euthanasia in the Netherlands'. Griffiths, above n. 33, 202.   [67] See below, Section III.B and Magnusson, above n. 43.

[68] Onwuteaka-Philipsen, above n. 9, Table 1 (95% CIs 0.6%-1.1% and 0.5%-0.9% respectively). These figures are based on death certificate studies. The 1990 survey did not collect interview data on this issue, but the relevant interview figures for the other two surveys are 0.7% (1995, 95% CI 0.5%–0.8%) and 0.6% (2001, 95% CI 0.4%–0.9%).

[69] Paul van der Maas & Linda L. Emanuel, 'Factual Findings' in Emanuel, above n. 31, 151, 160.

euthanasia and assisted suicide would cause an increase in the rate of non-voluntary euthanasia:

consistent with the law of demand, legalizing voluntary assisted suicide and euthanasia (and thus reducing the 'price' associated with the practices) would lead to an increase in the frequency of the practices when compared with baseline, prelegalization rates in any given country.... As nonconsensual killings become more acceptable – as they surely have in the Netherlands, where the government has sought to justify them as a 'necessity,' and where some, such as Griffiths, have urged their complete decriminalization – *one would expect the number of such cases to increase*, not remain constant as Kuhse seems to suppose. While an exception to the law of demand is not inconceivable, any theory that depends on such an extraordinary exception would require considerable proof.[70]

In the absence of evidence relating to the period before legalization, Gorsuch's argument would be more persuasive if, instead of remaining stable, the rate of non-voluntary euthanasia in the Netherlands had risen steadily during the period after effective legalization, particularly during the late 1990s following the decisions in the *Prins* and *Kadijk* cases of neonatal termination of life.[71] On the contrary, it has been suggested by Jocelyn Downie that the fact that the rate of non-voluntary euthanasia in the Netherlands has not increased over the period of the Dutch surveys indicates that there is no slippery slope.[72]

Neither the interpretations by Keown and Gorsuch, on one side, nor Downie on the other are sustainable on the basis of the current empirical evidence. The Dutch data does not precisely address the issue of legalization, as there is no evidence of the rate of non-voluntary euthanasia prior to legalization with which to compare the steady post-legalization rate. Similarly, no such evidence exists in relation to the period prior to legalization of assisted suicide in Oregon.[73]

In the absence of data on the rate of non-voluntary euthanasia in the Netherlands prior to legalization, the best hope for relevant data currently lies with a repeat of the pre-legalization survey in Flanders, Belgium which would allow a comparison between the rates of non-voluntary euthanasia in Belgium before and after legalization.[74]

2. An increase caused by legalization

Discussion of this second step of the causation argument is entirely speculative in the absence of any evidence of an increase in the rate of non-voluntary euthanasia

---

[70] Neil M. Gorsuch, 'The Legalization of Assisted Suicide and the Law of Unintended Consequences: A Review of the Dutch and Oregon Experiments and Leading Utilitarian Arguments For Legal Change' [2004] *Wis. L. Rev.* 1347, 1395–6 (emphasis added), citing Griffiths, Bood & Weyers, above n. 20, 267–98; Helga Kuhse, 'From Intention to Consent: Learning from Experience with Euthanasia' in Margaret P. Battin et al., eds., *Physician Assisted Suicide: Expanding the Debate* (New York: Routledge, 1998) 252, 263–6. Kuhse's argument is discussed below, text accompanying n. 126. [71] See Chapter Six, Section III.B.1.

[72] Downie, above n. 20, 135–6. [73] Ibid. 137, n. 56.

[74] Luc Deliens et al., 'End-of-life decisions in medical practice in Flanders, Belgium: a nationwide survey' (2000) 356 *Lancet* 1806, Table 5. The Belgian data is discussed below, text accompanying n. 88.

following legalization in any jurisdiction which has legalized. However, as John Griffiths points out, were there to be evidence of an increase in the rate of non-voluntary euthanasia following legalization, a causal link could not necessarily be inferred:

The contention assumes that the *reason* for the increase in the frequency of termination of life without a request – if it had taken place – would lie in the legalisation of euthanasia and not – for example – in the fact that such behaviour had come to be regarded as not always and under all circumstances objectionable.[75]

This argument does not preclude the possibility that changes in societal norms could be caused by legalization, in which case there could be a causal, albeit indirect connection between legalization and an increase in the rate of non-voluntary euthanasia. Eric Posner and Adrian Vermeule suggest that changes in norms might precede legalization, thus negating the possibility of a causal link between legalization and an increase in the rate of non-voluntary euthanasia:

Jochemsen and Keown, who are critics of Dutch euthanasia, argue that legalization has resulted in a slide down the slippery slope because the Dutch now condone some types of non-voluntary euthanasia.[76] But the authors cannot trace this change in attitude to legalization – legalization may have followed changes in attitudes – and in any event the change in attitudes can be attributed to benign causes: exposed to public debate about euthanasia practices, the Dutch view toward euthanasia, unsurprisingly, has evolved.[77]

It is true that evidence of causation is likely to be difficult to establish.[78] Nevertheless, a significant increase in the rate of non-voluntary euthanasia within a short time period during which legalization has taken place, would strongly suggest that legalization has had an influence on the rate of non-voluntary euthanasia. Although such evidence does not exist in relation to the Dutch model, again Belgium provides a good opportunity to collect evidence in the near future.[79]

In the absence of evidence of causation, or even of a post-legalization increase in the rate of non-voluntary euthanasia, critics of Dutch law and practice have drawn causative inferences simply from the evidence of the *existence* of non-voluntary euthanasia in the Netherlands. For example, Kumar Amarasekara and Mirko Bagaric argue that:

The...*only* cogent evidence...shows in a climate where voluntary euthanasia is openly practiced, there are also a large number of cases of non-voluntary euthanasia. It may be that the rate of non-voluntary euthanasia in Holland was not increased by the decision to give the green light to voluntary euthanasia. But given that we know that one state of affairs (ie where euthanasia is practiced with impunity) *definitely* leads to undesirable consequences and are unsure about the situation in the alternative state of affairs (where euthanasia is prohibited

---

[75] Griffiths, above n. 33, 202 (emphasis in original).   [76] Above n. 56, 20–1.

[77] Eric A. Posner & Adrian Vermeule, 'Should Coercive Interrogation Be Legal?' (2006) 104 *Mich. L. Rev.* 671, n. 67.

[78] John Arras has described this as 'an extremely difficult problem of empirical prediction.' Arras, above n. 4, 296.   [79] See above, text accompanying n. 74.

and this prohibition is enforced), logically we ought to opt for the later [sic] – speculative or possible dangers being accorded far less weight than certain ones.[80]

Logically, however, this does not follow. Amarasekara and Bagaric admit that there may be no link between legalization in the Netherlands and the rate of non-voluntary euthanasia, and yet in the next sentence assert that they 'know' that legalization '*definitely* leads to undesirable consequences'. How do they know this? Leaving aside the difficulty that there is no evidence of a post-legalization increase in the Dutch rate of non-voluntary euthanasia, the temptation to assume that the legalization of voluntary euthanasia causes non-voluntary euthanasia to occur, while understandable, should be resisted in the absence of evidence of causation. The presence of both legalization and non-voluntary euthanasia does not necessitate a causal connection between the two. As Stephen Smith has recently written:

> Groups may assume that the presence of A and B together leads to the conclusion that there is a connection. There may not always be such a connection or there may not be the right sort of connection for a slippery slope argument. In other words, the simple fact that A and B are present does not lend any authority to the claim that A led to B. More specific evidence, and more specific causal evidence, is required before a slippery slope claim can be verified.[81]

B. The comparative argument

The previous section illustrated that at present there is no *direct* evidence that legalization causes an increase in the rate of non-voluntary euthanasia. However, if rates of non-voluntary euthanasia are higher in jurisdictions which have legalized voluntary euthanasia than in those which have not, this may suggest *indirectly* that legalization has caused an increase in the rate of non-voluntary euthanasia. Conversely, if rates of non-voluntary euthanasia are higher in jurisdictions in which voluntary euthanasia remains illegal, the force of this empirical slippery slope argument is further attenuated. The first part of this section examines comparative evidence of the rates of non-voluntary euthanasia across jurisdictions in which the legal status of voluntary euthanasia varies. The second part of this section discusses the limits on the inferences which may be drawn from this comparative evidence.

1. Comparative evidence

There is no evidence demonstrating that the Netherlands has a greater rate of non-voluntary or involuntary euthanasia than other Western countries.[82] Indeed,

---

[80] Amarasekara & Bagaric, above n. 6, 190 (emphasis added). The argument is reproduced in Mirko Bagaric, 'The Kuhse-Singer Euthanasia Survey: Why it Fails to Undermine the Slippery Slope Argument – Comparing Apples and Apples' (2002) 9 *Eur. J. Health L.* 229, 233.

[81] Stephen W. Smith, 'Evidence for the Practical Slippery Slope in the Debate on Physician-Assisted Suicide and Euthanasia' (2005) 13 *Med. L. Rev.* 17, 22.

[82] Griffiths, above n. 33, 202; Griffiths, Bood & Weyers, above n. 20, 301, n. 4.

there is a significant amount of evidence demonstrating the prevalence of both voluntary and non-voluntary active euthanasia in various jurisdictions in which euthanasia has not been legalized, looking at criminal prosecutions,[83] admissions by doctors,[84] and anonymous surveys of medical professionals. The survey evidence is the most cogent and has been the most hotly contested.

a. Survey prevalence evidence

As discussed in the previous section, the rate of 'ending of life without explicit request' in the three Dutch surveys has remained stable.[85] While critics of Dutch practice tend to focus on the raw numbers of deaths in this category,[86] those in favour of legalization and those who defend Dutch practice have responded by citing surveys from other countries which indicate that the rate of non-voluntary euthanasia in some Western jurisdictions which have not legalized euthanasia or assisted suicide is higher than it is in the Netherlands. For example, a 1996 Australian anonymous postal survey of doctors based on the interview questionnaire used in the 1995 Dutch study found that the rate of termination of life without explicit request was 3.5 per cent of all deaths.[87] A 1998 death certificate study (based on the Dutch model) in Flanders, Belgium, prior to legalization, reported a rate of 'ending of life without the patient's explicit request' of 3.2 per cent.[88] The authors of this study have commented that 'the fact that the figure is four to five times higher in Flanders than in the neighbouring Netherlands supports the conclusion that the Belgian rate is unexpectedly high ... another possibility is that the Dutch rate is unexpectedly low'.[89]

However, a recent survey in the United Kingdom based on the same methodology as the Australian study reported a much lower rate of ending of life without explicit request from the patient of 0.33 per cent of all deaths.[90] A pan-European study based on data from 2001–2002 found rates of ending of life without the

---

[83] Some of the relevant cases are mentioned in Chapter 1, Section III and Chapter 4, Section III.A.1. See also, Otlowski, above n. 32, 140–8; Barney Sneiderman, 'The Case of Robert Latimer: A Commentary on Crime and Punishment' (1999) 37 *Alta. L. Rev.* 1017, [60], [85]–[87]; Downie, above n. 20, 137, n. 57; Laura Dietz et al., 'Aiding, abetting, or counseling suicide; euthanasia and assisted suicide' (2006) 40A *Am. Jur. 2d Homicide* § 623; James M. Thunder, 'Quiet Killings in Medical Facilities: Detection and Prevention' (2003) 18 *Issues in Law & Med.* 211, 213.

[84] See generally, Otlowski, above n. 32, 134–8; Magnusson, above n. 43.

[85] See above, text accompanying n. 68.   [86] See above, text accompanying n. 60.

[87] Helga Kuhse et al., 'End-of-Life Decisions in Australian Medical Practice' (1997) 166 *Med. J. Australia* 191, Box 4 (95% CI 2.7%–4.3%). Further Australian evidence is discussed below n. 94.

[88] Deliens, above n. 74, Table 5 (95% CI 2.7%–3.8%). The pilot study which preceded this study is described in Freddy Mortier et al., 'End-of-life decisions of physicians in the City of Hasselt (Flanders, Belgium)' (2000) 14(3) *Bioethics* 254. See also, Freddy Mortier et al., 'Attitudes, Sociodemographic Characteristics, and Actual End-of-Life Decisions of Physicians in Flanders, Belgium' (2003) 23 *Medical Decision Making* 502.

[89] Freddy Mortier & Luc Deliens, 'The Prospects of Effective Legal Control on Euthanasia in Belgium: Implications of recent end-of-life studies' in Klijn, above n. 9, 179, 184, n. 17.

[90] Clive Seale, 'National survey of end-of-life decisions made by UK medical practitioners' (2006) 20 *Palliative Med.* 3, Table 2. The survey was carried out in 2004–2005. A full comparison between the Australian and U.K. data is found in Table 2.

patient's explicit request varied between 1.5% in Flanders, Belgium (prior to legalization) and 0.06 per cent in Italy. This data is shown in the following table alongside the Australian data referred to earlier:

Table 1: Rates of ending life without the patient's explicit request (percentage of deaths and 95% confidence interval)[91]

Country	Australia	U.K.	Belgium	Denmark	Italy	Netherlands	Sweden	Switzerland
Including SUDs*	3.5 (2.7−4.3)	0.33 (0−0.76)	1.5 (1.12−2.01)	0.67 (0.44−1.04)	0.06 (0.01−0.29)	0.60 (0.43−0.84)	0.23 (0.11−0.47)	0.42 (0.25−0.70)
Excluding SUDs*		0.36 (0−0.87)	2.26 (1.59−2.93)	1.02 (0.57−1.47)	0.11 (0−0.26)	0.90 (0.59−1.21)	0.31 (0.08−0.54)	0.61 (0.29−0.93)

*SUDs = sudden and unexpected deaths

The rates of non-voluntary euthanasia in Australia, Belgium (pre-legalization), and Denmark were all higher than the rate in the Netherlands, the only jurisdiction in which termination of life on request was lawful at the time of these surveys. Other jurisdictions in which voluntary euthanasia was and remains illegal had significantly lower rates of non-voluntary euthanasia, including the United Kingdom, Italy, and Sweden.

b. Beyond non-voluntary euthanasia prevalence rates

Although comparable evidence of rates of non-voluntary euthanasia from other jurisdictions is unavailable,[92] there is considerable evidence that both non-voluntary and voluntary euthanasia and assisted suicide are practised in jurisdictions in which they are subject to criminal prohibition including Canada,[93] Australia,[94]

[91] This data is from Agnes van der Heide et al., 'End-of-life decision-making in six European countries: descriptive study' (2003) 362 *Lancet* 345, Table 2; Seale, above n. 90, Tables 2 and 3; Kuhse, above n.87, Box 4.

[92] '[E]pidemiological research concerning medical decision-making at the end of life is . . . rather scarce'. Agnes van der Heide et al., 'End-of-life Decisions in Six European Countries: A research note' in Klijn, above n. 9, 129, 131.

[93] See Neil Searles, 'Silence Doesn't Obliterate the Truth: A Manitoba Survey on Physician Assisted Suicide and Euthanasia' (1996) 4 *Health L. Rev.* 9, [22], Table 4 ('A little more than one in seven doctors indicated they had facilitated a patient's request for assisted suicide or euthanasia by hastening her or his death'); Downie, above n. 20, 137–8.

[94] See Kuhse, above n. 87, Box 4 (1.8% of deaths were due to voluntary euthanasia and assisted suicide (95% CI 1.2%–2.4%)); Charles D. Douglas et al., 'The intention to hasten death: a survey of attitudes and practices of surgeons in Australia' (2001) 175 *Med J. Australia* 511 (5.3% of respondents reported giving a lethal injection or providing the means to commit suicide on request); Helga Kuhse & Peter Singer, 'Doctors' practices and attitudes regarding voluntary euthanasia' (1988) 148 *Med. J. Australia* 623, 624 (29% of responding doctors had taken active steps to end a patient's life on request); Christine A. Stevens & Riaz Hassan, 'Management of death, dying and euthanasia: attitudes and practices of medical practitioners in South Australia' (1994) 20 *J. Med. Ethics* 41, 43 (18.8% of responding doctors had taken active steps to bring about the death of a patient; 49% of this group had never received a request from a patient); P. Baume & E. O'Malley, 'Euthanasia: attitudes and practices

New Zealand,[95] the United States,[96] and the United Kingdom[97] and other European jurisdictions. The pan-European study discussed above also includes data on rates of euthanasia and physician-assisted suicide. This data is shown in the following table alongside the corresponding Australian data:

of medical practitioners' (1994) 161 *Med. J. Australia* 137 (12.3% of reporting doctors had complied with a patient request to hasten death; 7% had provided the means for suicide).

[95] See Kay Mitchell & R. Glynn Owens, 'National survey of medical decisions at end of life made by New Zealand general practitioners' (2003) 327 *Br. Med. J.* 202 (5.6% of respondent doctors making an end-of-life decision at the last death attended had performed active euthanasia or physician-assisted suicide; 44% of these decisions had not been discussed with the patient, almost entirely because the patient was no longer competent). A direct comparison between this study and the most recent U.K. study is found in Seale, above n. 90, Table 4: the rate of active euthanasia or physician-assisted suicide at the last death attended across all respondents (not simply those who made an end-of-life decision) was 3.1% in the New Zealand study (95% CI 2.1%–4.1%) and 1.4% in the U.K. study (95% CI 0.3%-2.5%).

[96] The empirical evidence is reviewed in Ezekiel J. Emanuel, 'Euthanasia and Physician-Assisted Suicide: A Review of the Empirical Data From the United States' (2002) 162 *Arch. Internal Med.* 142, 146, Table 4 ('Many studies indicate that a small, but definite, proportion of US physicians have performed euthanasia or PAS, despite its being illegal. . . . [T]he data provide conflicting evidence on the precise frequency of such interventions, with reported frequencies varying more than 6-fold even among the best studies'). For individual U.S. studies, see, e.g., Diane E. Meier et al., 'A national survey of physician-assisted suicide and euthanasia in the United States' (1998) 338(17) *New Eng. J. Med.* 1193 (4.7% of respondent doctors had given at least one lethal injection; 3.3% had written at least one prescription to hasten death); Anthony L. Back et al., 'Physician-assisted suicide and euthanasia in Washington State. Patient requests and physician responses' (1996) 275(12) *J. Am. Med. Ass'n* 919, 920, 922 (24% of patients requesting assisted suicide received prescriptions; 24% of patients requesting euthanasia received parenteral medication and died); David J. Doukas et al., 'Attitudes and Behaviors on Physician Assisted Death: A Study of Michigan Oncologists' (1995) 13 *Clinical Oncology* 1055 (18% of respondents had participated in assisted suicide; 4% had terminated life on request); Lee R. Slome et al., 'Physician-Assisted Suicide and Patients with Human Immunodeficiency Virus Disease' (1997) 336(6) *New Eng. J. Med.* 417 (53% of respondent HIV physicians had assisted suicide at least once; the mean number was 4.2); Ezekiel J. Emanuel et al., 'Attitudes and Practices of U.S. Oncologists regarding Euthanasia and Physician-Assisted Suicide' (2000) 133(7) *Annals Internal Med.* 527 (3.7% of respondents had performed euthanasia and 10.8% had performed physician-assisted suicide during their career); Ezekiel J. Emanuel et al., 'The Practice of Euthanasia and Physician-Assisted Suicide in the United States: Adherence to Proposed Safeguards and Effects on Physicians' (1998) 280(6) *J. Am. Med. Ass'n* 507, 511 (10.7% of interviewed oncologists had performed either euthanasia or physician-assisted suicide; 'in 15.3% of cases, the patients were not involved in the decision but families wanted the patients' lives ended'); Dick L. Willems et al., 'Attitudes and Practices Concerning the End of Life: A Comparison Between Physicians From the United States and From the Netherlands' (2000) 160(1) *Arch. Internal Med.* 63, Table 4 (7% of responding U.S. doctors had assisted suicide on request; none had terminated life on request; 2% had terminated life without request).

[97] See Seale, above n. 90, Table 2; B.J. Ward & P.A. Tate, 'Attitudes among NHS doctors to requests for euthanasia' (1994) 308 *Br. Med. J.* 1332 (12% of responding doctors had taken active steps to hasten death on request); Sheila A.M. McLean & Alison Britton, *Sometimes A Small Victory* (Glasgow: Institute of Law & Ethics in Medicine, 1996) App. III, Table 17, 31–2, discussed in Keown, above n. 30, 61 and Michael Freeman, 'Denying Death its Dominion: Thoughts on the Dianne Pretty Case' (2002) 10(3) *Med. L. Rev.* 245, 249, n. 31 (4% of responding Scottish health professionals had assisted suicide). The House of Lords Select Committee on the Assisted Dying for the Terminally Ill Bill doubted some of the U.K. survey evidence: 'Bearing in mind however the trend towards death taking place in hospital rather than at home, the increasing prevalence of team-working in clinical care, the greater tendency for people to litigate where they suspect malpractice, and the potential for confusion with the legal administration of drugs to prevent restlessness and anxiety in the last hours of life, we would be surprised if covert euthanasia were being practised on anything like

Table 2: Rates of euthanasia and physician-assisted suicide (percentage of deaths and 95% confidence interval)[98]

Country		Australia	U.K.	Belgium	Denmark	Italy	Netherlands	Sweden	Switzerland
Including SUDs*	EUT**	1.8 (1.2–2.4)	0.16 (0–0.36)	0.3 (0.16–0.58)	0.06 (0.01–0.26)	0.04 (0–0.27)	2.59 (2.19–3.04)	—	0.27 (0.14–0.51)
	PAS***	0.10 (0.02–0.18)	0.00	0.01 (0–0.28)	0.06 (0.01–0.26)	0.00	0.21 (0.12–0.38)	—	0.36 (0.20–0.63)
Excluding SUDs*	EUT**		0.17 (0–0.51)	0.46 (0.17–0.75)	0.10 (0–0.24)	0.05 (0–0.15)	3.89 (3.49–4.29)	—	0.39 (0.13–0.65)
	PAS***		0.00	0.05 (0–0.15)	0.10 (0–0.24)	0.00	0.31 (0.13–0.49)	—	0.52 (0.22–0.82)

*SUDs = sudden and unexpected deaths
**EUT = euthanasia
***PAS = physician-assisted suicide

the scale which some of these surveys suggest.' House of Lords Select Committee on the Assisted Dying for the Terminally Ill Bill, *Report*, HL Paper 86-I (2005) [239], www.publications. parliament.uk/pa/ld200405/ldselect/ldasdy/86/86i.pdf, accessed 27 July 2006.

98 This data is from van der Heide, above n. 91, Table 2; Seale, above n. 90, Tables 2 and 3; Kuhse, above n. 87, Box 4.

2. Difficulties associated with the comparative evidence

a. Lack of reliable data

Not only is there a dearth of pre-legalization evidence in the Netherlands,[99] but studies similar to those subsequently undertaken in the Netherlands are rare,[100] although the recent Australian, United Kingdom, and pan-European research has provided some points of comparison.[101] However, the Australian survey has been heavily criticized on methodological grounds.[102] The more recent U.K. survey using similar methodology corrected one flaw in the Australian study which had the effect of 'artificially inflat[ing] the proportion of deaths receiving' end-of-life decisions.[103] The Australian data is nonetheless included here because it has become an important weapon in the armoury of pro-legalization commentators.[104]

A further difficulty with the comparative evidence is that 'legal and cultural differences' make valid comparisons difficult.[105] This is particularly true of comparisons between jurisdictions with very different health care systems.[106]

b. Effect of the topic

Collecting data about the prevalence of euthanasia and assisted suicide is a difficult enterprise. Even though most surveys focus on disclosure by individual practitioners given guarantees of anonymity, rather than on reports to the authorities,

[99] See above, text accompanying nn. 64–69.

[100] Raphael Cohen-Almagor, *Euthanasia in the Netherlands: The Policy and Practice of Mercy Killing* (Dordrecht: Kluwer, 2004) 26.

[101] See Kuhse, above n. 87; Seale, above n. 90; van der Heide, above n. 91.

[102] Some of the criticism was canvassed by the Australian Senate Legal and Constitutional Legislation Committee in its report on the Bill to overrule the Northern Territory legislation. *Euthanasia Laws Bill 1996* (1997) 88–9 (on the Northern Territory legislation, see Chapter Six, Section VI.C). See also, Kumar Amarasekara, 'Euthanasia and the Quality of Legislative Safeguards' (1997) 23 *Monash U. L. Rev.* 1, 15–16; Amarasekara & Bagaric, above n. 6, 191; Gorsuch, above n. 70, 1396–400.

[103] Seale, above n. 90, 6: 'Sudden and unexpected deaths are excluded from Table 3 to control for an artefactual effect that applied to this and the Australian study, which chose deaths according to the most recent one nominated by the respondent. Significantly fewer such deaths were nominated by UK and Australian doctors than in studies based on samples of death certificates. The effect of this is to artificially inflate the proportion of deaths receiving ELDs [end-of-life decisions], a point not appreciated by the Australian investigators.'

[104] See, e.g., Kuhse, above n. 87, 196 (noting that their study comparing Australia and the Netherlands weakens the assumption that countries openly practising euthanasia have higher non-voluntary euthanasia rates than countries not openly practising euthanasia); Margaret Otlowski, 'The Effectiveness of Legal Control of Euthanasia: Lessons from Comparative Law' in Klijn, above n. 9, 137, 141–3, 152–5; Dan Morris, 'Assisted Suicide under the European Convention on Human Rights: A Critique' (2003) 1 *Eur. Hum. Rights L. Rev.* 65, 84.

[105] Cohen-Almagor, above n. 100, 26. See also, Bregje D. Onwuteaka-Philipsen et al., 'End-of-Life Decision Making in Europe and Australia: A Physician Survey' (2006) 166 *Arch. Internal Med.* 921, 927–8. On social contexts as an influence on the strength of slippery slope arguments, see Lode, above n. 1, 1493–4.

[106] See van der Maas & Emanuel, above n. 69, 161; T. Howard Stone and William J. Winslade, 'Physician-Assisted Suicide and Euthanasia in the United States' (1995) 16 *J. Legal Med.* 481, n. 70; Griffiths, Bood & Weyers, above n. 20, 304–5; Otlowski, above n. 32, 452–4; Margaret Pabst Battin,

under-disclosure is likely. This is particularly so in jurisdictions in which these acts are illegal,[107] although some researchers have reported high response rates.[108] In Roger Magnusson's study of the euthanasia underground in the United States and Australia, he found evidence of practised deception amongst practitioners:

Deception permeates every aspect of illicit euthanasia practice. By all accounts, health care workers are remarkably accomplished in their deception. Deceptive practices contribute to the *invisibility* of euthanasia, and help to perpetuate the myth that because euthanasia is prohibited, it never occurs.[109]

The presence of criminal prohibitions makes the comparative evidence difficult to assess. Looking at the rather scant Canadian evidence, Lorraine Weinrib observes:

It may well be that the criminal prohibition in Canada hides the incidence of assisted suicide, particularly in respect to the terminally ill. Without any data for Canada, it is not possible to pinpoint our place on the slippery slope, i.e. whether there is a problem to avoid or a problem to regulate.[110]

Even post-legalization, practitioners may be reluctant to report cases which did not comply with the relevant criteria,[111] and this reluctance may extend to disclosure to researchers despite guarantees of anonymity. Practitioners who are involved in a number of assisted deaths may not remember each one, which may

'A Dozen Caveats Concerning the Discussion of Euthanasia in the Netherlands' in Margaret Pabst Battin, *The Least Worst Death: Essays in Bioethics on the End of Life* (New York: Oxford Univ. Press, 1994) 130, 140–1.

[107] Searles, above n. 94, [27] ('If the response rate is thought to be low, this is due predominantly to the controversial nature of the subject matter of this investigation. Physicians were asked if they have ever committed indictable offences, punishable by harsh professional and criminal sentences.'); Martien T. Muller et al., 'Euthanasia and Assisted Suicide: Facts, Figures and Fancies with Special Regard to Old Age' (1998) 13(3) *Drugs & Aging* 185, 189; Downie, above n. 20, 137; Seale, above n. 90, 6.

[108] Emanuel, 'The Practice of Euthanasia and Physician-Assisted Suicide in the United States', above n. 96, 512.   [109] Magnusson, above n. 43, 229 (emphasis in original).

[110] Weinrib, above n. 4, n. 77.

[111] Mortier & Deliens, above n. 89, 179; Cuperus-Bosma, above n. 53, 236–7; Barney Sneiderman, John C. Irvine & Philip H. Osborne, *Canadian Medical Law: An Introduction for Physicians, Nurses and other Health Care Professionals* (3rd edn.) (Scarborough, Ont.: Carswell, 2003) 727 (quoting Gerrit van der Wal, *Euthanasia en hulp by zelfdoding door huisartsen (Euthanasia and Assisted Suicide By Family Physicians)* (Rotterdam: WYT Uitgeefgroep, 1992) 12: 'physicians, having been informed about the requirements for prudent care, only report those cases of which they are almost certain that they will not be prosecuted'); Henk Jochemsen, 'Why euthanasia should not be legalized: A reflection on the Dutch experiment' in David N. Weisstub et al., eds., *Aging: Decisions at the End of Life* (Dordrecht: Kluwer Academic Publishers, 2001) 67, 77. The 1995 Dutch research indicated, however, that failure to report was generally related to a failure to meet one of the procedural requirements (such as obtaining a written request; consultation with another physician; or providing a written report). 'There were no major differences between reported and unreported cases in terms of the patients' characteristics or the basis for the decision to provide assistance (i.e., whether there was an explicit request and unbearable and hopeless suffering).' Van der Wal, above n. 57, 1708. Similar results were reported in later research (see Bregje D. Onwuteaka-Philipsen et al., 'Dutch experience of monitoring euthanasia' (2005) 331 *Br. Med. J.* 691, 692) and in earlier research amongst family doctors only (see Gerrit van der Wal et al., 'Euthanasia and Assisted Suicide II. Do Dutch Family Doctors Act Prudently?' (1992) 9(2) *Family Practice* 135, 137–40).

result in inadvertent under-reporting or under-disclosure.[112] Reports may also be moulded so as to better fit the relevant criteria, and this may also affect disclosure to researchers.[113]

3. Drawing inferences from the comparative data

a. The problem of the baseline

Even if the rate of non-voluntary euthanasia is higher in some jurisdictions which have not legalized (such as Australia) than in jurisdictions which have (such as the Netherlands) this could be consistent with the proposition 'that different countries have different baseline (pre-legalization) rates... because of unrelated cultural phenomena'.[114] For example, Clive Seale has proposed the following explanation for the low rates of both non-voluntary and voluntary euthanasia found in his recent U.K. survey:[115]

The lower relative rate of [end-of-life decisions] involving doctor-assisted dying in the UK, and the relatively high rate of [non-treatment decisions],[116] suggests a culture of medical decision making informed by a palliative care philosophy. Historically the UK developed palliative care approaches earlier than the other countries in which the survey has been done, supporting this interpretation. The situation may also reflect, amongst GPs in particular, fears arising from the Harold Shipman scandal in which a UK GP was convicted of causing the deaths of numerous patients by administering lethal injections.[117]

There is some evidence that the rate of non-voluntary euthanasia may be inversely proportional to the rate of discussion with patients and their families.[118] For example, Freddy Mortier and Luc Deliens suggest that one explanation for the relatively high Belgian rate of non-voluntary euthanasia is that 'in Belgium, the patient's autonomy is legally less clearly recognized and paternalistic medical practice appears to be more widely accepted.'[119] Patients' rights have only recently been recognized by statute in Belgium.[120] The higher Belgian rates of failure to

---

[112] Robert Pool, *Negotiating a Good Death: Euthanasia in the Netherlands* (Binghamton, N.Y.: The Haworth Press, 2000) 110, 114 (based on a small, non-scientific sample).

[113] Van der Wal, *Euthanasia and Assisted Suicide By Family Physicians*, above n.111, 12, translated in Sneiderman, Irvine & Osborne, above n. 111, 727.   [114] Gorsuch, above n. 70, 1395.

[115] See above, text accompanying nn. 90–91 and n. 98.

[116] The U.K. rate of non-treatment decisions as a percentage of non-sudden deaths was 33.4% (95% CI 27.1%–39.8%). Several European jurisdictions have significantly lower rates. For example, the rate in Belgium (pre-legalization) was 22.8% (95% CI 20.9%–24.7%). Denmark and Sweden had similar rates to Belgium. Italy's rate was much lower, at 5.6% (95% CI 4.6%–6.6%). The Netherlands and Switzerland had rates comparable to the U.K. Seale, above n. 90, Table 3, using data from van der Heide, above n. 91, Table 2.   [117] Seale, above n. 90, 8.

[118] See Clive Seale, 'Characteristics of end-of-life decisions: survey of UK medical practitioners' (2006) 20 *Palliative Med.* 653; Deliens, above n. 76, 1809–11; van Der Heide, above n. 91, 348–9; Seale, above n. 90, 6–8.

[119] Mortier & Deliens, above n. 91, 186–7. The Belgian data is discussed above nn. 88–89 and accompanying text.

[120] Law concerning the rights of the patient of 22 Aug. 2002, discussed by Herman Nys, 'Recent Developments in Health Law in Belgium' (2006) 13(2) *Eur. J. Health L.* 95.

discuss with the patient both non-treatment decisions and palliative measures intended to shorten the patient's life (in comparison to the Netherlands) are consistent with this explanation.[121] Helga Kuhse et al., in their Australian study, suggest that prohibition may be linked to low rates of discussion with patients and families: 'it may be that, because existing laws prohibit the intentional termination of life, doctors are reluctant to discuss medical end-of-life decisions with their patients lest these decisions be construed as collaboration in euthanasia or in the intentional termination of life.'[122]

Owing to the problem of the baseline, the comparative evidence does not rule out the possibility that legalization of voluntary euthanasia has caused or would cause a change in the rate of non-voluntary euthanasia. To repeat, the best evidence which could be obtained on this point would be evidence of a significant change in the rate of non-voluntary euthanasia within a short time period during which legalization of voluntary euthanasia has taken place. At present, no such evidence exists.[123]

b. Comparing jurisdictions which have legalized with those which have not

What *can* be inferred from the comparative data on the prevalence of non-voluntary euthanasia? Margaret Otlowski has argued that the inference to be drawn is that prohibition *causes* the higher prevalence rates in jurisdictions which have not legalized – Australia and pre-legalization Belgium – than in the one which has – the Netherlands:

These research data from Belgium suggest that these practices are not peculiar to common law jurisdictions or to the particular approach of the common law, but rather, *are the product* of an outright prohibition on euthanasia under the criminal law, however this might be achieved.[124]

Helga Kuhse makes a similar argument, drawing on the evidence that the rate of non-voluntary euthanasia in Australia is significantly higher than the Dutch rate:[125]

There seems to be good evidence to suggest that laws prohibiting the intentional termination of life, but permitting the withholding or withdrawing of treatment and the administration of life-shortening palliative care, do not prevent doctors from intentionally ending the lives of some of their patients. There are also good reasons to believe

---

[121] Mortier & Deliens, above n. 89, 186–7.   [122] Kuhse, above n. 87.

[123] See above, text accompanying nn. 78–79.

[124] Otlowski, above n. 104, 143 (emphasis added), 148. A similar argument was made by the Voluntary Euthanasia Society in its intervention in *Pretty v. U.K.* (2002) 35 E.H.R.R. 1, [27] (Eur. Ct. H.R.): 'The Dutch situation indicated that in the absence of regulation slightly less than 1% of deaths were due to doctors having ended the life of a patient without the latter explicitly requesting this (non-voluntary euthanasia). A similar studies [sic] indicated a figure of 3.1% in Belgium and 3.5% in Australia. It might therefore be the case that less attention was given to the requirements of a careful end of life practice in a society with a restrictive legal approach than in one with an open approach that tolerated and regulated euthanasia.'

[125] See above, text accompanying nn. 68, 87.

that such laws... encourage hypocrisy and unconsented-to termination of patients' lives.[126]

Once again, the inference of causation has not been proven. As Gorsuch has pointed out, factors other than the presence of prohibition could have caused these higher rates.[127] Indeed, the fact that high rates are not found in other jurisdictions which have prohibited assisted dying (such as the United Kingdom, Italy, and Sweden)[128] casts doubt on the inference proposed by Otlowski and Kuhse.

Kumar Amarasekara and Mirko Bagaric have argued that the Australian data does not refute the slippery slope argument but rather reinforces it. They contend that although voluntary euthanasia has not been legalized in Australia, the non-prosecution of such cases means that the description of Australia as a jurisdiction in which voluntary euthanasia is prohibited is inappropriate:

The surveys merely demonstrate that legislation is futile. If non-voluntary euthanasia is greater where it is illegal as in Australia than where it is practised openly as in the Netherlands, then the effectiveness of all legislation has to be questioned. Australian law which prohibits the intentional termination of life by an act or omission 'has not prevented the practice of euthanasia or the intentional ending of life without the patient's consent.' It is equally certain that decriminalising legislation which imposes conditions under which voluntary euthanasia may be administered will not be complied with.

The prevalence of non-voluntary euthanasia [in Australia] is attributable not to the ban on voluntary euthanasia but to the faulty exercise of a discretion not to prosecute violations of the ban.[129]

The logic of this argument is flawed. The evidence that 'non-voluntary euthanasia is greater where it is illegal as in Australia than where it is practised openly as in the Netherlands'[130] is equally consistent with the inference that legalization has a beneficial effect on the number of cases of non-voluntary euthanasia! Moreover, if the cause of non-voluntary euthanasia is the failure to prosecute those who commit it, then perhaps the fact that there have been a small number of such prosecutions in the Netherlands could explain the lower rate of non-voluntary euthanasia there.[131] Amarasekara and Bagaric's analysis also cannot explain the low rate of non-voluntary euthanasia in the United Kingdom, another jurisdiction in which such prosecutions are rarely brought.[132] Indeed, all of these inferences are entirely speculative. In order to determine which, if any, of these conclusions is valid, one would need to compare the rate of non-voluntary euthanasia in a jurisdiction where euthanasia is not legalized but is not prosecuted, with one (comparable in other respects) in which cases are vigorously prosecuted. No such data exists.

---

[126] Kuhse, above n. 70, 263.   [127] Gorsuch, above n. 70, 1395.
[128] See above, text accompanying nn. 90–91.
[129] Amarasekara & Bagaric, above n. 6, 191, citing Kuhse, above n. 87, 196. See also, Bagaric, above n. 80, 236–8.   [130] Amarasekara & Bagaric, above n. 6.
[131] See Chapter Six, Section III.B.   [132] See Chapter 4, Section III.A.1.

4. Beyond the rates of non-voluntary euthanasia

Although the paucity of the data does not allow us to reach any firm conclusions on the empirical slippery slope argument, insights from the survey evidence and other qualitative studies may provide evidence that legalization has some benefits in relation to the way in which voluntary, non-voluntary, and even involuntary euthanasia occurs, particularly in jurisdictions with relatively high apparent rates of covert voluntary and non-voluntary euthanasia such as Australia and Belgium. Roger Magnusson's study suggests that particularly 'disturbing practices, including "botched attempts", strangulations, and the practice of euthanasia in the absence of any prior relationship between doctor and patient, are disproportionately evident in countries where euthanasia is more difficult to access, and where it defaults to an invisible "underground".'[133]

If non-voluntary euthanasia is present regardless of legalization, open regulation may be preferable to a covert underground.[134] There is, for example, evidence showing that the presence of consultation with another physician as a safeguard in cases of assisted dying is far less likely to be present in jurisdictions which have not legalized.[135] Even if appropriate baseline-sensitive evidence were to show an increase in the rate of non-voluntary euthanasia following legalization in a particular jurisdiction, such an increase in an open, regulated environment might be preferable to the hidden world of disturbing practices described by Magnusson in which 'health care workers who perform euthanasia determine the conditions for their own involvement.'[136]

Moreover, prohibition may simply encourage doctors to terminate life in ways which are more difficult to detect, by using large doses of pain-relieving medications, for example:

To a considerable extent, a doctor can choose how to bring about a shortening of his patient's life and how to describe what it is that he has done. If one of the possibilities is unattractive for any reason, for example because it is illegal, he can accomplish the same result in a different way or under a different name. To the extent the horribles predicted should euthanasia be legalised were already taking place before legalisation but were characterised by the responsible doctor as deaths due to abstention or pain relief, it is not surprising that legalisation [in the Netherlands] has not led to a slippery slope. All that has happened is that what was taking place already has to some extent come out into the open as 'euthanasia', where it can be subject to some control. For precisely the same reason, no downward slippery slope is to be expected in other countries with similar levels of physician-negotiated death; they, too, have nowhere to go but up.[137]

---

[133] Magnusson, above n. 43, 262. See also, Emanuel, 'The Practice of Euthanasia and Physician-Assisted Suicide in the United States', above n. 96, 509. That is not to say that there are no clinical difficulties in jurisdictions which have legalized euthanasia. See, e.g., Johanna H. Groenewoud et al., 'Clinical problems with the performance of euthanasia and physician-assisted suicide in the Netherlands' (2000) 342(8) *New Eng. J. Med.* 551.

[134] Magnusson, above n. 43, 263; Searles, above n. 94, [25].

[135] Emanuel, 'The Practice of Euthanasia and Physician-Assisted Suicide in the United States', above n. 96, 511; Willems, above n. 96, 67.   [136] Magnusson, above n. 43, 4.

[137] Griffiths, above n. 33, 203. For evidence of this use of pain-relieving drugs, see Douglas, above n. 94 (36.2% of respondents reported giving pain-relieving drugs with the intention of hastening

However, the evidence from the pan-European studies does not indicate that those jurisdictions with low rates of voluntary euthanasia, assisted suicide, and termination of life without request have correspondingly higher rates of symptom alleviation with possible life-shortening effect.[138] Thus the advantages of legalization may be less significant in those jurisdictions whose baseline rates of covert practices are relatively low.

IV. Conclusion

Both the contours of any regulatory regime (as Chapter Six has shown) and the force of logical slippery slope arguments depend on the approach taken to legalization. In relation to logical slippery slope arguments, relevant moral distinctions exist between voluntary, non-voluntary, and involuntary euthanasia which could be adopted by a legislature in a jurisdiction with no judicial history of legalization based on either necessity or rights, and thereby become legally determinative. In such (rare) cases, logical slippery slope arguments would have little force. However, if legalization has occurred through judicial intervention based on either necessity or rights[139] then both categories of logical slippery slope arguments may have greater force. As the discussion in earlier chapters makes clear, neither necessity[140] nor rights[141] are likely to be used as mechanisms of legal change in most common law jurisdictions. Thus logical slippery slope arguments can be safely ignored in debates in these jurisdictions over proposals for legalization that do not proceed from either judicial acceptance of the defence of necessity or judicial vindication of individual rights claims.

In relation to the empirical slippery slope argument, greater caution is needed before relying on the 'Dutch experience' when discussing proposals for the regulation of assisted dying in other jurisdictions, and the possible consequences of such regulation. There is no evidence from the Netherlands that the legalization of voluntary euthanasia caused an increase in the rate of non-voluntary euthanasia. It is possible that post-legalization research in Belgium may eventually shed some

---

death); Seale, above n. 90, Table 4 (comparing U.K. and New Zealand rates of cases where the intention of intensifying alleviation of pain or symptoms was partly to end life among responding general practitioners: the U.K. rate was 4.0% (95% CI 2.1%–5.9%); the New Zealand rate was 13.7% (95% CI 11.8%–15.6%, calculated using data from Mitchell & Owens, above n. 95)); Deliens, above n. 74, Table 1 (among end-of-life decisions, the rate of alleviation of pain and symptoms with opioids in doses with a potential life-shortening effect and an additional intention to shorten the patient's life was 5.3% (95% CI 4.6%–6.0%)); Kuhse, above n. 87, Box 4 (6.5% of all Australian deaths were preceded by the alleviation of pain and suffering through the administration of opioids in sufficient doses to hasten death where the decision was partly intended to hasten death (no CI provided)).

[138] See Seale, above n. 90, Table 3; van der Heide, above n. 91, Table 2. In fact, the reverse may be true. See the data on Italy and Sweden in Onwuteaka-Philipsen, above n. 105, Table 3.

[139] In a jurisdiction which has accepted that a proxy may exercise rights on behalf of an incompetent individual. See above, Section II.B.2.   [140] See Chapter 4, Sections II and III.A.1.

[141] See Chapter 2, Section I.B.

light on this issue. Evidence in relation to other jurisdictions is mixed: while rates of non-voluntary euthanasia in some prohibitive jurisdictions are higher than the Dutch rate, in other prohibitive jurisdictions the rates are lower. Lacking solid baseline evidence, the current evidence does not support the drawing of inferences either that legalization causes an increase in the rate of non-voluntary euthanasia or that such rates are higher under a prohibitive approach. Furthermore, it seems likely that cultural factors may significantly influence baseline rates, thus further decreasing the possibility of drawing inferences from evidence in one jurisdiction as to what will happen in another.

Judges, commentators and interest groups have relied on arguments that the Dutch are sliding down a slippery slope with little attempt to consider the effect on such arguments of the use of the defence of necessity as the mechanism of legal change in the Netherlands and the vastly different social context. In the absence of evidence on the issues of causation and comparability, reliance on the slippery slope argument is suspect.

Slippery slope arguments, whether logical or empirical, often make distinctly unhelpful contributions to debates over legalization. It is to be hoped that we can move on from the divisive, polarized arguments over alleged abuses which have dominated foreign discussion of euthanasia in the Netherlands to take advantage of the open, systematic discussion, 'lack[ing] in ideological rigidity' which characterizes the Dutch public debate.[142] Instead, we should learn from the experience in jurisdictions which have legalized assisted dying, while recognizing that because of different social contexts and baseline rates of covert practices, and the use of diverse mechanisms of legal change, those experiences do not translate directly to other jurisdictions.

---

[142] Griffiths, Bood & Weyers, above n. 20, 305. See also van Delden, above n. 59, 27 ('medical decisions concerning the end of life ... are ... a part of modern medicine, and we had better openly discuss them').

Select Bibliography

INDIVIDUAL JURISDICTIONS

Australia

Amarasekara, Kumar, 'Euthanasia and the Quality of Legislative Safeguards' (1997) 23 *Monash U. L. Rev.* 1

Baume, P. & O'Malley E., 'Euthanasia: attitudes and practices of medical practitioners' (1994) 161 *Med. J. Australia* 137

Chesterman, Simon, 'Last Rights: Euthanasia, the Sanctity of Life, and the Law in the Netherlands and the Northern Territory of Australia' (1998) 47 *Int'l Comparative L.Q.* 362

Douglas, Charles D. et al., 'The intention to hasten death: a survey of attitudes and practices of surgeons in Australia' (2001) 175 *Med J. Australia* 511

Kissane, David W. et al., 'Seven deaths in Darwin: case studies under the Rights of the Terminally Ill Act, Northern Territory, Australia' (1998) 352 *Lancet* 1097

Kuhse, Helga & Singer, Peter, 'Doctors' practices and attitudes regarding voluntary euthanasia' (1988) 148 *Med. J. Australia* 623

Kuhse, Helga et al., 'End-of-Life Decisions in Australian Medical Practice' (1997) 166 *Med. J. Australia* 191

Magnusson, Roger S., *Angels of Death – Exploring the Euthanasia Underground* (New Haven, Conn.: Yale Univ. Press, 2002)

Otlowski, Margaret, 'Mercy Killing Cases in the Australian Criminal Justice System' (1993) 17 *Crim. L.J.* 10

Stevens, Christine A. & Hassan, Riaz, 'Management of death, dying and euthanasia: attitudes and practices of medical practitioners in South Australia' (1994) 20 *J. Med. Ethics* 41

Belgium

Act on Euthanasia of 28 May 2002 (2003) 10 *Eur. J. Health L.* 329

Adams, Maurice, 'Euthanasia: the Process of Legal Change in Belgium' in Albert Klijn et al., eds., *Regulating Physician-Negotiated Death* (Amsterdam: Elsevier, 2001) 29

Adams, Maurice & Nys, Herman, 'Comparative Reflections on the Belgian Euthanasia Act 2002' (2003) 11 *Med. L. Rev.* 353

Adams, Maurice & Nys, Herman, 'Euthanasia in the Low Countries: Comparative Reflections on the Belgian and Dutch Euthanasia Act' in Paul Schotsmans & Tom Meulenbergs, eds., *Euthanasia and Palliative Care in the Low Countries* (Leuven: Peeters, 2005) 5

Botbol-Baum, M., 'L'originalité du débat belge sur l'euthanasie: analyser et discuter les valeurs en question' ('The originality of the Belgian debate on euthanasia: an analysis and discussion of the values in question') (1999/2000) 9–10–11 *Espace éthique: la lettre* 92

Broeckaert, Bert, 'Belgium: Towards a Legal Recognition of Euthanasia' (2001) 8 *Eur. J. Health L.* 95

Burgermeister, Jane, 'Doctor reignites euthanasia row in Belgium after mercy killing' (2006) 332 *Br. Med. J.* 382

Chamber of Representatives, *Report by the Commission on Public Health, Environment and Societal Renewal on Federal Control and Evaluation Commission on Euthanasia, First Report to the Legislative Chambers (22 Sept. 2002–31 Dec. 2003)*, DOC 51 1374/002, 22 Nov. 2004, www.lachambre.be/FLWB/pdf/51/1374/51K1374002.pdf, accessed 29 July 2006

Comité Consultatif de Bioéthique de Belgique, *Opinion on the opportunity of the legal regulation of euthanasia*, no. 1, 12 May 1997

Comité Consultatif de Bioéthique de Belgique, *Opinion on the active ending of life of persons incapable of expressing their will*, no. 9, 22 Feb. 1999

Deliens, Luc & Bernheim, Jan, 'Palliative care and Euthanasia in countries with a law on euthanasia' (2003) 17 *Palliative Med.* 393

Deliens, Luc et al., 'End-of-life decisions in medical practice in Flanders, Belgium: a nationwide survey' (2000) 356 *Lancet* 1806

Halliday, Samantha, 'Regulating active voluntary euthanasia: what can England and Wales learn from Belgium and the Netherlands' in Austen Garwood-Gowers et al., eds., *Contemporary Issues in Healthcare Law and Ethics* (Edinburgh: Elsevier Butterworth-Heinemann, 2005) 269

Hennebel, Ludovic, 'La dépénalisation de l'euthanasie en Belgique' ('The decriminalization of euthanasia in Belgium') (2002) 2 *Journal de l'Institut International des Droits de l'Homme* 1

Mortier, Freddy & Deliens, Luc, 'The Prospects of Effective Legal Control on Euthanasia in Belgium: Implications of recent end-of-life studies' in Albert Klijn et al., eds., *Regulating Physician-Negotiated Death* (Amsterdam: Elsevier, 2001) 179

Mortier, Freddy et al., 'End-of-life decisions of physicians in the City of Hasselt (Flanders, Belgium)' (2000) 14(3) *Bioethics* 254

Nys, Herman, 'Advice of the Federal Advisory Committee on Bioethics Concerning Legalisation of Euthanasia' (1997) 4 *Eur. J. Health L.* 389

Nys, Herman, 'A Presentation of the Belgian Act on Euthanasia Against the Background of Dutch Euthanasia Law' (2003) 10 *Eur. J. Health L.* 239

Nys, Herman, 'Physician assisted suicide in Belgian law' (2005) 12(1) *Eur. J. Health L.* 39

Nys, Herman, 'Recent Developments in Health Law in Belgium' (2006) 13(2) *Eur. J. Health L.* 95

Provoost, Veerle et al., 'Medical end-of-life decisions in neonates and infants in Flanders' (2005) 365 *Lancet* 1315

Schotsmans, Paul, 'Debating Euthanasia in Belgium' (1997) 27(5) *Hastings Center Rep.* 46

Schotsmans, Paul, 'The Belgian Euthanasia Debate: Some New Developments since December 1999' (2000) 160 *Bull. Med. Ethics* E4

Schotsmans, Paul & Broeckaert, Bert, 'Debating Euthanasia in Belgium: Part Two' (1999) 29(5) *Hastings Center Rep.* 47

Senate and House of Representatives, 2003–2004 Session, Federal Control and Evaluation Commission on Euthanasia, *First Report to the Legislative Chambers (22 Sept. 2002–31 Dec. 2003)*, No. 3–860/1 (Senate), DOC 51 1374/001 (House), 16 Sept. 2004, www.senat.be/wwwcgi/get_pdf?50333038, accessed 29 July 2006

Senate, Bill on Euthanasia, *Annex to the Report of the Joint Commissions of Justice and Social Affairs by Mmes Laloy & Van Riet: Hearings*, No. 2–244/24, 9 July 2001, www.senat.be/wwwcgi/get_pdf?33576763, accessed 29 July 2006

Strubbe, Eva, 'Toward Legal Recognition for Termination of Life without Request? Remarks on Advice No 9 of the Belgian Advisory Committee on Bioethics Concerning Termination of Life of Incompetent Patients' (2000) 7(1) *Eur. J. Health L.* 57

Vermeersch, E., 'The Belgian Law on Euthanasia: The Historical and Ethical Background' (2002) 102(6) *Acta Chirurgica Belgica* 394

Weyers, Heleen, 'Legal recognition of the right to die' in Austen Garwood-Gowers et al., eds., *Contemporary Issues in Healthcare Law and Ethics* (Edinburgh: Elsevier Butterworth-Heinemann, 2005) 253

Canada

Browne, Alister, 'Assisted Suicide and Active Voluntary Euthanasia' (1989) 2 *Can. J. L. & Juris.* 35

Downie, Jocelyn, 'Voluntary Euthanasia in Canada' (1993) 14 *Health L. in Can.* 13

Downie, Jocelyn, *Dying Justice: A Case for Decriminalizing Euthanasia and Assisted Suicide in Canada* (Toronto: Univ. of Toronto Press, 2004)

Downie, Jocelyn & Anthony, Karen, 'The Push-Me/Pull-You of Euthanasia in Canada: A Chronology of the Nancy Morrison Case' (1998) 7(2) *Health L. Rev.* 16

Quigley, Tim, '*R. v. Latimer*: Hard Cases Make Interesting Law' (1995) 41 Crim. Rep. (4th) 89

Searles, Neil, 'Silence Doesn't Obliterate the Truth: A Manitoba Survey on Physician Assisted Suicide and Euthanasia' (1996) 4 *Health L. Rev.* 9

Sneiderman, Barney & Deutscher, Raymond, 'Dr. Nancy Morrison and Her Dying Patient: A Case of Medical Necessity' (2002) 10 *Health L.J.* 1

Sneiderman, Barney, Irvine, John C. & Osborne, Philip H., *Canadian Medical Law: An Introduction for Physicians, Nurses and other Health Care Professionals* (3rd edn.) (Scarborough, Ont.: Carswell, 2003)

Sneiderman, Barney & Kaufert, Joseph M., eds., *Euthanasia in the Netherlands: A Model for Canada?* (University of Manitoba: Legal Research Institute, 1994)

Special Senate Committee on Euthanasia and Assisted Suicide, *Of Life and Death – Final Report* (1995)

Weinrib, Lorraine Eisenstat, 'The Body and the Body Politic: Assisted Suicide under the *Canadian Charter of Rights and Freedoms*' (1994) 39 *McGill L.J.* 619

England and Wales

Assisted Dying for the Terminally Ill Bill, House of Lords, HL Bill 36, 9 Nov. 2005, www.publications.parliament.uk/pa/ld200506/ldbills/036/2006036.pdf, accessed 27 July 2006

Blake, Meredith, 'Physician-Assisted Suicide: A Criminal Offence or a Patient's Right?' (1997) 5 *Med. L. Rev.* 294

Brahams, Diana, 'The reluctant survivor' (1990) 140(6453) *New L.J.* 586 and 140(6454) *New L.J.* 639

Freeman, Michael, 'Death, Dying and the Human Rights Act 1998' (1999) 52 *Current Legal Problems* 218

Freeman, Michael, 'Denying Death its Dominion: Thoughts on the Dianne Pretty Case' (2002) 10(3) *Med. L. Rev.* 245

Grubb, Andrew, 'Euthanasia in England – A Law Lacking Compassion?' (2001) 8(2) *Eur. J. Health L.* 89

House of Lords Select Committee on Medical Ethics, *Report*, HL Paper 21-I (Session 1993–1994)

House of Lords Select Committee on the Assisted Dying for the Terminally Ill Bill, *Report*, HL Paper 86-I (2005) www.publications.parliament.uk/pa/ld200405/ldselect/ldasdy/86/86i.pdf, accessed 27 July 2006

Keown, John, 'No Right to Assisted Suicide' [2002] *Camb. L.J.* 8

Keown, John, 'European Court of Human Rights: Death in Strasbourg – assisted suicide, the *Pretty* case, and the European Convention on Human Rights' (2003) 1(4) *Int'l J. Const'l L.* 722

Leenen, H.J.J., 'Assistance to Suicide and the European Court of Human Rights: the Pretty Case' (2002) 9 *Eur. J. Health L.* 257

Lewis, Penney, '*Assisted Dying for the Terminally Ill Bill*: A Comparison with the Netherlands, Belgium and Oregon', Memorandum submitted to the House of Lords Select Committee on the Assisted Dying for the Terminally Ill Bill, 14 Sept. 2004, House of Lords Select Committee on the Assisted Dying for the Terminally Ill Bill, *Evidence*, HL Paper 86-II (2005) 27–31, www.publications.parliament.uk/pa/ld200405/ldselect/ldasdy/86/86ii.pdf, accessed 27 July 2006

McCall Smith, Alexander, 'Euthanasia: The Strengths of the Middle Ground' (1999) 7 *Med. L. Rev.* 194

Morris, Dan, 'Easing the Passing: End of Life Decisions and the Medical Treatment (Prevention of Euthanasia) Bill' (2002) 10 *Med. L. Rev.* 300

Morris, Dan, 'Assisted Suicide under the European Convention on Human Rights: A Critique' (2003) 1 *Eur. Hum. Rights L. Rev.* 65

Pedain, Antje, 'The Human Rights Dimension of the Diane Pretty Case' (2003) 62(1) *Camb. L.J.* 181

Price, David, 'Euthanasia, Pain Relief and Double Effect' (1997) 17 *Legal Stud.* 323

Seale, Clive, 'Characteristics of end-of-life decisions: survey of UK medical practitioners' (2006) 20 *Palliative Med.* 653

Seale, Clive, 'National survey of end-of-life decisions made by UK medical practitioners' (2006) 20 *Palliative Med.* 3

Ward, B.J. & Tate, P.A., 'Attitudes among NHS doctors to requests for euthanasia' (1994) 308 *Br. Med. J.* 1332

Williams, Glenys, 'The Principle of Double Effect and Terminal Sedation' (2001) 9 *Med. L. Rev.* 41

Europe

Bosshard, G. et al., 'Forgoing treatment at the end of life in 6 European countries' (2005) 165 *Arch. Internal Med.* 401

Clark, D. et al., 'Common threads? Palliative care service developments in seven European countries' (2000) 14 *Palliative Med.* 479

Council of Europe, Parliamentary Assembly, *Protection of the human rights and dignity of the terminally ill and the dying*, Recommendation 1418 (1999) http://assembly.coe.int/main.asp?link = /Documents/AdoptedText/ta99/EREC1418.htm, accessed 27 July 2006

Council of Europe, Parliamentary Assembly, Social, Health and Family Affairs Committee, *Report: Euthanasia*, Doc. 9898 (2003) http://assembly.coe.int/Documents/WorkingDocs/Doc03/EDOC9898.htm, accessed 27 July 2006

Council of Europe, Reply from the Committee of Ministers, *Protection of the human rights and dignity of the terminally ill and the dying*, Doc. 9404 (2002) http://assembly.coe.int/Documents/WorkingDocs/doc02/EDOC9404.htm, accessed 27 July 2006

Council of Europe, Steering Committee on Bioethics, *Replies to the questionnaire for member states relating to euthanasia*, CDBI/INF (2003) 8, www.coe.int/T/E/Legal_Affairs/Legal_co-operation/Bioethics/Activities/Euthanasia/, accessed 27 July 2006

Cuttini, Marina et al., 'End-of-life decisions in neonatal intensive care: physicians' self-reported practices in seven European countries' (2000) 355 *Lancet* 2112

Heide, Agnes van der et al., 'End-of-life Decisions in Six European Countries: A research note' in Albert Klijn et al., eds., *Regulating Physician-Negotiated Death* (Amsterdam: Elsevier, 2001) 129

Heide, Agnes van der et al., 'End-of-life decision-making in six European countries: descriptive study' (2003) 362 *Lancet* 345

Keown, John, 'No Right to Assisted Suicide' [2002] *Camb. L.J.* 8

Keown, John, 'European Court of Human Rights: Death in Strasbourg – assisted suicide, the *Pretty* case, and the European Convention on Human Rights' (2003) 1(4) *Int'l J. Const'l L.* 722

Leenen, H.J.J., 'Assistance to Suicide and the European Court of Human Rights: the Pretty Case' (2002) 9 *Eur. J. Health L.* 257

Morris, Dan, 'Assisted Suicide under the European Convention on Human Rights: A Critique' (2003) 1 *Eur. Hum. Rights L. Rev.* 65

Nys, Herman, 'Physician Involvement in a Patient's Death: A Continental European Perspective' (1999) 7 *Med. L. Rev.* 208

Pedain, Antje, 'The Human Rights Dimension of the Diane Pretty Case' (2003) 62(1) *Camb. L.J.* 181

Vickers, Lesley, 'Assisted dying and the laws of three European countries' (1997) 147(6789) *New L.J.* 610

France

Assemblée Nationale, *Rapport au nom de la mission d'information sur l'accompagnement de la fin de vie (Rapport Leonetti) (Report in the name of the inquiry into accompaniment at the end of life (Leonetti Report))*, No. 1708, 30 June 2004, www.assemblee-nat.fr/12/rap-info/i1708-t1.asp, accessed 20 July 2006

Aumonier, Nicolas et al., *L'euthanasie* (Paris; Presses Universitaires de France, 2001)

Boitte, P. et al., 'Point de vue sur le rapport n° 63 du Comité Consultatif National d'Éthique: "Fin de vie – Arrêt de vie – Euthanasie"' ('Point of view on CCNE Report no. 63: "End of life, ending life, euthanasia"' (2000) 24 *Les Cahiers du CCNE* 11

Boucaud, Pascale, 'Commentaire de l'avis du comité national consultatif d'éthique du 27 janvier 2000, intitulé "fin de vie, arrêt de vie, euthanasie"' ('Commentary on the opinion of the CCNE of 27 Jan. 2000 entitled "end of life, ending life, euthanasia"' (2000) 48(6) *Laennec* 10

Collange, Jean-François, 'Editorial' (2000) 23 *Cahiers du CCNE* 2

Collange, Jean-François, 'L'Avis 63 et l'éthique protestante' ('Opinion 63 and Protestant Ethics') Chaire Benjamin Edmond de Rothschild pour l'éthique bio-médicale, *Fin de vie, arrêt de vie, euthanasie: avis 63 du CCNE*, 16ème Entretiens consacrés à l'éthique bio-médicale, Palais du Luxembourg, 18 & 19 Nov. 2000, 4

Comité Consultatif National d'Éthique, *Avis concernant la proposition de résolution sur l'assistance aux mourants, adoptée le 25 avril 1991 au Parlement européen par la Commission de l'environnement, de la santé publique et de la protection des consommateurs (Opinion on the proposed resolution on assistance to the dying, adopted 25 April 1991 at the European Parliament by the Commission on the Environment, Public Health and Consumer Protection)*, no. 26, 24 June 1991

Comité Consultatif National d'Éthique, *Fin de vie, arrêt de vie, euthanasie (End of life, ending life, euthanasia)*, no. 63, 27 Jan. 2000

Comité Consultatif National d'Éthique, *Refus de traitement et autonomie de la personne (Refusal of treatment and autonomy of the person)*, no. 87, 14 Apr. 2005

Dunet-Larousse, Emmanuel, 'L'euthanasie: signification et qualification au regard du droit pénal' ('Euthanasia: significance and description in relation to the criminal law') (1998) 34(2) *Rev. Dr. Sanit. Soc.* 265

Ferrand, Édouard et al., 'Withholding and Withdrawal of Life Support in Intensive-care Units in France' (2001) 357 *Lancet* 9

Fortis, Elisabeth, 'Exception d'euthanasie et droit pénal: A propos de l'avis n° 63 rendu par le comité national consultatif d'éthique le 3 mars 2000' ('The euthanasia exception and the criminal law: CCNE Opinion no. 63 of 3 Mar. 2000') (2000) 48(7) *Laennec* 3

Hennette, Stéphanie, 'L'euthanasie est-elle pensable en droit?' ('Can one think of lawful euthanasia?') (1997) 29(3) *Les cahiers de la sécurité intérieure* 143

Legros, Bérengère, 'Sur l'opportunité d'instituer une exception d'euthanasie en droit français' ('On the opportunity of incorporating a euthanasia exception into French law') (2001) 46 *Méd. & Droit* 7

Lewis, Penney, 'The evolution of assisted dying in France: A third way?' (2005) 13(4) *Med. L. Rev.* 44

Mémeteau, Gérard, 'La mort aux trousses' ('Death on your heels') (2000) 3 *Revue de Recherche Juridique et de droit prospectif* 914

Michaud, Jean, 'A propos d'un avis du CCNE' ('About a CCNE opinion') (2000) 43 *Méd. & Droit* 1

Pousson-Petit, Jacqueline, 'Propos paradoxaux sur l'euthanasie à partir de textes récents' ('Paradoxical proposals on euthanasia from recent texts') (2001) 2 *Droit de la famille* 4

Prothais, Alain, 'Accompagnement de la fin de vie et droit penal' ('Accompaniment at the end of life and the criminal law') (2004) *J.C.P. G.* I 130

Py, Bruno, *La mort et le droit (Death and the law)* (Paris: Presses Universitaires de France, 1997)

Ricot, Jacques, 'Un avis controversé sur l'euthanasie' ('A controversial opinion on euthanasia') (2000) 11 *Esprit* 98

Senate, *Legislation Comparé: Euthanasie (Comparative Legislation: Euthanasia)*, No. LC 109 (2002) www.senat.fr/lc/lc109/lc109.html, accessed 26 July 2006

Senate, *Rapport fait au nom de la commission des Affaires sociales sur la proposition de loi, adoptée par L'Assemblée Nationale, relative aux droits des malades et à la fin de vie (Rapport Dériot) (Report in the name of the Social Affairs Commission on the Bill adopted by the National Assembly on the rights of patients and at the end of life (Dériot Report))*, No. 281, 6 Apr. 2005, www.senat.fr/rap/l04–281/l04–281.html, accessed 20 July 2006

Verspieren, Patrick, 'L'exception d'euthanasie' ('The euthanasia exception') (2000) 392(5) *Études* 581

Germany

Battin, Margaret P., 'Assisted Suicide: Can We Learn from Germany?' (1992) 22(2) *Hastings Center Rep.* 45

Becker-Schwarze, Kathrin, 'Legal Restrictions of Physician-Assisted Suicide' (2005) 12 *Eur. J. Health L.* 11

Sayid, M.D., 'Euthanasia: A Comparison of the Criminal Laws of Germany, Switzerland and the United States' (1983) 6 *Boston Coll. Int'l & Comp. L. Rev.* 533

Stauch, Marc, 'Euthanasia and assisted suicide in German law' (2005) 7(3) *Contemp. Issues in Law* 301

Netherlands

Law

Adams, Maurice & Nys, Herman, 'Euthanasia in the Low Countries: Comparative Reflections on the Belgian and Dutch Euthanasia Act' in Paul Schotsmans & Tom Meulenbergs, eds., *Euthanasia and Palliative Care in the Low Countries* (Leuven: Peeters, 2005) 5

Belian, Julia, 'Deference to Doctors in Dutch Euthanasia Law' (1996) 10 *Emory Int'l L. Rev.* 255

Chesterman, Simon, 'Last Rights: Euthanasia, the Sanctity of Life, and the Law in the Netherlands and the Northern Territory of Australia' (1998) 47 *Int'l Comparative L.Q.* 362

Cuperus-Bosma, Jacqueline M. et al., 'Physician-assisted Death: Policy-making by the Assembly of Prosecutors General in the Netherlands' (1997) 4 *Eur. J. Health L.* 225

Cuperus-Bosma, Jacqueline M. et al., 'Assessment of physician-assisted death by members of the public prosecution in the Netherlands' (1999) 25(1) *J. Med. Ethics* 8

Dijk, Marta van, Widdershoven, Guy A.M. & Meershoek, Agnes M., 'Reporting Euthanasia: Physicians' Experiences with a Dutch Regional Evaluation Committee' in Paul Schotsmans & Tom Meulenbergs, eds., *Euthanasia and Palliative Care in the Low Countries* (Leuven: Peeters, 2005) 71

Dillmann, R.J.M., 'Euthanasia in The Netherlands: The Role of the Dutch Medical Profession' (1996) 5(1) *Camb. Q. Healthcare Ethics* 100

Dillmann, Robert J.M. & Legemaate, Johan, 'Euthanasia in The Netherlands: The state of the legal debate' (1994) 1 *Eur. J. Health L.* 81

Dorscheidt, Jozef H.H.M., 'Assessment Procedures Regarding End-of-Life Decisions in Neonatology in the Netherlands' (2005) 24 *Med. & L.* 803

Driesse, Marian H.N. et al., 'Euthanasia and the Law in the Netherlands' (1987–88) 3 *Issues in Law & Med.* 385

Dutch Physicians' League, 'An Open Letter of the Dutch Physicians' League' (2000) 15 *Issues in Law & Med.* 325

Gevers, J.K.M., 'Final Report of the Netherlands State Commission on Euthanasia: An English Summary' (1987) 1(2) *Bioethics* 163

Gevers, J.K.M., 'Physician-Assisted Suicide and the Dutch Courts' (1996) 5(1) *Camb. Q. Healthcare Ethics* 93

Gevers, Sjef & Legemaate, Johan, 'Physician assisted suicide in psychiatry: an analysis of case law and professional opinions' in David C. Thomasma et al., eds., *Asking to Die: Inside the Dutch Debate about Euthanasia* (Dordrecht: Kluwer, 1998) 71

Griffiths, John, 'Assisted suicide in the Netherlands: postscript to *Chabot*' (1995) 58 *Mod. L. Rev.* 895

Griffiths, John, 'Assisted suicide in the Netherlands: the *Chabot* case' (1995) 58 *Mod. L. Rev.* 232

Griffiths, John, 'Self-regulation by the Dutch medical profession of medical behavior that potentially shortens life' in Hans Krabbendam & Hans-Martien ten Napel, eds., *Regulating Morality: A Comparison of The Role of the State in Mastering the Mores in the Netherlands and the United States* (Antwerp: Maklu, 2000) 173

Griffiths, John, 'Comparative Reflections: Is the Dutch Case Unique?' in Albert Klijn et al., eds., *Regulating Physician-Negotiated Death* (Amsterdam: Elsevier, 2001) 197

Griffiths, John, Weyers, Heleen & Adams, Maurice, *Euthanasia and the Law in Europe: With Special Reference to the Netherlands and Belgium* (Oxford: Hart Publishing, 2007 (forthcoming))

Griffiths, John, Bood, Alex & Weyers, Heleen, *Euthanasia and Law in the Netherlands* (Amsterdam: Amsterdam Univ. Press, 1998)

Haan, Jurriaan de, 'The New Dutch Law on Euthanasia' (2002) 10 *Med. L. Rev.* 57

Halliday, Samantha, 'Regulating active voluntary euthanasia: what can England and Wales learn from Belgium and the Netherlands' in Austen Garwood-Gowers et al., eds., *Contemporary Issues in Healthcare Law and Ethics* (Edinburgh: Elsevier Butterworth-Heinemann, 2005) 269

Kater, Loes, 'The Dutch Model for Legalizing End-of-life Decisions' (2003) 22 *Med. & L.* 543

Kater, Loes et al., 'Health care ethics and health law in the Dutch discussion on end-of-life decisions: a historical analysis of the dynamics and development of both disciplines' (2003) 34 *Stud. Hist. Phil. Biol. & Biomed. Sci.* 669

Kimsma, G.K., 'Euthanasia for existential reasons' (2006) 13(1) *Lahey Clinic Med. Ethics* 1

Kimsma, Gerrit K. & Leeuwen, Evert van, 'Euthanasia and Assisted Suicide in the Netherlands and the USA: Comparing Practices, Justifications and Key Concepts in Bioethics and Law' in David C. Thomasma et al., eds., *Asking to Die: Inside the Dutch Debate about Euthanasia* (Dordrecht: Kluwer Academic Publishers, 1998) 35

Kimsma, Gerrit K. & Leeuwen, Evert van, 'The New Dutch Law on Legalizing Physician-Assisted Death' (2001) 10 *Camb. Q. Healthcare Ethics* 445

Klotzko, Arlene Judith, 'What Kind of Life? What Kind of Death? An Interview with Dr. Henk Prins' in David C. Thomasma et al., eds., *Asking to Die: Inside the Dutch Debate about Euthanasia* (Dordrecht: Kluwer Academic Publishers, 1998) 388

Leenen, H.J.J., 'Dying with Dignity: Developments in the Field of Euthanasia in the Netherlands' (1989) 8 *Med. Law* 517

Leenen, H.J.J., 'Euthanasia in the Netherlands' in Peter Byrne, ed., *Medical Ethics and the Value of Life* (Chichester: John Wiley & Sons, 1990) 1

Leenen, H.J.J., 'Dutch Supreme Court about Assistance to Suicide in the Case of Severe Mental Suffering' (1994) *Eur. J. Health L.* 377

Leenen, H.J.J., 'The Development of Euthanasia in the Netherlands' (2001) 8 *Eur. J. Health L.* 125

Leenen, H.J.J. & Ciesielski-Carlucci Chris, '*Force Majeure* (Legal Necessity): Justification for Active Termination of Life in the Case of Severely Handicapped Newborns after Forgoing Treatment' (1993) 2(3) *Camb. Q. Healthcare Ethics* 271

Legemaate, Johan, 'Twenty-Five Years of Dutch Experience and Policy on Euthanasia and Assisted Suicide: An Overview' in David C. Thomasma et al., eds., *Asking to Die: Inside the Dutch Debate about Euthanasia* (Dordrecht: Kluwer Academic Publishers, 1998) 19

Lewis, Penney, 'The Dutch Experience of Euthanasia' (1998) 25 *J. Law & Society* 636

Möller, Maike & Huxtable, Richard, 'Euthanasia in the Netherlands: the case of "life fatigue"' (2001) 151(7006) *New L.J.* 1600

Netherlands Ministry of Foreign Affairs, *A Guide to the Dutch Termination of Life on Request and Assisted Suicide (Review Procedures) Act* (2001) www.minbuza.nl/binaries/ minbuza_core_pictures/pdf/c/c_56513.pdf, accessed 24 Sept. 2006

Schwitters, Rob, 'Medical Competence as a restriction on physician-assisted suicide: the Brongersma case' (2003) 7 *Newsletter MBPSL* 2

Sheldon, Tony, 'Netherlands sets up euthanasia advisory body' (1999) 318 *Br. Med. J.* 348

Sheldon, Tony, 'Dutch GP Found Guilty of Murder Faces No Penalty' (2001) 322 *Br. Med. J.* 509

Sheldon, Tony, 'Reported euthanasia cases in Holland fall for second year' (2002) 324 *Br. Med. J.* 1354

Sheldon, Tony, 'Being "tired of life" is not grounds for euthanasia' (2003) 326 *Br. Med. J.* 71

Sheldon, Tony, 'Court upholds murder verdict on doctor who ended woman's life' (2003) 326 *Br. Med. J.* 1351

Sheldon, Tony, '"Terminal sedation" different from euthanasia, Dutch ministers agree' (2003) 327 *Br. Med. J.* 465

Sheldon, Tony, 'Dutch doctors call for new approach to reporting "mercy killings"' (2004) 329 *Br. Med. J.* 591

Sheldon, Tony, 'Dutch reporting of euthanasia cases falls – despite legal reporting requirements' (2004) 328 *Br. Med. J.* 1336

Sheldon, Tony, 'Two test cases in Holland clarify law on murder and palliative care' (2004) 329 *Br. Med. J.* 1206

Sheldon, Tony, 'New penalties proposed for Dutch doctors who flout euthanasia law' (2004) 329 *Br. Med. J.* 131

Sheldon, Tony, 'Dutch euthanasia law should apply to patients "suffering through living," report says' (2005) 330 *Br. Med. J.* 61

Sheldon, Tony, 'Dutch murder case leads to talks with attorney general' (2005) 331 *Br. Med. J.* 473

Sheldon, Tony, 'Killing or caring?' (2005) 330 *Br. Med. J.* 560

Sheldon, Tony, 'The Netherlands regulates ending the lives of severely ill neonates' (2005) 331 *Br. Med. J.* 1357

Sheldon, Tony, 'Doctor who was remanded for murder wins record damages' (2006) 332 *Br. Med. J.* 443

Smies, Jonathan T., 'The Legalization of Euthanasia in the Netherlands' (2003–04) 7 *Gonz. J. Int'l L.* 1

Termination of Life on Request and Assisted Suicide (Review Procedures) Act 2001, (2001) 8 *Eur. J. Health L.* 183

Tol, Donald van, 'Physician-Assisted Suicide: The Brongersma Case' (2001) 5 *Newsletter MBPSL* 3

United Nations Committee on the Rights of the Child, *Concluding Observations: The Kingdom of the Netherlands (Netherlands and Aruba)*, 26 Feb. 2004, CRC/C/15/Add.227, www.unhchr.ch/tbs/doc.nsf/0/91e3134842f2024cc1256e76002b5ff8?Opendocument, accessed 29 July 2006

United Nations International Covenant on Civil and Political Rights Human Rights Committee, *Concluding Observations: Netherlands*, 27 Aug. 2001, CCPR/CO/72/NET, www.unhchr.ch/tbs/doc.nsf/0/dbab71d01e02db11c1256a950041d732?Opendocument, accessed 29 July 2006

Veer, B.A. van der & Sennef, A., 'Case Descriptions' in M. Malsch & J.F. Nijboer, *Complex Cases: Perspectives on the Netherlands criminal justice system* (Amsterdam: Thela Thesis, 1999) 123, 141–7

Vries, Ubaldus de, 'Psychological Suffering and Physician-Assisted Suicide: *Chabot* (1994)' in Eoin O'Dell, ed., *Leading cases of the twentieth century* (Dublin: Round Hall Sweet & Maxwell, 2000) 496

Vries, Ubaldus de, 'Can a Legal Right to Euthanasia Exist? A Dutch Perspective on a Universal Medico-Legal Dilemma' (2003) 9 *Medico-Legal J. of Ireland* 24

Vries, Ubaldus de, 'A Dutch perspective: the limits of lawful euthanasia' (2004) 13 *Annals Health L.* 365

Welie, Jos V.M., 'The Medical Exception: Physicians, Euthanasia and the Dutch Criminal Law' (1992) 17(4) *J. of Med. & Philosophy* 419

Weyers, Heleen, 'Euthanasia: the Process of Legal Change in the Netherlands' in Albert Klijn et al., eds., *Regulating Physician-Negotiated Death* (Amsterdam: Elsevier, 2001) 11

Practice

Aartsen, G.M. et al., 'Letter to the Editor' (1989) 19(6) *Hastings Center Rep.* 47

Anonymous Family Physician, 'In Death He Achieved a Stature that He Never Had in Life' in David C. Thomasma et al., eds., *Asking to Die: Inside the Dutch Debate about Euthanasia* (Dordrecht: Kluwer, 1998) 281

Bannink, Marjolein et al., 'Psychiatric consultation and quality of decision making in euthanasia' (2000) 356 *Lancet* 2067

C., Dr., 'The Euthanasia Mountain Gets Higher and Higher' (1996) 5(1) *Camb. Q. Healthcare Ethics* 78

Delden, Johannes J.M. van, 'Slippery Slopes in flat countries – a response' (1999) 25(1) *J. Med. Ethics* 22

Delden, Johannes J.M. van et al., 'Dances with Data' (1993) 7 *Bioethics* 323

Delden, Johannes J.M. van et al., 'The Remmelink Study: Two Years Later' (1993) 23(6) *Hastings Center Rep.* 24

Deliens, Luc & Bernheim, Jan, 'Palliative care and Euthanasia in countries with a law on euthanasia' (2003) 17 *Palliative Med.* 393

Groenewoud, Johanna H. et al., 'Physician-assisted death in psychiatric practice in the Netherlands' (1997) 336(25) *New Eng. J. Med.* 1795

Groenewoud, Johanna H. et al., 'Clinical problems with the performance of euthanasia and physician-assisted suicide in The Netherlands' (2000) 342(8) *New Eng. J. Med.* 551

Groenewoud, Johanna H. et al., 'Psychiatric consultation with regard to requests for euthanasia or physician-assisted suicide' (2004) 26 *Gen'l Hosp. Psychiatry* 323

Heide, Agnes van der et al., 'Medical End-of-Life Decisions Made for Neonates and Infants in the Netherlands' (1997) 350 *Lancet* 251

Jansen-van der Weide, M.C. et al., 'Implementation of the project "Support and Consultation on Euthanasia in the Netherlands" (SCEN)' (2004) 69 *Health Policy* 365

Jansen-van der Weide, M.C. et al., 'Granted, Undecided, Withdrawn, and Refused Requests for Euthanasia and Physician-Assisted Suicide' (2005) 165(15) *Arch. Internal Med.* 1698

Janssens, Rien & Have, Henk ten, 'The Concept of Palliative Care in the Netherlands' (2001) 15 *Palliative Med.* 481

Kimsma, Gerrit K., 'Assisted death in the Netherlands and its relationship with age' in David N. Weisstub et al., eds., *Aging: Decisions at the End of Life* (Dordrecht: Kluwer Academic Publishers, 2001) 49

Leeuwen, E. van & Kimsma, G.K., 'Acting or Letting Go: Medical Decision Making in Neonatology in The Netherlands' (1993) 2(3) *Camb. Q. Healthcare Ethics* 265

M., 'What Is There to Be Frightened About? After All, It's Not Like I Am Going to the Dentist!' (1996) 5(1) *Camb. Q. Healthcare Ethics* 83

Maas, P.J. van der et al., 'Euthanasia and other medical decisions concerning the end of life' (1991) 338 *Lancet* 669

Maas, Paul J. van der et al., 'Euthanasia and other Medical Decisions Concerning the End of Life: An Investigation Performed upon Request of the Commission of Inquiry into the Medical Practice Concerning Euthanasia' (1992) 22(1/2) *Health Policy* 1

Maas, Paul J. van der et al., *Euthanasia and other Medical Decisions Concerning the End of Life* (Amsterdam: Elsevier, Health Policy Monographs, 1992)

Maas, P.J. van der et al., 'Euthanasia, Physician-Assisted Suicide, and Other Medical Practices Involving the End of Life in the Netherlands, 1990–1995' (1996) 335(22) *New Eng. J. Med.* 1699

Muller, Martien T. et al., 'Active euthanasia and physician-assisted suicide in Dutch nursing homes: Patient characteristics' (1995) 24(5) *Age and Ageing* 429

Muller, Martien T. et al., 'Euthanasia and Assisted Suicide: Facts, Figures and Fancies with Special Regard to Old Age' (1998) 13(3) *Drugs & Aging* 185

Onwuteaka-Philipsen, Bregje & Wal, Gerrit van der, 'Support and Consultation for General Practitioners Concerning Euthanasia: The SCEA Project' (2001) 56 *Health Policy* 33

Onwuteaka-Philipsen, Bregje D. et al., 'Consultation with another Physician on Euthanasia and Assisted Suicide in the Netherlands' (2000) 51 *Social Science & Med.* 429

Onwuteaka-Philipsen, Bregje D. et al., 'Euthanasia and the elderly' (1997) 26(6) *Age and Ageing* 487

Onwuteaka-Philipsen, Bregje D. et al., 'Euthanasia and other end-of-life decisions in the Netherlands in 1990, 1995, and 2001' (2003) 362 *Lancet* 395

Onwuteaka-Philipsen, Bregje D. et al., 'Dutch experience of monitoring euthanasia' (2005) 331 *Br. Med. J.* 691

Pijnenborg, Loes et al., 'Life terminating acts without explicit request of the patient' (1993) 341 *Lancet* 1196

Pool, Robert, *Negotiating a Good Death: Euthanasia in the Netherlands* (Binghamton, N.Y.: The Haworth Press, 2000)

Rigter, Henk, 'Euthanasia in the Netherlands: distinguishing facts from fiction' (1989) 19(1) *Hastings Center Rep.* S31

Rigter, Henk et al., 'Euthanasia across the North Sea' (1988) 297 *Br. Med. J.* 1593

Rurup, Mette L. et al., 'Requests for euthanasia or physician-assisted suicide from older persons who do not have a severe disease: an interview study' (2005) 35(5) *Psychol. Med.* 665

Rurup, Mette L. et al., 'When being "tired of living" plays an important role in a request for euthanasia or physician-assisted suicide: patient characteristics and the physician's decision' (2005) 74(2) *Health Policy* 157

Rurup, Mette L. et al., 'Frequency and determinants of advance directives concerning end-of-life care in The Netherlands' (2006) 62(6) *Social Science & Med.* 1552

Sheldon, Tony, 'Dutch doctors choose sedation rather than euthanasia' (2004) 329 *Br. Med. J.* 368

Verhagen, Eduard, 'Developments with regard to end-of-life decisions concerning newborns in The Netherlands' (2005) 9 *Newsletter RSPMB* 3

Verhagen, Eduard & Sauer, Pieter J.J., 'End-of-life decisions in newborns: An approach from the Netherlands' (2005) 116(3) *Pediatrics* 736

Verhagen, Eduard & Sauer, Pieter J.J., 'The Groningen Protocol – Euthanasia in Severely Ill Newborns' (2005) 352(10) *New Eng. J. Med.* 959

Vermeulen, Eric, 'Dealing with doubt: Making decisions in a neonatal ward in The Netherlands' (2004) 59 *Social Science & Med.* 2071

Vrakking, Astrid M. et al., 'Medical end-of-life decisions for children in the Netherlands' (2005) 159(9) *Arch. Pediat. Adol. Med.* 802

Vrakking, Astrid M. et al., 'Medical end-of-life decisions made for neonates and infants in the Netherlands, 1995–2001' (2005) 365 *Lancet* 1329

W., Dr., 'The Moment Will Come When I Can Only Love Him by Killing Him' (1996) 5(1) *Camb. Q. Healthcare Ethics* 77

Wachter, M.A.M. de, 'Active Euthanasia in the Netherlands' (1989) 262(23) *J. Am. Med. Ass'n* 3316

Wachter, Maurice A.M. de, 'Euthanasia in the Netherlands' (1992) 22(2) *Hastings Center Rep.* 23

Wal, Gerrit van der & Maas, P.J. van der, 'Empirical Research on Euthanasia and Other Medical End-of-Life Decisions and the Euthanasia Notification Procedure' in David C. Thomasma et al., eds., *Asking to Die: Inside the Dutch Debate about Euthanasia* (Dordrecht: Kluwer, 1998) 149

Wal, Gerrit van der et al., 'Euthanasia and Assisted Suicide I. How Often is it Practised by Family Doctors in the Netherlands?' (1992) 9(2) *Family Practice* 130

Wal, Gerrit van der et al., 'Euthanasia and Assisted Suicide II. Do Dutch Family Doctors Act Prudently?' (1992) 9(2) *Family Practice* 135

Wal, Gerrit van der et al., 'Evaluation of the notification procedure for physician-assisted death in the Netherlands' (1996) 335(22) *New Eng. J. Med.* 1706

Willems, Dick L. et al., 'Attitudes and Practices Concerning the End of Life: A Comparison Between Physicians From the United States and From the Netherlands' (2000) 160(1) *Arch. Internal Med.* 63

Critics

Amarasekara, Kumar & Bagaric, Mirko, 'The Legalisation of Euthanasia in the Netherlands: Lessons to be Learnt' (2001) 27 *Monash U. L. Rev.* 179

Capron, Alexander Morgan, 'Euthanasia in the Netherlands: American Observations' (1992) 22(2) *Hastings Center Rep.* 30

Cohen-Almagor, Raphael, 'Euthanasia in the Netherlands: the Legal Framework' (2001) 10 *Mich. State Univ. – DCL J. Int'l L.* 319

Cohen-Almagor, Raphael, 'Why the Netherlands?' (2002) 30 *J. L. Med. & Ethics* 95

Cohen-Almagor, Raphael, 'Non-Voluntary and Involuntary Euthanasia in the Netherlands: Dutch Perspectives' (2003) 18 *Issues in Law & Med.* 239

Cohen-Almagor, Raphael, *Euthanasia in the Netherlands: The Policy and Practice of Mercy Killing* (Dordrecht: Kluwer, 2004)

Fenigsen, Richard, 'A Case Against Dutch Euthanasia' (1989) 19(1) *Hastings Center Rep.* S22

Fenigsen, Richard, 'Physician-Assisted Death in the Netherlands: Impact on Long-Term Care' (1995–1996) *Issues in Law & Med.* 283

Fenigsen, Richard, 'Dutch euthanasia revisited' (1997) 13 *Issues in Law & Med.* 301

Fenigsen, Richard, 'Dutch Euthanasia: The New Government Ordered Study' (2004) 20 *Issues in Law & Med.* 73

Gomez, Carlos, *Regulating Death: Euthanasia and the Case of the Netherlands* (New York: The Free Press, 1991)

Gorsuch, Neil M., 'The Legalization of Assisted Suicide and the Law of Unintended Consequences: A Review of the Dutch and Oregon Experiments and Leading Utilitarian Arguments For Legal Change' [2004] *Wis. L. Rev.* 1347

Have, H.A.M.J. ten & Welie, J.V.M., 'Euthanasia: Normal Medical Practice?' (1992) 22(2) *Hastings Center Rep.* 34

Hendin, Herbert, 'Seduced by Death: Doctors, Patients, and the Dutch Cure' (1994) 10 *Issues in Law & Med.* 123

Hendin, Herbert, *Seduced by Death: Doctors, Patients and the Dutch Cure* (New York: W.W. Norton & Co., 1997)

Hendin, Herbert et al., 'Physician-Assisted Suicide and Euthanasia in the Netherlands' (1997) 277(21) *J. Am. Med. Ass'n* 1720

Jochemsen, Henk, 'Life-Prolonging and Life-Terminating Treatment of Severely Handicapped Newborn Babies: A Discussion of the Report of the Royal Dutch Society of Medicine on "Life-Terminating Actions with Incompetent Patients: Part 1: Severely Handicapped Newborns"' (1992) 8 *Issues in Law & Med.* 167

Jochemsen, Henk, 'Euthanasia in Holland: an ethical critique of the new law' (1994) 20 *J. Med. Ethics* 212

Jochemsen, Henk, 'Dutch Court Decisions on Nonvoluntary Euthanasia Critically Reviewed' (1998) 13 *Issues in Law & Med.* 447

Jochemsen, Henk, 'Legalization of Euthanasia in the Netherlands' (2001) 16 *Issues in Law & Med.* 285

Jochemsen, Henk, 'Why euthanasia should not be legalized: A reflection on the Dutch experiment' in David N. Weisstub et al., eds., *Aging: Decisions at the End of Life* (Dordrecht: Kluwer Academic Publishers, 2001) 67

Jochemsen, Henk & Keown, John, 'Voluntary euthanasia under control? Further empirical evidence from the Netherlands' (1999) 25(1) *J. Med. Ethics* 16

Keown, John, 'The Law and Practice of Euthanasia in the Netherlands' (1992) 108 *Law Q. Rev.* 51

Keown, John, 'On Regulating Death' (1992) 22(2) *Hastings Center Rep.* 39

Keown, John, 'Physician-Assisted Suicide and the Dutch Supreme Court' (1995) 111 *Law Q. Rev.* 394

Keown, John, 'Euthanasia in the Netherlands: Sliding Down the Slippery Slope?' in John Keown, ed., *Euthanasia Examined: Ethical, Clinical and Legal Perspectives* (Cambridge: Cambridge Univ. Press, 1995) 261

Keown, John, *Euthanasia, Ethics, and Public Policy* (Cambridge: Cambridge Univ. Press, 2002)

Keown, John, ed., *Euthanasia Examined: Ethical, Clinical and Legal Perspectives* (Cambridge: Cambridge Univ. Press, 1995)

'Physician-Assisted Suicide and Euthanasia in the Netherlands: A Report to the House Judiciary Subcommittee on the Constitution' (1998) 14 *Issues in Law & Med.* 301

Proponents

Battin, Margaret P., 'The Euthanasia Debate in the United States: Conflicting Claims about the Netherlands' in Hans Krabbendam & Hans-Martien ten Napel, eds., *Regulating Morality: A Comparison of The Role of the State in Mastering the Mores in the Netherlands and the United States* (Antwerp: Maklu, 2000) 151

CQ *Interview* with Heleen M. Dupuis, 'Actively Ending the Life of a Severely Handicapped Newborn: A Dutch Ethicist's Perspective' (1993) 2(3) *Camb. Q. Healthcare Ethics* 275

Downie, Jocelyn, 'The Contested Lessons of Euthanasia in the Netherlands' (2000) 8 *Health L.J.* 119

Ethics

Haan, Jurriaan de, 'The Ethics of Euthanasia: Advocates' Perspectives' (2002) 16(2) *Bioethics* 154

Hartogh, Govert den, 'Euthanasia: Reflections on the Dutch Discussion' in Raphael Cohen-Almagor, ed., *Medical Ethics at the Dawn of the 21st Century* (New York: New York Academy of Sciences, 2000) 174

Kennedy, James C., 'The Moral State: How Much Do the Americans and the Dutch Differ?' in Hans Krabbendam & Hans-Martien ten Napel, eds., *Regulating Morality: A Comparison of The Role of the State in Mastering the Mores in the Netherlands and the United States* (Antwerp: Maklu, 2000) 9

Kimsma, Gerrit K. & Leeuwen, Evert van, 'Shifts in the Direction of Dutch Bioethics: Forward or Backward?' (2005) 14 *Camb. Q. Healthcare Ethics* 292

Proceedings of a European Conference (Maastricht, 10 and 11 June 1994), *Euthanasia and Assisted Suicide in the Netherlands and in Europe: Methodology of the ethical debate* (Luxembourg: Office for Official Publications of the European Communities, 1996)

Wal, Gerrit van der, 'Unrequested Termination of Life: Is It Permissible?' (1993) 7 *Bioethics* 330

Widdershoven, Guy, 'Beyond Autonomy and Beneficence: The Moral Basis of Euthanasia in the Netherlands' in Paul Schotsmans & Tom Meulenbergs, eds., *Euthanasia and Palliative Care in the Low Countries* (Leuven: Peeters, 2005) 83

New Zealand

Mitchell, Kay & Owens, R. Glynn, 'National survey of medical decisions at end of life made by New Zealand general practitioners' (2003) 327 *Br. Med. J.* 202

Oregon

Chin, Arthur E. et al., 'Legalized Physician-Assisted Suicide in Oregon – The First Year's Experience' (1999) 340(7) *New Eng. J. Med.* 577

Cohen-Almagor, Raphael & Hartman, Monica G., 'The Oregon Death with Dignity Act: Review and Proposals for Improvement' (2001) 27(2) *J. of Legislation* 269

Foley, Kathleen & Hendin, Herbert, 'The Oregon Report: Don't Ask, Don't Tell' (2000) 15 *Issues in Law & Med.* 336

Ganzini, Linda et al., 'Physicians' Experiences with the Oregon Death with Dignity Act' (2000) 342(8) *New Eng. J. Med.* 557

Gorsuch, Neil M., 'The Legalization of Assisted Suicide and the Law of Unintended Consequences: A Review of the Dutch and Oregon Experiments and Leading Utilitarian Arguments For Legal Change' [2004] *Wis. L. Rev.* 1347

Hedberg, Katrina et al., 'Legalized Physician-Assisted Suicide in Oregon, 2001' (2002) 346(6) *New Eng. J. Med.* 450

Hedberg, Katrina et al., 'Five Years of Legalized Physician-Assisted Suicide in Oregon' (2003) 348(10) *New Eng. J. Med.* 961

Martyn, Susan R. & Bourguignon, Henry J., 'Now is the Moment to Reflect: Two Years of Experience with Oregon's Physician-Assisted Suicide Law' (2000) 8 *Elder L.J.* 1

O'Brien, C.N. et al., 'Oregon's guidelines for physician-assisted suicide: a legal and ethical analysis' (2000) 61 *Univ. Pittsburgh L. Rev.* 329

Oregon Department of Human Services, *Annual Reports on Oregon's Death with Dignity Act*, http://egov.oregon.gov/DHS/ph/pas/ar-index.shtml, accessed 25 July 2006

Steinbrook, Robert, 'Physician-assisted suicide in Oregon – An Uncertain Future' (2002) 346(6) *New Eng. J. Med.* 461

Sullivan, Amy D. et al., 'Legalized Physician-Assisted Suicide in Oregon – The Second Year' (2000) 342(8) *New Eng. J. Med.* 598

Sullivan, Amy D. et al., 'Legalized Physician-Assisted Suicide in Oregon 1998–2000' (2001) 344(8) *New Eng. J. Med.* 605

Task Force to Improve the Care of Terminally Ill Oregonians, *The Oregon Death with Dignity Act: A Guidebook for Health Care Providers* (1998, revised on a continuous basis) www.ohsu.edu/ethics/guidebook.pdf, accessed 29 July 2006

Switzerland

Bosshard, Georg et al., 'Open regulation and practice in assisted dying: How Switzerland compares with the Netherlands and Oregon' (2002) 132 *Swiss Med. Wkly* 527

Bosshard, Georg et al., '748 cases of suicide assisted by a Swiss right-to-die organisation' (2003) 133 *Swiss Med. Wkly* 310

Fischer, Susanne et al., 'Swiss doctors' attitudes towards end-of-life decisions and their determinants: A comparison of three language regions' (2005) 135 *Swiss Med. Wkly* 370

Frei, Andreas et al., 'Assisted suicide as conducted by a "Right-to-Die"-society in Switzerland: A descriptive analysis of 43 consecutive cases' (2001) 131 *Swiss Med. Wkly* 375

Guillod, Olivier & Schmidt, Aline, 'Assisted suicide under Swiss law' (2005) 12 *Eur. J. Health L.* 25

Hurst, Samia A. & Mauron, Alex, 'Assisted suicide and euthanasia in Switzerland: allowing a role for non-physicians' (2003) 326 *Br. Med. J.* 271

U.S.A.

Alesandro, John A., 'Physician-Assisted Suicide and New York Law' (1994) 57 *Alb. L. Rev.* 819

Baron, Charles H. et al., 'A Model State Act To Authorize And Regulate Physician-Assisted Suicide' (1996) 33 *Harv. J. on Legis.* 1

Bopp, James Jr., 'Is Assisted Suicide Constitutionally Protected?' (1987) 3 *Issues in Law & Med.* 113

CeloCruz, Maria T., 'Aid-in-Dying: Should We Decriminalize Physician-Assisted Suicide and Physician-Committed Euthanasia?' (1992) 18 *Am. J. L. & Med.* 369

Destro, Robert A., 'The Scope of the Fourteenth Amendment Liberty Interest: Does the Constitution Encompass a Right to Define Oneself Out of Existence?' (1994) 10 *Issues in Law & Med.* 183

Doerflinger, Richard, 'Assisted Suicide: Pro-Choice or Anti-Life?' (1989) 19(1) *Hastings Center Rep.* 16

Dworkin, Ronald et al., 'Assisted Suicide: The Philosophers' Brief' (1997) 44(5) *N.Y. Rev. of Books* 41; 1996 WL 708956

Emanuel, E.J., 'Euthanasia and Physician-Assisted Suicide: A Review of the Empirical Data from the United States' (2002) 162 *Arch. Internal Med.* 142

Emanuel, E.J. et al., 'The Practice of Euthanasia and Physician-Assisted Suicide in the United States: Adherence to Proposed Safeguards and Effects on Physicians' (1998) 280(6) *J. Am. Med. Ass'n* 507

Engelhardt, H. Tristram Jr. & Malloy, Michele, 'Suicide and Assisting Suicide: A Critique of Legal Sanctions' (1982) 36 *Sw. L.J.* 1003

Garbesi, George C., 'The Law of Assisted Suicide' (1987) 3 *Issues in Law & Med.* 93

Kamisar, Yale, 'Are Laws Against Assisted Suicide Unconstitutional?' (1993) 23(3) *Hastings Center Rep.* 32

Kass, Leon R., 'Neither for Love nor Money: Why Doctors Must Not Kill' (1989) 94 *Public Interest* 25

Kevorkian, Jack, 'The Last Fearsome Taboo: Medical Aspects of Planned Death' (1988) 7 *Med. & L.* 1

Kevorkian, Jack, *Prescription: Medicide The Goodness of Planned Death* (Buffalo, N.Y.: Prometheus Books, 1991)

Magnusson, Roger S., *Angels of Death – Exploring the Euthanasia Underground* (New Haven, Conn.: Yale Univ. Press, 2002)

Marzen, Thomas J. et al., 'Suicide: A Constitutional Right?' (1985) 24 *Duq. L. Rev.* 1

Marzen, Thomas J. et al., ' "Suicide: A Constitutional Right?" – Reflections Eleven Years Later' (1996) 35 *Duq. L. Rev.* 261

Mayo, Thomas, 'Constitutionalizing the "Right to Die" ' (1990) 49 *Md. L. Rev.* 103

Meier, D. et al., 'A national survey of physician-assisted suicide and euthanasia in the United States' (1998) 338(17) *New Eng. J. Med.* 1193

Neeley, G. Steven, 'Self-Directed Death, Euthanasia and the Termination of Life-Support: Reasonable Decisions to Die' (1994) 16 *Campbell L. Rev.* 205

Neeley, G. Steven, *The Constitutional Right to Suicide: A Legal and Philosophical Examination* (New York: Peter Lang, 1994)

New York State Task Force on Life and the Law, *When Death Is Sought: Assisted Suicide and Euthanasia in the Medical Context* (1994)

Nicol, Neal & Wylie, Harry, *Between the Dying and the Dead: Dr Jack Kevorkian, the Assisted Suicide Machine and the Battle to Legalise Euthanasia* (London: Vision, 2006)

Note, 'Physician-Assisted Suicide and the Right to Die with Assistance' (1992) 105 *Harv. L. Rev.* 2021

Previn, Matthew P., 'Assisted Suicide and Religion: Conflicting Conceptions of the Sanctity of Human Life' (1996) 84 *Geo. L.J.* 589

Quill, Timothy E., 'Death and Dignity: A Case of Individualized Decision Making' (1991) 324(10) *New Eng. J. Med.* 691

Quill, Timothy E., *Death and Dignity: Making Choices and Taking Charge* (New York: W.W. Norton, 1993)

Quill, Timothy E., 'Doctor, I Want to Die. Will You Help Me?' (1993) 270(7) *J. Am. Med. Ass'n* 870

Quill, Timothy E. et al., 'Care of the Hopelessly Ill: Proposed Clinical Criteria for Physician-Assisted Suicide' (1992) 327(19) *New Eng. J. Med.* 1380

Richards, David A.J., 'Constitutional Privacy, The Right to Die and The Meaning of Life: A Moral Analysis' (1981) 22 *Wm. & Mary L. Rev.* 327

Risley, Robert L., 'Legal and Ethical Issues in the Individual's Right to Die' (1994) 20 *Ohio N.U. L. Rev.* 597

Roscoe, Lori A. et al., 'Dr. Jack Kevorkian and Cases of Euthanasia in Oakland County, Michigan, 1990–1998' (2000) 343(23) *New Eng. J. Med.* 1735

Sayid, M.D., 'Euthanasia: A Comparison of the Criminal Laws of Germany, Switzerland and the United States' (1983) 6 *Boston Coll. Int'l & Comp. L. Rev.* 533

Sullivan, Alan, 'A Constitutional Right to Suicide' in Margaret Pabst Battin & David J. Mayo, eds., *Suicide: The Philosophical Issues* (New York: St. Martin's Press, 1980) 229

Ubel, Peter A., 'Assisted suicide and the case of Dr Quill and Diane' (1993) 8(4) *Issues in Law & Med.* 487

Weir, Robert F., 'The Morality of Physician-Assisted Suicide' (1992) 20 *Law, Med. & Health Care* 116

Wolhandler, Steven J., 'Voluntary Active Euthanasia for the Terminally Ill and the Constitutional Right to Privacy' (1984) 69 *Cornell L. Rev.* 363

COMPASSION

Blum, Lawrence, 'Compassion' in Amélie Oksenberg Rorty, ed., *Explaining Emotions* (Berkeley: Univ. of Cal. Press, 1980) 507

Comité Consultatif National d'Éthique (France), *Fin de vie, arrêt de vie, euthanasie (End of life, ending life, euthanasia)*, no. 63, 27 Jan. 2000

Nussbaum, Martha, 'Compassion: The Basic Social Emotion' (1996) 13 *Soc. Phil. & Pol'y* 27

Pellegrino, Edmund D., 'Compassion Needs Reason Too' (1993) 270(7) *J. Am. Med. Ass'n* 874

Shepherd, Lois, 'Sophie's Choices: Medical and Legal Responses to Suffering' (1996) 72 *Notre Dame L. Rev.* 103

Shepherd, Lois, 'Face to Face: A Call for Radical Responsibility in Place of Compassion' (2003) 77 *St. John's L. Rev.* 445

Tribe, Laurence, 'Revisiting the Rule of Law' (1989) 64 *N.Y.U. L. Rev.* 726

West, Robin, *Caring for Justice* (New York: N.Y.U. Press, 1997)

Zipursky, Benjamin, '*Deshaney* and the Jurisprudence of Compassion' (1990) 65 *N.Y.U. L. Rev.* 1101

Zyl, Liezl van, *Death and compassion: A virtue-based approach to euthanasia* (Aldershot, U.K.: Ashgate, 2000)

COMMON LAW DEFENCE OF NECESSITY

Chan, Winnie & Simester, A.P., 'Duress, Necessity: How Many Defences?' [2005] *King's Coll. L.J.* 121

Coughlan, Stephen G., 'Duress, Necessity, Self-Defence and Provocation: Implications of Radical Change?' (2002) 7 *Can. Crim. L. Rev.* 147

'Editorial' (2001) 6 *Can. Crim. L. Rev.* 129

Fletcher, George, 'The Individualization of Excusing Conditions' (1974) 47 *So. Cal. L. Rev.* 1269

Fletcher, George, *Rethinking Criminal Law* (Oxford: Oxford Univ. Press, 1978)

Galloway, Donald, 'Necessity as a Justification: A Critique of *Perka*' (1986) 10 *Dal. L.J.* 158

Guy, Paul, '*R. v. Latimer* and the Defence of Necessity: One Step Forward, Two Steps Back' (2003) 66 *Sask. L. Rev.* 485

Huxtable, Richard, 'Logical Separation? Conjoined Twins, Slippery Slopes and Resource Allocation' (2001) 23(4) *J. Social Welfare & Family Law* 459

Huxtable, Richard, 'Separation of Conjoined Twins: Where Next for English Law' [2002] *Crim. L.R.* 459

McEwan, Jenny, 'Murder by Design: the "Feel-Good Factor" and the Criminal Law' (2001) 9 *Med. L. Rev.* 246

Michalowski, Sabine, 'Sanctity of life – are some lives more sacred than others?' (2002) 22 *Legal Stud.* 377

Rogers, Jonathan, 'Necessity, Private Defence and the Killing of Mary' [2001] *Crim. L.R.* 515

Sneiderman, Barney, '*Latimer* in the Supreme Court: Necessity, Compassionate Homicide, and Mandatory Sentencing' (2001) 64 *Sask. L. Rev.* 511

Sneiderman, Barney & Deutscher, Raymond, 'Dr. Nancy Morrison and Her Dying Patient: A Case of Medical Necessity' (2002) 10 *Health L.J.* 1

Trotter, Gary T., 'Necessity and Death: Lessons from *Latimer* and the Case of the Conjoined Twins' (2003) 40 *Alta. L. Rev.* 817

Wicks, Elizabeth, 'The Greater Good? Issues of Proportionality and Democracy in the Doctrine of Necessity as Applied in *Re A*' (2003) 32 *Common L. World Rev.* 115

Williams, Glanville, *The Sanctity of Life and the Criminal Law* (London: Faber, 1958) 286–8

Williams, Glanville, 'Necessity' [1978] *Crim. L.R.* 128

Yeo, Stanley, 'Private Defence, Duress and Necessity' (1991) 15(2) *Crim. L.J.* 140

COMPARATIVE WORKS

Chesterman, Simon, 'Last Rights: Euthanasia, the Sanctity of Life, and the Law in the Netherlands and the Northern Territory of Australia' (1998) 47 *Int'l Comparative L.Q.* 362

Emanuel, Ezekiel J., 'Euthanasia: where the Netherlands leads will the world follow?' (2001) 322 *Br. Med. J.* 1376

Gorsuch, Neil M., 'The Legalization of Assisted Suicide and the Law of Unintended Consequences: A Review of the Dutch and Oregon Experiments and Leading Utilitarian Arguments For Legal Change' [2004] *Wis. L. Rev.* 1347

Griffiths, John, 'Comparative Reflections: Is the Dutch Case Unique?' in Albert Klijn et al., eds., *Regulating Physician-Negotiated Death* (Amsterdam: Elsevier, 2001) 197

Hirsch, Dana Elizabeth, 'Euthanasia: Is it Murder or Mercy Killing? A Comparison of the Criminal Laws in the United States, the Netherlands and Switzerland' (1990) 12 *Loy. L.A. Int'l & Comp. L.J.* 821

Jost, Timothy Stoltzfus & Mendelson, Danuta, 'A Comparative Study of the Law of Palliative Care and End-of-Life Treatment' (2003) 31 *J. L. Med. & Ethics* 130

Lewis, Penney, 'The Dutch Experience of Euthanasia' (1998) 25 *J. Law & Society* 636

Lewis, Penney, '*Assisted Dying for the Terminally Ill Bill*: A Comparison with the Netherlands, Belgium and Oregon', Memorandum submitted to the House of Lords

Select Committee on the Assisted Dying for the Terminally Ill Bill, 14 Sept. 2004, House of Lords Select Committee on the Assisted Dying for the Terminally Ill Bill, *Evidence*, HL Paper 86-II (2005) 27–31, www.publications.parliament.uk/pa/ld200405/ldselect/ldasdy/86/86ii.pdf, accessed 27 July 2006

Magnusson, Roger S., *Angels of Death – Exploring the Euthanasia Underground* (New Haven, Conn.: Yale Univ. Press, 2002)

Nys, Herman, 'Physician Involvement in a Patient's Death: A Continental European Perspective' (1999) 7 *Med. L. Rev.* 208

Otlowski, Margaret, *Voluntary Euthanasia and the Common Law* (Oxford: Oxford Univ. Press, 1997)

Otlowski, Margaret, 'The Effectiveness of Legal Control of Euthanasia: Lessons from Comparative Law' in Albert Klijn et al., eds., *Regulating Physician-Negotiated Death* (Amsterdam: Elsevier, 2001) 137

Sayid, M.D., 'Euthanasia: A Comparison of the Criminal Laws of Germany, Switzerland and the United States' (1983) 6 *Boston Coll. Int'l & Comp. L. Rev.* 533

Vezzoni, Cristiano, 'Engineering Rights: The Legal Status and Social Practice of Advance Directives' in Albert Klijn et al., eds., *Regulating Physician-Negotiated Death* (Amsterdam: Elsevier, 2001) 67

Vickers, Lesley, 'Assisted dying and the laws of three European countries' (1997) 147(6789) *New L.J.* 610

ETHICS AND SOCIOLOGY

Ariès, Philippe, *Western Attitudes Toward Death: From the Middle Ages to the Present* (Patricia M. Ranum, trans.) (Baltimore, Md.: The Johns Hopkins University Press, 1974)

Battin, Margaret Pabst, *The Least Worst Death: Essays in Bioethics on the End of Life* (New York: Oxford Univ. Press, 1994)

Battin, Margaret Pabst, *Ethical Issues in Suicide* (Englewood Cliffs, N.J.: Prentice-Hall, 1995)

Bender, Leslie, 'A Feminist Analysis of Physician-Assisted Dying and Voluntary Active Euthanasia' (1992) 59 *Tenn. L. Rev.* 519

Bickenbach, Jerome E., 'Disability and Life-Ending Decisions' in Margaret P. Battin et al., eds., *Physician Assisted Suicide: Expanding the Debate* (New York: Routledge, 1998) 123

Brock, Dan, 'Voluntary Active Euthanasia' (1992) 22(2) *Hastings Center Rep.* 10

Brock, Dan, *Life and Death* (Cambridge: Cambridge Univ. Press, 1993)

Callahan, Daniel, *The Troubled Dream of Life: Living With Mortality* (New York: Simon & Schuster, 1993)

Foot, Philippa, 'Euthanasia' (1977) 6 *Phil. & Pub. Aff.* 85

Gay-Williams, J., 'The Wrongfulness of Euthanasia' in Ronald Munson, ed., *Intervention and Reflection: Basic Issues in Medical Ethics* (Belmont, Calif.: Wadsworth, 1983) 156

Kuhse, Helga, 'From Intention to Consent: Learning from Experience with Euthanasia' in Margaret P. Battin et al., eds., *Physician Assisted Suicide: Expanding the Debate* (New York: Routledge, 1998) 252

Nuland, Sherwin B., *How We Die: Reflections on Life's Final Chapter* (New York: A.A. Knopf, 1994)

Quill, Timothy E., *Death and Dignity: Making Choices and Taking Charge* (New York: W.W. Norton, 1993)

Rachels, James, *The End of Life: Euthanasia and Morality* (Oxford: Oxford Univ. Press, 1986)

Somerville, Margaret, 'The Song of Death: The Lyrics of Euthanasia' (1993) 9 *J. Contemp. Health L. & Pol'y* 1

PALLIATIVE CARE

Burt, Robert A., 'The Supreme Court Speaks – Not Assisted Suicide but a Constitutional Right to Palliative Care' (1997) 337(17) *New Eng. J. Med.* 1234

Campbell, Alastair V. & Huxtable, Richard, 'The position statement and its commentators: consensus, compromise or confusion?' (2003) 17 *Palliative Med.* 180

Chater, Susan et al., 'Sedation for intractable distress in the dying – a survey of experts' (1998) 12 *Palliative Med.* 255

Clark, D. et al., 'Common threads? Palliative care service developments in seven European countries' (2000) 14 *Palliative Med.* 479

Dutch Ministry of Health, Welfare and Sport, 'Palliative care for terminally ill patients in the Netherlands: Dutch Government Policy' International Publication Series Health, Welfare and Sport No. 16 (2003)

Francke, Anneke L. & Kerkstra, Ada, 'Palliative care services in The Netherlands: a descriptive study' (2000) 41 *Patient Education & Counseling* 23

Gevers, Sjef, 'Terminal Sedation: A Legal Approach' (2003) 10 *Eur. J. Health L.* 359

Gillick, Muriel R. 'Terminal Sedation: An Acceptable Exit Strategy?' (2004) 141(3) *Annals Internal Med.* 236

Gordijn, Bert & Janssens, Rien, 'The prevention of euthanasia through palliative care: New developments in the Netherlands' (2000) 41 *Patient Education & Counseling* 35

Gordijn, Bert & Visser, Adriaan, 'Issues in Dutch palliative care: readjusting a distorted image' (2000) 41 *Patient Education & Counseling* 1

Health Council of the Netherlands, *Terminal sedation*, Ethics and Health Monitoring Report 2004 no. 2, Publication no. 2004/12–02E (2004)

Janssens, Rien & Have, Henk ten, 'The Concept of Palliative Care in the Netherlands' (2001) 15 *Palliative Med.* 481

Janssens, Rien J.P.A. et al., 'Hospice and euthanasia in the Netherlands: an ethical point of view' (1999) 25(5) *J. Med. Ethics* 408

Janssens, R.J.P.A. et al., 'Palliative care in Europe. Towards a more comprehensive understanding' (2001) 8 *Eur. J. Palliative Care* 256

Jost, Timothy Stoltzfus & Mendelson, Danuta, 'A Comparative Study of the Law of Palliative Care and End-of-Life Treatment' (2003) 31 *J. L. Med. & Ethics* 130

Materstvedt, Lars Johan, 'Palliative care on the "slippery slope" towards euthanasia?' (2003) 17 *Palliative Med.* 387

Materstvedt, Lars Johan et al., 'Euthanasia and physician-assisted suicide: a view from an EAPC Ethics Task Force' (2003) 17 *Palliative Med.* 97

Meijburg, Herman H. van der Kloot, 'From the Netherlands' (2003) 17 *Palliative Med.* 176

Orentlicher, David, 'The Supreme Court and Physician-Assisted Suicide – Rejecting Assisted Suicide but Embracing Euthanasia' (1997) 337(17) *New Eng. J. Med.* 1236

Rietjens, Judith A.C. et al., 'Physician Reports of Terminal Sedation without Hydration or Nutrition for Patients Nearing Death in the Netherlands' (2004) 141(3) *Annals Internal Med.* 178

Rietjens, Judith A.C. et al., 'Terminal Sedation and Euthanasia: A Comparison of Clinical Practices' (2006) 166 *Arch. Internal Med.* 749

Royal Dutch Medical Association (KNMG) Committee on National Guidelines for Palliative Sedation, *Guidelines for Palliative Sedation* (2005), http://knmg.artsennet.nl/uri/?uri=AMGATE_6059_100_TICH_R171322439726668, accessed 24 June 2006

Wal, Gerrit van der, 'From the Netherlands' (2003) 17 *Palliative Med.* 110

Williams, Glenys, 'The Principle of Double Effect and Terminal Sedation' (2001) 9 *Med. L. Rev.* 41

RIGHTS

Ariens, Michael, 'Suicidal Rights' (1988) 20 *Rutgers L.J.* 79

Beschle, Donald L., 'Autonomous Decision-Making and Social Choice: Examining the "Right to Die" ' (1988–89) 77 *Ky. L.J.* 319

Blake, Meredith, 'Physician-Assisted Suicide: A Criminal Offence or a Patient's Right?' (1997) 5 *Med. L. Rev.* 294

Destro, Robert A., 'The Scope of the Fourteenth Amendment Liberty Interest: Does the Constitution Encompass a Right to Define Oneself Out of Existence?' (1994) 10 *Issues in Law & Med.* 183

Dworkin, Ronald, *Life's Dominion: An Argument About Abortion, Euthanasia, and Individual Freedom* (New York: A.A. Knopf, 1993)

Feinberg, Joel, 'Voluntary Euthanasia and the Inalienable Right to Life' (1978) 7 *Phil. & Pub. Aff.* 93

Freeman, Michael, 'Death, Dying and the Human Rights Act 1998' (1999) 52 *Current Legal Problems* 218

Freeman, Michael, 'Denying Death its Dominion: Thoughts on the Dianne Pretty Case' (2002) 10(3) *Med. L. Rev.* 245

Friedman, Roger F., 'It's My Body and I'll Die If I Want To: A Property Based-Argument in Support of Assisted Suicide' (1995) 12 *J. Contemp. Health L. & Pol'y* 183

Glendon, Mary Ann, *Rights Talk: The Impoverishment of Political Discourse* (New York: Free Press, 1993)

Kass, Leon R., 'Is There a Right to Die?' (1993) 23(1) *Hastings Center Rep.* 34

Keown, John, 'No Right to Assisted Suicide' [2002] *Camb. L.J.* 8

Keown, John, 'European Court of Human Rights: Death in Strasbourg – assisted suicide, the *Pretty* case, and the European Convention on Human Rights' (2003) 1(4) *Int'l J. Const'l L.* 722

Leenen, H.J.J., 'Assistance to Suicide and the European Court of Human Rights: the Pretty Case' (2002) 9 *Eur. J. Health L.* 257

Marzen, Thomas J. et al., 'Suicide: A Constitutional Right?' (1985) 24 *Duq. L. Rev.* 1

Marzen, Thomas J. et al., ' "Suicide: A Constitutional Right?" – Reflections Eleven Years Later' (1996) 35 *Duq. L. Rev.* 261

Mayo, Thomas, 'Constitutionalizing the "Right to Die" ' (1990) 49 *Md. L. Rev.* 103

Miller, Paul Steven, 'The Impact of Assisted Suicide on Persons with Disabilities – Is It A Right Without A Freedom?' (1993) 9 *Issues in Law & Med.* 47

Morris, Dan, 'Assisted Suicide under the European Convention on Human Rights: A Critique' (2003) 1 *Eur. Hum. Rights L. Rev.* 65

Neeley, G. Steven, *The Constitutional Right to Suicide: A Legal and Philosophical Examination* (New York: Peter Lang, 1994)

Note, 'Physician-Assisted Suicide and the Right to Die with Assistance' (1992) 105 *Harv. L. Rev.* 2021

Pedain, Antje, 'The Human Rights Dimension of the Diane Pretty Case' (2003) 62(1) *Camb. L.J.* 181

Richards, David A.J., 'Constitutional Privacy, The Right to Die and The Meaning of Life: A Moral Analysis' (1981) 22 *Wm. & Mary L. Rev.* 327

Risley, Robert L., 'Legal and Ethical Issues in the Individual's Right to Die' (1994) 20 *Ohio N.U. L. Rev.* 597

Rosenblum, Victor D. & Forsythe, Clarke G., 'The Right to Assisted Suicide: Protection of Autonomy or an Open Door to Social Killing?' (1990) 6 *Issues in Law & Med.* 3

Schneider, Carl, 'Rights Discourse and Neonatal Euthanasia' (1988) 76 *Cal. L. Rev.* 151

Sullivan, Alan, 'A Constitutional Right to Suicide' in Margaret Pabst Battin & David J. Mayo, eds., *Suicide: The Philosophical Issues* (New York: St. Martin's Press, 1980) 229

Wallace, Samuel E., 'The Right to Live and the Right to Die' in Samuel E. Wallace & Albin Eser, eds., *Suicide and Euthanasia: The Rights of Personhood* (Knoxville, Tenn.: Univ. Tenn. Press, 1981) 86

Wallace, Samuel E. & Eser Albin, 'The Rights of Personhood' in Samuel E. Wallace & Albin Eser, eds., *Suicide and Euthanasia: The Rights of Personhood* (Knoxville, Tenn.: Univ. Tenn. Press, 1981) 99

Wolhandler, Steven J., 'Voluntary Active Euthanasia for the Terminally Ill and the Constitutional Right to Privacy' (1984) 69 *Cornell L. Rev.* 363

SLIPPERY SLOPES

Bagaric, Mirko, 'The Kuhse-Singer Euthanasia Survey: Why it Fails to Undermine the Slippery Slope Argument – Comparing Apples and Apples' (2002) 9 *Eur. J. Health L.* 229

Burg, Wilbren van der, 'The Slippery-Slope Argument' (1991) 102 *Ethics* 42

Doerflinger, Richard M., 'Conclusion: Shaky Foundations and Slippery Slopes' (1996) 35 *Duq. L. Rev.* 523

Enoch, David, 'Once You Start Using Slippery Slope Arguments, You're On A Very Slippery Slope' (2001) 211 *Ox. J. Legal Studies* 629

Freedman, Benjamin, 'The Slippery-Slope Argument Reconstructed: Response to Van der Burg' (1992) 3 *J. Clinical Ethics* 293

Griffiths, John, 'Comparative Reflections: Is the Dutch Case Unique?' in Albert Klijn et al., eds., *Regulating Physician-Negotiated Death* (Amsterdam: Elsevier, 2001) 197

Kamisar, Yale, 'Physician-Assisted Suicide: The Last Bridge to Active Voluntary Euthanasia' in John Keown, ed., *Euthanasia Examined: Ethical, Clinical and Legal Perspectives* (Cambridge: Cambridge Univ. Press, 1995) 225

Kamisar, Yale, 'Some Non-Religious Views Against Proposed "Mercy Killing" Legislation' (1958) 42 *Minn. L. Rev.* 969

Lillehammer, Hallvard, 'Voluntary Euthanasia and the Logical Slippery Slope Argument' (2002) 61(3) *Camb. L.J.* 545

Lode, Eric, 'Slippery Slope Arguments and Legal Reasoning' (1999) 87 *Cal. L. Rev.* 1469

Mayo, David J., 'The Role of Slippery Slope Arguments in Public Policy Debates' (1990–91) 21–22 *Phil. Exchange* 81

Schwitters, Rob, 'Slipping into normality? Some Reflections on Slippery Slopes' in Albert Klijn et al., eds., *Regulating Physician-Negotiated Death* (Amsterdam: Elsevier, 2001) 93

Shauer, Frederick, 'Slippery Slopes' (1985) 99 *Harv. L. Rev.* 361

Smith, Stephen W., 'Evidence for the Practical Slippery Slope in the Debate on Physician-Assisted Suicide and Euthanasia' (2005) 13 *Med. L. Rev.* 17

Smith, Stephen W., 'Fallacies of the Logical Slippery Slope in the Debate on Physician-Assisted Suicide and Euthanasia' (2005) 13 *Med. L. Rev.* 224

Volokh, Eugene, 'The Mechanisms of the Slippery Slope' (2003) 116 *Harv. L. Rev.* 1026

Walton, Douglas, *Slippery Slope Arguments* (Oxford: Clarendon Press, 1992)

Whitman, Jeffrey P., 'The Many Guises of the Slippery Slope Argument' (1994) 20 *Soc. Theory & Prac.* 85

Williams, Bernard, 'Which Slopes Are Slippery?' in Michael Lockwood, ed., *Moral Dilemmas in Modern Medicine* (Oxford: Oxford Univ. Press, 1985) 126

Wright, Walter, 'Historical Analogies, Slippery Slopes, and the Question of Euthanasia' (2000) 28 *J. L. Med. & Ethics* 176

Index